Praise for *City in Europe*

'"Next stop Mars," said Malcolm Allison. Not quite ... but it's been a hell of a ride. A superb book and a must-read for any City fan.'

Daniel Taylor, senior writer, The Athletic

'A thorough and delicious retelling of perhaps not the most successful of European journeys, but definitely the most interesting, liberally sprinkled with the sort of humour that only a City fan could write. Fantastic.'

David Mooney, BBC Radio 5 Live

'A book that brilliantly explodes the myth that City have no history or pedigree in Europe. Curtis doesn't just detail the club's adventures on the continent from the late 1960s, he also captures their essence with accounts from fans who were there.'

Simon Mullock, chief football writer, *Sunday Mirror*

'Simon Curtis is a fine journalist with an extensive knowledge of the club – he is also a seasoned veteran of many European away trips. This book is essential reading for all City fans.'

Ric Turner, founder and curator, Bluemoon forum

'If you think that not winning the Champions League means there's no story to tell then think again. This book provides the story of every City game in Europe – a record that stretches back 54 years. Read the twists and turns of City's fortunes written in an engaging style with quotes from fans, players and broadcasters who were there.'

Gary James, football historian

'From Down the Kippax Steps to the latest rapture at the Etihad, Simon's gift for articulating how it's felt to support this undeniably unconventional football club has been unmatched. In times of comedy, tragedy, feast or famine, his writing has defined what it's meant to be City like no other.'

Mark Booth, head of content, New York City Football Club

CITY
IN EUROPE

FROM ALLISON TO GUARDIOLA:
MANCHESTER CITY'S QUEST
FOR EUROPEAN GLORY

SIMON CURTIS

ICON

Published in the UK in 2022 by Icon Books Ltd,
Omnibus Business Centre,
39–41 North Road, London N7 9DP
email: info@iconbooks.com
www.iconbooks.com

Sold in the UK, Europe and Asia
by Faber & Faber Ltd,
Bloomsbury House,
74–77 Great Russell Street,
London WC1B 3DA
or their agents

Distributed in the UK,
Europe and Asia
by Grantham Book Services,
Trent Road,
Grantham NG31 7XQ

Distributed in the USA
by Publishers Group West,
1700 Fourth Street,
Berkeley, CA 94710

Distributed in Australia and New Zealand
by Allen & Unwin Pty Ltd,
PO Box 8500, 83 Alexander Street,
Crows Nest, NSW 2065

Distributed in South Africa
by Jonathan Ball, Office B4, The District,
41 Sir Lowry Road, Woodstock 7925

Distributed in India
by Penguin Books India
7th Floor, Infinity Tower – C, DLF Cyber
City, Gurgaon 122002, Haryana

Distributed in Canada
by Publishers Group Canada,
76 Stafford Street, Unit 300, Toronto,
Ontario M6J 2S1

ISBN: 978-178578-732-4

Typeset in Palatino by Marie Doherty

Printed and bound in Great Britain
by Clays Ltd, Elcograf S.p.A.

To Barbara Curtis, whose early exhortations of 'good word that, my love, use it in your essays', started the ball rolling, and who, I hope, would have been proud to see this in print.

CONTENTS

ABOUT THE AUTHOR

Simon Curtis is a freelance journalist specialising in all things Manchester City. He has written extensively for the club's various official platforms, with regular columns in the matchday programme and articles on the official website spanning a number of years, in addition to many years writing Manchester City content for ESPN, contributions to *Champions* magazine and a variety of UEFA publications. He lives in Manchester.

ACKNOWLEDGEMENTS

In mentioning the following individuals' contribution to *City in Europe*, I am simultaneously acknowledging that none of this would have been vaguely possible without their input.

That the words you are about to read are reliable, factually accurate and in a vaguely coherent pattern is down to the eagle-eyed Graham Ward, who had the distinct challenge of reading the first draft (*'it hit his arm not his nose, Simon'*, *'Sané scored in the 87th minute not the 86th'* and my personal favourite, *'the attendance at Plzeň away was 11,281 not 11,282'*) and my long-suffering editor James Lilford, who had the unenviable task of putting the final version into readable shape on what was ultimately, after many unforeseen delays, a very tight deadline, and to whose wise counsel I am indebted. Thanks too to Philip Cotterell, Duncan Heath and the rest of the team at Icon and to Melanie at the Michael Greer Literary Agency, who persuaded Icon I could be trusted with telling the story.

Thanks also for time, help, access, encouragement, opinion, varnish, hyperbole, realism and inside information from Simon Mullock, Daniel Taylor, Gary James, Roger Reade, Simon Hart, Ian Cheeseman, Michael Cox, Rui Botica Santos, Vicky Kloss and Rob Pollard at the club, to Chris Dottie and Mike Hammond, without whose help with tickets I may never have seen the wonders that eventually passed before my eyes, and to stalwarts Gary Owen, Joe Corrigan and Tommy Booth, without whose stories my own would be so much the weaker.

I am also beholden to Paula, whose complete indifference to

football has reminded me every step of the way that it may be a frivolous practice that some of us have got inextricably caught up in, but there *are* other pleasures to be had in life if you keep your eyes and mind open. It is of course *'only a game'* and it is indeed inexplicable *'why anyone should get in such a state about it'*. Her plaintive cries of *'Oh no, the telly's gone green again'* will not go unremembered. Thanks too to our boys for understanding why their father appeared to have a greater affinity to Kevin De Bruyne's pass success rate than to their end-of-term meetings. Not even remotely true of course, but easy to assume during yet another Champions League match where Dad is either absent or busy upending all the furniture. Apologies to Lucas, who has been bitten badly by the bug, and congratulations to Sam, who has been strong enough to steadfastly avoid catching it.

Thanks too to my father for failing to have his own football affinity, liberating me to make my own disastrous lifestyle choice of Manchester City on the back of a simple dread for my cousin's bright red Sammy McIlroy tracksuit, worn every single day of a 1970s holiday on the Isle of Man. On such small and misshapen things entire lives are decided. That and Denis Law's backheel, it must be said.

And, finally, as this is a book interwoven with the stories of the fans who make this club tick, I would like to thank all of those who shared tales with me, some of which did not pass the censor's watering eyes, but who were there through thick and wafer thin following this marvellous club. You are as central to this story as Francis Lee, Fernandinho or, indeed, Martín Demichelis.

Finally, finally, to Malcolm Allison, Mario Balotelli, Stephen Ireland, Robinho, Craig Bellamy, Roberto Mancini, Jô, Gary Cook and Rodney Marsh, without whose unique taste for the ridiculous this story would be several grades less astonishing. If you enjoy the book half as much as they have enjoyed life, it will have been as well received as I could have hoped.

FOREWORD

I had never seen rain like it. Teeming down. Bloody pouring, it was. When you take a penalty, to get the accuracy needed, you have to put extra pressure on the standing foot, but I couldn't. If I'd put any more weight on my standing foot that night I'd have gone straight on my arse, like John Terry did in Moscow (in 2008). It was the only penalty of all the ones I took that I just whacked it. I used to hit all my penalties hard, but I always aimed for one corner or the other. This time I hit it with hope in my heart. Hope that I would stay on my feet and that the keeper would not be able to stop it, wherever it ended up going. I wanted it just under the crossbar. I took a long run-up. It went low. The keeper parried it with his legs, but it carried into the goal. It turned out to be the goal that won us the 1970 Cup Winners' Cup in Vienna and made me, makes me, to this day, the only person who can describe what it feels like to score the winning goal for Manchester City in a European final.

It is in my opinion a foregone conclusion that my record will fall. It is just a matter of time before City win the Champions League and somebody shares my feat of securing a continental trophy for the club. I don't think there is extra pressure on this generation of City players. It's just a matter of time. It's the only thing they've got left to win, isn't it?

The way City are structured these days, from top to bottom, the ladies' teams, the youths, right through to Pep Guardiola's brilliant squad, they are geared for winning. They spend wisely, they set up shrewdly, they are gaining that confidence all the time that comes from winning things. I just cannot see them being diverted from their goal of winning the Champions League. They have the structure running through the club for winning things. They replace players brilliantly. David Silva, Yaya Touré, Sergio Agüero and Vincent Kompany have all moved on and yet it hasn't disturbed the success of the team.

We had that too in 1970 under Malcolm Allison and Joe Mercer. Winning does that to you. You take on another level of calm, composure, a mentality that you know you are good. We were bloody good. We were strong, powerful and skilful. Malcolm was a visionary like Pep. He had us on the weights. He had us doing circuit training with pro athletes. The difference was that Pep Guardiola is more methodical. When we got the ball to the halfway line, Malcolm wanted us to shift it quickly; get it up to the target man as rapidly as we possibly could. Joe was the same. He used to say to us 'stick the fuckers in their own half and keep them there'. There were five of us all pressing. 'If they lose the ball there, we're in,' he would tell us.

Malcolm was ahead of his time in many respects, but he made mistakes like anyone does and he could be vain too. He was a terrific coach, so clever, but he sometimes did things just to get the limelight. Playing five at the back or something, just to be different. Think of Pep Guardiola in Porto for the final in 2020. No holding midfielder, just to be different.

Europe was a fantastic learning ground for us at City. That first year after winning the league in 1968, Fenerbahçe was like nothing we had seen before. We went out to Turkey and the ground was jammed. They were shooting rockets down the tunnel and everything. We had to have a police escort onto the pitch. I don't think poor Ken Mulhearn, our goalkeeper, played again after that. It shook a lot of the team up and right after Malcolm had said we would frighten the life out of them all. It was us who ended up being frightened!

But we were quick learners. You have to be in Europe. We won it the following year and nearly won it again the year after, reaching the semi-finals against Chelsea. We had a terrible injury crisis and Malcolm had to play the kids. There was only a squad of twelve or thirteen in those days. I remember Terry Venables playing in midfield for Chelsea and doing stepovers to waste time when they were ahead. We were calling him Charlie Cairoli for all his messing around. The year before, everything went right for us. After Fenerbahçe, we were determined to put on a good account of ourselves. We came up against some tough sides, but we were more than a match for them. Nobody roughed us up. Me and Mike Summerbee didn't take any funny business from the opposing defenders. We would switch positions. We knew how to look after ourselves too. In one game against Górnik, I rode a terrible tackle – just got into the air in time. The defender came flying through and we both ended on the floor. When I looked around, he was lying there with his shin bone sticking through his sock. Tough buggers they were. I couldn't believe it when he hopped off on one leg instead of waiting for a stretcher.

Everyone talks about the hardmen of the '70s, but some had a reputation without deserving it. Tommy Smith at Liverpool, Ron Harris at Chelsea and Denis Smith at Stoke always get a mention, but the toughest I played against was Jerzy Gorgoń of Górnik. He was in the Poland side that knocked England out of the 1974 World Cup as well. Never seen anything like him. He kicked me up the backside so hard I had a bruise there for weeks after. I had to take one of those little lifebelt things with me to sit on in restaurants it was so painful.

Of course, there is little of that today. Antonio Rüdiger might have finished Kevin De Bruyne's final early in Porto, but there aren't many thugs around in the game today. Teams still need a good hard player like Rüdiger, anyway – someone you don't take liberties with. The pitches play true too. You can let the ball run. You can rely on the path it will take. I would have loved playing on them, letting the ball go and relying on my turn of speed without having to worry where the ball was going. I played in quagmires at Maine Road and later in my career at Derby. In fact, in one European game for Derby vs Slovan Bratislava, the pitch was so muddy I went flying under a heavy challenge from one of their defenders and I put my hands out to break the fall. As I landed, my hands went into the mud, followed by my face. I propped myself up and wiped the mud out of my eyes and there was a bloody frog in the wet in front of me! You don't get so many frogs on the pitch today either.

The story of *City in Europe* is not one of toads though. It is about a football team that will win the Champions League very soon, maybe even next year, but also about a club that, when I left it in 1974, was already a very successful side with a rich history of winning things. In those days, there was no one-team domination. Every side reckoned they had a chance on their day. Derby, Everton, Stoke were all good sides that played in Europe. As did City, winning in 1970 before many of today's rivals had managed to do it. So, there's plenty of history to go through, plenty of games of which I am proud to say I took part in for City, and they are all covered in this book. I hope you enjoy reading about them as much as me and the lads enjoyed playing in them.

Francis Lee
Manchester City and England 1967–74

INTRODUCTION
CINDERELLA'S SLIPPERS

Don't look back in anger

> *'The Champions League is the beginning and the end; we want to do it; nobody knows if we can.'*
>
> Pep Guardiola

The broad church that is football punditry believes this statement to be true, but if you ask City supporters for their opinion, responses will be divided into three categories: 'it's inevitable', 'no way, we are cursed' and the equally sizeable third group of 'I don't care as long as we win the Premier League'.

To get behind this mindset, it is critical that we first explore its wonky trajectory through European club competition and itemise the different approaches that go together to represent 50 turbulent years of City in Europe.

Writing this the day after a tumultuous Champions League semi-final in the Santiago Bernabéu Stadium ended with the most unbelievable storyline even a club with City's gluttonous appetite for farce could summon up, it is easy to understand all opinions.

But then City's tale, at home or abroad, has always been liberally sprinkled with the most outrageous stories and the most eye-catching characters the sport seems able to produce.

The domestic rise and fall and rise again has been well documented elsewhere, but, when the up and down and around the corner tale of Manchester City's adventures in European football was first mooted as a story rich enough to warrant its telling, the original and symmetrical idea was to produce the work to coincide with City reaching (and perhaps – deep breath – even winning) their first-ever Champions League final.

The mirror image this would have produced with City's beginnings on the continent were far too delicious to ignore. From Vienna 1970 and the rain-drenched Cup Winners' Cup final to the ultimate deliverance of a club that has tried and failed more times than the rest have attempted to tackle a hot dinner.

Tony Book's bent-neck-lifting of the cup to a three-quarters-empty stadium juxtaposed by David Silva needing assistance to hoist a trophy bigger than his own upper body precisely 50 years later in 2020 just seemed too irresistible for words. Words, in fact, were all we possessed to do the idea justice.

Then, as has so often happened in this maverick club's patchwork quilt of a history, the story took on a whole new life of its own and all we could do was be tugged along, turning and bucking in its roaring slipstream.

Manchester City's history in European football has always been a curious case of the premature, the not to be and the not quite right, but, as of March 2020, we could add the maybe never will be.

Cup Winners' Cup winners before many British sides had even woken up to European football's potent promise, the club has followed early success with embarrassment, disinterest and a solid grasp for slapstick.

Between losing to Borussia Mönchengladbach in 1979 and beating Total Network Solutions (*what a re-entry to the boiling cauldron of European club football that was*) in 2003, a well-documented switchback of brave ups and laughable downs filled the gigantic void left by absolutely no European football whatsoever.

Twenty-four years of total network indifference, a blank canvas, a dark hole, a gaping crevasse.

City have always been a deeply contrary beast. Relegated scoring 100 goals as the reigning champions? No problem at all. (*In the 1937–8 season, City became the only team to date to be relegated as reigning league champions and, not happy with that alone, to be relegated as that season's top league scorers.*) Kicked out of the FA Cup by a Fourth Division side hypnotised by a man who crashed his car into a police van driving blindfold a week later? They can do it. (*In 1979–80, City were torpedoed from the FA Cup on a mudheap of a pitch at Fourth Division Halifax Town, their opponents having been apparently prepared for the event by a part-time soothsayer named Romark.*) Missing UEFA Cup qualification whilst playing a substitute goalkeeper up front? Yes, naturally, without as much as a blink of an eye, they can do that too. (*In May 2005, a win in the final game of the season at home to Middlesbrough would have taken City into the UEFA Cup. Manager Stuart Pearce decided, with time running out, to play goalkeeper David James in the centre-forward role. The beanpole James caused havoc, City gained an injury-time penalty, which was then punted into the waiting arms of Boro keeper Mark Schwarzer by Robbie Fowler. A relieved and sniggering Middlesbrough entered the 2005–6 UEFA Cup instead, and, naturally enough, reached the final.*)

More recent times have seen the club transformed from the limping, ugly duckling always one step from getting run over by a Gazprom truck to a preening would-be superpower of the modern game. And this is really where the going begins to get tough.

Through a clean, straight pinstripe of Roberto Mancini, Manuel Pellegrini and Pep Guardiola, City have just got better and better, scooping up domestic prizes like they are going out of fashion and playing a form of sumptuous passing football that has glittered and shimmered and bedazzled all who have gazed upon it. They have won more trophies since the takeover of the club in 2008 than in the rest of their preceding 114-year history, so these have certainly been what poetic types might call *the best of times*.

Champions League football was gathered in for the first time in 2011–12, a brave new world that had cost the club a king's ransom to even get close to. That supporters eyed the prospect of playing the likes of Real Madrid with glee was wholly natural. Before then, the only occasion City had entered the marble corridors of the Bernabéu in this correspondent's lifetime was to be beaten 5–2 in a chaotic 1979 friendly that saw multiple red cards and a collector's-item goal from Bobby Shinton of all people.

Real Madrid would be the natural benchmark.

In fact, the Spaniards have become much more than that. They form a central column of this bewitching story, first as difficult early opponents in the days when City's naive enthusiasm was not enough to carry them through the group stages; then as the club's first-ever semi-final opponent in the Champions League (2015–16) as Manuel Pellegrini's stint in charge carried City to the brink of greatness; in the spring of 2020, Real played the sacrificial lambs as City weathered attempts at Financial Fair Play derailment and a global Covid-19 pandemic to wipe the floor with the Spanish aristocrats; and in 2022, as the opponent that has once again given the dirty-faced upstart a firm slap in the chops to emphasise that new arrivals in these gilded corridors must sit and wait their turn.

So, *waiting their turn* is where City are. And just how long this process will take, in light of their most recent experience in the Spanish capital, is anyone's guess.

THE EARLY DAYS

The things we do for love

A little over an hour's sleep was all he had had time for. In somebody else's bed.

His head still throbbed, and the dizzying effects of the previous night's alcohol made getting up a task more fraught than normal, but Malcolm Allison struggled drowsily to his feet. A euphoric buzz was preventing him from sleeping more, although the low light from the street lamp outside told him he could have done so if he so wished.

The woman asleep alongside him did not stir as he dressed quietly and made his way out to the living room to collect his things. Jacket, tie, lighter, belt, some documents from the day before, notebook, a scarf given to him by an excited supporter and a small key fob.

The party at the Cabaret Club had seen him in typically brash form, swigging champagne from the bottle and puffing contentedly on his trademark cigars, while the whole world had seemed to file by to pay their respects.

The success he had promised had come at last and he had thoroughly enjoyed milking every second of it.

Big Mal – his showbiz alter ego – had made an immense evening of it, but it was a slow-moving Malcolm Allison that now made for the dimly lit street.

The press conference he would attend later that morning would become infamous in the history of Manchester City and its at times troubled relationship with European football, which at that stage was still to begin. Allison had just seen the side he and Joe Mercer had constructed just a few years before from the frozen ashes of a derelict and unloved Second Division base become champions of England.

With a typically buccaneering 4–3 win at Newcastle, they had sealed the title ahead of rivals Manchester United, two points the difference between them after a 42-game slog.

Allison, tired but elated, gazed out at the faces turned towards him in the crowded Maine Road press room. Some of them had been on the journey with him from the depths of the Second Division. There had been brickbats aplenty and widely aired criticism at the so-called cockney coach's highfalutin' ways. The assistant manager, brought up in Dartford and schooled at the West Ham academy, was the mouthy southerner who was heading for a fall, but that fall seemed to be long in coming of late, as everything he and Mercer touched turned to goals. His brashness, the cocky persona he had built as a juxtaposition to general manager Mercer's easy-going friendliness, the bravado and the boasting that often followed his colleague's tight little football homilies, all served to build him up for some as-yet unheralded but catastrophic tumble from the pedestal he occupied.

Waiting in vain for this descent to occur, many of the press pack had grown to like the City coach and enjoy the vivid audacity of his team, a side apparently built more in his own devil-may-care image than the relatively claustrophobic caution of Mercer. For his part, Allison nurtured the relationship expertly, often taking a gaggle of scribes with him through the narrow streets of Soho that he knew so well. They lapped up the glitz and the proximity to greatness and danger that a night out with Allison entailed.

As for Mercer, he had learnt to put up with his partner's outbursts, tolerating them at first, then growing to play them off as the enthusiastic outpourings of a larger-than-life character, a young buck, who needed to be given a loose rein in order to produce the heady cocktail of swagger and steel that had seen City punching so far above their weight with a squad of players almost entirely home-grown.

Mercer also understood two other things: firstly, that Allison's football brain and ability to innovate at a time when English football lay stagnant and sclerotic was almost peerless and, secondly, that Allison provided 'good copy' for the feverish press and was, therefore, always being trailed for a quote or two. James Lawton of the *Daily Express*, later to be Allison's ghostwriter on his racy autobiography *Colours of My Life* and later still the author of the excellent *Forever Boys*, a nostalgic look at Allison's late '60s City team, stated: 'He was pretty user-friendly and he liked the publicity, but he had his favourites. He had a particular respect for Ron Crowther of the *Daily Mail*. I always used to get a bit restive if Ron was at a press conference because he was a good old-style reporter who would ask pretty good questions and Malcolm respected him. It stuck in my mind that Malcolm was not just there to cultivate anybody who would write any crap.'

Lawton went on: 'It was obvious Malcolm had a very sharp intelligence and was lively company. Stockport County used to be run by a guy called Victor Bernard and their Friday night games were always a bit of a social occasion. Paul Doherty of Granada Television and Pat Phoenix of *Coronation Street* were there one night with Mal and they were obviously going out on the town, but Bernard was telling them how Stockport were going to get promoted and how he would get them into the

Second Division after that, then the First. He was going on a bit and Malcolm turned to Paul and said, "I think we'd better fuck off before he wins the European Cup!"'.

Ironically, on this occasion, in front of the press at Maine Road, with his sharp intelligence dulled by booze and little sleep, Allison's own boasting about Europe would come back to haunt him.

He looked out into the flashing light bulbs and announced in typical fashion: 'Gentlemen, there is no limit to what this team can achieve. We will win the European Cup. We will terrorise Europe.' Spurred on by his innate need to needle Manchester United at every turn, he continued, 'Manchester City will not play in Europe like some of the sides I have seen play Manchester United. I promise that City will attack these people as they have not been attacked since the days of the old Real Madrid.' Then he finished with the phrase that would live with him for the rest of his career: 'I think a lot of these Europeans are cowards. Their teams won despite their coaches not because of them …'

These ill-chosen words would rebound on the man who had uttered them and act as an albatross around the club's neck for the next 50 years, almost 30 of which would be devoid of any kind of European competition at all.

It was Allison's way, and it was typical City.

Worse still for Allison, within a month of uttering this infamous statement, his bête noire across the city would lift the European Cup at Wembley, beating Portuguese champions Benfica in a final that cemented the public's love affair with Bobby Charlton, George Best and their stoic leader Matt Busby.

Manchester United, it can be said with some authority, were quickly becoming a significant part of Allison's focus.

Soon after agreeing to join Second Division City, the ex-Plymouth coach had found himself at United's championship celebration gala, where he listened with increasing frustration to the various speeches. First, Busby, the iconic United manager and ex-City player, announced generously to the party that he considered 'Manchester had enough room for two teams'. It was another example of what Allison would later call their 'bumptious, patronising tones' that irritated him so much.

Later, a little too full of wine, he clashed with United's Scottish international Paddy Crerand and was told in no uncertain terms that 'City would never get a crowd over 30,000 in my lifetime'. In tone and sentiment, the statement would not stand the test of time. It would eventually resemble the 'not in my lifetime' outburst from Sir Alex Ferguson in its forced self-assurance when the manager was asked if City could be top dogs. Ferguson's 'noisy neighbours' quickly made mincemeat of his words, as Allison would of Crerand's.

If time has taught us anything, it is not to underestimate its cathartic powers of change. Angry and inebriated, Allison lurched back across the bar to corner Busby's son Sandy and muttered: 'Your father has got a twenty-year start, but I'll pass him in three.' As Allison would later admit, 'Now that was a bad thing to say, but a good thing to think.'

As things turned out, Allison and Mercer hauled City past United in less than three years and now they were heading to the continent to further rub United's noses in the dust.

Sunlit uplands

City's summer months in 1968 were full of high-spirited and badly organised travelling. The club undertook an arduous but light-hearted tour of the United States, Canada and Mexico, 'a great colourful swoop', as Allison himself called it in *Colours of My Life*. The trouble was that the 'swoop' through three sizeable nations took weeks and City started the season unfocused, distracted and in the wrong frame of mind to set about not only their first title defence since 1937, but also their first-ever tilt at a European trophy, in this case the prestigious European Cup.

As City physio Peter Blakey wrote in his account of the trip: 'It was an exhausted and depleted City party, which arrived back via Pan American jetliner on Monday 17 June from a 20,000-mile tour of three countries.'

There had been hi-jinks and trouble, ranging from disappointed hosts at the depleted squad that showed up, to shootings in the middle of the night, player arrests and the sight of a bored Franny Lee eating decorative flowers when his table ran out of alcohol at one of the many official functions the players were forced to attend.

Although City started the season with a pleasingly fluid romp in the Charity Shield game against West Brom at Maine Road, the 6–1 mauling masked the truth that the squad was not fit for purpose. Three league defeats followed in the first eight games, and by the time City's European campaign was set to start – they had been drawn against Turkish champions Fenerbahçe – the club was slumbering in 21st place, already a comfortable distance from the pacesetters Leeds, Everton and Liverpool.

Strangely, despite the virgin territory being traversed by both sides, they did have experience of playing each other, City having hosted the Turkish side in October 1953 in one of three matches to commemorate the completion of the new Maine Road floodlights. Although City were not expected to repeat the 5–1 score from 1953, confidence was high that a decent advantage could be constructed before the away leg in Istanbul two weeks later.

There was one unexpected element that would put a colossal spanner in the works, however.

Allison, one of the most accomplished and innovative coaches that English football had seen, committed the cardinal error of not bothering to have the Turks watched. Against Southampton at Maine Road, Fenerbahçe coach, Ignác Molnár, sat in the Main Stand taking copious notes. The 1–1 draw he witnessed did not faze him in the slightest. 'I wish my club had been playing City today,' he told the press afterwards, having seen the hosts labour terribly to bypass a defensive visiting side.

If Allison had been of mind to take a precautionary look at Fenerbahçe, he would have discovered a side that was defensively sound, with a young goalkeeper of outstanding talent. That he hadn't, reassuring himself that his City side could wipe the floor with Second Division-level players, meant that this information came as something of a surprise as the visitors held out for a 0–0 first-leg draw.

Despite young Yavuz Şimşek's tremendous showing between the posts on the night, City were presented with more than enough chances to score the necessary goals to make the second leg in Istanbul a formality. Francis Lee, Colin Bell and Tony Coleman all missed presentable opportunities, while Mike Summerbee snatched at the two best chances of all in a fitful, frustrating night for the near 39,000 packed into Maine Road for City's European debut. Allison spent an increasingly fretful 90 minutes fidgeting and shouting in the dugout, his strained instructions ringing out across the night sky towards a grumbling, uncomfortable Kippax.

MANCHESTER CITY 0–0 FENERBAHÇE | Att. 38,787
Mulhearn, Kennedy, Pardoe, Doyle, Heslop, Oakes, Lee, Bell, Summerbee, Young, Coleman

---

If Allison regretted not watching his opponents, Joe Mercer was unrepentant after the first leg, saying: 'Fenerbahçe are a good team, but I don't know if they can play any differently on their own ground than they did here. I don't plan to watch them in the meantime. I've seen all I want to see and I shall be very surprised if we don't win over there in Istanbul.'

After all the fevered anticipation of competing with some of the global names of football, both Allison and Mercer had kicked off by underestimating their medium-quality opponents. There was still time to recover, but it would have to be done the hard way, winning away from home in a place and against a team nobody knew anything about.

Admittedly, Turkish football at this stage of the late '60s had a reputation for amateurism and failure. The national team had not qualified for any finals tournaments and the biggest domestic sides were considered a soft draw in the early rounds of the continental competitions. That clubs from Turkey have since reached and – on one famous occasion – won European finals (Galatasaray's 2000 Europa League triumph), as well as developed talented players for a national team that is now a regular competitor in finals tournaments, belies the image of the footballing backwater Mercer and Allison mistook it for in the autumn of 1968.

Interestingly, Allison confessed to making what was for him, one of the greatest students of the game in English football, a beginner's error. He would later say in his autobiography: 'One basic misconception had undone me. It is one that is being slowly discarded by all but a few diehards in the English game. I mean the theory that the English football league is the toughest competition of them all ... I thought that because we had won the championship, that we were a great side. I was badly wrong.'

For Allison, schooled in the fluidity and movement of the Hungarian national side of Ferenc Puskás and Nándor Hidegkuti, the Milan side of Gunnar Nordahl and Helenio Herrera's Inter, this was a return to the small-time English parochialism that he hated and it was about to cost his club dearly.

Neil Young, quoted in Ian Penney's book *Manchester City: The Mercer–Allison Years*, agreed with his flamboyant boss: 'To this day I still don't know how we didn't beat them 10–1 at Maine Road. In that first leg, we did everything but score. I think this was one of Malcolm's biggest mistakes during his time at Maine Road.'

Teammate Colin Bell, City's focal point throughout the glory years, was equally adamant that their approach had smacked of ill-preparation, stating: 'It was unfortunate that it was our first experience of Europe. No English side had ever played against Turkish opposition either. They kicked us up in the air, picked us up and shook our hands and we accepted it. We weren't in the best of form at the time, but we still expected to win.'

Before the second leg, there were three domestic games to negotiate. In those days, a busy league and domestic cup schedule did not mean changing the team around to save legs for the more crucial games. In any case, European games were not seen as being more important than domestic matches.

Neither did the way the team played change greatly. City's 'up and at 'em' attacking style had served them well in the league and it was to be business as usual in European competition. As Allison had intimated, it was for the others to be frightened of City not vice versa.

League wins over Sunderland and Leeds were overshadowed by an embarrassing exit from the League Cup at lowly second-tier Blackpool.

Girl guides on the Bosporus

It was raining heavily in Manchester when the club's travelling party arrived at Ringway on 1 October. The squad of seventeen flew out into the unknown to find out what Fenerbahçe and the city of Istanbul had in store for them.

City would be housed in the Hilton Hotel – befitting their new-found status as glamorous league champions – on a hill overlooking the Mithatpaşa Stadium. It had also been picked to make sure the squad avoided the worst effects of the local cuisine.

Captain Tony Book, travelling with the squad but unable to play owing to an Achilles tendon injury, could not believe the sight that greeted him on pulling back the curtains the next morning: 'It was not much past 8 o'clock in the morning and already the queues to the ground were snaking back towards the hotel from the stadium. I realised straight away what this meant to the locals and that we were in for a hard time.'

By the time the squad headed for the stadium, its 32,000 capacity had been filled and another 10,000 fans were busy attempting to squeeze themselves inside its tall concrete walls. The bus carrying the City players edged slowly through the masses, affording the squad a close-up view of the fanaticism of the locals. 'The whole place', added Book, 'seemed to be sur-rounded by soldiers with guns. It is hard to ignore that sort of stuff when you have not experienced it before.' Once inside, a member of the local ground staff confirmed to an inquisitive Walter Griffiths, City's secretary, that the stadium was indeed over-full. Everything was set for a real test of City's sparse experience of such places.

At this point their coach's outspoken comments in the com-fort of a close-season Maine Road press conference must have felt hollow indeed. Without any kind of briefing on what to expect, the players were ashen-faced as they exited the bus to climb the steps into the heaving stadium.

Kick-off saw City led out into a wall of noise by Alan Oakes, captain in Book's absence, carrying a large bouquet of flowers and an apprehensive expression.

After a cagey start, City settled the better, with Oakes and Summerbee testing the home defence. City got an early feel of what might be in store for them if things went wrong, however, when Ogün Temizkanoğlu strode through a hesitant backline to score from Can Bartu's clever pass but was ruled offside. Not only had City been warned about Fenerbahçe's quick, incisive passing, but also the delirium that would greet any goal. As the referee whistled for the infringement, the City penalty area was already full of cameramen and cavorting club officials. However, Fenerbahçe, spurred on by the thoughts of an early goal and by the exhortations of the bubbling crowd, were in for a shock of their own.

In the twelfth minute, a moment of disaster for the Turks almost gave the tie to City. As Albert Barham wrote in his *Guardian* report the next morning: 'It seemed to knock the heart out of them for some time and gave City the lead they had wanted so desperately. It was a goal greeted in complete and shocked silence. Lee's long, looping pass which hovered over the penalty area was the cause. Ercan Aktuna, the big, burly strong man of the defence shaped to head it back. But he made a mistake. Deciding to fox the precocious Coleman with some of his own medicine, he anticipated that the ball would carry to Yavuz. It did not. Coleman, quick to spot the chance, pounced on it and as Yavuz came out to him, trying to tackle waist-high, Coleman popped the ball into the net.'

The 1–0 scoreline would see City through to the second round safely enough, if a little shaken. Oakes, playing superbly with the extra responsibility, and Neil Young, foraging back to aid the defence, were the stand-out performers as City held their ground.

Others were not faring so well in the cauldron of noise, though. As Allison later wrote: 'Before my eyes my players were simply freezing. The place was filled with hysterical Turks. Goalkeeper Ken Mulhearn was rooted in panic. George Heslop seemed unable to move coherently and even the swaggering "baby face" Tony Coleman found himself unable to play properly.'

Playing for survival, in the face of renewed Turkish efforts after the break, City could not hold out. In a wave of attacks, the home side drew level. The all-important morale-booster fell within two minutes of the restart and it was the substitute Abdullah Çevrim that scored it, finishing clinically after being put through a statuesque City defence by the clever passing of Ogün Altıparmak. Fenerbahçe's second, in the 78th minute, was scored by the provider of the first, after Can's quickly taken free kick.

In truth, City had not only committed the cardinal error of underestimating the Turks before a ball had been kicked, they had also compounded the mistake by repeating it in the second leg. As for Fenerbahçe, looking beaten and dispirited after City's early goal, they had been allowed back into a game they appeared to have given up as lost.

With Young pinned deeper and deeper by Fenerbahçe's clever running, Summerbee was left to run a lone furrow up front, often seeing the ball cut out before it reached him.

Molnár, the home coach, had thus got one over on his English counterpart. Allison's love of Hungarian football must surely have allowed him a wry smile, as he had been outfoxed by a countryman of his heroes Puskás and Hidegkuti.

City were out of the European Cup before they had had time to acclimatise. The bonfires being lit on the terraces as the teams left the pitch were a sure-fire metaphor for the heat being felt by Mercer and Allison. Having promised the earth, they were returning from their first-ever European trip empty-handed and embarrassed.

Barham's *Guardian* report concluded: 'City are out of the European Champions' Cup at their first attempt. It was not for the want of trying. They did their best. They covered as well as they could. They defended stubbornly. But three Fenerbahçe forwards were their betters. One sensed they would be from the brief glimpses seen in their attack in the goalless first leg at Maine Road ... By the standard one has seen elsewhere it was clean, fast and hard.'

As the excited crowd invaded the pitch, City's defeated players trooped off round-shouldered to face the gruelling task of picking up league form and saving some face from a season that was quickly turning sour.

FENERBAHÇE 2–1 MANCHESTER CITY | Att. officially 32,000 | Coleman

Mulhearn, Connor, Pardoe, Doyle, Heslop, Oakes, Lee, Bell, Summerbee, Young, Coleman

---

Fenerbahçe's progress in the tournament was halted immediately as they were dumped out without a squeak of complaint by an Ajax side playing the kind of 'clockwork' football under Rinus Michels that Allison had so admired from Puskás and his men.

For Allison, it was the bitterest pill to swallow. Ruminating in *Colours of My Life*, he remembered: 'It was a colossal flop. I had been so sure we would cut a fiery path through European football. At that Championship press conference in the spring, I had announced that European football was filled with cowards, people who would simply turn and run against the force and aggression that had become the style of Manchester City ... Maybe I had been a bit cocky about this first tie. I should have watched the Turks beforehand, if only to guard against complacency from the team. But the defeat had come simply because our team had not played. I remember groaning from the dugout "They look like girl guides."'

Thus, Allison, the great student of European football, had been tripped up by it at the earliest stage possible. Undone by poor finishing in the first leg, City were undressed completely when they arrived in Istanbul, as the culture shock dumb-founded many of the players. After not knowing what to expect, not briefed by the staff as to how much pressure, noise and excitement the game was likely to engender among the home supporters, certain players froze like rabbits in the headlights. It was a costly, painful, but ultimately useful lesson. City would be stronger next time, although when that would be was at this stage unclear, as the team returned to a growing relegation fight in the First Division.

* * *

The 1968–9 season would end in bitter disappointment in the league. City, champions twelve months before, finished in a des-ultory thirteenth place, 27 points adrift of first-place Leeds. For Allison and Mercer, who were just getting used to the glory they had brought to the club, it was a huge disappointment.

Saviour came in the shape of a run to the FA Cup final, a string of great performances, which really began to take shape in the fifth round at snowbound Ewood Park where City demol-ished Blackburn Rovers. A last-gasp winner from Tommy Booth in the Villa Park semi-final with Everton took the Blues through to Wembley where they would meet Leicester City.

Young's unerring left-foot winner from Summerbee's cut back was enough to seal the win. The season had been saved with practically the last kick of the campaign. On top of that, City would be back in Europe for a second season in a row and Allison was already working hard on a fail-safe plan to avoid the disasters of Turkey.

The summer began with disruption. Tony Coleman, scorer of the sole City goal in Istanbul, put in a transfer request. Worse still, as the goal frames came down at Maine Road and the ground staff got to grips with their summer chores, news broke that Malcolm Allison had flown to Turin where he was discussing terms to become the new manager of Juventus. The initial contact had apparently even come as Allison was preparing his side for the Cup final.

Allison, for ever the itchy-feet merchant, was at it again. Mercer felt dismay and hoped publicly that his colleague would see sense and come back to the fold. Allison himself, beguiled by the reception he received in Italy and the champagne treatment he was being afforded at every turn, was close to signing the lucrative contract that had been prepared for him. It included alluring clauses regarding frequent travel back to the UK, a rent-free mansion on the shores of Lake Como, a car of his choice (not necessarily one of the prosaic models from Juventus' main backers Fiat) and a salary that would have made his paymasters in Manchester blanch. In short, the only thing stopping him from taking out his pen there and then was the unfinished business that he and Mercer had talked about.

Instead, Allison took himself off on a flamboyant tour of the south of France and Rome with journalist friends, hooked up with what he euphemistically called an 'exotic dancer' – who, ironically, was Hungarian – whom he had met in one of Turin's seedier nightclubs and allowed his mind to wander from the subject at hand.

The moment had passed.

In addition to the unfinished business, there was also Allison's gnawing ambition to rub neighbours United's noses further into the dirt. The run-ins with Crerand and Busby, when Allison had just arrived in the city, had left an indelible mark on his psyche and he dearly wanted to finish the job of levering City onto a higher pedestal than United.

By winning the league ahead of them, Allison had begun to bask in the glorious power shift that he had foreseen. What he had not imagined was United trumping that by winning the

European Cup two weeks later, eclipsing City's achievement. For the final game of the season, the *Match of the Day* cameras had followed their instincts to Old Trafford, confident that they were in the correct location to witness the title being won. City's fantastic achievement was, thus, captured on grainy newsreel footage and half-forgotten when United triumphed so romantically at Wembley against Benfica.

On top of everything, it was here in Manchester, in the swirling vortex of European football, that Allison's urges burned brightest of all.

Allison's empathy with the City faithful had grown to such an extent he found it impossible to break the bond. Underneath everything, his failure in Europe was a stain on his credentials as a trailblazer. Having assiduously studied the intricacies of the continental game from the '50s onwards, Allison wanted to emulate the greats and storm the European stage with his swashbuckling side. The long periods he had spent learning about the philosophies of Helenio Herrera at Inter, Gunnar Nordahl's imposing AC Milan, Rinus Michels and his beautiful balance of steel and artistry at Ajax, Béla Guttmann's groundbreaking work at Benfica and of the great Hungarians he had idolised since he was a run-of-the-mill centre-back at West Ham were not to be wasted now, just as his City team was flowering to greatness.

Allison's mind was made up. He would stay in Manchester, shunning the bright lights of Europe, and he would bring the continental dazzle to Maine Road instead.

ALLISON'S PROPHECY COMES GOOD A YEAR LATE

This is the one

Without realising it at the time, Fenerbahçe had done Manchester City and Malcolm Allison something of a favour.

In dumping them out of their inaugural European adventure at the first hurdle, the Turkish champions ensured that City's flamboyant coach would, in his own words, 'never again' under-estimate an opponent. 'Never again' would he leave anything in the pre-match planning to doubt. Allison meant business. It also meant that as City began their preparations for the European Cup Winners' Cup campaign of 1969–70, there would be no outrageous statements of intent from City's boss.

Allison was just as focused and determined, but he was intent on letting his players do all the talking this time round.

Success would arguably mark Allison out as the innovative, outside-the-box thinker that certain aspects of his reputation concealed. Almost literally, the plumes of cigar smoke could occasionally veil the idea that here was a coach who thought about the game just as deeply as the grand masters. Allison's career at West Ham in the '50s had been cut short by tubercu-losis. Like many players whose careers had been curtailed by ill-fortune, Allison the manager was profoundly driven.

As a player, he would lead delegations of teammates to Cassettari's snack bar around the corner from Upton Park. There they would huddle round the tables and watch intently as Allison shuffled salt and pepper pots around, extolling the virtues of the great Hungarian side of Puskás and Hidegkuti. It became the daily meeting place for a group of Allison's disciples, who would all go on to manage in one capacity or another in the higher echelons of the sport: John Cartwright for the England under 18s, John Bond, who would follow Big Mal into the Maine Road hot seat when Allison's second coming at Maine Road failed, Frank O'Farrell, who would manage across the road at Old Trafford (and would be in charge of the Leicester side beaten at Wembley to allow City access to the Cup Winners' Cup) and Phil Woosnam, who went on to be a founding member of the North American Soccer League across the Atlantic. There was also Ken Brown, who would be a hugely influential figure in Norwich City's rise to the top flight, and Dave Sexton, who would carve out a successful managerial career at Chelsea, Queens Park Rangers and Manchester United. The list was almost endless. In the youth academy at West Ham, Allison took special care of another young prodigy that he felt had what it took. The spindly, star-struck youngster's name? Bobby Moore.

While Joe Mercer got plenty of plaudits for his behind-the-scenes work as the grand old sage, Allison's more boisterous reputation divided opinion. His players were cutting the mustard: his dietary regimes making them fitter, his exercise programmes making them nimbler and his team-building sessions making them mentally stronger. The City side about to unleash its effervescent attacking football on the continent would be doing it to Allison's unique blueprint.

City had been drawn against Atlético Bilbao in the opening round. Bilbao, with a strong English history, were led by ex-West Brom and England player Ronnie Allen and had a side containing various elements of the Spanish national team. Owing to a decree covering nationalism issued by Generalissimo Franco in 1941, the club had been obliged to change its name from the original anglicised *Athletic* to *Atlético*, but would revert to the original in the late '70s after the demise of the dictatorship.

Having started the season with mixed results, City were lower mid-table when a gap presented itself before they were due to play Chelsea. Taking advantage of the space, Allison and Mercer flew out to gain some inside information on their opponents. This time they were adamant nothing would be left to guesswork.

Although the Spanish season was yet to start, they took the chance to visit San Mamés, an intimidating 40,000-capacity arena that housed some of the most fanatical supporters in the country, to watch Bilbao in a pre-season friendly, where they were laughingly given seats behind a pillar. What Allison witnessed filled him with confidence. 'I know we can cause them problems,' he said on returning to Manchester. 'If we put Bilbao under pressure, we can beat them.' The old confidence was flooding back.

They even had time to check the hotel they would use on the outskirts of the city. As Mercer stressed: 'This time, we will miss nothing in our preparation.'

Asked about their opponents' style of play, Mercer continued: 'They are a straightforward, hard side, who play in a very British style.' Captain Tony Book, who had missed the previous excursion in Europe against Fenerbahçe, agreed: 'Malcolm's trip to see Bilbao play will be invaluable. He always weighs up a side very well, as we've found before with FA Cup opponents that he has spied on.'

If City were to fail this time, it would not be through a lack of preparation, nor from underestimating their opponents.

In an article in *Goal* magazine, dated 13 September 1969, under the headline, 'Last year's disaster won't happen again', Peter Barnard agreed that 'Manchester City go to Bilbao this week thoroughly acquainted with their opponents and well aware that they cannot afford to fail as they did in last year's European Cup'.

In the same magazine, Leslie Vernon ran the rule over Bilbao, writing: 'Ronnie Allen lost his chief aid, Rafa Iriondo, whose coaching was largely responsible for the club's cup success last season. The sensitive Iriondo did not like the idea of working under a new boss and now Allen has to shoulder the responsibility of preparing his squad for the needle games against City.' This kind of clash of personalities would resonate with City supporters soon enough, when Allison and Mercer's relationship foundered for similar reasons.

City's side had not changed unduly from the one defeated in Turkey twelve months earlier. Joe Corrigan had returned in goal, ousting Ken Mulhearn, and Tony Coleman's ongoing transfer talks with Sheffield Wednesday, which would come to fruition a month later, had brought about the promotion of promising youngster Ian Bowyer to first-team duties. Bowyer would, some ten years later, taste the pinnacle of European achievement in the Nottingham Forest side that defeated Malmö to capture the 1979 European Cup. Even more crucially, skipper Book was fit again. It should not be underestimated how much Book's steadying influence counted, particularly in hostile away games. The captain's solid character acted as a calming influence on the more volatile members of Allison's squad. His presence in San Mamés would be invaluable.

The squad arrived late in Bilbao after their flight from Ringway was delayed while a replacement plane was found, the original having run into technical trouble during an earlier flight. The afternoon arrival still afforded Allison and first-team coach Dave Ewing time to take a light training session before the players were ordered to rest in their rooms.

If the players were well briefed on what to expect, there were plenty of surprises in store for the travelling fans, however.

In order to get to Bilbao and find accommodation success- fully, City fan Steve Parish, an employee of British Rail, made his tortuous way courtesy of the national rail company to northern Spain. In Dave Wallace's book *Us and Them*, a com- pendium of fan recollections of travelling to City away games through the ages, he explained: 'The Spanish railway route to Bilbao goes the long way around, so I hitched the 80 miles from the border. It took five hours to get halfway, so I took the local train for the rest of the way. I wandered down to the San Mamés and interrupted Ronnie Allen's press conference asking, "Excuse me, where do I get tickets for the match?" I was sent to the City team's hotel, where I obtained three of the tickets we needed … Back at the stadium, I brandished my letter on MCFC paper and the Spanish official got excited and sent me down a tunnel underneath the stand. They opened a door for me, and I was in City's dressing room. I'd got my red- and-black-striped shirt on, so the official must have thought I was one of the players despite the glasses I was wearing! Malcolm Allison wasn't fooled, though. I explained why I was in the dressing room 30 minutes before kick-off. "Any tickets, lads?" Mal asked. With half a dozen comps in hand, I beat a hasty retreat. Three of these were given to Spanish urchins outside.'

Although Parish's trip home was badly affected by 'an allergic reaction to the paella', City fared slightly better after a shocking start.

San Mamés, named after a local child martyr and the loca- tion of several notable visiting sacrifices, was not a place for the faint-hearted. Packed to capacity, as the teams came out to an enthusiastic welcome, minds shot back to the exuberant welcome afforded City by the denizens of Istanbul.

The extent of the challenge became evident after eleven minutes. Bilbao raced into a two-goal lead through José María Argoitia and future national team boss Javier Clemente that thrilled the packed crowd and sent shivers down the spines of the away following tucked into one corner of the ground.

With dizzying speed and a blur of intricate exchanges of passes, the Spanish side had undone the City defence instantly. 'They were going through us like a dose of salts,' claimed Neil Young later. 'I have learned that the Europeans are much quicker – maybe twice as quick – at controlling the ball than we are,' the striker added.

Allison was quickly down on the touchline, barking instructions 'to get tighter' and deny Bilbao the space to create more havoc. City gradually calmed the home storm and began to get back into the match.

The coach, who had minutes before kick-off broken his enforced silence to predict a 3–2 win, telling the travelling journalists they would 'be proud to be British after you see the way we play tonight', must have once again been rueing opening his mouth, as his team laboured to keep the deficit to two. After his 'we will terrify Europe' gaffe the previous year, he had told himself not to utter anything to the press that could be used against him, but here he was again, heading for the morning's back pages for all the wrong reasons.

City rallied before half-time, however, and clawed it back to 1–2 after Young converted a sharp pass from Bowyer to score with a shot that went in off goalkeeper José Ángel Iribar's shoulder. The half-time break allowed Allison time to drill his thoughts into the players. 'You must concentrate, keep tight and not lose your man for a minute,' he insisted. The opening minutes of the second period saw the hosts regain their two-goal lead, Argoitia this time turning provider as his cross was headed past Corrigan by Fidel Uriarte.

Before things improved, Corrigan was again called into action, saving bravely from the lively Argoitia and José Ángel Rojo, as Bilbao sensed the chance to widen the gap further. City had other ideas, however, and reduced the arrears in the 68th minute, when Summerbee's corner was not properly cleared and, as the ball squirmed out as far as Tommy Booth on the edge of the area, the young stopper whacked it back through a forest of legs and inside the post. Despite the early pummelling, Allison's side came back well and an equaliser fell their way after 86 minutes.

The outstanding Book – how differently City's defence had played with him back in their ranks – sent Bell scampering down the right flank with a beautifully weighted through ball. Bell's cross scorched into the box and went in off a desperate Luis María Echeberría Igartua. Holding on for the final four minutes, City had revealed exceptional character after twice being two goals behind and had also racked up three goals away from home, which would help if the second leg was a tight affair.

Allison was delighted, stating: 'This is a wonderful result for us. We only started to play our normal game late in the first half. I knew we could come through once we got our game going. The lads are a bit niggled because they thought we might have won, but just wait for the second leg!'

Mercer was more circumspect but couldn't help revealing his delight, saying: 'Strangely enough, I did not feel too bad when their second goal went in. Once Young scored, I knew we would do well. However, the game's not over by a long way. We will start the next leg as favourites, but it's still going to be very difficult to beat this side. Bilbao surprised me. They played far better than I thought they would.'

Mercer's gentle words of praise fitted the level-headed

counterbalance that he offered to Allison's exuberance. He was the cup of tea and biscuits to the young coach's omnipresent champagne and cigars. The pairing had worked well on the domestic front, now Maine Road was about to see it in action in a totally different context. City, still to record their first European win, having drawn two and lost one of their first three continental games, were slowly beginning to get an idea of how to play wily, well-drilled foreign opposition.

For Young, the main difference had been the marking: 'Malcolm would play the reserves against the first team in training and have the reserves play the same way the Europeans would. That was a big help to us. One of the big things was man-to-man marking. We didn't really play that way, but we practised it in the reserve games, so that we knew what to expect on the night.'

Book remembers: 'The game against Bilbao was a really tough one. They looked a very good side, to be fair. Off the pitch there were no signs of the hostility we had experienced in Istanbul. Ronnie Allen made us feel very welcome. They gave us a bit of a chasing in the first leg. The papers said I personally had done well, which was pleasing but all this European stuff was new to me and I was enjoying it.'

ATLÉTICO BILBAO 3–3 MANCHESTER CITY | Att. 45,000 | Young, Booth, Echeberría (o.g.)

Corrigan, Book, Pardoe, Doyle, Booth, Oakes, Summerbee, Bell, Lee, Young, Bowyer

Two weeks later, on 1 October, City entertained Bilbao in the second leg and finally achieved their first-ever win in European competition.

'Exciting City banished a bad dream when they blasted their way through to the second round with a non-stop onslaught against defiant Atlético Bilbao,' enthused the *Guardian*'s report the day after the second leg.

The enthusiasm was matched in *The Times*: 'City's indomitable spirit and ceaseless attacking enthusiasm were the factors which proved decisive in their 3–0 win against Atlético Bilbao.'

City, winning as decisively as the score suggested, were through. Having told Allison to keep his mouth tightly shut, it was Mercer who was first to pipe up after the tie had been won. 'Bilbao are a predictable side,' he stated. 'We thought that we would be able to find a way through the middle, but I admit I was worried when we went so long without scoring and when young Bowyer hit the bar, I began to think it was going to be one of those nights, but the goal from Alan Oakes settled it.'

Oakes spoke of 'hitting it and seeing what happened' of the goal that finally broke the deadlock. Later, City's record appearance-maker would say of his feat: 'Joe and Malcolm had told us to go forward as Bilbao retreated and just have a go. I remember just running with the ball and shooting. It was one of the greatest moments of my career.'

As far as the Basques were concerned, the game may have hinged on an incident in the tunnel at half-time. As the sides came off, a scuffle broke out between Mike Doyle, always a staunch defender of the sky-blue faith, and José Ramón Betzuen. Ronnie Allen, speaking to the press after the game, said: 'I had to take him off as he could hardly breathe. After that we were finished.'

Indeed, Allen had a point. City's breakthrough had come in the 59th minute and Oakes' forward burst had come about as a direct result of the experienced midfielder being able to snatch possession away from the seventeen-year-old Josu Ortuondo, who had replaced the injured Betzuen at half-time.

Maine Road, with almost 50,000 roaring City on, exploded in joy. With the forwards well shackled by Bilbao's defence, it had fallen to Oakes to do the business from further back. With just 34 goals in a seventeen-year City career, Oakes tended to pop up at crucial moments, never more so than the goal that got things moving for an initially nervous-looking City side.

City were rampant after the goal, with Bell nodding in from close range after Young had seen his shot parried by the busy Iribar and the teenage sensation Bowyer picking up another loose save from Iribar to slot home from inside the box, as the Spaniards wilted in the face of wave after wave of vivacious attacking play.

Bowyer had proved something of a sensation in his first full season, exploding onto the scoring charts as the First Division's top scorer that autumn and knocking in his first European goal, all while just clear of his eighteenth birthday. The youngster would not stay long at Maine Road and the irony of his career blossoming at the City Ground under Brian Clough was not lost on Allison. Bowyer was the midfield mainstay and the scorer of a critical semi-final goal for Forest in the Müngersdorfer Stadium in Cologne that sent Clough's men through to their first European Cup final in 1979.

City's European credentials had now been hoisted back into the spotlight and the rest of the continent was sitting up and taking notice of the Blues as Allison had intended.

MANCHESTER CITY 3–0 ATLÉTICO BILBAO | Att. 49,665 | Oakes, Bell, Bowyer

Corrigan, Book, Pardoe, Doyle, Booth, Oakes, Summerbee, Bell, Lee, Young, Bowyer

The draw for the second round pitched City against the Belgians Lierse SK, whose campaign had begun effortlessly with an

11–1 mauling of APOEL Nicosia. Also in the pot for the second round were Rangers, taking on the little-known Górnik Zabrze of Poland, and Cardiff City, who were drawn to play Turkish side Göztepe SK. The tie of the round featured emerging Dutch giants PSV Eindhoven against AS Roma.

Peter Barnard, writing his preview in *Goal*, saw few pitfalls for City: 'Manchester City's progress should not be impeded by Lierse, who have been watching a film of City's first round game and must be feeling a shade pessimistic … In that form, Joe Mercer's men are a frightening proposition. They badly need a good run in Europe to erase memories of the early exit last year. Malcolm Allison's "we'll show those cowards of Europe" remark looked embarrassing – maybe he should have saved it for this year, because City's attacking style is certainly making them a feared name at present.'

Meanwhile, a twenty-strong spying mission from Lier had arrived in Manchester to see City in action against Southampton the weekend before the first leg. The south-coast side, playing a dour defensive game, managed to restrict City to a narrow 1–0 win. With Tony Towers deputising for the injured Young, City's performance had a lopsided, slow-moving look about it that failed to impress the Belgians. Bob Quisenaerts, the president, stated afterwards: 'I think City will have to play better than that when they visit us in Belgium next week. We were not particularly impressed with their performance.'

Four days later, the people of Lier would be impressed enough, however. With Young back in place of Towers, City, at full strength, had the game and the tie wrapped up after less than 45 minutes. Plenty of fans had made the short trip across the North Sea.

Alan Whitfield was one of the many hundreds who decided to travel to Belgium. 'It was a long day trip organised through a travel agent,' he says. 'On the way back we had to land at Blackpool airport because of thick fog in Manchester. All the booze and fags we had brought back with us was confiscated because we hadn't been out of the country for more than 24 hours! I had to coach it back to Manchester from there.'

Others braved the Social Club's special flight, arranged by Roy Clarke, who ran the club into the early '80s. Return flight, hotel bed and breakfast plus match ticket was an all-in bargain of £23.

Paul Priest from Gatley couldn't afford this sum so decided to hitch, beginning an odyssey that eventually got him featured in the City programme years later. 'We decided to hitch, leaving on the Sunday night to give us time to get there for the Wednesday!' he explains. 'Just as well, really, as the trip involved copious amounts of alcohol, a lift in an egg van and a night in a bus shelter. The ferry took eight hours, a queasy crossing, then we jumped a train to Antwerp, finally arriving Tuesday afternoon. Finding the ground, we decided to compare their social club with City's award-winning institution. It was our introduction to proper lager (considered a lady's drink in those days). For food it was chocolate bars.'

The tiny ground was packed as the two teams came out for the first leg. With the players in increasingly good form (City had begun a climb towards the top of the table after their poor start), there was every reason to feel confident. Runaway league leaders Everton had been dumped out of the League Cup and City had built up an eight-game unbeaten run which included seven victories.

With the Manchester derby looming at the weekend, Allison could have been forgiven for a conservative team selection, but City were at full strength and the result was a vindication of Allison and Mercer's approach. Ahead after seven minutes, City had the match tied up after 44, with two more. Lee scored two and Bell the other. City's vivid attacking play was unstoppable, but – with a comfortable half-time lead – the pace slowed and Allison's tactics became contain and hold, in order to save legs for the derby.

Young felt misled by the management team. 'Malcolm conned us before we played Lierse really,' he said. 'I remember after he came back from watching them, he said, "It's going to be very difficult against them. I've just seen them and they're a very good side. It won't be easy." In the end we *did* beat them easily. They were never in it. Malcolm knew we'd beat them easily and was trying to keep our feet on the ground.'

Paul Priest and his mates also managed to make it to the match after their marathon journey. 'We had fallen asleep in the Lierse Social Club the night before after drinking too many Belgian lagers and next day went to pick up our tickets. They were for a row of kitchen chairs just yards from the touchline. A great view but what would Lord Justice Taylor think today? I remember a great game but nothing of the long trip home. I went to work the following Monday and my manager docked me a week's wages instead of firing me, as he had threatened before I left.'

Once again, Allison had proved himself a master of the grand occasion. It may only have been a second-round first-leg match, in a tiny Belgian town, with barely 19,000 paying spectators, but for City it represented a leap forward. A first away win in Europe, achieved at a canter, playing City's by-now typical brand of swashbuckling attacking play. In delivering this result, Allison highlighted another facet of his managerial skills, which put him ahead of the field.

Early-era mind games might look a tad crude in the light of what has passed since, but in 1969, these little advantages being eked out by coaches prepared to look at every detail of match preparation stood City in good stead. It would be a generation before José Mourinho and Alex Ferguson took the whole mechanism to another level, but Allison's keen sense of the small detail often made a difference.

LIERSE 0–3 MANCHESTER CITY | Att. 18,000 | Lee (2), Bell
Corrigan, Book, Pardoe, Doyle (Heslop), Booth, Oakes, Summerbee, Bell, Lee, Young, Bowyer

With the players all on board, Allison felt he had carte blanche in how he went about the rest of the season. Never reticent at blowing his own trumpet, he kept his counsel and prepared feverishly for the derby, which City would win 4–0, and the relative formality of the return leg with Lierse.

If only a handful of intrepid fans managed to see the away game in the flesh, a few more wanted to see the return leg in Moss Side. Young fan Peter Thornton was wrestling with something of a problem, though: 'I was going to my first-ever night match and, despite my dad not being interested in football, it was a thrill that I was going with him. Instead of catching three buses like we did on a Saturday, we went straight to Maine Road in his car, which in itself was special at the time. The best part of the night for me was being the "official guide" showing him where we went in, the Kippax, where the toilets were, where you could buy a pie and a Bovril, and where we should stand. We must have got in quite early because we had no trouble getting my favourite spot behind one of the big white tunnels. The game was a blur to be honest. We absolutely murdered them. Slick City at their absolute best. I was so pleased because I probably hoped my dad would fall in love with City as I had.

'What I remember most is how different a night game felt. I'd never seen the floodlights on for one thing. They seemed to make the grass seem greener. The noise seemed louder, the smell of cigarette smoke and Bovril and pies was intoxicating. When we went on Saturdays, I was usually standing with lads my own age. Now I was standing among grown men and it was just the best. Sadly, he never did catch the football bug, but I was back for the next round.'

If the first leg had been a relative cakewalk, the second tie was like lambs to the slaughter with City running out 5–0 winners. On an icy night, Allison and Mercer chose to rest goalkeeper Corrigan and striker Young, replacing them with Mulhearn and eighteen-year-old debutant Derek Jeffries. In an odd twist of fate, it was Mulhearn's first outing with the first team since the ill-fated match in Istanbul.

The Belgians were torn asunder. A goal from Summerbee, firing in with a fierce low shot from eighteen yards, separated the sides at half-time, but Allison's attention to detail was about to come up trumps again. With a frosty night beginning to cool further, the players changed footwear at the break, the new boots giving them greater grip. Four more goals sailed past the Belgian goalkeeper, but a disappointing crowd of only 26,486, deterred by a combination of the freezing temperatures and what seemed like a foregone conclusion, was the only obvious negative from a night of flourishing attacking football.

Perhaps resigned to their fate, Lierse had fallen to a double from Lee, two more from Bell and the early Summerbee strike. 'If I could, I would come across to see City play every week,' said the Lierse manager Staf van den Bergh.

Expectations had now been raised. Lierse bowed out with nothing more than Lee's compliment. 'This performance by Lierse was one of the most sporting I can remember,' he said. 'It is an example to others. They knew they had little chance and we could have run the risk of real injury had they got stuck in hard, but they played fair and they played well. We all felt like going in their dressing room at the end to thank them.'

MANCHESTER CITY 5–0 LIERSE | Att. 26,486 | Summerbee, Bell (2), Lee (2)

Mulhearn, Book, Pardoe, Doyle, Booth, Oakes (Towers), Summerbee, Bell, Lee, Jeffries, Bowyer

---

Allison awoke the next morning in exuberant mood. City's 8–0 aggregate win had thrust them into the limelight of the tournament's last eight, where the Portuguese student side Académica de Coimbra awaited them. Allison's studious approach to continental challenges would now be met by real students, but few doubted City's ability to pass their exams.

Unusually for a quarter-final tie, Académica were as wet behind the ears as City in terms of European pedigree. This tie would be their seventh in Europe (and City's too). Their progress in the Cup Winners' Cup had brought them narrowly past Finnish side Kuopion and the Germans of FC Magdeburg to reach this stage. The other ties featured the Bulgarians of Levski Sofia against Górnik, Roma versus Göztepe and Dinamo Zagreb against Schalke 04.

Safely housed in a train rattling north through Portugal from Lisbon, Allison was in typically majestic form. Having spent lunch sitting in Rossio Square in downtown Lisbon drinking red wine with Joe Mercer, it was a lightly inebriated City coach who began explaining to journalist and confidant James Lawton how he saw football's role in life: 'A lot of people in football see football as an end in itself. They do not relate it to life. I'll never be trapped by the game. I love life and what I love about football is that you can compress into it all the strengths and weaknesses of life. It's a mirror to life … there is so much you can see in it. There's courage, there's weakness, there's real fear. You can see boys becoming men in front of your eyes. You can see characters stretching and dwindling.'

The irony of Allison's words would only really be recognised later, when the same Portugal he was now traversing at the peak of his coaching career would become a refuge as his life began to unravel and his reputation began to fade.

To the eyes of the waiting Portuguese journalists, however, there were other issues to report on.

'English football. Pretty, pretty, pretty, it isn't' screamed the headline of *A Bola* on the morning of 5 March 1970. 'Air of the second division, masked by two or three stars' cooed another headline, with the words of Vítor Santos continuing throughout the piece in a similarly disdainful tone. 'Lee, Bell and Summerbee distinguished themselves well above the others,' the report continued. Curiously, for those City aficionados, who remembered the two games with the team from Coimbra, the feeling was mutual. In the end, two horribly messy and unnecessarily quarrelsome matches saw City go through, but not without a mighty scare.

The press were more positive about the fans that had made the difficult journey to central Portugal. Alongside a picture of a huge 'Manchester City' banner in the stadium and an image of the FA Cup, *A Bola* ran the headline: 'Few but great'. The piece stated: 'There were only a small number of Manchester City fans to support their team at the game with Académica, but they were good ones. Throughout the game they noisily backed their team and, for long periods, could be heard above the home crowd, despite its numerical superiority.'

Befitting a town of ancient repute (Coimbra houses one of Europe's oldest universities), the pre-match courtesies looked nothing like the rough reception granted City on the pitch. The home side had gone to great lengths to welcome the City party. Each delegate, player, member of the coaching staff and administrator was given a bottle of vintage Port wine, Académica de Coimbra monikered ashtrays, guidebooks about Coimbra, cotton badges and pennants commemorating the match and, for the chairman, the special memento of a silver-plated ornamental Portuguese *caravela* ship.

No detail had been spared to make the City party feel welcome. But that was off the pitch.

'They kicked us all over the park,' remembers Tommy Booth, 50 years later. 'They were supposed to be £50-a-month students, but they were big and strong and played really dirty. Some of them looked way too old to be students too!' *A Bola* begged to differ, offering the home side the soaring title of 'Eleven little birds, alive and dancing'.

In a tough struggle, City were surprised not only by the physical presence of the Portuguese, dressed dramatically all in black, but also by their unwillingness to break ranks and attack. 'We were surprised they didn't come out and try and score,' said Francis Lee at the end of the game. 'I always expected that they would come out and attack us, but they seemed happy to pass in little triangles with little effect bar holding on to possession.' City would be making better use of similar little triangular passes under Pep Guardiola half a century later.

Colin Bell also offered his opinion, saying: 'It wasn't a good game, with everything strangled in the middle of the pitch. I must say I didn't really understand Académica's tactics. Surely they needed to try and score a goal?' If Bell and his teammates had listened to the home manager Julio Pereira's pre-match assertion that his side would be 'outclassed by City', they would perhaps have understood the home mindset better.

In truth, there had been one great opportunity for the home side, when António Jorge had managed to edge ahead of Booth but had been blocked by a typically brave dive from Joe Corrigan. 'I got so many injuries in those early games,' Corrigan told me. 'The pitches were very different to today's billiard tables. In Portugal it was a cold night with a hard pitch. Mind you the return in Manchester was a swamp.'

Noting the 'badly educated masseur', *A Bola* reported that the Belgian referee Robert Schaut was, during the second period, 'forced to address the Manchester City bench and ask them to retreat from the touchline and cease their shouting. Contrary to early reports that it concerned the trainer, Allison, the referee was actually directing his remarks to the "masseur" Ewing.' The strapping Ewing was a vociferous presence alongside Allison on the bench and, on this occasion, was banished to sit alongside Mercer in the stands after being sent off by Schaut, who later explained: 'The City trainer was sent to the stands for what I would call ungentlemanly conduct. He was doing too much shouting and I will not allow this.'

For his part, Ewing could only rue his behaviour. 'It was unfortunate,' he said. 'I always shouted as a player ... but I have never been in this sort of trouble before and certainly never sent off.'

Ewing's arrival in the crowd added a single digit to a surprisingly small attendance, due partly to the fact that national broadcaster Radio Televisão Portugal had decided to televise the game live, enabling many locals to watch in the warm comfort of their homes.

ACADÉMICA DE COIMBRA 0–0 MANCHESTER CITY | Att. 8,206
Corrigan, Book (Heslop), Mann, Doyle, Booth, Oakes, Pardoe, Bell, Summerbee, Lee, Young

A Bola had a column entitled, 'The Chronicles of A.F. Rebelo de Carvalho', a kind of Portuguese antecedent to today's widely read features on the game's shapes and forms by tactics gurus, such as Michael Cox. In his piece, Mr de Carvalho explained the intricacies of the different kinds of ball City might use in the second leg and how the shooting of Lee (whacking it as hard as he could) and the passing of Bell (caressing it like an early-form Kevin De Bruyne) might affect the trajectory of the Thistle or Mitre balls. De Carvalho insisted that Académica were missing a trick if they did not pay attention to Bell's column in *Striker* magazine that included his findings on the subject. The Portuguese press would be leaving no stones unturned in their preparations. If Académica could match their fastidious preparations on the pitch, they could still cause City some trouble.

By the time of the second leg, City had claimed the League Cup in a divot-strewn Wembley final with West Brom. With a delayed return from a fog-bound Portugal, the preparation could hardly have been worse. City eventually arrived back just 36 hours before their Wembley date with West Brom. Injury problems were mounting too, but out of adversity came a squad harmony and spirit of togetherness that could not be broken. Buoyed by their League Cup success, Allison drove his tiring squad on towards a unique climax to the season, packing the defence and encouraging left-back Glyn Pardoe to break into midfield in a new role, part-design, part-making-ends-meet. Pardoe had already scored the winner in extra time at Wembley and now the black shirts of Académica were about to stretch this second-leg tie to 120 minutes too.

Before the match could kick off, an argument over colours raged in the Maine Road corridors, with the referee insisting Académica's black shirts clashed with his own and that he would 'look like a clown' if he changed to red or blue. The Portuguese refused to change, claiming their colours were a centuries-old tradition that they could not countenance dropping. The referee acquiesced by changing into a smart white top for the occasion.

As in the first leg, the match turned into a war of attrition as the eager black shirts hounded the sky-blue ones out of their stride. In fact, they also found other ways of impeding City's stride, as Bell, Heslop and Doyle were all injured during a game that became increasingly bogged down. Doyle later wrote in his autobiography *Blue Blood*: 'They kicked us five times harder than they had done in Portugal. It was the first time I had ever come across a massed defensive system that involved all eleven men at the back. They were cynical and blatant in their defensive tactics. It seemed ridiculous that three weeks earlier everyone had been dismissing them as a bunch of students more interested in sitting their exams … They had degrees alright. In how to mix it out on the pitch.'

With both sides labouring into a desperate, untidy extra half-hour, Tony Towers – who was introduced after Heslop received a gashed knee – took things into his own hands. As *A Bola* put it the following day: 'After three and a half hours of resistance to English football, the English way – strong and ugly – finally prevailed.'

They were right in a way. The goal, when it finally came, was no thing of beauty, with seventeen-year-old Towers' shot securing passage to the last four, after the ball had bobbled to him in the very last minute of the additional thirty. It was Towers' first goal in senior football.

As the scorer drank enthusiastically from a bottle of milk in the changing room, his coach sat down next to him on the bench and slung a grateful arm over his shoulder. Big Mal's trademark glass of champagne was missing as he toasted Towers with a small bottle of beer. The bubbly would remain on ice for bigger and better nights to come.

MANCHESTER CITY 1–0 ACADÉMICA DE COIMBRA | Att. 36,338 | Towers

Corrigan, Book, Mann, Booth, Heslop (Towers), Oakes, Doyle, Bell (Glennon), Lee, Young, Pardoe

SEMI-FINALS AND FINAL:
AN EARLY BREAKTHROUGH

Champagne supernova

City approached the last four of the 1970 European Cup Winners' Cup with great expectation. Less than two years after the disastrous debut in Istanbul, Malcolm Allison's dream of continental domination was gliding into clear view.

After a heroic journey past Bilbao, Lierse and Académica, Schalke 04 barred the way to the glory City's coach yearned for. If the early rounds had produced confidence-inspiring victories, the quarter-final with Académica had been a real grind. Matching the quixotic nature of the tournament, City's chameleon spirit seemed to have found a kindred spirit in the Cup Winners' Cup. Not for them the gleaming aristocrats of the European Cup, nor the bear pit of the Inter-Cities Fairs Cup, filled with each European league's strongest nearly men. The Cup Winners' Cup was an entirely different beast, containing everything from Welsh minnows and unknown quantities from Finland to the armada of teams from behind the Iron Curtain, whose pedigree was unknown and whose resolve was untested.

This mysterious, unpredictable forest of brightly coloured kits seemed to suit the Blues well. Any Hungarian or Bulgarian side looking at the prospect of playing Allison's team would no doubt be faced with the same doubts Western clubs had about them. You could do your homework on Mercer and Allison's ways and then find yourself playing an unrecognisable side. This could work for or against you, depending whether you caught them on a dopey day or when they played like football royalty.

With the League Cup already on the sideboard, the situation had become similar to what would confront Pep Guardiola's side 50 years later. Europe had the club's almost total focus. The target was to become the first English side to secure European glory and a domestic trophy in the same season. Trailblazing City were hot on the scent.

City's extra challenge was dealing with a full repertoire of the Ruhrgebiet's worst weather. Rain was replaced by sleet, which was duly replaced by gale-force winds whistling around the confined surroundings of the Glückauf-Kampfbahn. A tightly packed crowd of 27,000 watched Schalke's own gale blow out relatively quickly, although a breakthrough finally fell after much stubborn resistance from the City defence, when Reinhard Libuda got the better of Glyn Pardoe on the right touchline, accelerated towards the box and shot low past Corrigan into the far corner.

There were just fourteen minutes remaining as a smattering of fans, officials, flag-wavers and a dog (predictably, in the circumstances, an over-excited German shepherd) entered the pitch to cavort with the players. With nothing left to give on a drenched pitch, Schalke fended off one last typically lung-bursting thrust from Colin Bell, whose low cross was fired wide by Alan Oakes, before claiming their win.

FC SCHALKE 04 1–0 MANCHESTER CITY | Att. 27,429
Corrigan, Book, Booth, Doyle, Pardoe, Jeffries, Bell, Oakes, Lee, Young, Summerbee

Two more defeats and a draw in the league had tugged City down into lower mid-table by the time of the second leg, reducing the tie to a crucial one-off chance to perpetuate the club's hopes of a double trophy haul.

Hans-Jürgen Wittkamp played for Schalke in both ties and remembered the away game and the welcome his team encountered at Maine Road. 'The English had heavily watered the pitch,' he laughed. 'We travelled over with some confidence. The atmosphere in their stadium was unbelievable. It took your breath away to be honest. My first experience of English fans was overwhelming. The hairs on my neck were sticking up. As we ran out, the 50,000 crowd made a hell of a din, which without a shadow of doubt reflected in the final scoreline.'

With the band of the Manchester and Salford City Police attempting to make themselves heard on the pitch too, Maine Road prepared itself for a memorable night. Fate had chosen that future BBC radio commentator Ian Cheeseman would experience a City match for the first time on this night: 'My mother was born in Gelsenkirchen, so Schalke was her team. My uncle Karl and some of his friends were over for the game and I managed to tag along with them, despite my mum's overprotective nature. It was my first game and I was completely knocked out. Having only seen City on television in black and white, the green of the pitch and the blue of the City shirts was a real memory, along with the smell of Bovril.'

On nights like this the old ground could kick up an atmosphere that was utterly exhilarating. Certainly, Wittkamp and his teammates, as they waited for the whistle to blow, were struck by the wall of noise rolling off the packed Kippax. Over 46,000 were present as City began what Denis Lowe in his *Daily Telegraph* report the next day would call 'an onslaught'.

The start that Allison had wished for duly arrived after eight minutes. Lee found Oakes in space on the left and, as his diagonal ball into the box skidded across the wet turf, Klaus Fichtel, a stalwart of what would be 556 first-team games for Schalke, failed to cut out the pass. It bobbled through to Doyle, who stroked it past goalkeeper Norbert Nigbur.

Any pretensions the German side had of holding strong until the break were blown sky-high by two more quick-fire goals. First Bell cut in from the right wing and pushed Oakes through ahead of him in the middle. His flick to the on-running Young was finished with aplomb inside the far post. Within minutes, in a carbon copy of the second goal, Bell again found the willing Oakes through the middle. He slid it through a forest of defenders to Young on the edge of the box. Without hesitation, the striker allowed the ball to bounce through in front of him as he ran on to wallop a left-foot shot into the top corner.

Young would later say that Oakes had 'laid two goals on a plate for him', but the goals also required eye-watering accuracy from the scorer. City were untouchable, Schalke flattened. Half-time came unwanted on one side and as a blessed relief on the other.

Wittkamp remembers the problems building up for his side: 'The pitch was wet, the crowd was incredible and on top of that City had turned the heating up full blast in the dressing rooms, so we were sweating like mad too. We were sweating on the pitch too. City put us under immediate pressure and kept us under it. This "pressing" allowed us no room to play our game whatsoever.'

Fichtel agreed, stating, 'It was so hot in the "*kabine*". We were all sweating like madmen. City had arranged every detail to knock us out of our stride. The early goals broke our neck.'

There would be no sign of a Schalke comeback after the break. Further goals from Lee, with a right-foot smash past Nigbur and Bell, with a wonderfully stylish flick from Young's low cross in from the left, buried Schalke without trace.

City were through to their first final despite a late consolation goal from Libuda. A season after Allison's infamous speech and the embarrassment it had provoked, the coach could bask in the glory of his players' achievements. He said elatedly: 'We are not worried whether it is Górnik or Roma in the final. Both are good sides, but we fear nobody.'

'A great performance. It was really thrilling to watch,' was Joe Mercer's immediate reaction. Denis Lowe stated in the *Daily Telegraph* that 'City strode magnificently into the final of the Cup Winners' Cup last night with a handsome, commanding performance over Schalke. This notable performance was certainly the best by Manchester in their two seasons of European competition.'

MANCHESTER CITY 5–1 SCHALKE | Att. 46,361 | Doyle, Young (2), Lee, Bell

Corrigan, Book, Pardoe, Doyle (Heslop), Booth, Oakes, Summerbee (Carrodus), Bell, Lee, Young, Towers

---

It was a week before City knew whom they would be playing in Vienna. They had just seven days to gen-up on Górnik, after they had defeated Roma, and get themselves prepared for the biggest night in the club's short European history.

There were two league games to fulfil to complete the programme, the first of which saw the Blues beat Cup finalists Leeds 3–1 at Elland Road. They then travelled to Hillsborough to relegate a jittery Sheffield Wednesday side in front of over 45,000 expectant Yorkshiremen and secure a tenth-place finish for themselves. It wasn't all good news for City either, however, as Summerbee tweaked a long-standing injury that had troubled him since the League Cup win over West Brom and would be unavailable for the final.

The morning of 29 April 1970 dawned wet in Austria's capital and gradually got worse. By kick-off, the pitch had gone from lush and watered to something akin to the Danube delta. For Allison, it was a return to the city where he had learnt some early lessons in life. Stationed in nearby Klagenfurt for National Service, Allison befriended a local girl called, almost inevitably, Heidi. They had met at a fair in the Viennese woods and Allison eventually persuaded her to take him home. He recalled: 'To get to her room, we had to pass the place where her father slept. He was a 17-stone butcher. I crept past his room with my army boots slung around my neck.'

Allison's knowledge of the Viennese woods and the contours of the local females would not be of much use to his players against Górnik, but the feeling of pride that he had felt all those years ago after his first Viennese whirl, was about to be replicated by the actions of his players.

While Oakes would make the starting line-up, Summerbee would not. Allison remembered in *Colours of My Life*: 'We tried desperately to get Summerbee fit. We gave him injections. We considered gambling on his courage and his fierce instinct for competition, but in the end we had to leave him out.' In his place came the stout defender George Heslop, hardly a like-for-like swap with the waspish winger. Heslop would slot into a defensive foil in midfield, allowing Bell, Lee and Young more freedom to run at the Poles. Allison was channelling his inner Guardiola. Meanwhile, Górnik would be at full strength, with no fewer than 190 Polish caps spread through their ranks.

In the twelfth minute, the freedom Heslop's inclusion was designed to bring saw Lee clear to cut in from the left and try a potshot at Hubert Kostka. The goalkeeper could not hold it, allowing Young to run in the loose ball. With Doyle suffering a bad injury to his ankle, substitute Bowyer deputised, as the rain lashed the open bowl of the Prater Stadium. Just at the most opportune moment, with the half-time break approaching, City notched a crucial second goal. Young, picking up a slovenly pass from Górnik captain Stanisław Oślizło, advanced into the area and was upturned by Kostka. Lee steadied himself for the spot kick and, despite the long run-up, did not get the customary power on his shot, but the ball still reached the back of the net via Kostka's legs.

With water now visible on the pitch, Górnik began the fight-back. Despite Oślizło pulling a goal back after 68 minutes, it remained an uphill task against resolute City defending.

Colin Bell, talking to Ian Cheeseman in his autobiography *Reluctant Hero,* stated: 'There had been no doubt about the game going ahead. In those days the majority of pitches were passed fit. The truth is that it was waterlogged and still would have been two days later, there was that much rain. There were pools of water all over the place. Once we got started, the ball stuck in the mud and you would have to go back and hook it out, as the pitch was like a swimming pool.'

In a second half punctuated by even more rain, Bowyer's chance to sew things up ended on the running track. The match ended with the ball refusing to run cleanly and Górnik slicing hopeful long passes towards the City defence. All to no avail. City had made it to the summit. The large contingent of soaked City fans made their way onto the pitch to celebrate with staff and players. As was often the case in those days with finals featuring Eastern European teams, whose fans were banned from travelling (Górnik had released fewer than 100 'fans' to voyage to Austria), there were only 7,000 to 12,000 fans in the vast ground. With more than 4,500 intrepid travellers from the north-west of England, City's support could now mainly be found on the pitch.

Brian Bright was one of those travelling fans who made it to Vienna. His daughter, Maria Lester, remembered: 'Dad was a blue through and through for his entire life. He had been a season ticket holder as long as he could remember. He was an electrician working at N.B. Baileys so when City got through to the final, he booked a couple of days off work. He was to travel in the morning and return the same evening. With this being the case there was no reason for him to pack any spare clothes.

'So, he left home on a cold Wednesday morning wearing a grey two-piece suit along with shirt and tie, as was the norm for "men about town" going to an important football match abroad! Anyway, the heavens opened, drenching the City supporters. My poor dad, sodden down to his underwear, made the return journey home to Manchester, his polyester suit eventually drying out along the way. Unfortunately, the suit hadn't braved the weather as well as he had and he arrived at the front door of our house wearing a suit which was now two sizes too small, much to the merriment of his family. Even now, nearly 50 years later, the family still laugh about it.'

Back home, City fans were forced to wait for the highlights of the game and Barry Davies' familiar voice on *Sportsnight*, as the first FA Cup final to go to a replay had transfixed the nation. Both the BBC and ITV carried the Leeds vs Chelsea game live, leaving City's noteworthy triumph to a highlights package in the post-watershed slot.

Speaking to Corrigan 50 years after the event, the emotion remains in the big man's voice: 'I was very proud to represent City in every single game, in Europe and at home, but this was something else. That team in 1970 was absolutely brilliant and I was extremely proud to be a part of it.'

It is strange the things you remember at times of overwhelming emotion. Tommy Booth has a clear recollection, for example, of facing up to teammate Doyle on the pitch after the presentation of the cup: 'The medals were in a square presentation case and inside the medals were also square. I shouted at Mike, "They've given us the wrong bloody medals." We had the losers' medals!'

The party moved on from the packed changing rooms to Vienna City Hall, where all of the players' partners and guests were invited. 'All the wives were drenched through from watching in that downpour,' Booth remembers. 'They had to go back to the hotel first to get changed, as there was no way they could go to the do looking like that. It was a right mess, but none of us cared. We were just so happy to have won the cup. When we got to the reception three-quarters of an hour late, we discovered the Górnik party were next door, so we invited them through and we all spent the night together in the best of spirits.' BBC man Barry Davies also recalled the same scene in his autobiography *Interesting, Very Interesting*: 'The celebrations, though, were somewhat marred for the players' wives and sweethearts, whose hairdos lost many curls to the weather.'

The fun continued back at the team hotel, where Harry Godwin, the chief scout, commandeered a piano with Francis Lee serenading the group from a position on top in his underpants. It was a rip-roaring Mancunian end to a fine Viennese waltz from City.

The next morning, after barely two hours sleep, Allison watched dawn break over the majestic spires of the city from his hotel balcony. Vienna, a city he had known in the flourishing moments of early manhood, as the follies of youth had begun to crystallise into something more serious. He later reflected: 'I could not have imagined that, in fact, Vienna was the climax to the rampaging years which had carried City out of the shadows of United and into the forefront of English and European football. I saw Vienna as simply a milestone on a road to be littered with broken opponents.'

What it was, in retrospect, was the end of a good thing, not the middle of it. In pulling in their first European trophy, City were also landing their last. For Allison too it would be the last time he tasted glory of this kind with the Blues. For the fans, the long wait has stretched on to 2022.

Despite the burning desire for things to be otherwise, the first great era of City success was at an end.

MANCHESTER CITY 2–1 GÓRNIK ZABRZE | Att. 7,968–12,000 | Young, Lee (pen.)

Corrigan, Book, Pardoe, Doyle (Bowyer), Booth, Oakes, Heslop, Bell, Lee, Young, Towers

TROUBLE IN THE BOARDROOM, PROGRESS ON THE PITCH

Confusion

Bright sunlight is shining across the playing fields. Birdsong mingles with the exuberant sound of young men shouting and laughing. A suburban train rattles past in the distance. A small crowd of boys and their parents stand along the edge of the area watching intently as Malcolm Allison, wearing a crisp purple adidas tracksuit and blowing regularly on his whistle, goads the City squad into the first days of boisterous pre-season activity.

It is a bucolic scene, bubbling with energy and good humour, a seemingly homogenous gathering of honed athletes preparing to meet their destiny. That City's destiny was about to lose the sprinkling of stardust that had coated everything they touched for the past three years could not have been evident to even the closest of observers in this late summer of 1970.

The World Cup in Mexico had ended badly for England with quarter-final defeat to the West Germans, but a sunlit land of Cinzano ads and smiling street urchins had etched itself onto the public's mind and hunger for the new season was pronounced. In Manchester, as in many other football cities, the fever was returning after the shortest of summer breaks.

Thus, City approached the 1970–71 season in the highest possible spirits. The squad photograph, arranged during a subsequent pre-season training session at Platt Lane, saw the League Cup and Cup Winners' Cup sitting proudly on the freshly cut grass in front of the players. A decent push in the league was expected and a further cementing of their newly found European pedigree seemed a likely by-product of any strong domestic form the club could muster. That said, nothing was being taken for granted, as City's chameleon nature meant that most observers were unable to forecast with any certainty what might come next.

Allison, along with Mike Summerbee, Tony Coleman and Franny Lee, helped lock this image of unpredictable rascals into the public's awareness with their own fast lifestyles outside the game. Allison's cigars-and-champagne image was in fact a bit of an act for the newspapers, but he lived up to it well enough, pictured in London's hotspots on a regular basis, often surrounded by bunny girls and models, and featuring as a floral-shirted and deeply opinionated expert on Brian Moore's Sunday football show, *The Big Match*.

Some of Allison's players were attempting to follow their coach's example.

Summerbee ran a bespoke shirt shop in central Manchester with George Best; Lee had started his own waste-paper business and was on his way to becoming one of the game's first player-millionaires, while Coleman was a law unto himself, proving a difficult case even for Allison to get to grips with. All in all, the sassy, modern image of the team tied in well with the spirit of the time and the club's winning brand of football. Swashbuckling and fearless as it often was, the style sat comfortably with the bright, confident aura around the place. The misplaced bravado of the club's first foray into European competition already seemed a long time ago, although in truth it had been little more than a couple of years.

How things had changed in that short period, however.

Having won the league in 1967–8, despite the disaster against Fenerbahçe in their first European outing, the previous two seasons (1968–9 and 1969–70) had seen two trophies gathered on each occasion (the FA Cup and Charity Shield, followed by the League Cup and Cup Winners' Cup). The club was on the crest of a wave and the widely held feeling was that talent, energy and organisation existed to emulate this success in 1970–71. Breaking their European duck so early also meant City could approach what was only their third European campaign in a relaxed state of mind. Beating Górnik in Vienna had exorcised the ghosts of Istanbul and put City on the map.

With the league campaign starting well, City were in a strong second place behind early leaders Leeds as the continental season opened in September. Drawn against Linfield of Belfast, City were expected to make a smooth start to their second successive attack on the Cup Winners' Cup. With Chelsea's FA Cup win pitching them into the same competition (City played as holders), domestic interest was high in what was in those days often seen as the second of UEFA's prestigious competitions. (The winners of the Cup Winners' Cup would in later years play in the following season's Super Cup against the European Cup holders.) Like City, Chelsea also represented something of the avant-garde of English football, with the swinging set from the King's Road drawn to Stamford Bridge, where the playing staff also contained a number of individuals liberally sprinkled with stardust.

In stark contrast to this, the manager of Linfield was ex-Everton, Sunderland and Luton Town player Billy Bingham. He would later manage the Toffees in the First Division and take Northern Ireland to their greatest-ever triumph, beating the host nation at the 1982 World Cup in Spain. Bingham, unlike Allison, was already totally absorbed by one thing and one thing only:

football. 'This is a higher grade of football – much higher – but if we get a good result in the away game, then our hopes will be raised for the return leg at Windsor Park,' he said breezily on the eve of the first leg in Manchester.

Linfield had been quietly revamped in the summer with a number of high-profile signings. Joe Mercer was also at pains to underline the quality of their European pedigree, the club being the only Irish side to have reached the quarter-finals of the European Cup, in 1966–7, where they had only lost out to CSKA Sofia by one goal.

Having beaten local rivals Glentoran, they topped the nascent Irish League once again and the fluid, simple style engendered by Bingham promised to give City a run for their money. Mercer and Allison highlighted the front-running danger of striker Billy Millen, as well as home-grown stars Dessie Cathcart and Phil Scott. In goalkeeper Derek Humphreys (ex-Sunderland), forward Eric Magee (ex-Oldham) and midfielder Willie Sinclair (ex-Chelsea), Linfield also possessed a spine with experience of the English professional game. They were a side worth taking seriously, despite the relative poverty of the league they played in.

Despite a strong start in the First Division, City's early season had not been without ructions. Dumped out of the League Cup at unfancied Carlisle, off-pitch rumblings were reaching a head of steam by the eve of the Linfield fixture. As usual, it involved money, intrigue and – in the middle of it all – the smoke-shrouded figure of Malcolm Allison.

News of a takeover bid by double-glazing tycoon Joe Smith, who was trying to buy a large-enough chunk of shares to take control of the club, had by now reached the papers.

Joe Mercer – ever the traditionalist and searching as usual to maintain the status quo that had served the club so well in the previous two and a half seasons – was set against any power change, feeling that chairman Albert Alexander should stay in charge of the club.

Predictably, Allison saw things differently. Itching for more glory, and further appreciation for his own role in City's success, he had swiftly thrown his weight behind the takeover. Part of the reason for this was that he had been promised full control of the management of the team by Mercer, but this now appeared to be the last thing on his senior colleague's mind. Allison's London Weekend Television stints in the studio with Brian Moore, Paddy Crerand and Rodney Marsh had given him the taste for the big stage, a platform that he considered his rightful place for the game-changing role he had played in the glittering revival at Maine Road.

Allison would later provide an interesting insight into what was happening at the time in *Colours of My Life*, stating: 'I didn't want to clamber over Joe; I wanted recognition of my work with the team. I wanted to be a team manager. Joe could have had any title he wanted. He threw me a sprat. I could be called team manager, but he would still make the final decisions. I realised, bitterly, that Joe was hanging on. I suppose it was then I decided to organise a takeover of Manchester City.

'I knew that the City vice-chairman Frank Johnson was ready to sell a huge chunk of shares for £100,000 and that the man who bought them had only to forge one or two available alliances and he could win control of the club. I said to Ian Niven, a fanatical City supporter, "Find me a man with £100,000 and we will get control of the club." Niven came up with the man in a fortnight, Joe Smith, a double glazing "tycoon" from Oldham.

'He was ready to do all he could to develop City. He wanted to give me a twenty-year contract. I was apparently in business ...'

The other directors did not take this hostile move lying down, however, and the Linfield fixture approached with the club in significant turmoil. Allison now thought that his days at Maine

Road might be numbered, the takeover having been blocked by those supporting Mercer and Alexander. No one was to know it, but far greater seeds of doom were being sown at this time, the seeds of disaster that would end the club's golden era almost before City's new prestige had properly sunk in. Soon enough, the off-field troubles would see Allison gone, the squad broken up and the club thrust into a 40-year spiral of dust and tears, devoid of European football.

For now, though, preparations for European combat in Northern Ireland were in place. A 1–0 win at the City Ground against a tough-tackling Nottingham Forest put City a point behind Leeds at the top. Anyone watching in Belfast had better prepare themselves was the general opinion in Manchester.

What transpired on a cold night at Maine Road did not exactly match expectations. With Chelsea held in Salonika, Ajax surviving a scare in Tirana, Real Madrid held in Malta and Liverpool scraping a 1–0 home win over Ferencváros, it was not a good night for Europe's so-called big names.

* * *

Like those in Amsterdam and Madrid, City's heads were bowed. A solitary goal from Colin Bell in an almighty struggle with Linfield set up the second leg in Belfast perfectly. Fielding a side almost identical to the one that had progressed to the final a year earlier, the result differed markedly from those glory nights of the 1969–70 campaign. Of the side that had played so brilliantly a year earlier against Bilbao, only Ian Bowyer was missing, replaced by Tony Towers in midfield.

City laboured for the entire game against gallant opponents. Bell's breakthrough, with only seven minutes remaining, told its own story, the England midfielder ghosting in to beat the keeper from close in after Alan Oakes had swung in a long ball. For

83 long minutes, Bingham's men had frustrated City, putting in tackle after tackle and relying on lady luck when all else failed.

Bell's winner, facilitated by an error of judgement from Ivan McAllister, had also come about just minutes after the inspirational Isaac Andrews had been forced off the pitch with a badly gashed eye. These two burly defenders had formed dual pillars of resistance to anything and everything City had to offer in the way of attacking intent, and Andrews had shadowed Bell with great success all night.

MANCHESTER CITY 1-0 LINFIELD | Att. 25,184 | Bell

Corrigan, Book, Pardoe, Doyle, Booth, Oakes, Summerbee, Bell, Lee, Young, Towers

Writing in the *Belfast Telegraph*, Bill Ireland reflected: 'Linfield reduced the City superstars to the realms of ordinary mortals. They came within seven minutes of achieving a modern miracle against one of the best club sides in Britain.'

Manager Bingham was understandably upbeat afterwards, saying: 'I think City may have been surprised by our level of fitness.' The fabled 'good result' that the Northern Irishman had breezily talked of before the game had duly landed. Linfield could now look forward to shaking City again in the noisy confines of Windsor Park in three weeks' time. Jubilant too were 'the hordes of Ulstermen', who had made the trip across the Irish Sea to back their side. As they boarded the ferries in Heysham and Holyhead, the chatter was all about how their side would complete the greatest triumph of their European history back in Belfast.

By the second leg, City's domestic form had begun to falter. A big home win over Stoke had been followed by defeat at Tottenham in the league and a home draw with Bologna in a short-lived flirtation with the Anglo-Italian Cup. After their dogged performance in the first leg, it was clear to all that Linfield would put up quite a fight on their home turf.

Prior to the game, the first of a catalogue of disasters occurred that would eventually sink City's entire European campaign. It did not seem unduly worrying at the time, but Tommy Booth – who had started the season in commanding form – had limped out of the Stoke victory with a damaged knee. This would keep him away from first-team duty for over three months and his deputy George Heslop travelled to Belfast as a doubt himself. Heslop and Francis Lee were put through a rigorous fitness test on the eve of the match, the striker making it but Heslop failing to convince Allison's medical staff. This opened the door for young Derek Jeffries, who notched an odd record for himself in the process, being involved in two European ties before establishing himself in the league squad after making his first appearance in the 5–0 home win over Lierse a year earlier.

In the end, City received the shock of their lives and escaped only by the skin of their teeth, this good fortune taking physical form in Francis Lee's away goal in a 2–1 defeat that sent them home with their tails between their legs.

A crowd of 25,000 watched what went down in Belfast sporting history as one of Linfield's all-time great performances. To add to the febrile atmosphere, the game took place during a heightened period of the Troubles, with a fatal shooting having taken place the day before the game. Joe Corrigan remembered the feeling of trepidation around the away leg, feeling 'sure' there had been a police escort to the ground and that there were 'SAS men' on board the team coach.

With the home side ahead with barely four minutes on the clock, things were not looking good.

Cathcart's quick pass to Magee caught City's defence asleep and, when the ball found striker Millen in space, he managed to steer a shot wide of Corrigan's flailing arms.

At this point the game had to be stopped to relieve Corrigan of missiles that were landing behind his goal. Corrigan's recollection was of a potentially game-threatening situation: 'Behind my goal, bottles and other missiles began raining down from the terraces and the people throwing them made no secret of their intended target: ME. It was unnerving to say the least and Linfield manager Billy Bingham had to come out and plead with the fans not to force the game to be abandoned,' he wrote in his autobiography *Big Joe: The Joe Corrigan Story*.

Luckily for City, the bubbling atmosphere created by Millen's early strike was quickly doused when Lee fired in the equaliser just a couple of minutes later.

Bell fed Lee but his shot seemed to be covered by Linfield keeper Derek Humphreys. In truth, Lee had not hit it cleanly and perhaps this helped confuse Humphreys, whose dive had followed the ball's path until it hit a divot and bounced over him and into the net: 1–1 and City had secured the critical away goal.

Humphreys made amends with a series of good saves, and shortly after the break the home side were in front again, with plenty of time left to get the third goal they needed to go through. For the goal, Cathcart was again the thorn in City's side, feeding Millen, who, collecting the defender's short free kick, blasted it home. An inspired Linfield attacked with vigour, but a relieved Joe Mercer said at the final whistle: 'If this was one of the easy draws, give me a hard one every time. You have got to hand it to this lot. They played magnificently and we're just very thankful to be through to the next round.'

LINFIELD 2–1 MANCHESTER CITY | Att. 25,000 | Lee
Corrigan, Book, Pardoe, Doyle, Jeffries, Oakes, Summerbee, Bell, Lee (Bowyer), Young, Towers

Corrigan felt the crowd disturbances had taken something away from Linfield's performance, insisting: 'The crowd trouble took the focus away from a fantastic performance by Linfield and I don't believe they got the credit they deserved for the victory. I heard a teenager had been shot by security forces after running through a roadblock while we were there and that seemed to have heightened the tensions. We were relieved to get on the plane and fly home straight after the match.'

After the game, Linfield's Isaac Andrews added: 'I would rather lose to a British team than a foreign one and City will improve along the way.' Indeed, the feeling of elation was shared by both sides coming out of the tie. City's relief was matched by the joy of the home supporters that their heroes had put up such a stout fight.

There was a lingering feeling at this stage that City, unlike the previous season, were saving their best performances for the league. Coasting nicely in the slipstream of leaders Leeds, the league campaign had started smoothly, while cup performances had so far delivered the League Cup disappointment at Carlisle and this closest of scrapes against Linfield. Striker Neil Young felt a certain sense of déjà vu with the disorganised situation before the Fenerbahçe games two years previously, stating in an interview twenty years later: 'I think the games with Linfield were very similar to the one in Turkey in as much as I don't think Malcolm had them watched. We all thought it was going to be an easy game. However, we'd got to the point where there were no easy games any more. They had one or two useful players and the whole side played above itself, but we had played badly. Had it not been for the away goals rule, we would have been eliminated there and then in the first round.'

Allison's assurances that he would not repeat the mistakes of Fenerbahçe were in danger of falling on deaf ears. City's slovenly showing against Linfield had suggested once again that some still carried a blasé attitude to so-called minnows. In truth, Allison was preparing his staff for the long run and City's next opponents would resonate particularly strongly with the studious coach.

With almost all the home nations sides through in the various European competitions, City were drawn against the one team, Budapest Honvéd, who had managed to dispose of a British side in the first round. The Hungarians had turned around a 1–3 defeat from the first leg against Aberdeen and, Mercer insisted, were a team to be respected.

Strangely, in the climate of developing awareness of the ins and outs of European competition rules, the tie threw the two sides together thanks to two intricate new details of continental competition: City had beaten Linfield on away goals, while the Hungarians had equalled Aberdeen's 3–1 success from the home leg in the Budapest return, prevailing on penalty kicks.

Good fortune in the previous round hardly dampened the appetites for what promised to be a fascinating clash of styles and philosophies, especially for Allison. The City coach had based much of his philosophy on the musings and formations of the pioneering Hungarian coaches of the '50s. The pairing with Honvéd, of all the possible opponents City could have drawn, was an appropriate draw.

During his national service in Austria, Allison had studied the great Austrian and Hungarian sides of the time. His interpretation of what these avant-garde football folk from the East were doing formed the basis of City's invigorating passing game that seemed light years ahead of the prosaic surroundings of English football.

If there had been one event above all that had coloured Allison's approach to the sport, it was the international game at Wembley in 1953 when England were thumped 6–3 on their own patch by Hungary, a day infamous in English football as signifying a wake-up call for the country that had invented the game.

Allison had travelled to Wembley with West Ham teammate Jimmy Andrews on the day of the Hungary international and had been initially unimpressed by the sloppy training sessions they had witnessed outside the stadium, remarking particularly on the pot-bellied man stretching the number ten jersey over his somewhat full figure.

But when Ferenc Puskás began flipping 25-yard volleyed passes to colleagues with a nonchalance that took the breath away, Allison knew that English football was utterly ill-prepared for what was to come.

To exacerbate England's problems when the game got going, the Hungarians wore lightweight boots and shorts cut away high on the thigh. Allison's delight at such little details and the improvements they might bring would later be transferred into attention for every preparatory detail possible for his City side.

From Halifax to Honvéd

Honvéd had been domestic league champions five times between 1949 and 1955, supplying the great national team that Allison had so admired with many of its best players, but the side had fallen from grace after the Hungarian uprising in 1956. The match with City found them in a healthy second place in the Hungarian league behind rivals Újpesti and making a strong attempt to climb back out of the doldrums.

The match, taking place on the afternoon of 21 October 1971, was televised live in Hungary. The combination of live TV coverage and a kick-off time coinciding with a normal work afternoon in the city meant a low turnout of around 14,000 and a dismal atmosphere in the Kispest Stadium in the shabby outskirts of a marvellously ornate city. Once again, City's dreams of alighting in the football capitals of the continent had been dashed.

After Belfast's petrol bombs came the grey suburbs of Soviet-era Budapest and a stadium hardly able to rustle up a murmur of encouragement.

Much to Allison's delight, his weakened side took control of the game from the start. Evidently aware of the perils of under-estimating their opponents after the embarrassing scrape with Linfield, City had the tie wrapped up after 90 minutes with a comfortable 1–0 win, courtesy of a majestic strike by Francis Lee. In truth, City could have been well clear by the time a late scramble almost brought Honvéd an equaliser, so imperious had their performance been.

City's elegant football had been a joy to watch and had vindi-cated their coach's adherence, all those years ago, to the virtues of good passing and faultless technique that he had witnessed from Hungary's national team. After the match, a Honvéd offi-cial approached Allison to congratulate him for 'the best football we have seen from an English side in our country'.

Later, Allison was escorted to a little restaurant where Puskás' infamous paunch was said to have been fostered in the early days and to the house with the red chimney pot where the mas-ter of Hungarian football had grown up. Despite his defection to Spain, the place had remained a shrine to the player.

Fascinated by tales of how Puskás had been encouraged to hone his left-foot skills and how Sándor Kocsis had been aided with what would become a prodigious ability to head the ball, the City coach lapped it all up. 'He could control a football how another man holds a fountain pen,' Allison would say later. 'I was entranced by the stories they told me. I could see elements of what they were telling me that were totally alien to English coaching methods.'

Unlike Pep Guardiola in technically brighter times for English football, Allison could not 'point to one single player in England who had been trained and coached with similar greatness'. From the unpolished diamonds that Allison lamented over in the '70s, Guardiola's vision would produce a City team in the late 2010s that glittered with some of the most precious jewels in world soccer.

'In England we have been sloppy,' Allison concluded. 'We do things out of habit and without properly enquiring about their value. There is no deep conditioning which is an inbuilt thing in South America and on the continent.'

BUDAPEST HONVÉD 0–1 MANCHESTER CITY | Att. 14,000 | Lee
Corrigan, Book, Pardoe, Doyle, Heslop, Jeffries, Summerbee, Bell, Lee, Hill, Towers

If live television had restricted the attendance in Budapest, Manchester produced another barrier for the return leg. The day of 4 November 1970 dawned wet and got progressively worse. The Hungarian party, housed in a central Manchester hotel, watched forlornly as the rain teemed down on Deansgate and Oxford Road. Any hope they had harboured of sneaking out to buy some luxury Western titbits to take home was dashed by the unrelenting onslaught of a Manchester downpour.

By kick-off, the streets of Rusholme were awash and the Maine Road pitch resembled a duck pond punctuated by a smattering of muddy islands. In a programme feature earlier in the season, the City squad had been asked what their favourite playing conditions were. Not one had replied Amazonian morass, yet here it was.

Both sides were challenging for top-four positions in their respective leagues coming into the second leg, but opinion had City as clear favourites to go through. Nobody had reckoned with one great levelling factor, however: the execrable state of the pitch.

Although City's efforts on a truly dirty night were somewhat hampered by the atrocious conditions, the performance in winning 2–0 was hailed as a masterclass by the press gathered in the Main Stand. Colin Bell and Francis Lee were ascendant throughout, showcasing that special blend of grit and guile that had brought City to the English game's pinnacle. Bell was in typical driving form and, having sustained a gash near his eye that needed lengthy treatment and stitches, returned at the beginning of the second half wearing a clean, numberless shirt.

Bell opened the scoring in the seventeenth minute, with a cleanly hit shot after one of his trademark runs through the Honvéd defence. Alan Oakes had a goal ruled out, before Lee's mishit shot made it 2–0 after 65 minutes. With Joe Corrigan a drenched and inactive figure in City's goal, the score somehow remained at two.

Peter Gardner, writing in the *Manchester Evening News*, gushed: 'City emerged as saturated supermen when effortlessly thrusting aside a dual obstacle on their way to the quarter-finals of the European Cup Winners' Cup. They shattered a Honvéd side that lacked both physical challenge and conviction in their own ability, but what is more important is that they conquered almost farcical conditions, on a waterlogged pitch, to win.'

Bob Russell, writing in the *Daily Mirror*, called the Maine Road pitch 'a morass topped by two hours of continuous rain', and christened City the 'aquanaut champions of European football', while the *Telegraph*'s Derek Hodgson stated that 'City could blame their own climate for not managing the anticipated slaughter.'

Ronald Crowther in the *Daily Mail* was also fulsome in his praise, stating that 'City powered their way through pouring rain and a paddy field of a pitch … against hopelessly inferior and ill-equipped opponents', while John Bean's *Daily Express* report alighted on Honvéd's military status, as the army team of Budapest, by hitching some apt metaphors to his opinions: 'The regimented ranks of the famous old Hungarian army side last night were given the full blast of what Joe Mercer calls the superb professionalism of the English player. I've rarely seen a side conquer conditions such as these better than City as they frisked like water babes through a superb opening twenty minutes.'

The conditions had at least conspired to offer Kálmán Preiner, the Honvéd coach, a ready-made excuse in his after-match assessment: 'My players were lost in the heavy going. City rose above it, but we had it on our minds and we got worse and worse. If they continue to play like that, they must surely win the trophy again.' For the fans, bedraggled but happy, the night had been memorable.

MANCHESTER CITY 2–0 BUDAPEST HONVÉD | Att. 28,770 | Bell, Lee

Corrigan, Book, Pardoe, Doyle, Heslop, Oakes, Summerbee, Bell, Lee, Hill, Towers

---

Years later, Tony Book reflected that the conditions had not been a problem at all for City, saying: 'When we played Honvéd, it poured down all night, but – bad as it was – we used to really like playing in those sorts of conditions. Whatever type of conditions we used to come up against, we could always adapt to them better than the opposition and I felt that was one of the strengths of our team. When I think of some of the surfaces we played on back then and the pitches today, well there's no comparison.'

Book's point was perhaps overlooked at the time. The Maine Road pitch in those opening months of the decade was about as bad as anything the First Division had to offer. Although Derby County's Baseball Ground would soon join it as a glorified mud-heap, the first few months of 1970 often saw City playing on a surface that glistened like a mirror, so little grass did it contain.

Grainy YouTube images reveal players skating around on a surface as bald as it was treacherous, where simply staying vertical was a major challenge. Having to play on it week in, week out, as Derby County did at the Baseball Ground to win their league titles of 1972 and 1975, must have made the players incredibly adaptable.

In athletes like Colin Bell and Neil Young, however, their grace and nimbleness of foot would have given them an advantage on any surface.

City were through to the quarter-finals where old foes Górnik Zabrze awaited them. The beaten finalists from City's triumph the year before would certainly be out for revenge, but the team held the psychological advantage of victory from another damp night in Vienna the previous year and that of playing the away leg first. They would, however, have to wait for three months until the following March to see if their good form could be continued on the European stage.

REACHING THE CROSSROADS EARLY

New dawn fades

By March 1971, the atmosphere at City had changed. An explosive three-year spell of great football and unparalleled success would later be looked back upon as City's glory days, as viewed in the austere light of the subsequent 45 years of emptiness. Success had bred greed off the pitch too, as the takeover of the club rumbled on in the shadows. Things were returning to the plodding mundanity of before, but nobody was to know it quite yet.

City's league title push was over, sunk by patchy form and an unprecedented run of injuries to key players. Having trailed early leaders Leeds and eventual champions Arsenal for much of the season, they had fallen away badly. Knocked out of the League Cup in the early stages by Carlisle and out of the FA Cup in the fifth round at the hands of Arsenal, who would go on to win that too, emulating north-London rivals Tottenham's magnificent 1961 double, City were looking to the Cup Winners' Cup to restore some gloss to a dented season.

A tough quarter-final with Górnik awaited them. With fellow favourites Chelsea and Real Madrid still going strong too, City's challenge to end the season with at least one trophy (they had finished each of the previous two with two) was looking tricky.

Górnik, still smarting from their loss in the 1970 final, would clearly be out for revenge. City, meanwhile, were hanging on for dear life as several factors threatened to sink their trophy hopes completely. The takeover rumours had taken away focus. The players were aware of the off-field manoeuvring rumbling in the background. Form had disintegrated, leaving that imperious side of the 1967–70 period looking eminently beatable, an invitation an increasing number of opponents were taking up with gusto. Injuries were also beginning to cut deep, with Bell, Lee, Summerbee, Young, Book, Booth, Doyle and Oakes all out for lengthy spells during the winter and spring.

Opponents were becoming wise to City's tactics: the driving fulcrum that was Colin Bell; the snappy, aggressive wing play of Mike Summerbee; the gliding efficacy of Neil Young and the never-say-die probing of Francis Lee.

Lady luck had also deserted the club at just the wrong moment. It would take more than four decades of shambolic trying to rekindle any semblance of a relationship with her. Eventually, the thought would dawn on supporters that perhaps this was a club that had to get completely lost before it could properly find itself. Nobody knew quite to what levels that theory might be taken, however.

In March 1971, such dramatic thoughts would understandably have been deemed ridiculous. Success was a new experience that no one had considered might be fleeting. Fans were generally optimistic that retaining the European title was still on, if City could steer clear of more injuries. Already Freddie Hill and Derek Jeffries had been introduced to the starting line-up, while Tony Towers was also being asked to play a much more prominent role.

Scottish defender Arthur Mann had also been drafted in at left-back. Mann's ferocious fear of flying did not bode well for a trip to Poland, although it would really become problematic a little later. The Scot was a competent-enough footballer, but this seemed to represent a kind of tipping point for the club. He had been brought in to replace Glyn Pardoe, whose shattered right leg had been just 30 minutes from requiring amputation after a reckless tackle by George Best in the Manchester derby.

The balance tips

Peter Gardner of the *Manchester Evening News* went as far as to say that this incident was the watershed moment in City's season. It tipped, he maintained, the whole balance of the season out of kilter and set Joe Mercer and Malcolm Allison impossible problems to solve.

Only three more league wins would come City's way after that fateful afternoon in December at Old Trafford. Of that paltry total, one came the week after the derby, before the full meaning of the injury and its consequences had sunk in. That win, at Burnley, had left City in fifth position. Three weeks later, a 1–0 win over Crystal Palace left four months of the season remaining, a period in which only Everton would be beaten in the league.

With the away leg in Poland fast approaching, City were fading fast in the league and had witnessed Tottenham snatch away their League Cup, beating Aston Villa 2–0 in a dull Wembley final. The same weekend Spurs were winning at Wembley, City lost at Portman Road to an Ipswich side struggling just above the relegation zone. The 2–0 defeat put them eight points behind sixth-place Southampton, seventeen points down on leaders Leeds.

Europe really would be all or nothing.

The theme of revenge and the 'bleak winds of winter' sure to be raging across the untamed wastes of Eastern Europe at this time of the year had the press in a froth of anticipation. Warwick Jordan, writing in *Goal*, said: 'This industrial mining city [Chorzów] will be humming with expectation of a glorious win. They will be willing the defending champions to defeat.'

The Poles' lack of competitive practice would play against them, however. With a three-month winter break recently completed, Górnik had undergone a month-long fair-weather tour of South America, topping that up with friendlies in Scotland, Tunisia, Yugoslavia and Spain. While perhaps casting envious glances at their warm-weather schedule, Francis Lee underlined the evident adverse effects. 'This must cause them great problems, especially when they are involved in one of the major European tournaments,' he said. 'British sides have no such break, so we can be said to have a decided advantage at this stage.'

When asked how he rated Górnik, Lee's attention fell on their forwards. 'When we beat them in Vienna, I rated them as a very good side,' he continued. 'They have a couple of excellent forwards and we must look out for them with special care.'

Jan Banaś and Włodzimierz Lubański, the two players in question, had indeed been key to the Polish side's progress, helping them smash eight past Aalborg BK of Denmark and three more against Göztepe.

Lee had an interesting tactical insight to add to the growing air of positivity: 'Against these continental defences we have always enjoyed some freedom, because you can throw the sweeper off his game by playing up tight on him or by ignoring him completely and having an extra man in midfield.' With the blanket defences of the early '70s beginning to stifle scoring at an alarming rate in the First Division, this 'freedom' felt like a breath of fresh air to the likes of Lee and Young, used as they were to being tethered and battered by old stalwarts such as Ron Harris, Norman Hunter and Peter Storey.

The feeling was City's defence would be under pressure, but the attack should find the space to create some chances. Putting those chances away would be paramount.

City's games against Górnik came towards the end of a golden era for Polish club football, a charge led by Legia Warsaw, the northern army team, and Górnik, the miners' side from the Silesian coalfields in the south. Between them they won seventeen of the twenty leagues and cups contested in the 1963–72 period. Both sides contained real strength in depth and untypically delicate skills for Soviet-era Polish teams.

Star man Lubański was at home right across the forward line and showed poise and elegance in his finishing. While capital club Legia had climbed above their rivals to claim the Polish league title in 1970, Górnik were in the middle of a five-year run of winning the national cup. Within this time frame, Lubański remained Polish league top scorer for four of those five seasons.

City's own woes were in stark contrast. Serious decline was imminent. For the Poles, though, good times were just about to start. Despite this, hopes remained high that Lee's suggestion of a lack of competitive match practice might be decisive. The forecast of bad weather might just play into City's hands too, given their sprightly display in the mud against Honvéd.

City's preparation had not been ideal. Aside from the raft of injuries affecting the squad, a nine-game unbeaten streak had turned into six games without a victory.

As the entourage from Manchester touched down in Kraków, the piles of scooped snow lying thick at the sides of the runway did nothing to encourage positive thoughts among the travelling party. By kick-off, the temperatures had dropped to –7°C, making the Poles' choice of tights and roll neck shirts under their kit a wise move against premature frostbite. City, with only adapted leather studs flown in by Allison from Germany to help, had to be content with slapping their sides to keep warm as 90,000 Poles cleared their voices for kick-off. Great plumes of smoke rose from the packed terraces and a roar of anticipation wafted down towards the nervous-looking players.

On seeing the brown legs of the local players, Lee later mused:

'I knew they had been on a sunshine tour of Spain and other places, but I remember thinking their legs can't be as brown as that. Then it dawned on me they were all wearing tights!'

The game will be best remembered for two things: City's complete inability to stay on their feet and the incessant tooting of claxons and air horns in the crowd. Lubański opened the scoring after 55 minutes with a scorching shot, which was quickly followed by a second from Erwin Wilczek, following up on Corrigan's fumble on the hard ground. City had not adapted, while the Poles – with their tails up – had mastered the frozen conditions to clinch a promising winning margin.

Afterwards, Allison lamented a lack of firepower on City's part, saying: 'We were all right at the back but produced nothing up front.'

Colin Bell acknowledged Górnik's ability, suggesting: 'They played very well in difficult conditions … the ground was rock hard, it was blowing a gale and really cold out there. They showed a lot of skill and control, though they were not particularly physical, and stamina did not really come into it in the conditions. It's impossible to compare them to a year ago in the final. That was water polo. On a normal surface I'd say we would beat them, but if they score in Manchester, we will need four goals … so we can't afford to give anything away at the back.'

Joe Mercer was more bullish, stating: 'We cannot complain. It was a fair result. But I have not given up on this one yet. Let's see what we can do at Maine Road!'

GÓRNIK ZABRZE 2–0 MANCHESTER CITY | Att. 90,000
Corrigan, Book, Towers, Doyle, Booth, Oakes, Summerbee, Bell, Lee, Young, Jeffries

Peter Gardner's post-match report stated: 'City took their out-of-tune First Division form with them into Europe and now stand perilously close to having had their last major trophy within sight torn from their grasp.'

In the *Express*, Derek Potter agreed: 'The miners' team had everything from pitch to fanatical crowd in their favour on this emotionally charged, bleakly cold evening. Another factor is that Górnik on an ice rink pitch revealed they are a formidable and skilful side.'

It was left to the *Sun*'s Peter Fitton to sum up the barrier now facing the Blues: 'Manchester City must now grimly prepare for their toughest-ever ordeal since they marched into Europe three years ago. After the near-disaster of this quarter-final in the hostile atmosphere of the Chorzów Stadium, their chances of surviving in the Cup Winners' Cup are almost as harsh as the deep freeze Polish winter.'

Supporters had only two weeks to wait to see whether Mercer's bullish tones or the pessimism of Gardner and his press colleagues would be proved right.

What became clear after a disastrous game at Derby's Baseball Ground, on a pitch that resembled the Somme, was that City's ranks would be even more depleted by the time the game came around. In this one match, Summerbee broke his leg, Oakes damaged cartilage in his knee, Book dislocated his shoulder and Corrigan injured his elbow. The fallout of war was not an unreasonable metaphor in the circumstances. City were down to the bare bones of their squad at the most inopportune moment.

As 24 March 1971 dawned, it was clear that if the brittle, hard snowfields of Silesia had proved beneficial for Górnik, Manchester's diluvial rain was again intent on evening things up for City in the return leg. With gangly ex-postman Ian Mellor drafted in, City attacked from the off, knowing anything less than a four-star display would mean the end of their season.

By the time Mellor headed in City's opener before half-time, the Blues had already found the goalpost three times in a whirlwind of attacking football reminiscent of the greatest days of the era.

Mellor's 70th-minute pass then sent Doyle through and, as he collided with goalkeeper Jan Gomola, the ball squirted up into the air for Doyle to head into the empty net to put City level on aggregate. With a fully committed crowd behind them, City came agonisingly close to clinching the tie with Bowyer's last-minute effort scooped from the line by a defender, who – mysteriously – had been receiving treatment behind the goal seconds earlier.

As Gardner admitted in the *Evening News*, Joe Mercer had been right to issue his fighting talk in Poland. 'Magnificent Manchester City stood by Joe Mercer's pledge to the letter,' he wrote. 'They smashed into Górnik with an explosion in a glittering tension-jammed Cup Winners' Cup quarter-final on a night of torrential rain and heat-hugging emotion.'

Scorer Mellor was delighted with the start of his career: 'Four days after making my debut, I have played in Europe and scored,' he enthused. For all City's bluster, however, all they had done was earn the right to take part in a play-off, chosen for Copenhagen. Worst of all, there would be just seven days to prepare for it and no time at all to reintegrate the injured players.

MANCHESTER CITY 2–0 GÓRNIK ZABRZE | Att. 31,950 | Mellor, Doyle

Healey, Connor, Towers, Doyle, Booth, Donachie, Jeffries, Bell, Lee, Young (Mann), Mellor (Bowyer)

With Malcolm Allison banned from Maine Road on match-days in a somewhat heavy-handed punishment for comments made to referee Bob Matthewson in the league win at Burnley in December, the build-up to the crucial play-off was fraught with problems. As well as organising flights, accommodation and training facilities in Denmark's capital, Joe Mercer's team selection was done for him, with youngsters Healey, Donachie, Towers and Jeffries all assured of a start as there was hardly anybody else fit to play.

An incident at Ringway on departure further clouded the mood when Arthur Mann's fear of flying hit a new height. Having taken some pills to calm his nerves, Mann then made his way through half a bottle of whisky. Still trembling uncontrollably in the departure lounge, a teammate unknowingly bought him a double brandy to 'help calm him down a bit'. Once lugged into a seat at the back of the plane, preparations for take-off got under way. In a conversation nearly 50 years on from the incident, Tommy Booth remembers exactly what happened next: 'We had somehow managed to get Arthur onto the plane without Malcolm noticing the state he was in. All was set for take-off, and we thought no more of it. Then there was a commotion at the back of the plane and Arthur was going mental. You wouldn't believe the scene. They had to drag him off and take him to hospital.' Joe Corrigan, staring out of the window further forward saw Mann's stretcher laid down on the tarmac. 'Arthur sat up and, as the medic leaned down to ask if he was all right, he headbutted him! The medic was then laid out alongside Arthur by the side of the plane! It was like a scene from *Monty Python*!'

Taking the piss

A cold wet night in Copenhagen brought the old foes together for a fourth time in two seasons of close-fought European combat. As Mercer and Allison strolled into the ground and took their bearings pitch-side, neither could suppress a smile. With all the worries about personnel, something had at last gone their way. Unlike the skating rink in Chorzów and the mudbath in Manchester, the Idrætsparken was in immaculate condition. Allison was immediately at ease with the thought that his game plan could be properly carried out in optimal conditions. With so much hanging on the outcome and so many of his old dependable players absent, the stakes were intolerably high. For the most successful English club of the past three years, everything now hung on the outcome of a single game.

For Allison, it was also a return to a city where the most eccentric of his excesses had taken place. Drinking late into the night with John Charles, then of Juventus, the bar owner had warned the players that his premises were about to shut. Discussing Charles' business interests, Allison persuaded him to add the Copenhagen bar they were about to be asked to vacate to his growing portfolio 'so that they could decide when it shut'. Allison wrote a cheque for £27,000 on the spot. It was the kind of crackpot behaviour that had endeared him to many but drove Joe Mercer to distraction. Mercer rightly asked, if the manager had a reputation for flouting so many rules, how could he expect his players to be disciplined? On this occasion, however, Mercer needn't have worried. The players were about to deliver one of their most disciplined European performances of all.

Nevertheless, before a ball had been kicked in anger, the Poles managed to launch a campaign of dirty tricks. Revealing a staggering lack of grace, club president Eryk Wyra demanded a drugs test on City's players as he claimed they must have been taking performance-enhancing cocktails to have produced such a high-energy display in the return leg. The unprincipled Wyra had enacted a similar trick on AS Roma in 1969–70 when Górnik had won on the toss of a precariously balanced coin in the semi-final.

Mercer, ever the pragmatist, told the players to ignore such gamesmanship, saying: 'I don't want you wasting energy by getting worked up by this sort of business. You must ignore it, no matter how distasteful it may sound and concentrate on beating them.' It was in situations like this where the Mercer–Allison partnership worked so well. The younger coach's brash hyperbolic approach would no doubt have stirred up a hornet's nest before the game and taken his players' focus away from the task facing them. Mercer was not made of the same material, preferring a softly, softly approach and remaining the ultimate diplomat.

So, on a surface like a moist bowling green, City proved the absolute masters on a night of scintillating football that took many back to the side's greatest performances of the era. After a convincing 3–1 win saw them through to the semi-finals, Allison enthused: 'I'm a proud man tonight. I would have been proud if our top strength team had pulled off such a performance, but with all the boys in the side, it was superb. They gave me all I wanted.'

Goals from old hand Neil Young, scoring for the first time in weeks, Tommy Booth and a Francis Lee tap-in, after Colin Bell had beaten five men in a terrific run, turned the game into something of a procession as City maintained steely control for most of the 90 minutes. City's impressive stamina, built up after months of specially organised fitness training by Allison, had seen them through to the end of a demanding three-game marathon against the very best the emerging Polish football nation could throw at them. Lubański's goal to make it 1–2 quickened City fans' heartbeats for a short while, but Bell's majesty, setting up the third, put the tie to bed.

Watched by a bigger crowd than the one who had witnessed the Vienna final between the same two sides, City had made it through to the semi-final, a heroic feat in what would be their second and last appearance in the tournament. It represented arguably the best performance, percentage-wise, of all competitors in the tournament up to its demise in 1999.

The only real failure proved to be in the corridors below the ground afterwards, as the drug-testing unit requested by Wyra was made to wait for over an hour as Bell, Dave Connor and Jeffries found it nigh on impossible to produce a usable sample for their test tubes, despite offers of physio Blakey's bottles of orange juice and, appropriately, the arrival of their overjoyed coach with a trademark bottle of champagne. 'They won't allow them to have this,' Allison beamed to waiting pressmen as he returned down the narrow corridor, swinging the Moët & Chandon as he went. Mercer was less amused, shouting: 'It's an absolute farce in there. I am disgusted.'

MANCHESTER CITY 3–1 GÓRNIK ZABRZE | Att. 12,100 | Young, Booth, Lee

Healey, Connor, Towers, Doyle, Booth, Donachie, Jeffries, Bell, Lee, Young, Hill

---

City's semi-final opponents would be Chelsea, a first-ever all-English European clash for the Blues to get their teeth into. Real Madrid, after a titanic struggle with Cardiff City and PSV Eindhoven, who had overcome Vorwärts Berlin in a similarly tight contest, would be the teams fighting for a place in the final against one of the two English sides, a match already scheduled for Athens' Karaiskakis Stadium on 19 May.

By the time the first leg of the semi-final came into view in mid-April, little had changed on the injury front. City's league form had continued to tail off in a mediocre league season. Stamford Bridge would host the first game with City still unable to call on the services of Pardoe, Oakes and Summerbee. Having beaten Everton 3–0 at Maine Road on 3 April, what would become a ten-game winless finish to the season was already well under way.

This run would include no fewer than three matches with Chelsea to add to the two away games already played against the London side that season.

The Stamford Bridge first leg attracted a crowd of just under 46,000. With the First Division down to a straight scrap between Leeds and Arsenal, the west Londoners found themselves fourth and still fighting for a UEFA Cup place for next season. For City, some seven points further back in eighth place, it was paramount that they kept their eyes firmly on the European front as it represented the only way to get back there for the next season.

City lined up with seventeen-year-old Jeff Johnson included in the injury-ravaged side. Goalkeeper Joe Corrigan was at least back on duty, but still sporting a black and partially closed eye, after being kicked in the face during a dull goalless draw at Newcastle. Incredibly, the Newcastle game also saw Bell and Doyle pick up serious injuries. The fallout riled Allison and put one of the final nails in the coffin of his failing relationship with Mercer. Mercer had decided to go with a full-strength side on Tyneside and now Allison (still suspended and leaving full matchday responsibility to Mercer) ripped into him before the Chelsea match, saying: 'You've wrecked our relationship and you've wrecked our chances of going through.' In a final ironic flourish, Allison accused his colleague of being 'full of ego', which even he was later moved to describe in his autobiography as a 'remarkable statement coming from me'. Allison had pleaded with Mercer to leave Doyle and Bell out at Newcastle for what was to his mind 'an unimportant league game'. His refusal to do so produced what Allison would later call 'my blackest moment'.

Meanwhile, Mercer, hitting a different tone altogether, announced to the *Evening News*: 'May God bless this ship and all who sail in her.' It had been meant as a tension-breaking aside, but Peter Gardner was later moved to write: 'How gallantly that ship performed in the rough-going at Chelsea…'

Skipper Tony Book's presence in the starting line-up was a boost so soon after dislocating a shoulder. With Francis Lee deployed as a lone striker, it was a hard-pressed defence, marshalled expertly by Book, that possessed the key to surviving the first leg intact.

Both sides took to the pitch wearing their away kits. Chelsea in yellow tops and blue shorts, City in their now famous red and black 'Milan' stripes.

With seven back passes to Corrigan in the first six minutes, it was clear that City had come to contain the Londoners' attacking threat.

With many of City's fans housed in the rickety North Stand, an upright, truncated piece of wood and corrugated iron that sat in the corner opposite the Shed End, City had noisy if nervous support. Those there spoke of the stand vibrating to their songs. The ramshackle building was demolished in 1976.

City held out well, with Corrigan in safe form despite having the use of only one good eye. South African schemer Derek Smethurst scored the solitary goal for Chelsea minutes into the second half, finishing a diagonal cross clinically with his left foot, but the consensus was that City had come out of a difficult situation surprisingly unscathed.

Derek Wallace in the *Daily Mirror* spoke of City's 'unquenchable spirit', while Derek Potter's *Express* report described Chelsea's first-leg lead as a 'fragile thread'.

CHELSEA 1–0 MANCHESTER CITY | Att. 45,595
Corrigan, Book, Connor, Towers, Booth, Donachie, Johnson, Hill, Lee, Young, Mann

---

Before the second leg could be played there was the small matter of a league game between the sides, also at Maine Road. City's injuries meant more of the same gap-plugging with reserves and youth team players, while Chelsea manager Dave Sexton was able to juggle his squad, making eight changes to rest important players before the second leg. A 1–1 draw satisfied only pools punters. The programme for this game featured an update by Gerry Harrison on City's walking wounded: Bell cartilage operation needed, Summerbee in plaster, Doyle in plaster, Corrigan eye problems continuing, Bowyer in plaster, Jeffries ankle injury, Healey dislocated finger, Carrodus ankle trouble, Pardoe in plaster, Oakes back in light training, Glennon in plaster. Even secretary Walter Griffiths was in hospital for surgery to his back.

City were then faced with three games in five days, less than perfect preparation for the crucial second leg, losing at Stoke, then drawing with Liverpool, who fielded an entire reserve side as they were also engaged in European combat two days later. As luck would have it, yet another player fell injured in this game, centre-half Booth damaging his already suspect knee in an accidental clash with Alun Evans.

Things were looking grim, but by the time the second leg arrived, Chelsea too had been afflicted by an injury crisis of their own. City's league form was showing no signs of improving and, on the eve of the game, Corrigan – with 20–20 vision restored – suddenly reported in with 'a boil on his knee' and was replaced by a reportedly 'jittery' Ron Healey, still fresh from dislocating his finger. It seemed as if City had enough main characters and plot lines for an entire series of *General Hospital*.

In the end, the two sides registered a grand total of eleven first-teamers unfit to play between them. With City forced to name the semi-fit Jeffries and Summerbee, plus the rookie Johnson once again, their plight looked worse and so it turned out.

Mercer's forced gamble failed to take off on a night of searing disappointment at Maine Road. The two unfit players were unable to play a proper part and Johnson's inexperience was frequently exposed as the away side smoothly took control. George Heslop fought manfully in Booth's place, but Chelsea possessed too much firepower and the tie was sealed by the only goal, scored in the 43rd minute.

Sadly, this too had an otherworldly air about it.

Keith Weller's free kick swung over into the box from out on the touchline in front of the Main Stand and, as it arced towards the flailing Healey, the nervous keeper flapped it inexplicably into his own goal. It was a totally unforced error, with nobody challenging the goalkeeper as the ball floated in. It entered the net via Healey's outstretched arms, down his leg and into the back of the goal via his shins. A more comical attempt at unsuccessfully keeping a football from entering the net could not be remembered on the Kippax as the half-time chatter centred on whether City could come back from such a farcical error and whether Healey's visibly declining confidence would offer the visitors more gifts.

For the unfortunate goalkeeper, it would represent the biggest error of his career in the most important game he would play in.

Chelsea held off City's threat throughout the second half to make it to the final on a 2–0 aggregate. City's gamble had failed to pay off – the unprecedented injury crisis had crippled their chances at just the wrong moment. The superb performances against Honvéd and Górnik had been for nothing. The European adventure was over and there would be no return the following season. An era was coming to a close. The next time City would feature on the playing fields of continental Europe, much would have changed and the triumphs of the glory period would be committed to the dusty record books in the club's wood-panelled boardroom.

'I was disappointed in the attitude of the players towards the game,' said Allison afterwards. 'They were afraid before they even started and you should never be afraid. They did not really try to win. I have never seen a Manchester City team go into a big match like that. It looked as if they were playing for a draw.'

Despite this, the press had begun to talk of the 'Mercer's Minors', as the young recruits had adapted well to being thrown in en masse at the deep end. This too irked Allison, as he wrestled with his colleague for recognition. The truth was that neither man was the same without the other, much like Brian Clough and Peter Taylor in later European crusades for Nottingham Forest. Partnerships are difficult balances, but City's early European success could be put down to the remarkable synergy created between these two most unlikely bedfellows.

MANCHESTER CITY 0–1 CHELSEA | Att. 43,663

Healey, Book, Connor, Towers, Heslop, Jeffries, Summerbee (Carter), Lee, Bowyer, Young, Johnson (Donachie)

There would be a great deal of – often justified – criticism aimed at subsequent City efforts abroad in the 45 years that followed, but Allison's words, delivered about the club's golden generation, seemed to carry extra weight and poignancy. Perhaps, if the outspoken coach had known what was to follow, he might have been less scathing in his assessment. As it was, his sharp words effectively brought an end to the first great period of City success. Those that had been enthralled along the way would be approaching a half-century older by the time the club could once again call itself a competitive force against Europe's finest sides.

For Allison, it represented a last hurrah under the European floodlights at Maine Road. Ebullient under the bright glare of success, the City coach could be acerbic in defeat. The latter years of his career would see him wearing a suit of armour made up mainly of his mistakes, of which there were many. A return to City later in the decade would coincide with more European football but a return to winning ways would evade him. He would taste success briefly and gloriously in Lisbon with Sporting Clube de Portugal in 1982, but he would never again match what he and Mercer had achieved at Maine Road.

Chelsea would go on to defeat Real Madrid in the replayed final, while City lumbered home in eleventh place in the First Division.

6

STUMBLING BLOCKS AND LAUGHING STOCKS

Every day hurts

Pre-season training had started at an alarming pace. Players began gathering at the edge of the Platt Lane training pitches, preparing themselves for the off with nervous laughter and the usual round of backslapping and glad-handing, after a few weeks away with families, girlfriends and acquaintances. The usual groups of inquisitive kids and dog walkers drifted slowly past, offering the first words of encouragement for the new season.

Among the group ribaldry, coaching staff carried out equipment and kit for the opening sessions. A phalanx of staff stood waiting as Mike Summerbee turned to the others and whispered: 'Where's Joe when you need him?'

Allison, troubled by City's fitness levels, had arranged a tough start for the squad with specialised help in the form of running coaches and fitness gurus. A meticulously prepared squad would enter the Charity Shield opener at Villa Park wearing a stylish sash on their shirts, another nod to the continental style and exuberance that the coach sought. As usual, City could not be faulted for their sartorial elegance, nor for their physical condition.

One crucial element *was* missing, however.

Joe Mercer had been rolled out of the front door to allow Allison the broad ambit he had long desired. A smutty and tasteless end to a regal partnership, a palace coup of sorts, ignited by the Machiavellian antics of Big Mal.

Without the knowledge of the playing staff, changes had been made behind the scenes, which would set a grand and prolonged rot in motion. Even though City's one-season absence from the fields of Europe would be remedied by their fourth-place league finish in 1971–2, which allowed them to enter the rebranded UEFA Cup, their reappearance would not last long. The whole decade, in fact, would be peppered with brief continental sightings of a club that was slowly but surely going as mouldy as a French Camembert and as dried out as the skin on a Spanish chorizo. If the ups and downs recorded thus far had seemed like a roller coaster, it soon became clear that the club had in fact been mainly coasting on the high bends. The sweeping, stomach-churning drops characterising the '70s were just around the next coil of track.

With Mercer sent to Coventry with the firing shot at the club: 'You don't have to be young to be enthusiastic,' Allison finally had what he wanted. Anything the club achieved from now on would bring a warm spotlight to rest on him and nobody else.

Tactically speaking, City had hardly evolved. Allison's brief had always been 'play it fast and loose', but Colin Bell, who was the pivot for everything positive in his philosophy, started the 1972–3 season in subdued form.

City's personnel were undergoing the first phase of significant change. With the smooth front running of Neil Young now replaced by the bargepole Wyn Davies, the attack appeared ready to be both more blunt and more airborne, while youngsters Derek Jeffries and Tony Towers were now first-teamers, rather than the emergency fill-ins they had been when City were turfed out of the Cup Winners' Cup by Chelsea.

There was one even more noticeable alteration, though, that no one could take their eyes off. Rodney Marsh had arrived from Queens Park Rangers.

A London Weekend Television colleague of Allison, Marsh cut a similarly cavalier look, with tousled hair and trend-setting brown leather jackets. His arrival during the four-way title run-in the previous March had so unbalanced a City side looking odds-on to be champions that they had fallen away inexplicably to finish 'last' of the four contenders.

Now Marsh's unpredictable input was expected to gel with the workmanlike Davies. Allison's idea in forking out a record £200,000 for his extravagant skills was to allow him to switch between a traditional 4–3–3 and a more adventurous 4–2–4. Tactics during this time were beginning to get bogged down in offside traps, over-cautious defences and a deep fear of losing. Marsh brought an innate ability to improvise, a flamboyant disregard for authority and occasional bloody-mindedness.

'Rodney is a player of great ability,' Allison intoned. 'His greatest value will be coming through on the left flank. This allows us to set up different points of attack and will help us to stretch defences more. He gives us more variation. Rodney's arrival has taken weight off Lee, Summerbee and Davies. They are now able to find more space and freedom.'

While this was undoubtedly true, Allison failed to mention that it also placed a huge amount of pressure on Marsh himself and, when the team switched into a 4–2–4 to stretch the opposition, it diverted much of that pressure on to Bell and Oakes, who were left holding the midfield together as everyone flooded forward. This would later be replicated to some extent under Guardiola, when a similar urge to play too many creative players left whoever was holding midfield dangerously exposed. As City would find in 1973, 2018 and critically in the Porto final of 2021, this would lead to a raft of problems against teams prepared to counter-attack in numbers.

Writing in *Goal* on 2 September 1972, Ray Bradley saliently pointed out: 'Perhaps Marsh's greatest problem will be to discipline his individual talents for the collective good of the team, without sacrificing his flair. But painters must paint, writers must write and entertainers must entertain. It's instinctive.'

Another element in the acquisition of Marsh was City's 'maverick quotient' being sent over the tipping point. There is no telling what the correct ratio of water carriers to mavericks did the trick in 1972, but City were clearly beginning to push the envelope.

In Alan Hudson's autobiography *The Working Man's Ballet*, the Chelsea midfielder talked about joining the England squad around the same time. Breaking a curfew set by Alf Ramsey, Hudson was immediately led astray on a late-night drinking trip by Bobby Moore (whose mentor at West Ham had been Allison), Summerbee and Marsh. As a snapshot of where the City squad's influences were beginning to lie, this was a poignant one.

Allison had long been preoccupied by the shadow cast by Manchester United. He was in some part jealous and in some part irked by the infamous 'bumptiousness'. He wanted to divert some of that awe and mystique to City and this occasionally moved him to do what others viewed as 'strange things'. For many the signing of Marsh fell into this category.

For those that knew Allison well, however, it was typical of the man. He was managing a club in a city that was unique in its pressure levels. United were already a global entity, thanks to George Best, Bobby Charlton and to global sympathy after the Munich air crash. Allison had quickly found that he had taken on a particularly difficult challenge at City. He wrote later in *Colours of My Life*: 'In Manchester we had extraordinary competition.

Our rivals were not merely another football team, they were woven into the fabric of the city. If Bell, Lee and Summerbee were extremely gifted players, they *did* lack that quality of fantasy. Marsh brought our fantasy levels higher.'

By the time of the club's UEFA Cup debut, new levels were indeed being reached, at the foot of the league. Marsh's game-changing form was nowhere to be seen and Bell was misfiring in a low-profile midfield. It was far from the fantasy football that Allison had been plotting, and an air of restlessness was beginning to settle over the club.

Suddenly, Joe Mercer's departure was beginning to look more meaningful. Fissures started to appear that Mercer's grandfatherly presence may have kept sealed. Mike Doyle claimed that Allison socialised with some of the players and not others. 'Mal, Mike and Franny were the champagne set, we were the black and tan brigade,' he said of himself, Alan Oakes and Glyn Pardoe, although Colin Bell always steadfastly argued that 'Allison had no favourites. His best eleven were his favourites and that eleven could change depending on who was playing well.'

As ever, though, a successful squad tends to show greater togetherness than one out of form. Europe, as has often been the case, would be the litmus test.

The draw had pitted City with Valencia, a strong-running and delicately skilled side built in the persona of coach Alfredo Di Stéfano, the ex-Real Madrid legend. Like Allison, Di Stéfano was a student of the great international teams of the preceding era. Having been the centrepiece of the Real Madrid side that launched the European Cup with five successive victories, his legacy was the sort of gold-plated benchmark Allison enviously coveted. While Di Stéfano's fledgling management career was not reaching the heights of his playing days, clashes with European royalty of this kind were beginning to pitch Allison into the company he craved.

City warmed up for Europe with defeats at Derby, Chelsea, Palace and Birmingham and found themselves in the bottom three with West Brom and neighbours Manchester United as the match approached.

However, as Ronald Crowther was to remark in his *Daily Mail* piece the day after the first leg: 'The sweet scent of the big occasion brought Manchester City out of their slump in an exhilarating, all-action tie.' The match would also revisit upon the club a problem experienced two years before and one that would dog them for the next two domestic seasons.

The visitors had only just started their league season, having beaten Atlético and lost to Barcelona four days before the tie in Manchester. If City were expecting an opponent still finding its gear, they were in for a surprise.

The Spaniards, cool under pressure, clever in possession and fast on the counter, quickly brought the best out of City in a pulsating match. José Claramunt Torres, in the eighth season of a thirteen-year association with the club, rapidly became the star of the show, running a fast-passing operation that had City chasing shadows.

It was his butter-fingered colleague in goal, Juan Meléndez Alberdi, who started the ball rolling, however, when he fluffed an easy clearance. In what Tom German, writing in *The Times*, called 'a remarkable lapse in judgement', Meléndez caught a simple lob and elected to roll the ball to the right of his area, where the unseen Mellor stuck out one of his trademark gangly legs to tap the ball into the goal.

This gift galvanised City, with Doyle and Towers strong in the middle and Marsh and Mellor running the Spanish side ragged. There were warnings of what Valencia could do in return, however, as Claramunt sent the little Argentinian winger Óscar Valdez scurrying through towards Corrigan's goal on three occasions. With City's defence spread thinly, Valencia duly got the equaliser they deserved when Valdez again slipped through and slotted in as Corrigan and Booth dithered.

Twelve minutes into the second half, things got significantly worse, as Valencia's other Argentinian, Miguel Ángel Adorno, found space to head past Corrigan after more good work from Valdez. Following a corner, Marsh managed to equalise, provoking an onslaught by City, with Towers, Doyle, Bell and Lee all going close.

In a repeat disaster, echoing problems in the club's last appearance on the European stage, City were forced to bring on goalkeeper Ron Healey, after Corrigan went down injured. The 2–2 draw clearly suited Di Stéfano's men more, but City had at least woken up from their domestic slumber and proved they had it in them to proceed. To do so, they would need a performance on a par with their only other Spanish trip, the 3–3 draw in Bilbao in 1969–70. That result had paved the way for a run to the final. Allison was hopeful something similar in Valencia might have the same effect.

In a field containing Feyenoord, Red Star Belgrade, Torino, Inter Milan and Slovan Bratislava, Allison knew all he needed to know about the strength in depth of UEFA's new competition. With holders Spurs plus Stoke and Liverpool in the mix too, City were up against it.

MANCHESTER CITY 2–2 VALENCIA | Att. 21,698 | Mellor, Marsh

Corrigan (Healey), Jeffries, Donachie, Doyle, Booth, Oakes, Mellor, Bell, Marsh, Lee, Towers

There were only two weeks between the home and away legs against Valencia, but a fair amount of drama was squeezed into that period. First Wyn Davies was announced as a cross-city transfer, making a move few others had dared in the past. City then produced some form beating Tottenham, with Marsh looking like a man with a weight lifted from his shoulders. Within a week, however, a 1–5 setback at Stoke sent City to the foot of the table. To top things off, deposed chairman Albert Alexander died.

City attempted to gain focus for Valencia. In *Goal*, TV talking head Jimmy Hill weighed in with his take on Allison: 'A bad start to the season will be taken by Allison's critics as a sign that he is losing his grip. He faces his biggest challenge yet. He has to find a new role for himself and part of this should be one in which he can build a solid relationship between himself and the board. It is an open secret that the City board is not the most united one. If he can solve his problems upstairs, those downstairs on the field will fade away.'

Hill's point was a salient one. The ructions off the field were beginning to overshadow what occurred on it. What he called City's 'football of poetic beauty' was on display less frequently. Rifts were beginning to show. 'Why don't you have Franny and I on your television show instead of Mal?' Summerbee apparently said to Hill. 'We're two lads that will say something. Malcolm's gone soft and has nearly become one of the Establishment.'

Allison had been quoted saying he had become 'less interested' in winning. Time's sands were shifting. The restless coach was showing signs of distraction.

With City on six points from ten games, something had to change. Only Manchester United and Leicester had started as badly and both had superior goal difference. Four months earlier, Allison's highly tuned squad had been on the brink of a second title in four years. Now here they were sitting in 22nd spot.

Valencia, meanwhile, were still only four games into a season that would see them finish sixth in La Liga. Since the first leg they had registered two draws and City could have been forgiven for thinking their opponents might still be stretching muscles gingerly for bigger things to come.

Wrong again.

In a tense game that snapped and sizzled through to the 72nd minute before a goal was scored, City were eased out 2–1.

By the time Rodney Marsh's touch worked its fantasy effect on the 35,000 spectators gathered at the Estadio Luis Casanova, the home side had scored twice, through Valdez and Quino Sierra. The City striker's 91st-minute response was too little, too late and a despondent party headed for the airport knowing that the glory days were running out.

By the time City studs once again dug into the lush turf of Europe, Allison would be gone – to weave his fading magic at Crystal Palace, where he would preside over two consecutive demotions – as would his immediate successors Johnny Hart and Ron Saunders. The likes of Lee and Summerbee would be gone too.

Although many of the squad assembled with such elan by Allison and Mercer would soldier on into the late '70s, the magic was gone and the struggle to relocate it was just beginning. Who could have thought that the rain-soaked triumph in Vienna would herald not the club's entry into the annals of European fame, but a slide away from the arc lights towards three decades of blundering into some of English football's most offbeat cul-de-sacs?

Before the embarrassment of league engagements at Wrexham and Bristol Rovers, FA Cup defeats at Halifax and Shrewsbury and a season in the third tier that was followed by honest talk of the club folding, however, City's European odyssey through the '70s would encompass three more seasons of continental jousting. There would be embarrassment here too, but also a last, eventful burst of meaningful activity under the auspices of none other than Malcolm Alexander Allison.

VALENCIA 2–1 MANCHESTER CITY | Att. 35,000 | Marsh

Healey, Book, Barrett, Doyle, Booth (Mellor), Oakes, Summerbee, Bell, Marsh, Lee, Towers

GLORY IN MILAN, PEANUTS IN POLAND

Heaven knows I'm miserable now

That the '70s would eventually be regarded as a period of relative progress for the club could be put down to one reason only – that the two decades that followed were, respectively, desperately uncomfortable and an incomparable nightmare for City. In effect, the '70s would be City's last hurrah on several fronts, included among them trophy winning of any kind and carefree participation in European competition.

Licking wounds at Malcolm Allison's flight to Crystal Palace and the departure of European stalwarts Young, Lee and Summerbee would be put into context later, but for now the club's fans had to become accustomed to mere inconsistency and the fact that everyone else had caught up with them.

It took three years from Allison's departure and over five from the last trophy win in Vienna to lay hands on silverware again. Dramatic goals from new heroes Dennis Tueart and Peter Barnes secured the 1976 League Cup final win over Newcastle United and captured a UEFA Cup place for City the following season.

Three blank seasons had passed since the two UEFA Cup games with Valencia in 1972. The club, now managed by ex-skipper Tony Book, was embarking on a new era of attacking

football that would hoist it briefly back among the main protag-
onists in English football during the second half of the decade.

Although the League Cup had been won in style, City had
finished the 1975–6 season in eighth place, the same position as
the year before, seventeen points adrift of champions Liverpool.
As the new season opened, however, there was some hope that
things might turn out differently under Book, who had gathered
exciting new players to fuse with the old dependable faces.

The major summer acquisition certainly ticked the 'European
experience' box. Brian Kidd, brought in from Arsenal, had been
a United player before his spell at Highbury and had partici-
pated in United's greatest moment, the extra-time de-robing of
Eusébio's Benfica at Wembley in 1968. That European Cup final
win, in front of an adoring London public, was just the sort of
thing Malcolm Allison had dreamed of for City.

Book was more of a pragmatist. Although he liked a cigarette or two, there were no clouds of blue cigar smoke wafting
out of the tight confines of the manager's office. The sound of
champagne corks popping had gone too, replaced by the incessant grinding of spoons in teacups. The sprightly quotes that
had fed a voracious press pack for six long years were also a
thing of the past.

Book was a man of few words, his West Country burr a low
volume crackle in the cut and thrust of post-match press con-
ferences. For City, it was a new era of taking up the chase with
neighbours United, but one that would be carried out without
the pompous promises, the sound bites and the flamboyant
hand signals to the Stretford End that had been his predecessor's
party piece.

'And Manchester City will play ... Italy!'

There was to be no gentle reintroduction to European competition. City were drawn to play Italian champions-in-waiting

Juventus, one of the biggest names in European football, who, despite never having won a continental trophy in sixteen consecutive years of trying, had been beaten finalists in the Fairs Cup against both Leeds and Ferencváros and had also gone down narrowly to defeat in the 1973 European Cup final against Ajax in Belgrade. Their side featured Italian football royalty, names synonymous with the national team's most high-profile efforts.

In contrast, City's four seasons of European travails had delivered the Cup Winners' Cup, giving them – in one respect at least – the upper hand. Along with Kidd, the new intake of Asa Hartford (West Bromwich Albion), Joe Royle (Everton) and Dennis Tueart (Sunderland) had, albeit sparse, European experience.

City's squad could still count on stalwarts from earlier continental campaigns too. Mike Doyle and Colin Bell had 40 European appearances between them, while Tommy Booth, Joe Corrigan and Glyn Pardoe (who would announce his retirement because of injury just weeks after the Juventus home game) were not far behind. Willie Donachie, a young tyro when thrown in against Chelsea in 1971, was well established at left-back. Europe would not be a complete novelty.

What *was* a novelty, however, was being drawn against such a giant of the continental game. This kind of bad luck would become commonplace in City's early participation in the Champions League 30 years later, when low UEFA coefficients (words that were still a foreign language in the '70s) meant drawing the big guns several years running, but in 1976 City's European roll of honour had only taken in the likes of Linfield, Lierse and Coimbra. Never before had they drawn an Italian team, if one disregarded a brief and disastrous flirtation with Bologna in the ill-fated and short-lived Anglo-Italian Cup.

All at Maine Road were in a state of excitement. Roger Reade, just installed in secretary Bernard Halford's admin team, remembers the feeling in the office: 'There was genuinely great excitement among everyone at Maine Road about this – particularly as it had been three years since City's last participation in European competition. City were on a great run of form in the league and there was great optimism about the possibilities for the team. There seemed to be a much greater togetherness than people had felt for some time.'

A glance through the Juventus squad profile for the match reads like a *Who's Who* of Italian World Cup history. From goalkeeper Dino Zoff, through a granite-hard defence of Antonello Cuccureddu, the elegant Gaetano Scirea, Claudio Gentile (the most inappropriately named defender in the history of the sport) and Marco Tardelli, a midfield of captain Giuseppe Furino, Franco Causio and the kryptonite Romeo Benetti, through to strikers Roberto Bettega and Roberto Boninsegna, the squad was liberally sprinkled with star quality.

Reade, dispatched on special errands by his boss, was about to come face to face with two of them: 'Bernard asked me to deliver something to the UEFA match official staying with the Juventus team … So, I set off, envelope in hand, duly arriving in good time to deliver said envelope. What I wasn't ready for was the chance to meet some of the players – all dressed in club blazers and looking a million dollars. Among the players I was introduced to were Gentile and Cuccureddu and all I can recall was that they seemed to be about seven feet tall! They were huge! One of them gave me a Juventus badge which I still treasure to this day.'

Few fans in those days had a football knowledge wider than that covering their club's immediate domestic interests. The weekly magazines *Goal* and *Shoot!* covered world football in single pages each week and newspaper coverage of the continental game was scarce. Had fans known in greater detail what had landed on our shores when the Juventus side arrived, they may well have turned and run for the hills.

A solid start to the new season had been made, with three draws plus wins over Aston Villa and Bristol City putting City third. The side was settled, with Book playing practically an identical eleven in all six games thus far. Corrigan and Doyle were the mainstays from City's last European adventures, with the central defence bolstered considerably by the ex-Sunderland colossus Dave Watson. A broad and well-staffed attack comprising wingers Barnes and Tueart, plus Royle and/or Kidd was supported by the all-action, no-nonsense midfield scheming of Asa Hartford.

Immediately after a League Cup defeat at Aston Villa at the start of September, Book had flown out to Turin in the company of assistant Bill Taylor to take stock. In a low-key league game against Sambenedettese, Juventus had won 4–0 with two goals from star man Boninsegna.

Oddly, Book made note of the 'incredible crowd noise', although the match had been attended by only 20,000. What the City men had witnessed, in effect, was a low-key warm-up to the real thing.

Book was in no doubt that Juventus 'will have tried to disguise some of their customary style and ploys', but the manager felt that it had nevertheless been a worthwhile fact-finding trip, helping him and Taylor gather valuable information that would serve the club well.

At least, unlike the prematurely cocksure Allison, Book could say that his opponents had been watched, vetted and properly planned for. On that front there would be no excuses.

Chairman Peter Swales was in no doubt that the public had a treat coming their way. 'To be involved again in European competition after an absence of four years is a great thrill,' he wrote in the match programme. 'The anticipation is heightened by the fact that for our first test in the UEFA Cup we have been paired with one of the greatest clubs in world football. No task could be stiffer, and anyone who has knowledge of the record books will know that this is not flattery for the purpose of being courteous.'

Boninsegna, meanwhile, was equally sure that City's style would suit Juventus. 'I can understand why our football is not well received in England,' he said in an interview in *Shoot!* 'We are too defensive and not spectacular enough. This may not be good for the game, but it has brought Italian clubs many trophies!' That none of the trophies he mentioned were European ones in Juventus' case puzzled the striker as much as it puzzled everyone else. 'There is no logical explanation for our European performances,' he said. 'Ever since the days of John Charles, Juve have made the league almost their own exclusive property. Maybe it's because the approach to knockout football is so different.'

The only doubt beforehand concerned new signing Kidd, who had played on the opening day of the season at Leicester but pulled up injured in the second game at home to Villa. Kidd had returned against Bristol City the previous Saturday, forming a potent front three with the free-scoring Tueart and Royle, but playing them all against Juventus seemed a little foolhardy.

City's other summer signing, the unheralded Jimmy Conway, would take up the midfield place of the European stalwart Alan Oakes, who had been sold to Chester.

As news filtered through that Kidd would indeed be playing, and that he would be joined up front by both Royle and Tueart, the pre-match beers flowed more swiftly. Book, the quiet man of English soccer, evidently intended to make a big noise on City's ceremonial re-entry into Europe.

The manager had been accused in some quarters of producing a more pragmatic style of play, but he insisted that, although it might not resemble the all-out attack from the glory days, it was his intention to bring goals from all areas of the pitch, just as the side he had played in had done.

City now had more season ticket holders than ever before, and it was decided that for the Juventus game entry to the Platt Lane Stand would be by ticket only. Fans used to entering by simply paying the admission at the turnstiles had new habits to learn. On this occasion, only those climbing onto the Kippax could pay at the gate. The princely sum of 80 pence (£6.14 in today's money) would be the price for getting into the standing area. Youngsters and old-age pensioners could make it in to see these giants of European soccer for just 50 pence (£3.84 today). Seats would cost up to £1.40 (£10.75 today).

Pre-match chat in the pubs and chippies was all about whether City's front three could breach the seemingly impregnable Italian rearguard. Infamous for adopting the 'catenaccio' style coined by Helenio Herrera at Inter, Juventus' back four played together for the national team and would comprise a formidable barrier to City's attacking aspirations.

With Benetti hoping to nullify Hartford's combative energy in midfield, City would need every player to be on top of their game if they hoped to take any sort of advantage to Turin. One chink of light remained, however. Top scorer and talisman Boninsegna, whom Book had watched dismantle Sambenedettese, would be unavailable due to a suspension.

Book had identified the wings as the route around Juventus' blockade. As the Italians massed in defence in the opening minutes, it was clear that City would be trying to go around the outside and loft balls into the middle for the three strikers to move in on.

For Roger Reade, by now back in the office after his trip to Northenden, night games at Maine Road meant something special: 'Night matches were exciting, as the darkness seemed to "draw in" the crowd and create a special atmosphere. For the staff, it was exciting too as the club would buy us fish and chips before the game!'

Italian fortress cracked but not destroyed

The Italians were solid and quick into the tackle, as Book had forecast, and spent the first half repelling everything City threw at them. The Blues attacked with a vigour and intensity hardly seen since the glory days of Mercer and Allison, a non-stop effort that pressed Juventus deep into their own half for long periods. In midfield, despite the illustrious company, Hartford was setting the tempo to what was becoming a thrilling match.

Tueart also seemed energised by the challenge. In the 38th minute he came closest yet to breaking the deadlock. Letting fly with his left foot from fully 30 yards out, his shot raced past the outstretched arms of Zoff and catapulted off the top off the crossbar. Kidd was also coming closer, with a flying drive and a steep header that the apparently unbeatable Zoff managed to claw away at the foot of his post.

The shuddering Maine Road crowd did not have long to wait before Zoff's resistance was broken, however. Tueart's corner was met at the near post by Royle, glancing the ball behind him, where Kidd rose to dart his header inside the post.

With the goal falling a minute from half-time, the referee's whistle came as an unwelcome intrusion to City's growing superiority. The Italians had no intention of changing their safety-first tactics after the break and were evidently prepared to go home to Turin a goal down.

Odd chances began to fall their way, as City legs tightened. Twice Causio wriggled through to one-on-ones with Corrigan but was thwarted.

Barnes, making his European debut on the left wing, had been followed all night by the irascible Gentile and in the 57th minute received a tackle so ferocious that his game was over, replaced by another European debutant, Paul Power.

As David Barnes suggested in the following morning's *Daily Mail*: 'Juventus, masters of negativity, walked off the pitch at the end with the smug air of men who had done their jobs well. They showed enough skill in control and ruthlessness in the tackle to suggest a second leg ordeal for City.'

Sensing the need for positivity after a monumental effort, Book opined: 'It could have been three or four. But the ball is now in our court and we intend to keep it there. We can defend as well as anyone.'

Counterpart Giovanni Trapattoni sounded an equally positive note: 'I am well satisfied. It will be difficult in the second leg, for they are a good side, but we are happy with the scoreline and feel that we can get through.'

Barnes' report concurred with the Italian: 'Though they are far from finished, City came desperately close to destroying Juventus' pursuit of their first European trophy in sixteen years of steady campaigning.'

Speaking to Tommy Booth in the spring of 2020, the City centre-half was adamant that City's efforts in the '70s were hindered by the naivety that had been present in the early days in Europe too. 'We didn't know how much to defend,' he told me. 'The Italians were very cynical, knew how to block our game for long periods. They also knew how to get the refs onside. Some of the things going on wouldn't have been allowed in our league games. Juventus in '76 were like this. Hard, disciplined and they knew what they were doing!'

MANCHESTER CITY 1–0 JUVENTUS | Att. 36,955 | Kidd
Corrigan, Docherty, Donachie, Doyle, Watson, Conway, Barnes (Power), Kidd, Royle, Hartford, Tueart

---

City played two league fixtures before the return leg in Turin, winning at Sunderland to go second and then entertaining Manchester United in the first derby match of the season.

Hopeful of a decent confidence booster before travelling

south, City suffered a 3–1 defeat instead. Reports made a great deal of United manager Tommy Docherty's son Michael playing at right-back for City. Docherty, another of Book's low-key signings, had played in every game so far and would be picked for the match in Italy, which would curiously be his last game for the club.

Like Docherty, former Fulham schemer Jimmy Conway was also judged by the fans to be surplus to requirements. Having played in the home game, Conway missed the trip to Turin after picking up an injury at Roker Park, as did Barnes, injured in his jousting with gentleman Gentile.

Bolton away

Book, convinced that City needed to be strong-minded in Italy, again chose a side heavily endowed with attackers. Tueart, Royle and Kidd would all start, with Conway and Barnes replaced by Booth and Gerard Keegan. If the former, with his links back to the trophy-winning side that had beaten Górnik in 1970, would add great solidity in front of the back four, the latter was a gamble. One of many youngsters coming through at the time, Keegan, along with Kenny Clements, Peter Barnes, Paul Power, Gary Owen and substitute on this occasion Mike Lester, represented a new wave of emerging talent. Booth was anxious, nevertheless. 'The Italians were very clever at Maine Road,' he told me. 'They knew what they were doing and we didn't always know quite as much when we played in Europe, especially away from home. We attacked too much sometimes, played too much like we did in the First Division. You have to remember it was a learning curve for us even then. Foreign sides, particularly the Italians, wanted you to come out and attack like that. Then they just picked you off.'

City travelled to Italy in good spirits, not at all unusual at the time, according to Roger Reade: 'There was a great atmosphere behind the scenes at Maine Road at the time. What I would call a *togetherness*. I'm not sure why this was, but there seemed to be a collective spirit at the time. The staff and players would sit together for lunch at the City Social Club ... There were no mobile phones, no laptops or computers of any sort – so personal contact was the only way to communicate in those days. With a small number of non-playing staff, players and coaches, the collectiveness was palpable. Much credit for this must go to Book and Taylor.'

Book's intention for City to bare their teeth in the lion's den perhaps now revealed the first signs of a more gung-ho approach. Certainly, something needed to give, as City's eighth-place finish the previous season had been built almost entirely on a watertight home record. Away from Maine Road, City had managed to gather only ten points. If they were to escape the Stadio Comunale with a draw, Book felt boldness was the key.

With Boninsegna back in the line-up after suspension, the Italians would be stronger in attack and could be expected to come out more than they had in Manchester. 'I hope City will attack us,' the striker stated ominously before the game, 'as that usually gives me more room to operate in.'

Back in Manchester, with the party preparing to fly out, Reade was about to get a surprise. 'I was loving working in the office. I had supported City since boyhood ... Bernard had asked me and Ian [Niven Junior, another office employee] if we would be interested in being observer/stewards on the Official Supporters Club trip for the second leg. Was the Pope a Catholic?! I jumped at the chance. We arrived after an uneventful flight and were dropped in the middle of Turin. It was pouring down. City fans headed for cover in the bars; many, I recall, ended up in the square where much of the movie, *The Italian Job* had been filmed in 1969. Then the coach took us to the old Stadio Comunale, where there seemed to be very little cover from the rain. In fact, from our seats, we could only see a small section that had a roof and that seemed to be where the directors went. We all got drenched! Despite it being the city where all those glamorous films had been made, Turin was not a place I would have wanted to revisit. Some wag said it reminded them of Bolton, which was hardly a recommendation.'

With 55,000 fans undeterred by the weather, the challenge was obvious. City started competently enough, soaking up the early forays by the home side with a coolness that belied the tense atmosphere, even going close as Brian Kidd, suffering from a heavy cold, just failed to reach a chance. With Kidd toiling, neither Royle nor Tueart were able to impose themselves against a resolute Italian backline.

The first scare came in the 27th minute when the Belgian referee Francis Rion decided against awarding a penalty after Doyle had slipped and Corrigan took Bettega's ankles away with a desperate dive. If City were lucky to survive that incident, the roof fell in less than ten minutes later when Docherty's block on Scirea's shot bounced straight back to the defender, who stroked it past Corrigan with an unerring calmness.

The second half began with Booth and Hartford swapping roles, the former pressing forward more. As a ploy to allow Hartford to mark Causio, it failed. Causio, comfortable on the ball and intelligent in his positioning, was swapping wings at will and beginning to pull City all over the place. Three fine saves from Corrigan ensued, as Juventus pressed for the decisive goal.

The dreaded moment came when Gentile ventured forward and hit a speculative cross, which reached the head of Bettega. From there the ball was knocked back into the path of Boninsegna, who volleyed in from twelve yards.

On came Lester with the express instructions of evening a few scores. Read recalls: 'The City players all seemed to take a kicking until Lester came on just before the end and he was the only player who kicked them back. In fact, he was kicking them first.'

One final attack almost brought salvation when Royle heaved his giant frame at a cross and flicked the ball backwards. A goal at this point would have taken City through on the away goals rule, but Zoff – just as he had done in Manchester – got a hand to the header. The chance was gone.

Flattened and exhausted, City departed the ground to the sound of firecrackers and wild celebrations. They had shown great spirit, played with heart and endeavour, but Juventus' greater experience had seen them through.

Book had been right to say that the winners of this tie could go on to lift the trophy, but it was Juventus who would do so and not City.

'They were too experienced for us,' he said. 'We were sixteen months together and only knew one way to play. We did not adapt to the needs of the European game, the slow build-up, patient passing game.'

Forty-three years on, speaking with Gary Owen, the unused substitute was adamant that there was no way past Juventus for the likes of City in those days. 'If we'd have played all night and all the next day, we wouldn't have beaten them. The ref kept blowing up for infringements that did not exist. It felt like we would never score over there. I still believe that something untoward was going on. Plus, the Italian players knew every trick in the book. I was asked to warm up at one point by Tony and the Italian subs were warming up down the same stretch of the touchline. Even off the pitch their subs were standing on our feet and trying to trip us up as we went past.'

Owen has clear and unpleasant memories of the whole trip: 'It was cold, it was wet, there was smoke everywhere from the flares. The atmosphere was hostile. I'd made my debut at the tail-end of the season before, but this was different. The following season I played both games versus Widzew Łódź and we felt happy playing against anyone, but it still went wrong for us. We were still learning. There was a lot to take in, but you'll never persuade me to think differently. Juventus had it all sewn up with the referee.'

Joe Corrigan had been closer to the fans' animosity than most and recalled an incident that typified the night in his biography *Big Joe*: 'It was the first time I'd come up against a team that would do anything to come out on top. Their attitude resulted in cynical challenges, time wasting, shirt tugging, you name it. Juventus had mastered every trick in the book and while I don't think ability necessarily won the day, experience and gamesmanship edged it.

'One challenge summed up their philosophy perfectly. A cross came in and as Tommy Booth leapt to head the ball clear, Tardelli launched himself horizontally at Tommy and clattered him. The challenge could have broken Tommy's spine, so I grabbed hold of Tardelli, who was theatrically protesting his innocence. Meanwhile, Freddie Griffiths our physio ran on to treat Tom who had two sets of stud marks down his back. I was pulled away before I chinned him and that's when I noticed the Juventus players had an intense look in their eyes, a look that said defeat just wasn't an option. They did a very professional job on us.'

As for Reade and the rest of the supporters on the official trip, the long, wet night was not yet at an end. 'After the game, we got the coach back to the airport, where we had a lengthy wait before getting the flight home. I recall that there was an "incident" where a sink unit was smashed – though, to be fair to the City fan concerned, this did seem to be a genuine accident as I think he had simply sat on the unit and it fell away. As a trip for a twenty-year-old kid, it was truly memorable, in spite of the disappointing result.'

Dennis Tueart looked back on it less positively, striking a frustrated tone: 'We just didn't have a European head on. We were very inexperienced at this level. Very, very poor in that European tie. No real European steel.'

JUVENTUS 2–0 MANCHESTER CITY | Att. 55,000

Corrigan, Docherty, Donachie, Doyle, Watson, Booth, Keegan (Lester), Kidd, Royle, Hartford, Tueart

Book's adventurous tactical policies would see the Blues finish just short of champions Liverpool in second place come the following May. As a pointer for England's November game in Rome for the first of two World Cup qualifiers against the Italians, there had also been a clue or two for manager Don Revie. Roberto Bettega would again be the thorn in the English side with one of the two goals in a 2–0 home win that set the Azzurri on their way to Argentina. England, like City, would be left to lick their wounds.

For all City's huffing and puffing, they were out at the first hurdle. Another abrupt end; another harsh lesson. Small consolation came in the next round when Manchester United were dumped out by Juventus on a 3–1 aggregate.

Gary Owen was sure Juventus were on their way: 'The way their games were refereed there was no way they were going to concede goals in Turin. If you check the records, I'll wager they didn't have many go in against them in that run.' Juventus progressed past Shakhtar Donetsk, Magdeburg, AEK Athens and Athletic Bilbao to win the trophy, conceding only one goal in Italy. The *Vecchia Signora* shimmied all the way to the final and a glorious first-ever European trophy win, while City's blues began an inexorable slump that would end up with the team face down in the mud at Macclesfield in 1998.

Between those mid-to-late '70s nights and the 2003 UEFA Cup

match with Total Network Solutions FC (TNS), there was not a European sausage, bratwurst or chorizo worth its name for City fans to savour. The drought has long since ended and these days the likes of Inter, Roma and Juventus look at Manchester City in a different light to how Juve must have approached the 1976 encounter. The relative naivety of Book's approach, when a tight defence might have helped, is seldom echoed in the approach of City's modern-day European opponents, many of whom shy away from going toe to toe with giants.

These days the football boot is on the other foot.

City would be back in the UEFA Cup the following season, thanks to their efforts in the league, but would they have learnt their lessons? The fans, eager for more continental nights under the Maine Road lights would not have long to find out.

Łódź to think about

The 1977–8 season dawned with City among the favourites for honours. Book's judicious team-building had hoisted City back into English football's elite. In order to try and win the league, the manager had turned to England striker Mike Channon for goals. The £300,000 cheque to sign him may have brought tears to the eyes of chairman Peter Swales, but it was evidence that City meant business. Just how Book intended to keep four strikers (Channon, Tueart, Kidd and Royle) happy at the same time was unclear. Pre-season in Holland and Belgium, where City played future UEFA Cup opponents Lokeren, gave few clues.

By September, City were firing on all cylinders. Channon's brace in the 4–0 win over Norwich confirmed an unbeaten start to the season and brought him back into the England fold. A thrilling 3–1 win over United was a perfect warm-up for European action. City were top of the First Division and playing a brand of scintillating attacking football reminiscent of the grand old days.

Drawn against the unknown Widzew Łódź, confidence was high, despite Polish football enjoying a golden period. Knocking England out of qualification for the 1974 World Cup with the likes of Grzegorz Lato, Jerzy Gorgoń and the flying Lubański (whom City had met against Górnik) represented a first phase, now giving way to a second generation that would see the national team push on in Argentina in 1978 and finish third in Spain in 1982.

Unbeknown to them, City were to become the victims of the next phase of Polish development. In particular, they were about to be introduced to the man who would be the undisputed leader of a fresh generation of Polish success. The trouble was, in the autumn of 1977, nobody in England knew anything about him. They would all know soon enough. Unhappily for City, the legendary status about to be bestowed upon Zbigniew Boniek would only look appropriate after the night of 14 September 1977.

Book had found the perfect balance between exciting young blood (Barnes, Owen, Keegan and Clements would all play against Łódź) and solid experience in Booth, Corrigan and Donachie. Add the star quality of Tueart, Hartford, Kidd, Channon and Watson and City were a formidable opponent for anyone.

Owen, enjoying his first full season, was adamant that City were good enough. 'That side had balance, strength and personality. You knew, playing with the likes of Doyley and Dave Watson, Asa and Kiddo, Willie at the back, that you had a great chance against anyone,' he told me when I spoke to him in 2021. 'We had international players all the way through the side. I was one of the few that wasn't, but, even then, I ended up playing twenty-odd matches for England under 21s. We had goals across the front and we always felt we would score, wherever we were playing.'

Łódź had also qualified by finishing domestic league runners-up in 1976–7. This would be their European debut.

Book's enthusiasm reached Allison-esque levels the day before the game. 'A three-goal cushion will give us a pressure buffer before the second leg,' he enthused. 'I am convinced my boys can do it. We must take as much advantage as possible of the home leg.'

An expectant 34,000 crowd awaited the teams on a still autumnal evening in Manchester. All seemed set as City sailed into an eleventh-minute lead. Keegan (replacing the injured Power) was heavily involved in the slick build-up, linking well with Owen and Hartford. As the latter's cross found Kidd, his fierce shot was parried by the overworked Stanisław Burzyński. Barnes, who was first to react, swept in a close-range volley with his 'wrong' right foot.

Within four minutes of the start of the second half, City had increased their lead to within one goal of the confident target set by Book, Channon's close-range effort doing the damage. Owen compared what happened next to the plight of City in more modern times: 'Sometimes, if you take your foot off the accelerator, something just goes in your mind and it's difficult to explain. We've seen it with City loads of times in recent years. You go in at half-time three or four up and the second half ends 4–1 or stays the same. Once you throttle back, it's difficult to get going again. I don't know whether this is what happened with Łódź, but we allowed them back in and they took their chances. Or at least Boniek did. This was the first we had seen of him. What a player he was.'

As the game wore on, tempers frayed, with City's focus switching from pretty football to the possibility of a punch-up. The Irish referee Dominic Byrne boldly attempted to write the names of Ryszard Kowenicki and Zdzisław Kostrzewiński into his notebook, adding the more prosaic Hartford shortly after with the relieved expression of a man returning to his own language. Owen, providing fewer problems with his desultory two syllables, was also written down. City had allowed themselves to become distracted and Boniek took full advantage.

Within four minutes, the youngster took the game by the scruff of the neck and brought Łódź level through a misplaced shot and a well-struck penalty. First his 70th minute shot was deflected off Watson, after Booth had lost possession, then Booth clattered Jerzy Krawczyk in the box and Boniek buried the spot kick.

It had been a scintillating smash and grab from Boniek and a disastrous four minutes for Booth.

City then added attempted suicide to mortal injury when Donachie decided to upend the author of his side's downfall and was promptly sent off. This was too much for City supporter George Beddows to put up with, and the steaming Kippax was treated to a brief moment of comedy as the ever-threatening Boniek came face to face with one of Glossop's finest. Graham Ward, watching enthralled from the North Stand, remembers: 'I couldn't see whether a blow was landed on Boniek or not, but it was a disastrous end to the game.'

A fast-moving policeman curtailed Beddows' conversation with the player and Boniek promptly got back to bossing the game for the final few minutes. Another City fan Martin Stubbs remembers Beddows from the Gamesley estate in Glossop: 'He was a couple of years ahead of me at school, was George. We were all gobsmacked when we recognised the intruder as him, as he was a really quiet lad at school.'

Book's after-match tones bore little resemblance to the triumphalism before the game. 'With the benefit of hindsight, we can all see what was wrong,' he stated. 'We got involved in physical tussles, were too easily baited and concentration lapsed. The team's rhythm disintegrated and they took advantage of the problems we caused ourselves. I set the target of three goals to act as a confidence booster for the return leg, but now we will need victory to see us through.'

Asa Hartford revealed some of the skulduggery perpetrated by the Łódź players: 'My booking was unfortunate, because I felt that I was right. Their goalkeeper was blatantly time-wasting as he went into the net to retrieve the ball. I pushed him out of the way to get the ball back into play. I get booked and he gets off free despite provoking the situation.' He added: 'It's definitely going to be difficult in Poland, but I am more comfortable going to Łódź with a 2–2 than I was last year going to Juventus with a 1–0 advantage.'

Goalscorer Barnes was thrilled to get a goal, but rued City's approach: 'I always enjoy scoring, but it is a special thrill to get a goal in Europe. We should have taken things easier when we were leading, but we began to rush to obtain a bigger lead.'

Perhaps Book's pre-match exhortations had affected the way City had played but not how the manager had hoped. In 'rushing things', City had stumbled.

Without realising it, the team had helped launch a Polish football phenomenon that would see Łódź gather fans from all over the country as a result of their daring antics in European competition. The legend was starting here – thanks to City's customary generosity of spirit – and would be cemented by a tense and fruitless second leg.

For Roger Reade, the let-down was palpable: 'I recall the home match very well. When Donachie was sent off, in essence because City had become frustrated by the way the Polish team were diving and winding us up, the supporters also became frustrated. The fan who ran onto the pitch created a new kind of administrative problem for our staff to manage.'

A UEFA fine would follow, something the club would become more familiar with in later years.

MANCHESTER CITY 2–2 WIDZEW ŁÓDŹ | Att. 33,695 | Barnes, Channon

Corrigan, Clements, Donachie, Owen, Watson, Booth, Barnes, Channon, Kidd, Hartford, Keegan (Royle)

Meanwhile, City drew with QPR and beat Bristol City to remain top of the league. Talk of a title challenge was realistic enough. They were unbeaten in nine games. The party travelling out to Poland on 27 September felt special responsibility, as league leaders, to take the game by the scruff of the neck.

Dennis Tueart, hopeful of a recall after being injured in a League Cup tie at Chesterfield, stated: 'We have to go and attack. At Maine Road we fell into their trap of intimidation. Now it all depends on our attitude.'

Book agreed. 'I have no doubts that we are the better side,' he told Derek Potter of the *Daily Express*. 'We must go there and attack them with the fervour of a home game, adding a bit of common sense. But we cannot afford to fall for their intimidation, like we did in the first leg.'

A sixteen-strong squad flew out from Ringway, with Book said to be tempted to play both Tueart and Barnes in order to open the Poles up down the flanks. This mirrored the thinking a year earlier when the same ploy had failed to get City through in the Stadio Comunale and it would fail again on this occasion.

Widzew had shifted the game to rival LKS Łódź's stadium to accommodate a bigger crowd. By kick-off, 40,000 were crammed into the open-sided ground, kicking up a fuss, reminiscent of City's first-ever European away day at Fenerbahçe. The result, ignominious departure, would be exactly the same for City here as it was in 1968.

Łódź, with an appalling start in the league, actually entered this game bottom of the Ekstraklasa. With City's propensity for mishaps, there could really be only one outcome.

With Channon failing a fitness test, Royle deputised. Book chose Tueart and Barnes on the wings, with Power also making the cut in place of the suspended Donachie. Book had been experimenting with an early production of inverted wingers, where the left-footed Barnes often started on the right with the predominantly right-footed Tueart on the other side. With Tueart cutting inside, the theory was that space would be created for Power to overlap and produce something for the lurking Royle.

Had Royle scored from an easy opportunity in the 24th minute, this might now be recorded as a tactical master stroke. Burzyński dropped a swinging cross at his feet and Royle, perhaps startled by the goalkeeper's sudden return to fallibility, made two wafting gestures with his foot, neither connecting.

With Widzew happy to defend their position, City had the better of the second period but could not break the home side down. With tempers fraying and patience running out, Power found his way into the referee's notebook and the final breathless whistle was greeted by the now customary home exuberance. City were once again out of Europe at the first hurdle and had only themselves to blame.

'We just didn't stick the ball in the back of the net,' was Book's neat attempt at stating the obvious, alluding to Royle's moment of elephant ballet six yards out. Tueart and Royle were both unhappy, the former with City's continuing naivety in continental football, the latter for being made a scapegoat for the exit: 'The players would joke about it. Asa would say, "What's it like to cost the club £250,000!?" It was immaterial really. I had been thrown in because of Channon's injury. I knew I was on my way out with him in the squad. I was probably the first of that great side to go. In the game I had chased the ball down and the keeper had dropped it. I had an empty net to slot into, but I lost it as it was coming down. I should have volleyed it first time ...'

Another European chance had thus been cast to the four winds. City would have to wait and see if the domestic season's efforts would bring them another continental opportunity in 1978–9.

WIDZEW ŁÓDŹ 0-0 MANCHESTER CITY | Att. 40,000
Corrigan, Doyle (Clements), Power, Owen, Watson, Booth, Barnes, Kidd, Royle, Hartford, Tueart

---

A strong finish to the league campaign brought Book's men home in fourth place, high enough to qualify for the UEFA Cup. The summer would be spent recuperating after a long chase behind surprise winners Nottingham Forest. Few changes were made to the star-studded squad in the close season. At the time, one A-list signing was usually the extent of City's transfer activity, and this year the club's money (for a club record of £350,000) was spent on Luton Town's promising centre-half Paul Futcher, who came in to replace the long-serving Mike Doyle, sold to Stoke City. To help Futcher acclimatise, in came his twin brother Ron, after a summer with Minnesota Kicks. They had played together at Chester, then Luton. Now they had hit the big time in stereo too. In a busy summer for Paul, he also got married. 'It has been the most fantastic month of my life,' added Futcher afterwards, unaware that his future at City would not be quite so fantastic.

Just before the season kicked off, Book swooped on title rivals Ipswich to collect midfielder Colin Viljoen, as chairman Swales reluctantly made a further £100,000 available for his manager's war chest. The late signing was concluded with just three hours to spare for registration for European games.

Elsewhere, City's squad contained one or two gaps that would eventually prove costly. Dennis Tueart, with 59 goals from 140 appearances, had been lured away to the all-star project at New York Cosmos, where he would rub shoulders with Mick

Jagger off the pitch and Carlos Alberto and Franz Beckenbauer on it. Joe Royle had joined a slightly different scene at Bristol City, where showbiz infiltration was restricted to the cider-themed folk combo The Wurzels. Of City's multi-pronged attack of the 1977–8 season, only Mike Channon and Brian Kidd remained.

The outlay on new players had been restricted by a steep bill for ground improvements. Included in these, explained director Ian Niven, were safety requirements from UEFA to enable City to participate in their competitions. New seats had been placed at the edge of the Main Stand and, as a result of the altercation between Boniek and the over-enthusiastic fan George Beddows from the North Stand, 'a £10,000 portable fence needed to be erected behind each goal for our subsequent European games', confirmed Niven, after City were fined '£400 for the intrusion'. Curiously, the club had not been asked to erect fencing in front of the Kippax terracing, where most of City's hard-core support was housed.

Fines levied by an increasingly agitated UEFA half a century later would continue to rain down on City. By 2020, the club would be dealing with more than just financial punishments, however.

City had started the season slowly, with 1–1 draws against Derby, Arsenal and Norwich interrupted by a heavy defeat at Maine Road to an already slick-looking Liverpool. With Paul Futcher appearing nervous in his opening games, Book's job was becoming more complicated than the pre-season predictions had suggested. However, a 3–0 win over Leeds steadied the ship somewhat ahead of the opening European tie of the season.

City had been drawn to play the Dutch side FC Twente Enschede. Part of a characteristically tortuous pre-season had been spent in Holland the previous month, with a win against SC Heracles, but a 5–1 rout from lowly AZ Alkmaar. Twente were of higher calibre to Alkmaar and Book went out of his way to warn against any complacency.

Coach Bill Taylor had spent some of his summer at the Argentina World Cup and had been particularly captivated by the Dutch squad. 'They were situated 50 miles from Mendoza in the hills,' Taylor enthused. 'The players wanted for nothing. They had video television with tapes involving matches of their opponents, plus feature films, table tennis, snooker and a superb music centre. You name it, they had it. Even down to two-way radio for them to communicate with their families back home. That's organisation.' Taylor had reported back on various aspects of match preparation that could be of use to the City squad on their travels.

Taylor would also have noted that Twente right-back Piet Wildschut was one of the Dutch international squad he had so admired during his working holiday. Also on the books at Twente were three players who would subsequently make a name for themselves in the First Division: Romeo Zondervan (later of West Brom and Ipswich), Heini Otto (Middlesbrough) and Frans Thijssen (destined to become one of Ipswich Town's most famous sons).

Twente, thus, well stocked with quality and, having matched City's fourth-place finish in the Eredivisie, would be a tough nut to crack.

The 600-or-so City supporters expected to travel to eastern Holland for the game were also asked to prepare themselves properly. After the incident against Łódź, the club were sensitive to the danger of further fines. The curse of hooliganism was rife and the '70s had seen several British clubs having problems in European competition. Manchester United's match in Saint-Étienne had involved a riot of such proportions they were ordered to play the home leg in Plymouth, and Liverpool's excursion to Mönchengladbach had seen widespread misbehaviour by returning fans, looting and vandalising in various Belgian towns on the route back to the ferry ports. City were not without their troublemakers, and a message in the last home programme before the tie in Holland urged all fans to remember the import-ance of decorum.

If City were to get something from the first leg, the goal-scoring prowess of Brian Kidd, already evident in the first three games of the season, would be missing, after he chipped a bone in his foot. This was an early rumble of what would become a full storm later in the season regarding City's striking pos-itions. Ex-paper boy Roger Palmer had stepped into Kidd's shoes against Leeds and scored twice, making himself a shoo-in for Enschede in place of Ron Futcher.

Book explained why he chose Palmer and not Futcher: 'I am not taking Ron with us this time, because he needs some heavy training sessions. He will be the first to admit that he returned from America nowhere near fit enough for the demands of First Division football. For this reason, he won't be considered for the Twente game.'

At the Bad Boekelo Hotel, a spa resort just outside Enschede, the team were welcomed by the Dutch club's general manager Tom van Dalen, impressing Peter Swales with his knowledge of City and English football. The limpid waters, dotted with lily pads and stretches of reed beds, provided the squad with a calm retreat before the game, perhaps coach Taylor's first opportun-ity to copy some of the good habits he had witnessed the Dutch adhering to in Mendoza.

With bicycles, a spa, sauna and a bowling alley, Boekelo's facilities allowed the players to recuperate away from the prying eyes of the press after a hectic start to the season.

Come the night of the match, a cold dark evening and a tightly packed ground welcomed the two teams. City were quickly into their stride in an attempt to end their bad run of first-round collapses, new boy Palmer inches from finishing off a piercing second-minute cross from Barnes. Palmer then twisted a magnificent header onto the crossbar and side-footed another chance wide of the post during a busy first-half showing.

By the break City were ahead anyway, thanks to a typically bold header from Watson, who had foxed the defence with a blindside run to meet Hartford's free kick. Having battered Twente's defence in a lively first half, City took a pounding in the second, with Watson again prominent in the next goal.

Thoresen's fiercely hit free kick flicked up off Watson's boot, diverting the ball past Corrigan. Twente then unleashed a formidable effort to attempt to gain the lead, with Viljoen and Owen booked as the temperatures rose, but City held out, much to the delight of the hero of the hour Watson. 'It will be hard, but I think we can beat Twente at home,' he said after the game. Book was understandably satisfied: 'We would have settled for this result before we kicked off.'

With Book's praise falling on newcomers Palmer and Viljoen, the press were keen to focus on a more customary performer, Joe Corrigan. Peter Gardner's *Manchester Evening News* report stated that 'once again Corrigan emerged the battered hero, pulling his side out of the wood when Twente were well on top'.

Denis Lowe's *Telegraph* piece enthused: 'Corrigan, as consistent as ever, produced three notable saves in quick succession, from Thoresen, Otto and Ierssel.' While Ronald Crowther in the *Daily Mail* suggested that 'the result might well have gone against City – and it might even have been a crushing one – but for the ever-dependable Corrigan'.

The goalkeeper's high-profile troubles in the early part of the decade had been put behind him thanks to hard work and a resolute attitude. Widely lambasted for some regrettably high-profile mistakes, the big goalkeeper had hauled himself back into the limelight as England third-choice keeper.

Once again part of the official trip organised by the club, Roger Reade remembers a well-run, well-behaved and culturally productive visit to Holland: 'Again, Bernard approached Ian Niven Junior and me to ask us if we wanted to go on the Official Supporters Club trips … Once again, the City fans were really well behaved, so there was little for me to do in the form of "stewarding". In fact, most City fans were perfectly happy with the 1–1 draw, so there was no real likelihood of any difficulties. I remember that the ground was small, about the size of Edgeley Park, and there was no threat of any trouble. In fact, the crowd was only around 12,000, including a good 500 or more City fans. The arrangements were spot on and a really enjoyable time was had by all in Amsterdam itself.'

A slightly more eventful and less successful trip is remembered by City fan Johnny Waters, who was already working in Holland, based in Haarlem at the time. He recalls: 'I had been up all night at a girlfriend's, got back to the squat in the morning absolutely shattered, when Don Price came out with the lads from Prestwich and persuaded me to come across to Enschede to meet up with them. I was skint, but he paid for us to get down there. Train full of Blues all the way. The centre was full of Blues when we got there too. Had a good session that afternoon, but sadly I fell asleep in a bar and when I woke up everyone had gone. Missed the match completely. Then, somehow, I managed to find Don and a gang of Blues, looking for somewhere to drink afterwards, or they found me perhaps. The bars wouldn't let us in. We missed the last train back to Haarlem and slept on the station platform guarded by local police. Great day out, that was.'

Martin Stubbs recalls a train and ferry trip that diverges slightly from Roger Reade's *official* account: 'The trip was eagerly anticipated, certainly by us younger ones. First part of the journey was train to Piccadilly, plenty of cans en route. Into The Brunswick for a few more pints then to the off-licence, before the aptly named boat train, because it was swimming with piss, to Harwich. The train journey was bedlam with lads scrapping with each other; the emergency cord pulled at least three times en route. Anyway, onto the ferry for the overnight sail to the Hook of Holland. More beer was consumed and the sight of loads of pissed-up blues attempting to find their cabins was hilarious. Others were being sick over the side. After an eventful night we were eventually shuttled by bus to our accommodation in Amsterdam the day before the game. Well, chaos ensued as there were hundreds of drunk fans all over the place, some obviously visiting the local establishments for cakes and sweets. Well, that's what they said anyway. Others made their own amusement. It was rumoured that somebody actually went sightseeing. A late night was had, back to the hotel morning of the game, arriving for breakfast then out on the beer again in Amsterdam. A central meeting point was arranged for transfer on coaches to Enschede from Amsterdam. On arrival, we were greeted by some not-so-friendly Dutch fans and a bit of a fracas ensued. Anyway, the local police soon had it under control. The game was a decent 1–1 draw followed by more *festivities* with the locals, as we were escorted back to our coaches. Back to Amsterdam where the next few hours can only be described as surreal: an impromptu game of football against locals at three in the morning and finally in bed at 5.30. The return journey was chaos, lads scrapping with each other, sick everywhere, staff at their wits end. Eventually we got back on the train to Piccadilly, where the mood was slightly more subdued, but still lively enough for me to have a row with one of the travel club stewards, and subsequently getting a ban from the travel club. A truly memorable journey.'

FC TWENTE ENSCHEDE 1–1 MANCHESTER CITY | Att. 12,000 | Watson

Corrigan, Clements, Power, Viljoen, Watson, P. Futcher, Channon, Owen, Palmer, Hartford, Barnes

---

The day after the game, a story circulated that Book was being considered for the vacant manager's job at Leeds, who were falling on hard times after a glittering decade of trophy winning. Book quickly put the rumours to bed. Roger Reade was well aware of the qualities of City's manager: 'Tony must have been under constant pressure from the board and Peter Swales in particular, but he was a terrific bloke to work alongside, always positive and always good company. I felt for Tony a little, as I believe that his player's background at City meant that he didn't carry as much "clout" as if he had been an outsider. An example was when he wanted to sign Graeme Souness from Middlesbrough and the board simply refused his request. Souness went to Liverpool instead of City and we all know what his influence was in winning so many trophies there.'

There is no telling what the acquisition of Souness would have done to City's chances at a time when Colin Bell's career was stuttering to a tragic close. Suffice to say, Souness would lift the European Cup wearing the red shirt of Liverpool in London, Paris and Rome in 1978, 1981 and 1984, respectively. City's European pedigree would take many decades more building and missing out on Souness can be seen as one of a selection of *sliding doors* moments for a club that was on the cusp of experiencing a dramatic downturn instead.

A midfielder of even more elevated all-round ability than the imperious Souness was available to Tony Book for the return leg with Twente, however.

Colin Bell, proud owner of 48 England caps and one of City's all-time greats, had hauled himself back from a cruciate ligament injury in 1975 and would play his first game of the season for the return leg against Twente. Bell knew full well that his knee was 'not right', yet he soldiered on. His manager, conscious of Bell's potential influence, would use him in the remaining European games City played in 1978–9, rightly judging his experience would add something crucial to the mix.

In Ian Cheeseman's reflective biography of the player, Bell stated: 'My only concern was to prove to myself that I could still play like I'd done in my mid-20s. I was 32 now and, as much as I wanted to believe things would improve, I was beginning to have doubts. I started the new season in the reserves again and – apart from a game with Derby County – only played a few games in the UEFA Cup.'

To those of us watching from the sidelines, the sight of Bell with obviously restricted flexibility was hard to take. The man Malcolm Allison had nicknamed 'Nijinsky' for his incredible stamina, was now moving with little fluidity and, visibly from the terraces, a slight stoop and a relative slowness that spoke volumes.

While Bell attempted to climb back on the regular first-team roster, another teammate was about to cause problems of a different kind for Book.

The supposedly unfit and overweight Ron Futcher bagged a hat-trick in a win at Chelsea and then scored again against Tottenham. Futcher's sudden rich form was to be rewarded against Twente with replacement by the fit-again Kidd, a clear sign to him of his place in the pecking order. City's stuttering start had cleared and the Spurs win pushed them up to fourth. Donachie, still excluded owing to his indiscretion against Widzew Łódź, threw the only minor spanner in the works, necessitating Power to be drafted in at left-back.

Rumours that Bell would be named as substitute began to circulate in Manchester on the morning of the match, adding to the already sharp sense of anticipation. In the *Manchester Evening News*, Bell explained that he was back to make a difference, not to make up the numbers: 'When the time comes that I am on the pitch just to inspire the others, without being able to play my part, then I'll quit.' These were prophetic words for more than one reason. Bell had made his comeback the season before in a Christmas game at home to Newcastle, where the warmth of the reception to his substitute appearance had reduced a usually phlegmatic man to tears. Little did he know it, but that evening's European game would have a similar effect on him.

The near-30,000 Maine Road crowd were treated to an emotionally charged, switchback of a game, thanks not only to Bell's appearance, but to an unendingly brave performance from the Dutch visitors, who just refused to accept defeat.

As John Roberts wrote in the *Guardian*, 'City took their supporters on the accustomed rollercoaster ride before defeating the resilient Dutch technicians of Enschede to reach the second round of the UEFA Cup after failing at the first round in their three previous attempts.'

Even though Twente conceded an early own goal from Wildschut, after Owen's prodigious dummy in the build-up left experienced left-back Kees van Ierssel contemplating his own shadow. Owen's firmly hit cross was impossible to deal with and the ball squirted into the net past reserve keeper Eddie Pasveer.

With a seemingly good goal from Kidd disallowed and Owen firing against a post, City were punishing Twente, who nevertheless persevered with a bold attacking ploy themselves. In an era suffused with the flexible attacking theories of the Dutch national side under Rinus Michels, Twente seemed to embody what football fans had seen on their television sets from West Germany and Argentina.

With City ahead at the break, the feeling in the ground was that the job was on the way to being done. That illusion was shattered before the half-time cup of tea had been properly digested, as Twente forced themselves level through Niels Overweg's low free kick, which squirmed past an unsighted Corrigan.

Colin Bell's 60th-minute introduction for the struggling Viljoen lifted everyone. The old master began by threading a simple pass through to the overlapping Clements, who almost scored. Following this with a lob that almost put City back in front, Bell was quickly showing the fans what they had been missing.

Gary Owen remembers another individual from a packed midfield that night: 'Romeo Zondervan! He was a clever player, who I played with later on at West Brom. We had another Dutchman at the Hawthorns, Martin Jol. They played a style that suited the English game.'

Soon City had a breakthrough that came screaming off the toe of Brian Kidd that had been mending for the previous five weeks. As Derek Potter wrote in the *Express*: 'The savagely struck swerving left-foot shot from 25 yards out blasted City's jinx to oblivion.' As the ball fell to Bell on the edge of the box in the next attack, the midfielder did not hesitate for a second and smashed a third past Pasveer.

Twente stormed forward in an attempt to salvage something. Kidd and Channon came close to putting City further clear, but it was Ab Gritter who scored next, pulling the score back to 3–2. The agitated crowd were forced through six more minutes of end-to-end football before being put out of their misery.

It felt like a troublesome cycle of failure had been put to bed at last. This energetic win against testing opponents would allow a different mindset to foster among the players. It would be the start of City's last heroic push through European competition for more than three decades. Although the adventures that would follow in the coming months would supply great memories, nobody was contemplating what would be a generational void that would last into the next century.

For Colin Bell, nursing a painfully swollen knee, there was also a feeling of deliverance. 'The crowd's reaction to my appearance, then my goal was something special,' he said. 'Something I had never dreamed of; something really special. It has made the months of hard work worthwhile.'

MANCHESTER CITY 3–2 FC TWENTE ENSCHEDE | Att. 29,330 | Wildschut (o.g.), Kidd, Bell

Corrigan, Clements, Power, Viljoen (Bell), Watson, P. Futcher, Channon, Owen, Kidd, Hartford, Barnes

---

With Everton easing past Finn Harps on a 10–0 aggregate, West Brom knocking six past Galatasaray over two legs and Arsenal beating Lokomotive Leipzig 7–1, City would be accompanied into the second round by all the English teams that had started the competition. With Ajax, Benfica, Stuttgart, AC Milan and Mönchengladbach all through too, plus dark horses Dinamo Tbilisi, a strong field was assembling.

Despite lurking danger, the draw could have been worse for City, pitching them against Standard Liège. The Belgians would provide another trip of short dimensions for the supporters. Roger Reade, waiting to be told about travel arrangements, was informed there would be no tickets available to staff, 'presumably because they felt we were going through without too much trouble' he suggests.

One minor problem was UEFA's confirmation that Gary Owen would be suspended for the first leg, after picking up bookings in both Twente games. The midfielder would be available for the second leg in Liège. Of all the youngsters Book and Taylor were attempting to integrate into the side, Owen was faring the best. Only an infamous short fuse hindered him from making one of the midfield berths his own.

'It was part of my game to be feisty,' he told me. 'But it meant that I missed a few games suspended.' The topic would rear its head again in Liège and this time the consequences would follow Owen to the present day.

Standard fare

By the time of the home leg, City were in good form. Four goals from Owen, three of them from the penalty spot, in the previous two games had seen City through to the third round of the League Cup and they were sitting fifth in the league.

Standard arrived in Manchester showcasing half the Belgian national team. If Juventus had been Italian royalty in 1976, Standard were Belgian princes too. Goalkeeper Michel Preud'homme was one of the best in Europe, while captain Eric Gerets also led the national side. With injuries still affecting Book's selections, Palmer again played. In Owen's absence, Viljoen deputised alongside Hartford and Bell.

The game itself did not run smoothly for City. For long periods a stubborn Standard held their own. What Michael Carey in *The Times* called 'one of City's uneven performances' was beginning to be a feature of the season. Scintillating on their day, Book's men were beginning to stack up the pedestrian displays, despite possessing a squad which looked more than good enough to challenge for honours.

Half-time arrived with the two sides separated by an early back-post header from Hartford, which bounced down and through Preud'homme's legs. It was an uncharacteristically sloppy lapse from the keeper, but nobody at Maine Road was complaining.

By the 84th minute, almost everyone was complaining, however, as City looked to be heading to Belgium with an exasperatingly slender lead. Becoming ever more fitful, a host of chances had been spurned. But for Hartford's goal-line clearance from Philippe Garot, it would have been all square.

The picture suddenly changed dramatically in the 85th minute, when Watson's goal-bound header was handled in the box. Kidd smashed home the penalty. With unexpected haste the *other City* woke up and started to pulverise the Belgian defence. Barnes, jinking through a field of legs, squared for Kidd to head a third. Then the winger, already at odds with Book about selection issues, tore down the other side and fed Palmer for a fourth. A six-minute cameo had flattened the Belgian challenge completely. Barnes, unplayable in this form, switching wings at will, was a swerving menace.

All at once the second leg looked a formality. 'This is where we sometimes had problems,' Owen told me. 'It's so difficult to keep focused. Even when the manager has said what to do and what not to do … We were a good side, professional. I was the youngest one there, so I got a bit over-excited, but we knew what we were doing.'

For young fan Alistair Wade, the match presented other problems: 'I remember the win over Liège well. At seven years old it was my first night match. Season 1978–9 was the first year my dad and I had season tickets. With an hour's drive home to Chester, it was a late night and I missed the start of school the next day. My mum said I would not be allowed to go to a night match again if I couldn't get up for school. My love for City meant I was never late for school again.'

MANCHESTER CITY 4–0 STANDARD LIÈGE | Att. 27,489 | Hartford, Kidd (2, 1 pen.), Palmer

Corrigan, Clements, Donachie, Booth, Watson, Viljoen (Keegan), Palmer, Bell, Kidd, Hartford, Barnes

Draws at Bolton and West Brom occurred before the second leg. City's form appeared to have peaked.

In Liège, the players appeared focused, but – as Owen had intimated – it was impossible to escape the fact that, barring an absolute collapse, City were through. By half-time, that thought had become a certainty in many minds, as Standard had failed to find a way past Corrigan.

However, in the 62nd minute City suddenly fell a goal behind when Booth fouled Gerets and Ásgeir Sigurvinsson scored with the resulting free kick. When the same player whipped in a second on 84 minutes from the penalty spot, the mercury began to rise. Owen's moment in the limelight was also about to happen.

'It started getting rough in the second half, as we tried to slow Standard down a bit,' Owen reflects. 'They had got a bit of a head of steam going and the tackling was getting tasty. One of their players reacted badly to one of Asa's typical digs and, with Asa flat on the floor, he was about to stamp on his head. Well, I wasn't having any of that, so I rushed over. I always liked to get my retaliation in first. My dad was a rugby league player, small like me, and always told me that I had to hold my own otherwise I'd get bullied. He even gave me a bat to take to school with me!

'Anyway, I ran in and walloped the Standard player who was leaning over Asa. The referee sent me off. As I was going off, I was shaking. Tony Book ushered me off and asked Bernard Halford to take me down to the dressing rooms. Unfortunately, the door was locked when we got there. Bernard was such a gentle fellow and he had to watch as I kicked the dressing room door in. At the hearing Bernard said to me: "Gary, don't worry I am representing you at the hearing and I'll get things sorted for you." Well, suffice to say you wouldn't have wanted Bernard as your defence lawyer. I thought I might get two games, but they gave me six! City only had four more games in Europe that season and when I moved to West Brom we had a UEFA Cup game and I was picked. I got changed ready when one of the staff came in and said: "You can't play, you're banned!" I'm 61 years old and I'm still fucking banned now. We never played another European game, so I never played out the ban...'

City had scraped through, nevertheless. If Owen's red mist had been a hindrance on this occasion, it helped him on many other occasions to fight his corner against larger, stronger opponents. It was part of the little midfielder's game and made him the quintessential foil – along with the equally robust Hartford – for Bell and Viljoen's quiet probing. City, with a shock to their system, were through to fight another day.

STANDARD LIÈGE 2–0 MANCHESTER CITY | Att. 25,000

Corrigan, Clements, Donachie, Booth, Watson, Owen, Channon, Bell, Kidd, Hartford, Palmer

The third round would be the last round played before the winter break. With Everton edged out by Dukla Prague, City entered the draw with Arsenal and West Brom. Arsenal would play Red Star Belgrade and West Brom had drawn Valencia, while City had the toughest draw of the lot: AC Milan.

Liverpool were already ten points away at the top of the league, so City concentrated their powers on Milan. *Football Monthly* magazine's Leslie Vernon wrote: 'Now, as the season moves towards its critical phase, it is to Europe, where the club has had so many disasters, that they must look for their main hope of success.'

Nils Liedholm's side was liberally decorated with quality, although Gianni Rivera's final season was coming to an end after nineteen seasons and approaching 650 games. Along with national team player Fulvio Collovati plus a young Franco Baresi, the Italians were expected to provide a test for a misfiring City.

No British team had ever won a competitive game in Milan's San Siro. To make matters worse, Channon had pulled up with an injury and Clements broke his leg against Ipswich. As usual, things were never straightforward for City.

A defeat to Derby had seen spies from Milan in the Main Stand. Pictured in the next home programme, the shady characters were named as Fernando Benzoni, aiming a primitive movie camera towards the pitch from his position in front of puzzled-looking fans. The man to Benzoni's right was apparently 'Alvaro Gasparini, who made careful mental notes of the tactics and formations employed by the Blues'. Needless to say, 'neither of the Milan officials were over-impressed with City's form against Derby. Gasparini, through an interpreter, did make mention of Mike Channon, Asa Hartford and Brian Kidd though,' the programme concluded.

Arriving in Milan, the first thing City's official party noticed was the thick fog. City, without Owen, Channon and Barnes, would have to make changes. With kick-off less than 30 minutes away and the stadium filling up, the referee took one look at the mists curling around the ground and called the game off. Paul Power, drafted in as cover for Owen in midfield, remembered noise, adrenaline and relief: 'There were firecrackers going off everywhere and flares being lit on the upper tiers. It was more intimidating than we had expected, but due to the conditions, the game was called off at the last minute. We ended up playing at lunchtime on the Thursday and only half the ground was occupied.'

Although the atmosphere had lost much of its hostility, City fans would have a problem due to the prearranged charter flights back to Manchester planned to leave halfway through the game. Still the match was played in front of around 40,000 spectators. Book would later confirm that the sting had been taken from the crowd, bringing with it a big advantage to City. 'What

I remember most vividly is that there is always such a special atmosphere in grounds for night games,' he said. 'In Milan it was going to be extra special with a full house expected. So, when the game was fogged off it was definitely an advantage to us.'

Book had brought a gaggle of untried youngsters with him for the bench: Gerard Keegan, Tony Henry, Russell Coughlin, Paul Futcher and Keith MacRae all took their places as the crowd settled.

Watson swapped pennants in the centre circle with Gianni Rivera and City, with Viljoen, Power and Palmer making the starting line-up, immediately found themselves under the cosh, as Collovati shot wide in the first minute. By half-time Milan had added only one more effort of note, from Ruben Buriani, as the twin towers of Booth and Watson at the back had repelled everything they had managed to throw at them. At the other end, City had not only had six presentable opportunities of their own, they also had the lead, with Kidd's soaring header from Hartford's cross rocketing past Enrico Albertosi.

Twelve minutes into the second half came one of Power's career highlights. The midfielder began an electric run down the right wing. Seventy yards later, Power found himself staggering into the Milan box with the teenage Franco Baresi before him. Dropping a shoulder, Power cut back inside and unleashed a left-footer that bounced in front of Albertosi and clipped over the diving keeper.

Possibly dazzled by their sterling efforts and the prospect of becoming only the third side to win at the San Siro in European combat, City were caught cold by Bigon's header, which reached Corrigan tamely, but somehow disappeared under the goalkeeper and into the net. Then came the onslaught. Three times Corrigan was beaten in the City goal only for the linesman's flag to come to the rescue. What was left of the crowd began to pelt the big City keeper with rubbish, fruit and cans of drink as a sign of their bubbling discontent, barracking the referee Heinz Einbeck at the same time. With only eight minutes remaining, Bigon, ironically from what looked like an offside position, took advantage of a deflection and netted past Corrigan. The big keeper's stunning save from Bigon's last-minute hat-trick attempt gained City a 2–2 draw that felt less of a reward than it should have done.

The City party was kept inside the San Siro afterwards as a mob busied itself conducting a minor riot. Bricks, bottles and beer cans were thrown in the direction of the coach waiting to take City to the hotel. Neither the tear gas filling the concourses, nor the distant echoes of excited locals disturbed the City party deep in the bowels of the old ground. A heroic stand had been made, one that deserved a proper second helping in two weeks' time at Maine Road.

'Their equaliser was two yards offside,' said Book afterwards, conveniently ignoring the three Milan goals that *had* been marked off for offside, 'but we are delighted with the result, especially with the two away goals.'

Derek Potter in the *Express* put City's achievements succinctly enough: 'The legend of the San Siro was destroyed by a clinically efficient City side in the sunshine of Milan yesterday and City's two away goals will be priceless when the two sides meet in the second leg.'

Norman Fox, in *The Times*, noted a tactical flexibility: 'City had started with a mainly defensive attitude. Preferring not to man-mark Rivera, who at first strolled the pitch caressing passes, City had Watson and Booth grandly coping with Milan's attacking. Rivera's prompting gradually became less inspiring as the two City defenders closed in hard on the men who should have been profiting from Rivera's approach work.'

City fan Glenn Ellaby, working at the time for Swinton Insurance in Salford, had an afternoon similar to many Blues that Thursday. 'I spent the afternoon darting in and out of the bogs to listen to the game on the radio,' he said. 'Luckily, our boss was a Blue so he didn't mind too much.'

Fellow teenage Blues fan Simon Mullock, destined later to write about the club for the *Daily Mirror*, also remembers keeping up to date with the game thanks to a flexible teacher: 'I was gutted when the first game in Milan was postponed and subsequently rearranged for the following afternoon because I knew I would be in a metalwork class when it kicked off. Thankfully, our teacher Mr Gartside was a big football fan – even if he did support Liverpool. He also ran our third-year football team and knew there would be plenty of Blues turning up to file down our fish slices and coat hooks, when all we'd really be thinking about was how the boys were going on in Italy. When sir pulled a radio out of his bag and asked who fancied listening to the game, the place went mad. We were warned that any noise would result in the wireless being turned off, so when Brian Kidd scored it was just a case of muttering "yes" under your breath. But when Paul Power got number two, there were City fans dancing around the lathes in triumph. Those of a different persuasion weren't impressed – and neither was Mr Gartside. The radio was off. We spent the rest of the lesson begging for normal service to be resumed – when it was it was the United fans giving it out when the commentator said the score was now 2–2.'

The flight home involved a heady combination of champagne and cheer, the scorers famously photographed holding up a copy of the *Corriere dello Sport*. The headline was clear enough even for non-Italian speakers: '*DELUSIONE!*' it screamed, '*MILAN 2–2 MANCHESTER*'.

AC MILAN 2–2 MANCHESTER CITY | Att. 40,000 | Kidd, Power
Corrigan, Clements, Donachie, Booth, Watson, Power, Viljoen (Keegan), Bell, Kidd, Hartford, Palmer

Was City's season, stuck in the middle of the table domestically, set to take off for the stars in Europe instead?

There was only one game between the away leg and the now highly anticipated return game. Needless to say, in a season that was fast unravelling, it turned out to be a complete disaster. The 1–2 defeat against Ipswich showcased Kazimierz Deyna's debut, but the Polish national captain was left bewildered by what he witnessed. Clements broke his leg in a match that shot before the new man's eyes like a downhill skier pursued by an avalanche. 'The match was so much faster than what I was used to at Legia Warsaw,' he said afterwards. As a warm-up for Milan, it had not been great either. Home form was suddenly becoming a problem and a growing list of injuries were adding to Book's woes.

Graham Ward remembers the build-up: 'AC Milan! One of the original greats of the European game, at that stage twice champions of Europe. They had the golden boy Rivera and I knew the goalkeeper Albertosi from the World Cup. It was a cold December night and I don't think the Italians were up for it. I could see as they came out that Albertosi had tracksuit bottoms on and he soon looked all of his 39 years of age, as City piled into them from the start.'

For Keegan, replacing Clements, the invigorating feeling of breaking into the side for such a big event was a false dawn. It would be his penultimate game for City before moving to Oldham in the new year. Ironically, it would turn out to be Keegan's best performance in a sky-blue shirt, watched from the Main Stand by Oldham boss Jimmy Frizzell.

City were in no mood to repeat the slack finishing that had sealed their fate the previous weekend against Ipswich. By half-time, a whirlwind performance had blown the Italians away. The scoreboard at the back of the North Stand, for so long a malfunctioning jumble of hieroglyphics and asterisks, read clearly enough: *City 3–0 Milan*.

Gary Owen told me on more than one occasion during our interview how these early leads could play on the minds of players. How it was almost inevitable that minds and bodies relax, even though the task is not complete. Owen had been referring to the second leg in Liège, but here, in the tumult of a rip-roaring contest with the Italian aristocrats, something similar happened, with City content to hold on to what they had gained in a second half that produced no more goals.

Nevertheless, the effect was stunning. 'Magical Manchester City didn't just beat the Italian league leaders last night … they demoralised them,' wrote Derek Potter in the *Express*. 'A blend of slip-streaming attack and Chianti-red aggression killed this UEFA Cup tie as a spectacle by half-time.'

Shining brightly in an all-round team performance of excellence were Peter Barnes and Asa Hartford. For the wiry Scot in particular, this was one of *the* performances of a brilliantly consistent career. So dominant had he been in midfield that Gianni Rivera failed to reappear for the second half. Potter called the Scot a 'creative and energetic blur' and the critical second goal a 'viciously dipping shot from 30 yards out against the stiff wind'.

Milan, 'reduced to a band of desperate hatchet men', according to Patrick Barclay in the *Guardian*, left with their tails between their legs.

Fan Simon Mullock returned from the Kippax elated: 'It was a freezing night and we just blew them away in the first half. It felt like we completely overpowered them, which was great because I had been expecting them to do what Juventus had done to us a couple of years earlier and kick us off the park.'

Joining City in the quarter-final draw would be West Brom, who had managed to dispose of Valencia, but Arsenal, held at Highbury by Red Star Belgrade, were out.

MANCHESTER CITY 3-0 AC MILAN | Att. 38,026 | Booth, Hartford, Kidd

Corrigan, Keegan, Donachie, Booth, Watson, Power, Channon, Viljoen, Kidd, Hartford, Barnes

In his column in the New Year's Day programme for the match against Middlesbrough, Book felt the need to state 'we are not in turmoil', despite the fact that City's league form had dropped away alarmingly – the side were occupying fifteenth spot as they entered 1979. Peter Swales looked ominously fidgety as City lost at Goodison Park and then drew at Bristol.

On Sunday 4 January, the *News of the World* broke the astonishing news: '£40,000 Big Mal'. Swales had swooped for City's ex-manager and paid Plymouth off for the remainder of his contract. Allison would step in with immediate effect as City's new 'coaching overlord', as Swales was calling him.

With Allison possessing a personality as big as an oil tanker, it was clear that Tony Book was headed for the reeds at the edge of the river. Allison's territory had always been midstream and his presence was soon looming large over training ground and press room alike. Book's aim was to 'bring back the good old days'. Sadly, the reality would usher in a sour new chapter of disaster. The first brick to fall from the wall was quick in dropping. Coach Bill Taylor resigned with immediate effect. The playing staff would soon be coming under pressure from Allison's no-nonsense scrutiny too.

Two weeks before the Manchester derby, which was lost 0–3 at a disbelieving Maine Road, City had found out who their quarter-final opponents would be: Borussia Mönchengladbach. The decorated German side, having lost in both UEFA and European Cup finals to Liverpool, barred City's way to the last four. In a final eight dominated by German sides, West Brom had drawn Arsenal's conquerors, Red Star Belgrade, while

MSV Duisburg would play Honvéd, another name from City's European past, and Hertha Berlin would face up to Dukla Prague, Everton's nemesis in the second round.

Book and Allison flew out to see Mönchengladbach in action. What they saw gave them some hope. Despite City being in freefall, there was perhaps one small chink of light. Gladbach were coming to the end of what would become known as their *'goldenes jahrzent'* ('golden decade'), comprising five Bundesliga titles and two runners-up spots; five European finals, including one victory, and a variety of other minor trophies. Like City, they were trailing in fifteenth place in the Bundesliga and the UEFA Cup offered the one hope of glory in a season of gradual decay.

Shortly after the draw, Liverpool boss Bob Paisley announced that he would be offering several files on City's opponents to Book and Allison. 'There's not a lot we don't know about Borussia's style of play,' said Paisley, 'and we'll help City all we can. We have played them five times in six years and won three of them, including two finals. Our files are at City's disposal.'

Bundesliga star Kevin Keegan, ploughing an exciting furrow in Hamburg, was also quickly in touch. The man who would be in charge of City 25 years later when they resurfaced in European competition, stated in the *Express*: 'It's probably a disadvantage to City to be at home first and I think they'll need a two-goal lead to take to the second leg, but if they play to their full capability, they will get through. The fascinating thing for me is that both City and Borussia are in false positions, well down their own leagues and are keen to do well in Europe. Mönchengladbach are nowhere near the side they were when I played against them for Liverpool. Players like Heynckes, Wittkamp, Stielike and Bonhof have all left and the present side is young.' Keegan continued: 'But they still have Allan Simonsen, who got them through to the quarter-final with a hat-trick against Śląsk Wrocław in Poland.

They also have a menacing midfield man Hans-Günter Bruns. It's evenly balanced but I'll back City and I hope to be there for the second leg.'

Allison's arrival had shaken everything up. Pitiful defeat on an ice rink at Shrewsbury in the FA Cup added to the confusion. A home defeat to a desperate Chelsea side that would go down at the end of the season was met by hoots of derision from the Kippax. Ronald Crowther, writing in the *Daily Mail* under the headline 'Book Faces a Probe', wrote: 'Manchester City chairman Peter Swales will launch a personal investigation today into the astonishing crack-up of one of Britain's most glamorous clubs.'

With Channon listening to offers and Watson having to deny that he was a 'cry baby', the playing staff was also in a state of bubbling ferment as the UEFA Cup quarter-final drifted into view. Every day seemed to bring new transfer rumours, with Watson, Barnes, Hartford and Channon all said to be 'reviewing their positions' and Johan Neeskens, Herbert Prohaska, Trevor Brooking, Gerry Francis and even Kevin Keegan said to be 'interesting' Allison. Despite the cavalcade of star names, Big Mal's first venture into the market brought in Barry Silkman of Plymouth Argyle.

In typical Dartford gunslinger style, Allison told his big-name stars that he had five youngsters on the brink of the first team and that 'over the next month you will be fighting for your places'. Whether the sight of the youngsters in question, Russell Coughlin, Tony Henry, Ray Ranson, Tommy Caton and Nicky Reid, would have the desired effect on the form of Channon, Kidd and Watson was another question. The first result of Allison's return to the back-page headlines was that the latter of this budding group, Nicky Reid, would find himself marking European Footballer of the Year Allan Simonsen on the big night.

Forty years on, Tommy Booth remembers Allison's return vividly: 'The board were all for Malcolm. I had no problems with him at all. He had put me in the side as a teenager to play against Fenerbahçe in City's first European game. Malcolm's problem was he wanted to do it all and when he came back, that was impossible. He wanted to run everything. Bill Taylor went, Tony felt a bit sidelined. Mal had his favourites too. He and Brian Kidd didn't really get on. Nicky Reid was one of Mal's boys. But he wouldn't take advice from anyone. We'd run in to training and say: "What are we going to do for this game, boss?" I think it was Liverpool at Maine Road on this occasion. "Sweeper system tomorrow!" he'd say. We'd not played it before, so we played, it went horribly. Anyhow, second half, I changed it back to a normal back four and he didn't even notice!'

The Norwich programme brought news of ticket prices for the big night. The cheapest way of seeing City's quest for the UEFA last four was, as usual, to head for the Kippax and pay £1.90 (£11.64 today) at the gate. For those with a bit more floating cash, however, 'reserved chairs' were available in the Main Stand next to Peter Swales and Freddie Pye for the princely sum of £2.90 (£17.76 today). Juniors and old-age pensioners could still sneak in for 70 pence (£4.29 today).

More elaborate prices were quoted under the Travel Club details for the second leg. A two-day trip by air would knock a supporter back £130 (£796). This would include two flights, match ticket, bed and breakfast and transfers. Those on a tighter budget could, for £85 (£521) all-in, complete the same trip by coach and ferry and have two breakfasts and two dinners thrown in on top.

In the meantime, Channon had played himself back into contention with three goals in three games leading up to the first leg. On the weekend before the game, City took on Bolton, with Gladbach manager Udo Lattek in attendance. Channon stood out with a goal in a 2–1 win. *Manchester Evening News'* Peter Gardner was convinced he had witnessed the City plan, stating:

'Tony Book and his Manchester City wide boys are poised to take Europe by storm. Peter Barnes' skills on the flank are well documented but the watching *Gladbach* trainer also saw Channon hugging the touchline for much of the game. In this way Bolton had been pulled out of position, allowing City to get through and score twice.'

Meanwhile, Allison's first look at the reserve and youth teams in action told him sixteen-year-old Caton and eighteen-year-old Reid were ready for action. With Owen still suspended, a stand-in was sought. Allison's willingness to gamble meant Reid was suddenly, despite never having played in the first team, in pole position to take the role of tracking the ghost runs of Simonsen.

If the youngster made it, 150 caps' worth of international expertise in Colin Bell and Kazimierz Deyna would be making way for him. Allison's runaway enthusiasm pointed to only one conclusion: 'Reid will be another Dave Mackay one day. He has no fear whatsoever.'

In the end, we were restricted to just two *Big Malapropisms* for the first leg. Reid was indeed in to shackle Simonsen and experienced left-back Willie Donachie would play at right-back.

Fan Glenn Ellaby remembers two things from the night: 'Yes, Mal's madcap idea to play Reid on Simonsen in midfield and getting beaten up when the special dropped us back in Salford. United weren't playing, but some of theirs were waiting for us when the bus dropped us back at Salford precinct. There was only one special going back to Salford, so we stuck out a bit sadly.'

In a match of grinding tension that City never fully gained control of, the Germans left happy with a draw. 'We go to Germany with high hopes,' said Book afterwards. 'Borussia are no better than the three teams we have beaten so far.' If the first statement was the usual positive sound bite expected of such occasions, the second was also true enough. City had had chances to win. Going ahead through Channon's 26th-minute shot, City held out until Simonsen shed himself of Reid's enthusiastic marking and fed Ewald Lienen, who scored with aplomb.

Bruns, whom Keegan had warned City about, struck the foot of the post and brought Corrigan into a neat save before the final whistle. Lattek, after undertaking a little jig of joy on the touchline at the final whistle, added a note of caution: 'We expect to see a different City in the second leg. An away goal is priceless, but we have to start all over again.'

As for the fans filing out of Maine Road, nobody could have thought that the old ground had just witnessed its last-ever European game. City had played only sixteen European matches at Maine Road, winning eleven, drawing four and losing just one, ironically to the only English opponent played during those opening ten years of competition, Chelsea. The next opponents, English or otherwise, to visit Manchester to engage City in European combat would be doing so in very different circumstances.

MANCHESTER CITY 1–1 BORUSSIA MÖNCHENGLADBACH | Att. 39,005 | Channon

Corrigan, Donachie, Power, Reid, Watson, Booth, Channon, Viljoen, Kidd, Hartford, Barnes

If City were beginning to find some form in a stale winter, the weather put paid to further momentum being gained. Between the two legs, City had matches scheduled at West Bromwich and at home to Aston Villa. Both were postponed owing to the ferocious winter weather.

Despite this, there remained some reason for hope. City's away form had picked up markedly, while Borussia had made heavy weather of their last home game in the UEFA Cup, being held by Śląsk Wrocław and needing an exhilarating, seat-of-the-pants 4–2 win in Poland to go through.

Book's confidence ('We have only lost twice away in Europe in the three UEFA Cup campaigns we have played in, at Juventus and in Liège') was matched by Allison's typically robust exhortation to fellow gamblers ('If you've got some spare cash, get it on us now').

In truth, the fans should have kept their money in their pockets.

City travelled across the North Sea with hope in their hearts. Future BBC reporter Ian Cheeseman travelled too. 'It was my first away game in Europe. We were in town before the game and I bumped into Peter Barnes on the hotel steps where City were staying. I was so honoured to meet him, but then he and Big Mal invited me inside to sit in the lobby while the team talk went on. Unbelievable.

'I had already been to Schalke games with the family so it didn't feel so exotic and different for me. We went back to Gelsenkirchen after the game to visit my Uncle Karl and we were confronted by Schalke fans when we got off the train! If you ask me if these were the halcyon days, I'd have to say no. The halcyon days are now.'

A first half low on quality and chances kept the fervour of the packed Bökelburgstadion down to a gentle background hum. In that first 40 minutes, dotted as it was with misplaced passes by the Germans, Allison's tactics appeared to be working a treat. With Hartford and Viljoen working hard in midfield alongside youngster Reid, Borussia's passers were being hustled out of their rhythm. Another Allison favourite, Tony Henry, had also made it into what was a packed midfield, wearing the unaccustomed number nine shirt on his European debut.

With Power's inclusion at left-back, Donachie again started on the right, while Booth and Watson repelled anything Simonsen, Lienen and the marauding Kalle Del'Haye could muster. The best chance of the first half-hour fell to Channon, playing alone up front. Barnes surged down the left, giving Kulik problems, and when the ball pinged into the area, it took a deflection to the England striker, whose close-range flick was charged down by the towering Borussia keeper Wolfgang Kneib.

The crowd was brought to its feet by Lienen's willingness to run at Donachie. With City coping well enough and the boisterous away fans making themselves heard, Borussia broke through just before half-time. Kulik's finish to a swift counter-attack occurred seconds after Henry had rocketed a powerful shot against the bar at the other end. As has always been the case, on such fine margins are football dynasties built or demolished.

With City suddenly in disarray in the second half, chasing the game became difficult and the wily Germans picked them off twice more on the break before Allison, tiring of his own mazy patterns, replaced the ineffectual Reid with Deyna. The Pole promptly hit a searing angled volley into the top corner to illustrate the folly of the returning coach's ways.

With Kidd's foraging missing up front and Barnes cutting a lonely figure down the left, City had come up short. The inexperienced Reid, eclipsed by Borussia's powerhouse Bruns and the clever positioning of Lienen and Kulik, had proved a failure. With the sun setting fast on City's season, experience and guile had been needed against a side packed with European know-how. As with Juventus in 1976, Borussia would go on to win that year's UEFA Cup, beating Red Star Belgrade in the final. City had again been beaten by classy opponents, but they had brought a deal of the bad luck down upon themselves.

BORUSSIA MÖNCHENGLADBACH 3–1 MANCHESTER CITY |
Att. 30,000 | Deyna

Corrigan, Donachie, Power, Viljoen, Watson, Booth, Channon, Reid (Deyna), Henry, Hartford, Barnes

There would be plenty of time to pick at the bones of the carcass, as City limped home in the league just clear of the relegation zone. The exhilarating European run had juxtaposed fiercely with a feeling of general decay. Allison's return felt like another wrong move. The backbone of Book's carefully fashioned squad was to be sold off, with a kamikaze leaning towards new blood that was untested at the top level.

It was the end of an era for the once-lauded coach, but also for the club where he had made his name. In trying to emulate earlier triumphs, City had swum too deep too quickly. They were about to sink without trace with two relegations in the coming decade, but, before European football was once again partaken of, much worse would land on City's doorstep. In fact, even the doorstep would be taken away.

For Allison, restless and contrary, his best work was behind him. He had made his name with innovation and daring, but since becoming enthralled by the idea of 'Big Mal', success had evaded him. When he died, alone and consumed by alcoholism and depression, Simon Kuper's 2010 obituary in the *Financial Times* noted simply: 'The Allison of Cassettari's café and *Soccer for Thinkers* had disappeared long before – his loss and English football's …'

In fact, arguably, the greatest loss of all was Manchester City's.

AN UNCONVENTIONAL RETURN

Kicker conspiracy

There were two elephants in the room as City prepared to play their first-ever competitive game at the City of Manchester Stadium. By yet another strange turn of events – we should really have been used to this by now – City's inaugural romp on the new turf would also be their first European tie for nearly a quarter of a century.

If the lights had long gone out over Europe after Malcolm Allison's badly calibrated fiddling in Mönchengladbach, City's return would be orchestrated by another man who had had more than his fair share of gung-ho moments of misdirected enthusiasm. Kevin Keegan had dragged City out of yet another period of Second Division navel inspection with a brand of swashbuckling football that Allison would have been proud to call his own. Promotion gained in the summer of 2002 with the mini marvels of Ali Benarbia, Eyal Berkovic and Shaun Wright-Phillips meant City had returned to the big time with a burst of colour not seen since the late '70s.

Keegan steered City to a lofty final placing of ninth in their return to the Premier League. The final day was yet another moment of glorious inadequacy as 80 years of football at Maine Road was brought to a tear-filled finale with abject defeat to

Southampton. After all the glory, including the never-to-be-forgotten European nights chronicled here, the doors were locked for the last time at Maine Road.

Raising a tremulous fist to the sky that afternoon was a shaky Malcolm Allison, drawing one last throaty roar of appreciation from the packed stands. Stooped visibly, his bewildered expression alighted on us fans in the Main Stand as if he were regarding a flock of gulls taking off into a strong easterly wind. It was impossible not to think of his swashbuckling team of Bell and Doyle, Pardoe and Oakes all down there now on the pitch with him, suited and booted and silver-haired, and the glorious European nights he had produced with them. 'Next stop Mars!' Allison had whooped when City qualified for Europe, although in truth they had had to suffice with Turkey. As Allison trudged off the pitch, a sad and diminished sight, Keegan performed an awkward little bow in front of him, an acknowledgement of the old man's greatness that was more gravity than gravitas.

Awkward was also the word attached to the news a week later. City had qualified for the UEFA Cup, despite finishing below Everton, who would not be going to the party. The 'back door' return had been delivered thanks to the UEFA Fair Play Award, with City's disciplinary record landing the available place in 2003–04.

From Allison to Keegan, no fewer than fifteen good men had tried and failed to get City back into Europe. Neighbours United had played 140 European games in the ensuing period. Prime ministers and presidents had come and gone, wars had blown themselves out and supporters had grown old with dread and frustration. A whole new generation would fill the stands of the new ground who knew little of Bilbao and Coimbra, of Liège and Gelsenkirchen. Soon they would have their own memories of Santander and Paris, of Naples and Nicosia.

Short-term solutions

There was some serious catching up to do and, looking back from within the prism of all that has been achieved under Pep Guardiola, it is possible to say that the wheels were set in motion in the summer of 2003 in the lowest key possible.

Chairman John Wardle expressed his delight. 'We are back in Europe's elite,' he enthused with glee. 'I'm very pleased because it has been a long time since City were there,' he explained. 'It's not the best way to qualify, but I'm sure everybody is happy to take the place on offer.'

'We didn't earn it by conventional means,' added Keegan with a hint of regret. 'It doesn't sit quite right for me, to give this reward when there are others who have won ten points more than us and missed out.'

Being in Europe meant greater bargaining power in the transfer market for City. The lure of Europe would ensure that stars of the calibre of Nicolas Anelka, David Seaman, Steve McManaman and Michael Tarnat would be in the squad before the new season got under way, each one fired up for City's first tilt at Europe since the 1970s. That tilt, stoked by the sight of Allison in May and the rhetoric of Wardle, looked a little comical when the names came out of an expensive felt hat on 20 June.

After precisely 24 years of waiting to get back into the thrust of top-class European competition, City's first European challenge would be in Wales.

Total Network Solutions were the runners-up in the League of Wales, four times European participants and had played in the Champions League more times than City (admittedly just the once, but still). 'I feel sorry for Manchester City,' joked the TNS owner Mike Harris getting into the mood of things. 'They have waited all this time, only to be knocked out in Wales!'

If the feeling of anti-climax was palpable, the names of City's fellow preliminary round contestants made it even more real.

Dundee would play KF Vllaznia; Derry City would play APOEL Nicosia; Portadown had drawn Malmö, Coleraine had União de Leiria and Cwmbrân Town would travel to face Maccabi Haifa.

By the eve of the tie, Keegan had changed his tune to fit the occasion. 'I'm delighted we're in Europe,' he told Dominic King of the *Manchester Evening News*. 'It's tremendous for the players and staff but also for the fans. The supporters are tremendously excited.'

If Keegan was prone to hyperbole, it was at least true that a new era was starting. With a 2–1 win over Barcelona in the inaugural friendly match in the City of Manchester Stadium, what better way to christen it properly than with a European game? If the fanfare only greeted TNS' Jimmy Aggrey and his mates, rather than Ronaldinho, Marc Overmars and Patrick Kluivert, no matter. You have to start somewhere.

Aggrey, rejected by Keegan during a brief stay at Fulham, was keen to show his old manager what he had missed, an eagerness shared by TNS' ex-league journeymen Gary Brabin (Blackpool), Simon Davies (Manchester United) and manager Ken McKenna (Tranmere). Non-executive director Ian Rush was also expected to impart some gems of wisdom. The stadium was geared to receive a small TNS following for the first leg. Based in the mid-Wales village of Llansantffraid-ym-Mechain (population 1,000), their average home gate was a meagre 258. In fact, the only thing the Welsh side had in common with City's previous opponents in Europe was the possession of a name that would give a ventriloquist a bad night's sleep.

The game was played in one direction, towards the man whose various errors would decorate the evening. Goalkeeper Gerard Doherty, a Derry man in the middle of a 233-game career for the Welsh side, could do little with Trevor Sinclair's first-half volley, but of the four that sailed into the net in the second half, two seemed to go straight through the keeper and another came about as a direct result of a feeble punch at a corner that David Sommeil touched in.

City should have had more, as Keegan noted, but the profligacy of Wright-Phillips and the poor touch of Robbie Fowler put paid to that. Nevertheless, the five they did score equalled the club's best-ever in Europe (against Lierse) and reduced the second leg, already switched to the Millennium Stadium in Cardiff to enhance the Welshmen's earning potential, to a formality even for City.

One was left with the feeling that, had the match been played at Maine Road, the occasion might have been wrapped in the usual fog of impending doom. Instead, it had been played out in the euphoric atmosphere of a palatial housewarming. Perhaps the slick new ramparts would draw out the professionalism needed to be successful again and the old City penchant for disaster would slowly fade from view. We would see in time, but throwing this opening party had certainly taken on the air of unusually upbeat self-confidence.

MANCHESTER CITY 5-0 TOTAL NETWORK SOLUTIONS | Att. 34,103 | Sinclair, Wright-Phillips, Anelka, Sun, Sommeil

Seaman, Sun, Tarnat (Tiatto), Sommeil, Distin, Wright-Phillips, Bosvelt (Barton), Berkovic, Sinclair, Anelka, Fowler (Wanchope)

By the time of the second leg, City were flying. Top of the league after wins at Charlton and Blackburn, Keegan felt comfortable to travel to the Principality with the intention of playing mainly second-string squad members. Thus, City's role of honour in Europe would now boast the likes of Willo Flood, Mikkel Bischoff, Glenn Whelan, Christian Negouai and Jon Macken. All good Manchester City stories are made of the epic and the comic.

For those that had dreamed of seeing their team walk out at one of the cathedrals of European football, there was on this occasion what the locals might have called a double whammy:

the cathedral in question was a rugby stadium and it would be all-but empty.

In fact, precisely 10,123 seats were occupied in the Millennium Stadium, leaving 64,400 unoccupied. The echoes outdid the applause, which in any case was only sporadic in a dour game. It took a burst of electricity from Wright-Phillips to finally illuminate a dull evening that had thus far only witnessed Negouai's close-in goal. The diminutive winger's 81st-minute run on to Bosvelt's clever pass left him clear of an ailing defence. Darren Huckerby, waiting for the simple square ball, did the rest.

TOTAL NETWORK SOLUTIONS 0–2 MANCHESTER CITY | Att. 10,123 | Negouai, Huckerby

Weaver, Flood, Dunne, Wiekens, Bischoff, Tiatto, Bosvelt, Whelan, Berkovic (Barton), Negouai, Huckerby, Macken (Wright-Phillips)

A day later, the draw for the first round paired City with struggling Belgian outfit Lokeren. Elsewhere an eclectic starting field included Southampton, due to face Steaua Bucureşti, Newcastle, who would play NAC Breda and Blackburn, awarded a trip to Gençlerbirliği. Liverpool would take on NK Olimpija Ljubljana in a draw featuring more vowels than thrills.

In any steady build there is a need for some glamour. Keegan knew a thing or two of this and was indifferent to the effects his spending might have on the board. City's chequered past had often demanded *coups de théâtre* on a grand scale. They are an integral part of any club who court success and disaster in the same breath and with the same devil-may-care attitude.

Lokeren director Patrick Orlans wasted no time cooking up some good feeling: 'We are proud to host this game, but the important thing is that everyone has a good day,' he enthused. 'City got into the cup through fair play, so I expect there will be a pleasant atmosphere.'

Orlans' optimism was exemplary, although those City fans getting a pasting for spilling over into the home areas of the tiny Daknam Stadium on the night of a quite chaotic second leg will have questioned the lines of his logic.

But first the Belgians had to travel west.

Founded in the year City had won the Cup Winners' Cup, Lokeren were involved in their sixth European campaign, but had been made to wait sixteen years since their last participation when they had been turfed out in the first round by Malcolm Allison's old friends from Honvéd.

Those certain of an easy home win were rewarded with the opportunity to bite their fingernails down to the quick as City entered the final thirteen minutes 2–1 down. With David Seaman claiming his fourth calamitous error of what was about to become an extremely short career in Manchester, the Belgians could scarcely believe their luck. While their supporters bounced excitedly around the away enclosure, home fans took to shaking their heads, then their fists. Two goals in three minutes would help Keegan's men to a slapstick, slipshod victory.

Seaman, running down an illustrious career at Eastlands, had just been announced as a captain in the TV show *They Think It's All Over*. By Christmas it would also be a literal description for his football career.

When the big moment came, Seaman would blame recurring injuries, but clearly recurring mistakes were also part of the decision process. This one involved Sun Jihai and an obvious opportunity for communication failure. Communication was the least of Seaman's problems, however, as Sun's back-header fell gently into his path. The 40-year-old keeper looked to be carrying every one of his years as he crept forward to gather the ball at a less than electric pace. In stepped Patrick Zoundi to lob it over the pony-tailed television host and into the net. City fans, known for their undying patience with a team that had earlier taken them into the depths of the third tier, enthusiastically clapped every clean catch by the keeper thereafter and cheered wildly when he picked up a shot dribbling towards him slower than a marble heading up a hill.

To everyone's astonishment, including, you imagined, the visitors, Rúnar Kristinsson then took advantage of loose defending by Sylvain Distin to put the Belgians 2–1 ahead. Inexperience in European games could now be offered in mitigation. Keegan's team overhaul was also proving dramatic rather than piecemeal. Not for the first time, City were attempting to run before they could walk. Never the pragmatist, Keegan's answer would be to keep overloading on creativity and trust the rest to luck.

When the equaliser fell, scorer Fowler knew next to nothing about it, the ball running down his leg and into the net through a field of limbs, while Anelka's penalty winner came after Sun collapsed like a deck of cards on the edge of the area. The Chinese international blew out his cheeks in relief at the chance to make up for the calamity with Seaman.

It had been a deeply uncomfortable night.

MANCHESTER CITY 3–2 LOKEREN | Att. 29,067 | Sibierski, Fowler, Anelka (pen.)

Seaman, Sun, Tiatto (Dunne), Sommeil, Distin, Bosvelt (Wright-Phillips), Reyna, Sibierski, McManaman, Fowler, Anelka

---

One positive development from the lacklustre display stemmed from the torpidity of the crowd. The evening had been concluded to a backdrop of sighs and limp hand signals. Interpreting this as gentlemanly conduct, the superintendent of Lokeren police, Dirk de Smet, announced that he would be ripping up emergency measures put in place at the time of the draw to keep City fans outside his town and ship them in by bus just for the match.

'The behaviour of the Mancunians convinced us of their good intentions,' de Smet gurgled. 'So, I want to make clear that every Manchester fan with a ticket is welcome in Lokeren.'

This would prove a less-than-prescient change of mind, as travelling fans Martin Stubbs, Glenn Ellaby and Simon Mullock explain:

'What a trip!' exclaimed Ellaby. 'We drove over, getting the Dover–Calais ferry. Found a hotel in Bruges, which was clean enough apart from the open can of cat food in our fridge. I then mislaid my passport and went looking for it in the car. I reached over to the glove box from the driver's side and collapsed. It felt like I'd been shot. My back just gave way. When my mates saw me, they thought I'd had a heart attack. Went to a chiropractor, costing me €150 to work his magic.

'We set off for the train but got on the wrong one. A kindly local informed us with just enough time where to catch the correct one. Ended up pre-game buying a bottle of J.D. and plastic cups from a local supermarket, while it was being looted by other City fans. We paid obviously. Finally, due to my bad back, Simon volunteered to drive my car home. It was a brand-new Audi A4, which he very kindly reversed into a post on the ferry caving in the back panel. A good time was had by all.'

For Martin Stubbs it was also a trip to end all trips: 'We all had tickets for the away end, but no one had theirs checked. You could have gone in using a beer mat. The away stand was a temporary thing made of wood and must have been hundreds over the safety limit, as it was a free-for-all getting in. It was actually pretty dangerous, joking aside. You could feel the whole structure wobbling around. Earlier we had all been drinking in a small village nearby and drank the place dry. I remember being on the Duvel (8.5 per cent) at the end and – possibly as a result – I couldn't even remember the name of the little place. We all liked a punt and all our lot lumped on Anelka first and last scorer at 5/1. Virtually paid for the trip! It was the best away trip I've been on with City.'

Ian Ladyman, writing in the *Mail*, translated the fun and games differently in his match report, stating that '4,000 travelling City fans gave the town a festival air'. If it was a festival, superintendent de Smet was working up quite a sweat.

The 8,000-capacity ground had had its capacity swollen to 12,000, with most of the City fans in the temporary stand behind one of the goals. Others found themselves squeezed into less hospitable parts of the ground, where conspicuous bouts of fighting continued to break out throughout the first half.

If TNS had been a false start, football-wise, for those members of the press housed on the top deck of a converted double-decker bus, this hardly represented the dreamed-of banquets at the Nou Camp and the Estádio da Luz. 'Weirdest place I have ever had to do a commentary from,' agreed Ian Cheeseman when I spoke to him. 'And I've seen City from some strange places, including the Faroes.'

The only goal of the night fell early. There had been more action on the terraces than on the pitch when Paulo Wanchope was impeded by the hulking Mamadou Coulibaly and referee Damien Ledentu pointed to the penalty spot. Anelka's confident kick sailed past Sven Van Der Jeugt into the corner of the net to the delight of City's support packed in behind the goal.

Steve McManaman, playing his first European game since turning out for Real Madrid against Juventus in the previous season's Champions League semi-finals, seemed becalmed by the downsized surroundings. The Bernabéu's towering precincts were hardly comparable to the ramshackle Daknam, where McManaman's wide role took him past the parked press bus, inside which the story of the game was being knitted together. 'We couldn't see much inside that bus to be frank,' said Cheeseman. 'But it was certainly memorable, which is more than you could say for the performance. I think Kevin wanted a little bit too much too soon from that squad. It was certainly a roller coaster, which is how we like it of course and I'll never forget that bus as long as I live.'

LOKEREN 0–1 MANCHESTER CITY | Att. 12,000 | Anelka (pen.)

Seaman, Sun, Tarnat, Distin, Sommeil, Wright-Phillips, Bosvelt, McManaman, Sinclair (Barton), Wanchope (Reyna), Anelka

---

If McManaman's opinion of the Daknam was low, his reaction to City's next venue remains unrecorded. Dyskobolia Grodzisk Wielkopolski's ground, the even less well-appointed Stadion Dyskobolia, held just 6,800 supporters.

'We didn't know anything about Groclin when the draw was made, but we know all about them now,' claimed Keegan optimistically.

That Groclin is nowadays a fifth-division Polish team is more because of failed mergers than a drastic dip in form. In 2003, however, they were in their pomp, if that is not pushing the phrase too far. Having seen off Hertha Berlin, they were ready to receive Manchester City.

Bankrolled by local car magnate Zbigniew Drzymała, known throughout the region as the larger-than-life owner of the Inter Groclin Auto Company, Groclin were on the up. Notwithstanding this, nobody in England had ever heard of them and they were about to dispatch City from the UEFA Cup.

Paulo Wanchope, still clinging to the vain hope that Manchester might furnish him with temperatures approaching his homeland, confided: 'I don't know much about them, but I do know that it will be very cold when we go to Poland at the end of November. Much colder than Costa Rica!'

In fact, it would be freezing and, on the night, so would half of Keegan's team.

Employing a mindset contrary to contemporary football fashion, as well as an unreconstructed feel for political correctness,
Keegan suggested playing at home first was good news: 'It's
helpful. We start favourites to go through and that is because
we are from the Premiership and they are Polish.' To add to the
wisdom, Keegan had dispatched Stuart Pearce to Poland on a
spying mission. No stone would be left unturned. Pearce came
back with the news nobody wanted to hear. 'We've got a decent
game on our hands here,' he confirmed.

In retaliation, Groclin boss Dušan Radolský went himself to
Southampton, where he witnessed a slick win for City, sending
Keegan's men into fifth place in the table. 'Obviously, we have
respect,' he said. 'But there is no fear.'

Keegan suggested: 'In terms of Europe we are still a young
club and fans have to learn that sometimes a scrappy 1–0 win
is all you need. It's not all about brilliant, dazzling football.'
Replacing his usual overwhelming enthusiasm with clairvoyance,
he hazarded: 'If we are not capable of beating Groclin over two
legs, then we are not ready for the kind of teams that lie beyond.'

Keegan's programme notes on the night started with what
could loosely be taken as a quip. 'The UEFA Cup is starting to get
very exciting,' he wrote. 'You only have to look at the calibre of
the top clubs in the competition tonight.' While his words were
not exactly untrue, once again the City of Manchester Stadium
would not be welcoming one of them.

A 32,506 crowd suggested many City fans were also keeping
their powder dry until those *top clubs* shipped up. To be drawn
against Welsh part-timers, then the bottom club in Belgium and
now a Polish side the name of which nobody could pronounce
was something of an anti-climax. City were about to provide an
even bigger anti-climax of their own, however.

If fans had been waiting patiently for Keegan's scattergun
transfer policy to pay dividends, this was where all hope died.

The idea that Robbie Fowler, whose signature Keegan had chased so doggedly the previous season it had almost led to his resignation, might at some point rediscover his Liverpool goal form alongside Anelka had been niggling away for months. Anelka would score, gloriously, early on, after a pass through the middle from Fowler that was precision itself. Thereafter, however, Fowler's profligacy took over.

Anelka and Fowler fluffed two chances each. Sun Jihai missed another, but it was left to Claudio Reyna to raise the bar, when he sidestepped a defender and, with just goalkeeper Mariusz Liberda to beat, the American wafted the ball over.

Plucky Groclin swarmed back after the break. The equaliser was as inevitable as the headache from standing too close to the Groclin supporters' band. Happily, for those losing patience with the action on the pitch, the oompah band from Grodzisk knew all the tunes the locals did, with 'When the Saints', 'You're not singing any more' and even 'You fat bastard' parping out from their noisy brass and percussion section.

By this time, Fowler had faded entirely from proceedings, replaced in the spotlight by Sebastian Mila, who curled in a luscious free kick to make it 1–1. That the supposed indiscretion from Distin on the edge of the box had been a perfectly clean tackle did nothing to brighten the mood.

As the minutes ticked by, Polish players were struck by injuries that reduced them to silent mounds that only came back to life when carried over the touchline. The healing properties of the white lines running down the touchline were tested time and again before City were finally put out of their misery by the final whistle.

MANCHESTER CITY 1-1 GROCLIN | Att. 32,506 | Anelka

Seaman, Sun, Tarnat, Dunne, Distin, Wright-Phillips, Barton, Reyna (Bosvelt), McManaman (Tiatto), Anelka, Fowler (Wanchope)

'The orders have already gone in for our tights!' quipped Richard Dunne, as City prepared to travel out to Poland for the second leg. If Francis Lee and Mike Summerbee had been surprised to find Górnik parading in 'lady's clothing' in 1971, it would be City in tights in Poland this time.

In effect, there was little room for joking. A 3–0 home defeat to bottom-three Leicester ensured minds were firmly focused on City's fading form. To avoid the worst effects of the freeze, the match would kick off early. City hoped for the same effect as the last time this had happened, in the San Siro for City's famous 2–2 draw with AC Milan in 1978.

Peter Ferguson, travelling for the *Daily Mail*, remembers basic amenities on arrival: 'My big memory was the state of the pitch. It was like a farmer's field. It wasn't apparent during the game so much, but there was no press room in the ground, so we all trooped onto the pitch afterwards to speak to Keegan. You felt like you could have found a few spuds to take home with you. It was a tiny place in the middle of nowhere.'

Interviewing Keegan by the centre circle after a dismal 0–0 draw, Ferguson found him disconsolate. What he and the estimated 987 intrepid City fans (in a crowd of 5,500) had witnessed was a low-energy run-out that asked more questions than it provided answers.

While the small pamphlet serving as a programme referred to the Blues as 'The Magic Manchester City', all Keegan's men could manage was a disappearing act. With pages devoted to the romantic story of Widzew Łódź in Europe, another tale of woe for City, and to star striker Sebastian Mila's dreams ('I just want to be like David Beckham'), the planets appeared to be aligning against City.

Indeed, Seaman had watched Tomasz Wieszczycki's header rebound from the post and Dunne had cleared off the line from Andrzej Niedzielan. Nothing went right. As fireworks lit up the village sky at the end of the game, the slope-shouldered players returned to their spartan dressing room to consider how they had managed to add the name of Groclin to Widzew in City's roll of dishonour in Poland.

City's season would quickly disintegrate from here, relegation avoided thanks to a May win over Newcastle. As far as Europe was concerned, they had been found out. Only participating because they played fair, they discovered that all the other competitors were there because they could play good football. The last words were left to Keegan: 'If you look in terms of ability, we probably have more gifted players than them, but, apart from the first twenty minutes at our place, they have been our equals. We lost the tie at home. We got in through the back door and we go out of the back door. I wanted to play a bigger team than Groclin in a bigger stadium.'

It was impossible not to like Keegan, but enthusiasm alone can only take you so far. Naive tactics on the pitch and in the transfer market had undone his grand plans for City. By the time the club hit the European trail again, thanks bizarrely to another fair play advancement in 2008, City would have chewed their way through his replacement, Stuart Pearce, and Pearce's successor Sven-Göran Eriksson. At a club where nothing stood still for long, the next incumbent, Mark Hughes, was in for a bigger shock than all his immediate predecessors put together.

GROCLIN 0–0 MANCHESTER CITY | Att. 5,500
Seaman, Sun, Distin, Sommeil, Dunne, Wright-Phillips (Reyna), McManaman, Barton, Sinclair, Fowler (Wanchope), Anelka (Macken)

9

FISHING FOR SUCCESS

Life is a minestrone

The expression on Mark Hughes' face told its own story, as it would at various times during his eighteen-month stint at the helm of City.

Sitting between the deposed Prime Minister of Thailand Thaksin Shinawatra and the beaming chief executive Garry Cook, the new City manager was struggling to make himself heard above the crackle and sizzle of excitement. A shy man at heart, Hughes looked at a loss for words as the arc lights beamed off Cook's melon grin.

With excited talk of Shinawatra's dubiously acquired gains helping to bring in the double act of Ronaldinho and David Bentley, the wires were positively frying. Hughes' studious approach to spending the owner's money was expected to raise City's profile from the car-crash end to predecessor Sven-Göran Eriksson's season in charge.

Indeed, a 1–8 defeat at Middlesbrough in the last game of the season had left Shinawatra with little room for manoeuvre with the Swede. Hughes, a straight-faced, serious type, would court none of the publicity the lothario Eriksson had done. There would be no Nancy Dell'Olios, no Ulrika Jonssons and no Faria Alams shimmying around the precincts. He was to tighten the reins on a sloppily run crew too. The face he would be pulling when Shinawatra upped and left, to be replaced by Sheikh Mansour bin Zayed Al Nahyan, was still two months in the future. For now, it was a blink-and-grimace introduction to the big time that City genuinely thought should be theirs.

'I had a fantastic time at Blackburn. I knew there was a limit to how far I could take the club. But I'm now at a club that can match my ambitions,' Hughes offered. 'The ambition here is to challenge at the top table – not only in this country but also in Europe.'

It's a trawlerman's life for some

With transfer speculation filling the back pages, City were preparing for an early start, in the shape of the qualifying rounds of the UEFA Cup. Beneficiaries once again of a fair play slot, the draw had pitched City with EB/Streymur. Atlases informed us this meant a trip to the Faroe Islands. For Hughes, targeting success on the continent as well as progress at home, the match offered supine opponents to kick off his reign.

A steady trickle of fans had started arriving after a complicated journey through northern Europe. Peter Ferguson of the *Daily Mail* remembers: 'The press flew with the official party, including VIP fans, while some others paid a trawler for passage out of Aberdeen, to the red tops' delight. I remember Tórshavn being so small you could walk round it in ten minutes and the bars were closing at 10pm. I just missed last orders at two different pubs. The ground was small and basic, but the press boxes were like mini executive boxes, two reporters to each. Lovely weather while we were there and never a hint of an upset for City … It had the feel of a pre-season friendly with the bonus of the second leg if it didn't go to plan, but Mark was already bringing his standards to bear. He told us all that Carrington was to be regarded as a "football factory" from now on, with no hangers-on at training and no mobile phones.'

This professional approach brought its reward with two 2–0 wins over the Faroese. It was perhaps not the grand entry into City life that Hughes had been thinking of when he talked of the 'great project' that had enticed him to choose City over Chelsea, but it was a start. A start to what turned out to be one of the most tortuous routes through a European season anyone would be able to remember.

Talk of Hughes' 'football factory' suggested a tightening on player excesses. With a nod to greater discipline and sensible planning, Hughes brought in Tal Ben Haim, a signing that had nobody uncorking champagne bottles.

'A quite unique trip. I was privileged to be the only radio reporter there,' said Ian Cheeseman. 'I had the opportunity to try whale meat, go on a rigger around the islands, talk with local whale catchers and puffin shooters and interviewed some of the fans who had arrived by trawler. I had wondered about travelling with them in the interests of "good radio" but ended up getting there by more conventional means. It was a trip to remember, that's for sure. Brilliant place, lovely people, incredible stadium and a commentary delivered from the top of a bunk bed!'

With 5,400 assembled in the national stadium (Streymur's ground held fewer than 1,000 fans and was deemed unsuitable for the tie), City quickly took control.

Well-taken first-half goals from Martin Petrov and Dietmar Hamann underlined the difference between the expensively assembled Premier League outfit and the eager part-timers. With the Atlantic flipping gentle waves onto the pebbled beaches, the small group of journalists who had made the trip could have been forgiven for dwelling a moment on a nice gentle start to City's campaign. Who could have guessed at that stage that a month and a half later, the entire football world would be turning its gaze on Manchester City.

EB/STREYMUR 0–2 MANCHESTER CITY | Att. 5,400 | Petrov, Hamann

Hart, Ball, Onuoha, Dunne, Richards, Ireland, Hamann (Gelson), Johnson, Petrov, Vassell, Jô (Evans)

If anything, City made harder work of the second leg, which was played at Oakwell, Barnsley, because the Eastlands pitch was still receiving treatment after an unexpectedly energetic reaction to a Bon Jovi concert had ruined the turf. Travelling across the Pennines appeared to have more of a debilitating effect on the team's performance than flying to a set of rocks in the North Atlantic and a lethargic display was lucky to net two more goals.

It took City until the 49th minute to ease in front, despite a first half containing no fewer than 22 attempts on René Tórgarð's goal. Again, it was Petrov breaking the deadlock, with a clinical finish from Vassell's driven cross.

Vassell himself got the second, but a patient crowd had to wait until the 90th minute for it to happen. Those that had not already started filing out to hit the road back to Manchester saw Ched Evans climb well to flick on a long ball, sending the striker through to round Tórgarð and score.

MANCHESTER CITY 2–0 EB/STREYMUR | Att. 7,344 | Petrov, Vassell

Hart, Ćorluka, Ball, Dunne, Richards, Elano, Gelson (Hamann), Johnson, Petrov (K. Etuhu), Vassell, Sturridge (Evans)

As City's name entered the draw for the second qualifying round, news broke that the chairman had jumped bail in Thailand and was holed up in a London hotel rereading the FA's fit and proper persons file for fine detail. For a club being bankrolled by Shinawatra's cash, this was not quite what everyone had had in mind as pre-season preparation. The stakes would also be upped following City's pairing with the Danes of FC Midtjylland. With doubts over Hughes' new rules and regulations, a misunderstanding with Stephen Ireland over whether he had been picked or not, problems with the attitude of Michael Johnson and Danny Mills, plus Vedran Ćorluka's supposed deal with Tottenham vacillating between on and off, clarity of focus had also suddenly become clouded. Hughes was beginning to enjoy the rotten fruit of Eriksson's holiday-camp tenure.

Power, corruption and lies

As ever at City, the pot was coming nicely to the boil and the first leg against the Danes would see it boil over completely. A home defeat in front of just 17,200 supporters encompassed the oft-seen tragicomedy of a club determined to do things the hard way. FC Midtjylland, a club that had only come into being in 1999, managed to draw out the same reaction from supporters that Lokeren had under Keegan. Boos rang out after just twenty minutes, as misplaced pass followed misplaced pass. By this time, the visitors were already ahead, after Richard Dunne's ball out of defence had been charged down, allowing Mikkel Thygesen to advance and feed the supporting Danny Olsen. Olsen slotted calmly past Joe Hart with a low shot.

On ITV, meanwhile, summariser David Pleat was sufficiently moved to invent a new word to describe what he was witnessing: *slaphazard*. Most watching could vouch for the new adjective's plausibility.

With Jô, Benjani and Vassell unavailable, Daniel Sturridge and Felipe Caicedo were making particularly heavy weather of things. Sturridge later hit the crossbar and Petrov fizzed a shot of his own onto the woodwork, but to no avail. City's continued vulnerability surfaced in Ćorluka's attempted own goal and the petulance of Johnson as he swung an elbow into the face of substitute Dennis Flinta.

Hughes, meanwhile, was pulling another of his faces in the post-match press conference. 'I think maybe we were behind them a bit in terms of sharpness and match fitness, but that's no excuse,' he stated glumly. His counterpart, Thomas Thomasberg, wore the contented expression of a man who had just seen his name in capitals on the press conference identity cards.

It had been five years since the debacle in Groclin, but here we were again, facing an exit to another European minnow.

MANCHESTER CITY 0–1 FC MIDTJYLLAND | Att. 17,200

Hart, Ćorluka, Ben Haim, Richards, Dunne, Elano (K. Etuhu), Johnson, Gelson, Petrov, Caicedo (Bojinov), Sturridge

With players looking unfit and confused, the opening of the Premier League at Villa Park brought more chaos in a 2–4 reverse. City, playing in a hideous orange kit, played like a set of freshly planted pumpkins, with Ćorluka's 89th-minute goal his penultimate parting gift, as the Croat would finally get his wish to move to Spurs. Transfer speculation was rife. With striker Valeri Bojinov rupturing his Achilles tendon in the Villa Park warm-up and the chairman's assets frozen in Bangkok, a list of potential targets ranging from Barcelona's Thierry Henry to Diego Milito at Zaragoza was everything but understated.

The official party set off for the bright lights of Herning and Ikast in the west of Jutland with the sole target of saving their European skins at this earliest of hurdles. The rounds of the UEFA Cup still carried the moniker 'qualifying' at this stage. The season was yet to enter September, not a month usually associated with exits in European competition and certainly not one envisaged to contain regime change at the top of the club.

But that was precisely what was about to happen.

In two games' time City would entertain Chelsea with Robinho de Souza, the returning Shaun Wright-Phillips, Pablo

Zabaleta and the legend-in-making Gláuber Berti on board after a transfer deadline day nobody would ever forget, but anyone predicting a £200 million takeover from investors in Abu Dhabi, as fans sheltered in bars from the slanting Danish rain on Thursday 28 August, would have been certified a clear and uncomplicated lunatic.

First, this curious club would have to take things to the limit in a way only it seemed able to carry off, with a seat-of-the-pants performance which had become something of a trademark.

Fan Pat Rose had travelled from Leeds and remembers a smooth trip but a chaotic match: 'It was a quiet trip with my daughter, Erin. We met Vedran Ćorluka outside the ground after walking there from town and Erin had her photo taken with him. The picture was in the programme for the Chelsea game the week after. I had my umbrella confiscated but managed to retrieve it from an umbrella mountain after the match. There was a lot of singing about Shaun Wright-Phillips coming home and about City going to Istanbul. It was Erin's first experience of a penalty shoot-out, so that livened things up at the end.'

The match kicked off at 3.25pm, as if someone knew in advance that it would take a while to complete. Half-time would also be extended as the eagle-eyed referee demanded someone stitch up a hole he had found in the goal netting.

In a tight first half, Petrov's angled drive was all City could muster, but the match became stretched after the break as City looked for the winner that would level the tie overall. That this finally came in the last minute was hardly a surprise. Michael Ball's cross gained the slightest of touches off Ched Evans, confusing the defenders behind him. One of them, the Californian Danny Califf, took Ball's cross full on the nose and watched in horror as it shot off his face and past Lasse Heinze.

City looked the more likely in extra time with Sturridge's no-backlift left-footer pinging against Heinze's crossbar in the

103rd minute. Both keepers remained steadfast and the tie was forced into penalties. With the referee constantly having to warn Hart about his gamesmanship (he spent the shoot-out talking to the Danish penalty-takers about their varying deficiencies), the tension was racked up another level. Hart produced two daring saves to present the match-winning opportunity to none other than Ćorluka. His parting gift to the faithful was a drilled penalty to Heinze's left to put City into the hat for the first-round proper. It had been a long and tortuous route, but City had made it. As it happened, this was just the start of a journey that would bring the club and its supporters back to Denmark twice more, as well as trips to Cyprus, Germany and Spain as the odyssey began in earnest.

Hughes, wearing a slightly different expression to the one he showcased after the first leg, was clearly relieved. 'It's a bit of a lottery with penalties, but we're delighted we've overcome this hurdle,' he said. 'You're always relieved. There are no easy games. I know it's a cliché, but it's true.'

With Ćorluka and Hart to thank for saving his Danish bacon, Hughes would be wearing a much bigger smile the next time he faced the press.

FC MIDTJYLLAND 0–1 MANCHESTER CITY | Att. 9,552 | Califf (o.g.)

Hart, Ćorluka, Ball, Dunne, Ben Haim (Hamann), Ireland, Richards, Johnson, Petrov, Elano (Sturridge), Jô (Evans)

The next game would take City to Cyprus for the first time. Before that, City won 3–0 at Sunderland with a brace from the returning hero Shaun Wright-Phillips and then faced Chelsea at Eastlands with new owners in place and a war chest for new signings the like of which the football world had never seen before.

Things would never be the same again. Hughes, suddenly wearing the smile of the cat that got the keys to the cream factory, explained the breathless advances as best he could: 'It has been quite a fortnight, hasn't it?'

By the time of City's next European appearance, Pablo Zabaleta, Vincent Kompany and £32.5 million Robinho had been added to the mix. To keep feet firmly on the ground, however, Omonia Nicosia were the next opponents. Real Madrid would have to wait.

The first European tie under the aegis of Abu Dhabi United Group began tentatively, with a well-placed free kick by Albanian Klodian Duro giving the Cypriots the lead. Some things, it seemed, were meant to stay the same. By this time, City had already hit the post twice through Jô and Ireland, and the Irishman had seen his pinpoint cross missed amazingly from five yards out by the Brazilian.

With the impish Wright-Phillips beginning to call the shots down the right and Elano Blumer setting the pace in midfield, City found a way back, but not before Jô had hit the goal frame again with a raking left-foot shot.

When the goals eventually fell, the lanky Brazilian was the unlikely hero. A shaky connection from close in made it 1–1 and an angled shot from Zabaleta's cross sealed things in the 72nd minute. 'It was frustrating we didn't convert all the chances we created,' said Hughes afterwards. 'When that happens, you fear it is going to be one of those nights. But once we scored, I knew we would go on and win.' It was a fear that subsequent City managers would get used to.

First sightings of Robinho in Nicosia could also be seen as a precursor to this new era of success, adorned as it would be with some of the world's most talented footballers. His eye for a pass was immediately evident, making him look like he was operating on a different plane to the rest. But for now, Hughes would have to make do with a collection of last-minute purchases and a hotchpotch squad inherited from Eriksson.

OMONIA NICOSIA 1–2 MANCHESTER CITY | Att. 15,907 | Jô (2)

Hart, Zabaleta, Garrido, Dunne, Richards, Ireland, Kompany
(Gelson), Elano (Hamann), Wright-Phillips, Jô (Sturridge), Robinho

As with the first leg, the return with Omonia made it to the second half before anybody could find the net. This time City scored first, with Elano's shot finding the corner after great work down the left by Robinho. Persistence allied to a trademark bullet finish brought Wright-Phillips the second seven minutes later and the tie was sealed.

Omonia pulled a consolation goal back after 77 minutes when Rasheed Alabi climbed in front of the lacklustre Ben Haim to head home. The tournament then entered a new format of group games at this point. 'I felt it was important for the development of the side that we qualified for the group stages,' said Hughes. 'We now have a number of games to look forward to.'

MANCHESTER CITY 2–1 OMONIA NICOSIA | Att. 25,304 | Elano, Wright-Phillips

Hart, Zabaleta, Garrido, Richards, Ben Haim, Wright-Phillips, Ireland, Kompany (Hamann), Elano, Robinho (Petrov), Jô (Evans)

The group stage was an odd beast. Each team would play each other once only. As things transpired, City were pitched into a well-balanced section comprising Racing Club of Santander, Schalke 04, Paris Saint-Germain and FC Twente. If the format was new, at least two old foes had glided into view. In Twente and Schalke, City would be renewing ties with opponents from the '70s.

City's up-and-down season was continuing apace by the time the Twente game appeared. A difficult start for Hughes had seen his side languishing in tenth spot, with inconsistency a major problem. Robinho's hat-trick against Stoke suggested he was settling in adequately, but a 2–0 defeat at Middlesbrough and then Bolton the week after proved others were not.

The little Brazilian would have notched another hat-trick in the Twente match, had two raking right-footers not both rebounded off the inside of Sander Boschker's post. Having already swung in a brilliant curling shot from the left-hand side of the box for City's second (Wright-Phillips had whacked the first in in the second minute), Robinho's artistry was in full flow in what developed into a pulsating match.

Twente, under new boss Steve McClaren, had been removed from the Champions League qualifying rounds in no uncertain terms by Arsenal. With guile and pace throughout the team, they matched the effort and indeed the score of their previous visit to Manchester in 1978, when they had been the first-ever Dutch visitors to Maine Road.

A lively, well-balanced side contained future Premier League stars Cheick Tioté and Marko Arnautović. By the end of a fascinating struggle, both sides had spurned enough chances for the five goals to have been doubled to ten and it was Twente coach McClaren in familiar pose, doubled up on the touchline with his head in his hands, as late substitute Stein Huysegems missed the final chance for the visitors in the 89th minute, which would have made it 3–3.

McClaren was pleased with his side's effort, stating: 'We felt we should have got something from the game. We certainly had chances.' The coach would take his side on to be runners-up to AZ Alkmaar in the domestic title race and losing finalists in the KNVB Cup.

MANCHESTER CITY 3–2 FC TWENTE | Att. 21,247 | Wright-Phillips, Robinho, Benjani

Hart, Zabaleta, Garrido, Richards, Dunne, Wright-Phillips, Ireland, Gelson, Vassell (Elano), Robinho, Jô (Benjani)

City's second game took them to group leaders Schalke, managed by McClaren's predecessor at Twente Fred Rutten, and it was a typically grey sky that met supporters boarding the trains from Düsseldorf to make the journey to Gelsenkirchen. Those of us nursing bad heads from the previous evening's revelry in the Christmas market of Cologne were not aided by the sight of City in their luminescent orange kit at the Glück auf Schalke Arena. The throbbing drumbeat from the 54,142 spectators packed in helped little either.

With thousands holding up euro notes, one could have been forgiven for thinking it was an early protest against City's new spending power, but the German supporters were decrying the sparse buying policy of the home management. The jokes about City's lucky fortune would come soon enough, however.

Even without Robinho, City had the lead by half-time, when Sturridge hit a deep cross which found its way to the back post, where Christian Pander contrived to carry out the most exaggerated of air kicks, allowing Benjani to tuck the ball away easily. With the tannoy announcer sending out messages for the after-match transport for what she called 'the Man United fans', the 3,000 travelling supporters were kicking up quite an atmosphere of their own. Although there was an apology from the announcer, City were still not done chasing United's shadow.

In the 66th minute, City clinched the game and early qualification from Group A, as Benjani's pass looped up off a defender and rookie goalkeeper Manuel Neuer failed to challenge Ireland, who nipped in to finish coolly.

Hughes was radiant, claiming: 'It could not have gone any better … We were really comfortable out of possession, got our shape back very quickly and looked to break with pace and that's what we did on many occasions, causing them some real problems.'

For fan Simon Bell, the trip highlighted the hazards of travelling away: 'Following City in Europe, you effectively had three options for travelling: Endurance – one day; Compromise – two days; DIY – three or more days. For the Schalke trip we stayed in Cologne. I have nothing against Cologne, but it is more than 50 miles from Gelsenkirchen. I guess the drive would normally take around an hour, and clearly that was the thinking of the organisers, but the traffic was very heavy. As time ticked away it became clear we were not going to make kick-off. Attempts were made to exit the coach prior to arrival, but we managed to reach our destination and get into the stadium just in time to see Benjani put us ahead. This was the first game with Vincent Kompany dropping into the back four. The rest you could say is history.'

SCHALKE 04 0–2 MANCHESTER CITY | Att. 54,142 | Benjani, Ireland

Hart, Richards, Garrido (Ball), Kompany, Dunne, Wright-Phillips, Hamann, Ireland, Vassell, Benjani (Jô), Sturridge

A stultifying 0–0 draw with Paris Saint-Germain followed at Eastlands before the group was wrapped up with a trip to Santander. The group's dynamics meant qualification had been decided after just two of the four games, while Parisian hopes receded with this solitary point against the Blues. UEFA's inexplicable tinkering with the tournament meant the French team could still qualify despite the prospect of winning just one of their games. With third-placed Champions League teams parachuting into the next round, it would shortly become even more of a lottery.

A decade on, a City–PSG match would have experts from Manila to Massachusetts salivating and human rights critics jumping up and down on their sofas, but in 2008 neither side was ready for the full glare of the arc lights. The Parisians, fielding an ageing Claude Makélélé and the unruly Mateja

Kežman (lucky not to be dismissed for what Andy Hunter in the *Guardian* reported as a 'series of reckless indiscretions'), were still three years away from their own moment of transition under Qatari riches and City's transformation was still in its infancy. The stellar attack of Jô, Vassell and Sturridge bore testament to this.

A modest crowd of 25,626 told its own story. The visitors were far from box office and UEFA's tinkering had also left the group with hollow areas. Little hung on the outcome and little was offered to warm the hands of those fans that had bothered to turn up.

Instead of putting the group to bed, as Hughes had wanted, City put the crowd to sleep.

'Tonight was part of a learning experience,' he insisted, following a line of thought that Malcolm Allison and Tony Book had used and Roberto Mancini would also enthusiastically adhere to. 'We have not got a great deal of experience. In Europe you have to show patience to draw people out.' Assistant Mark Bowen offered a less profound piece of insight when asked if fans could have expected a little more from the evening's spectacle. 'From our side?' the Welshman asked, before departing. It was as much analysis as anyone deserved.

MANCHESTER CITY 0–0 PARIS SAINT-GERMAIN | Att. 25,626
Hart, Zabaleta, Garrido, Dunne, Ben Haim, Kompany, Elano (Benjani), Ireland, Sturridge, Jô (Evans), Vassell (Hamann)

If the Paris game had left everyone cold, defeat in Santander posed many more questions than it answered. City's third competitive visit to Spain produced rows between stand-in goalkeeper Kasper Schmeichel, making his European debut, and his defenders, but also handed them top spot in Group A, after PSG beat Twente. If ever there was reward for little effort, this was it.

As Sid Lowe, reporting for the *Guardian* in the wonderfully named El Sardinero, stated: 'One team did nothing and got it all, the other did it all and got nothing.' So much for UEFA's dreadful experiment with five-team groups.

It was not an understatement to say that Racing, playing in Europe for the first time, ran rings around Hughes' side.

The 1,000-strong City support – keen to see City's 50th game in European competition – had to wait until the final minute to witness City's consolation goal, elegantly placed by Caicedo. But this was no coronation, nor was it a night to remember. In time-honoured style, City had limped into the knockout rounds in first place.

REAL RACING CLUB 3–1 MANCHESTER CITY | Att. 18,360 | Caicedo
Schmeichel, Zabaleta, Garrido, Ben Haim, Richards, Hamann, Gelson, Elano (Kompany), Vassell, Robinho (Ireland), Evans (Caicedo)

Elano out, Kaká in?

The manager's ire descended, rightly or wrongly, on his Brazilians and on Elano in particular. After what the press agreed had been a 'woeful' exhibition from the schemer, Hughes dropped him from the side. The *Mirror* also talked of 'a lack-lustre display in training' after the Santander game. A difficult character at the best of times, Elano had gained a reputation for leading player revolts at previous club Shakhtar, and Hughes was becoming convinced that he was attempting to get fellow Brazilians Robinho and Jô to down tools too. In the case of Jô, it was difficult to tell from the outside whether he had already followed his teammate's instructions or not.

Having only had six hours of deadline day to bolster playing depth after the club takeover was confirmed, the inadequacy of the rest of Hughes' squad was becoming obvious. A disastrous defeat at The Hawthorns on 21 December left City in the relegation zone. Just at the most inopportune moment came reassurances from Abu Dhabi that Hughes' position was safe, a poisoned chalice in football if ever there was one. 'They have been very positive,' the manager insisted, pulling fitfully at his hair. 'They understand where we are in our development.'

As attempts to take everyone's minds off the crisis went, putting in a sudden bid for AC Milan's Kaká was up there with the best. It would ultimately fall into the Lionel Messi bracket of failed *grands gestes*, but for 34 breathless days the drama held everyone spellbound. *'Follie per Kaká!'* screamed *La Gazzetta dello Sport*. '£100 Million' shouted the *Daily Mail*, scarcely able to believe itself. Meanwhile, Nigel de Jong of Hamburg, Chelsea's Alex, Sporting anchor Miguel Veloso, Craig Bellamy of West Ham and Inter bone-cruncher Marco Materazzi were all apparently City-bound too. Full-back Wayne Bridge's arrival had gone unnoticed amid the general hoopla.

The draw for the knockout round paired City with FC Copenhagen. The prospect of a second trip to Denmark on top of the Faroese adventure did not exactly ignite the imagination, but hope for advancement was palpable.

By the first leg, City had climbed the table to ninth and had added de Jong, Bellamy and Shay Given to the squad. With no domestic cups to worry about, minds could be trained on Denmark and a city that had played host to a City game in Europe before, just not against the team that actually played there (the play-off with Górnik in 1971). The tie would be City's eleventh of the UEFA Cup campaign, two more than it had taken to actually win the Cup Winners' Cup against Górnik in 1970.

Domestic away form was causing Hughes headaches, with defeats at West Brom, Stoke and Portsmouth suggesting his side had a soft underbelly. In Europe, things were different, however, and City were looking to notch a fifth away win of the season, after victories at Streymur, Omonia, Schalke and Midtjylland. Copenhagen had also been in action since the middle of the summer holidays, playing Cliftonville, Lillestrøm, FC Moscow, Saint-Étienne, Valencia, Rosenborg and Club Brugge to get through.

In the build-up, Ståle Solbakken, Copenhagen's coach, became what was quite possibly the first opposition manager post-takeover to take up the dual subjects of money and City's standing in world football. It would become a tediously well-trodden path, but Solbakken can proudly claim to be the first to start bleating. 'I think that such incredible sums will destroy football,' he told the BBC. 'They are creating too big a mental distance between what we call reality and then Manchester City. The hardest part for City is that they, by tradition, are not a big football club and, therefore, all the money in the world does not make a difference for them.'

With temperatures at freezing, Solbakken's words cooled the atmosphere further. It would reach −8°C during the game but there was no surprise that City had a spring in their step. Firstly, they had a point to prove to Solbakken and, secondly, they might have frozen solid had they stood still for too long.

One player quickly rooted to the ground was home goal-keeper Jesper Christiansen, who let Nedum Onuoha's gentle shot through his legs and into the net for the opener. It wasn't clear whether the hardening pitch had played a part or whether, as Hughes put it later, the defender 'had given Christiansen the eye'. Those present were left wondering how Christiansen had been elected Danish Goalkeeper of the Year three times and what the second- and third-placed men might look like. Onuoha, delighted at doubling his career goals total with a single, badly hit strike, celebrated gleefully with the painted faces on the giant mural hanging behind the goal. 'A few of us were talking about the mural before the game and I said that I would do it. I just didn't think I would score!' he admitted afterwards.

Newcomer Bellamy gave the sulking Elano a lesson in commitment, running the channels without letting up and adding bite to City's play. Just after the break, Onuoha was involved in the equaliser, as he grazed on the edge of the penalty area while Aílton José Almeida headed past Given. When Wright-Phillips managed to escape from a seemingly impossible position by the corner flag in the 61st minute, his cross found Ireland, who dispatched the ball with one touch. Copenhagen were level again right at the end, when Dunne and Micah Richards lost substitute Martin Vingaard and he nodded in from the edge of the area.

Nearly 2,000 City fans had made the journey and Hughes was quick to acknowledge their part in the evening. 'Following your team in Europe is an expensive and time-consuming thing and we really appreciate the following that we always get,' he said. With Aalborg leading Deportivo 3–0 from their first-leg game, the pre-packaged draw for the last sixteen looked like sending those fans straight back to Denmark again, if City could progress.

FC COPENHAGEN 2–2 MANCHESTER CITY | Att. 30,159 | Onuoha, Ireland

Given, Richards, Bridge, Dunne, Onuoha, Zabaleta, Kompany, Ireland, Wright-Phillips, Robinho (Caicedo), Bellamy

Manchester's air was thick with rain rather than snow for the return leg and a pitch pocked with puddles bore reminiscence to the old Maine Road mudbath against Coimbra in 1970. It was City who were quickest into their stride and gilt-edged chances for Robinho, who headed against the bar, Bellamy, who hit the post, and Ireland, who slid in on Wright-Phillips' diagonal ball just too late, all went begging. An urgent crowd finally had a goal to celebrate after 72 minutes, when Bellamy broke on to Zabaleta's pass and finished with aplomb under Christiansen.

More chances were missed before Bellamy claimed his second, confirming a fast-growing understanding between him and Robinho, which belied press reports of arguments between them. Bellamy's work rate was no doubt an eye-opener for the languid Brazilian and his sharp tongue had been a surprise in the dressing room too. Nevertheless, Latin nonchalance and Welsh fire-breathing proved a workable combination again in the 73rd minute, when Robinho skipped through on the left and his cut-back found Bellamy. An unerring shot finished off the Danes, for whom Vingaard again scored in the final minute. This time it counted for nothing.

Bellamy, with five goals in seven games, had provided a spark to what he described in his autobiography *GoodFella* as a volatile camp. 'I realised I was playing with the big boys now. But I arrived at the club's winter training camp in Tenerife to find all hell had broken loose. Robinho had walked out. I wasn't complaining. City had paid £14m for me and Mark Hughes had fought tooth and nail to sign me, above the objections of some people at the club who weren't keen on paying that money for a 29-year-old with a lot of injuries on the clock. Oh, yeah, and they were trying to sign Kaká from AC Milan for £91m. That deal broke down on the day I arrived, too. Garry Cook, City's chief executive, said famously that Kaká had "bottled it" … It was chaos even without any help from me.'

MANCHESTER CITY 2–1 FC COPENHAGEN | Att. 26,018 | Bellamy (2)
Given, Richards, Bridge, Dunne, Onuoha, Zabaleta (Elano), Kompany, Ireland, Wright-Phillips, Robinho, Bellamy

Pablo Zabaleta, embarking on a career that would see him become a cult hero, was also beginning to contribute beyond the call of duty, with an ability to slot into a hard-running midfield role when needed. As a right-back, he had already caught the eye as a spirited, never-say-die player, who would help lift the side to greater heights. Defensive midfielder Vincent Kompany would also change position to add value to his performances and would join the Argentinian as one of the club's finest-ever servants. A dynasty that would last for a decade was beginning under Hughes' stewardship.

With new recruit Nigel de Jong also revelling in what he called a 'lively' dressing room, Hughes had stumbled across the recipe for partially managed chaos, for what would soon enough in another's hands become a formidable dish.

Aalborg rolled up in Manchester with their own story of recurring coincidence. Danish champions, their Champions League campaign had involved a draw with Manchester United. This then was their second trip of the season to the city (a feat already achieved by Juventus in 1976–7), while City were entertaining their third Danish opponents of the campaign.

The Danes' 6–1 aggregate win over Deportivo told of a formidable opponent, while fifth place in the league domestically told a different story. Had City's interest in Kaká borne fruit, there would have been another nice coincidence, as the Danes showed up with midfielder Cacá in their own squad.

Club-icon-in-waiting Gláuber Berti would also be reunited with ex-Nürnberg teammate Michael Beauchamp, a player who would be in the news by full time.

With City two up after half an hour, smooth progress to the quarter-finals seemed assured. That it would take an unbelievably tense penalty shoot-out a week later in Denmark to finally separate the two sides seemed impossible at this point. City, as is often the case, had other plans for us all.

The Blues were quickly into their stride. The 24,596 crowd – perhaps growing tired of a never-ending UEFA Cup campaign (this was the thirteenth tie of the season and another six would be needed if City were to reach the final) – was on its feet to applaud Caicedo's opener after eight minutes. Wright-Phillips' cracking second seemed to tie things up, and when Robinho was upended by Beauchamp, a penalty seemed the only outcome. Referee Alain Hamer offered only a Luxembourgian shrug and play continued.

Elano, excellent at last, was prominent throughout in a fast-moving, well-fought tie. Onuoha, Wright-Phillips and Robinho saw chances spurned before the final whistle, but City had to be content with a two-goal advantage to take north in the away leg.

MANCHESTER CITY 2–0 AALBORG BK | Att. 24,596 | Caicedo, Wright-Phillips

Given, Richards, Bridge, Dunne, Onuoha, Wright-Phillips (K. Etuhu), Zabaleta, Ireland, Elano, Robinho, Caicedo (Evans)

With a defensive midfield shield of Zabaleta and Kompany doing its work with confidence, the second leg was cruising to a satisfying and uneventful 0–0 draw until five minutes before the end, when Aalborg suddenly scored twice to turn the tie on its head. Quite how City had invited this last-minute madness was unclear, but 700 highly strung City fans were there to testify. In a game that had not seen a single shot on target until the 57th minute, things were about to change radically.

The catalyst for the desperate cave-in appeared to come when Andreas Johansen was impeded by Javier Garrido but the referee, Stéphane Lannoy, ordered play to continue. Incensed, the home side got the two goals they needed anyhow, with former Sheffield United striker Luton Shelton hammering home the first, to maintain City's unhappy relationship with the word *Luton*, the club that had sent City down in such harrowing circumstances in the final minutes of the final game of 1982–3.

Robinho had hit the underside of the bar three minutes earlier to add to the drama. To offer more gloss to the moment, Shelton had been the scorer for Sheffield United in the infamous FA Cup match in 2008, when the ball reached him after a ricochet off two party balloons lurking in the area.

With time running out, Evans handled in the box and Michael Jakobsen powered home the penalty to scenes of absolute disbelief.

Extra time proved inconclusive, leaving penalties to separate two tired teams. With four penalties successfully dispatched, Given dived low to his right to keep out Thomas Augustinussen. The keeper then blocked Shelton's effort, matching Hart's heroics in Midtjylland. Having been beaten by a penalty in the 90th minute, Given had taken City through by dint of saving two more in the shoot-out. The team had made an unnecessary meal out of things and a wobbly Hughes stressed: 'Maybe lady luck smiled on us, maybe that's a good sign. You scratch your head and wonder how that situation developed ...'

Many had scratched their heads at the antics of a club that knew only complicated solutions to simple challenges. If Hughes was pondering how situations like that could develop, a cursory glance at the club's crater-pocked history would have helped him understand.

With SV Hamburg waiting in City's first quarter-final since 1979, it was clear that they would have to rely on a lot more than just lady luck.

AALBORG BK 2–0 MANCHESTER CITY | Att. 10,734
Given, Richards, Bridge (Garrido), Dunne, Onuoha, Wright-Phillips, Zabaleta, Kompany (Elano), Ireland, Robinho (Caicedo), Evans

'The stadium felt huge, the atmosphere electric, with the City section singing its collective head off from start to finish,' remembers Pat Rose, who travelled to Germany with her daughter for the game. 'Security was tight at the ground and I can remember them going through the usual checks outside. When they got to Erin's backpack, they found her (un)lucky monkey inside. The security woman called her supervisor over and his suggestion was to cut it open to see if there was anything offensive hidden inside.'

The monkey would not be the only defenceless beast being surgically breached on a cold night in northern Germany. Before the invasive surgery, however, City stunned the boisterous crowd, with Ireland side-footing into Frank Rost's net after 30 seconds. Within eight minutes, however, Given had already been forced into two point-blank saves and the writing was clearly on the wall. By the end, City would have the Irishman to thank for keeping the score down to 3–1.

Joris Mathijsen's header brought the Germans level after nine minutes. Piotr Trochowski made it 2–1 from the spot after Richards handled the ball and, with City being totally overrun in the closing stages, the home side got the all-important third from Paolo Guerrero, who tapped in at the far post after yet more good work from Trochowski. As the HSH Nordbank Arena (now renamed the Volksparkstadion) wobbled on its foundations, little did fans know that the return leg would reach a boiling point that made this cauldron look like a pan of gently simmering soup.

What was also continuing to simmer was ill-feeling in the squad. Ireland complained afterwards of 'people hiding'. Eyes swiftly turned towards Robinho. Daniel Taylor, in the *Guardian*, maintained: 'The only defence for Robinho was that he was far from the only City player to have a negligible impact in a match that may have caused irretrievable damage to the club's hopes of reaching the UEFA Cup semi-finals. Hughes could be without 10 players for the return leg.'

Chief executive Gárry Cook also chose this moment to ladle on some pressure of his own. 'Mark doesn't need anyone to remind him what he needs to do,' he stated, marking the Welshman's departure date for the foreseeable short-term future.

To the public, Hughes' utterances remained straight-faced and positive. 'It's not on an even keel, but it will be,' he promised. 'We are very good at home and need to get off to a good start in the second leg and dictate the play, which we did not do in Hamburg. Hopefully, we will get the first goal and kick on from there, but we have to take the game to them.'

SV HAMBURG 3–1 MANCHESTER CITY | Att. 50,500 | Ireland
Given, Richards, Bridge (Garrido), Dunne, Onuoha, Zabaleta, Ireland, Wright-Phillips (Gelson), Bellamy, Robinho, Sturridge (Benjani)

Getting off to a good start is not how the opening at Eastlands would be described in the papers, but Hughes' brave battlers would carry out the rest of his instructions with heart-warming accuracy.

For twenty minutes at the start of the second half of the second leg, the atmosphere inside the City of Manchester Stadium was as good as it gets. A pulsating game had increased the already fervent crowd to a level of frantic activity that occurs only rarely in modern grounds. If the new stadium was yet to endear itself, here was a night so throbbing with energy and drama that you could have argued the place was finally coming of age. The great wave of noise that used to rumble off the Kippax at Maine Road on wintry cup nights in the '60s and '70s was perhaps never to be repeated, but in the sterile, deep-washed environment of post-Taylor Report British football, 'Hamburg at home' still creates a frisson of excitement when it surfaces in pub conversations a decade after the event.

But first, Hamburg scored.

Of all the things that needed to happen, this was not top of the manager's list. Missing Bellamy and Wright-Phillips, there was the boost of seeing Zabaleta and Kompany, nursing simultaneous toe and hamstring problems as a foretaste of years at City scarred by injuries, make the starting line-up.

Tearing into the Germans, who had won all five of their away ties, the first five minutes were a shambolic festival of breakneck football. Dunne's agricultural swipe at Jonathan Pitroipa went unpunished, while at the other end Richards' headlong fall in the area resulted in panicked keeper Rost smashing his clearance into the small of Mathijsen's back. With the crowd in a rare froth, Guerrero tore into the box and, as Kompany's balance betrayed him, scored. Twelve minutes gone and a mountain to climb.

Five minutes later, Elano's low cross struck Trochowski on the arm. The Brazilian, bristling with new-found endeavour, stroked the penalty in. With Ivica Olić pulling Dunne out to the flanks, Guerrero's running behind Zabaleta and Kompany was leaving Onuoha exposed in the centre. At the other end, Robinho and Elano were running Hamburg a merry dance. With three minutes to half-time, another surge from Robinho left him flattened on the turf. Elano's 25-yard free kick hit the meat of the crossbar with a power that saw it rebound halfway to Piccadilly Gardens. Uproar ensued with the combative Zabaleta winning a series of 40:60 tackles.

An unwelcome blow of referee Nicola Rizzoli's whistle brought the show to a temporary close.

Within five minutes of the restart the dream was back on, however, as Caicedo side-stepped Jerome Boateng to score. Panic now set in completely. Boateng, struggling with the pace of the game, got the wrong side of Elano and brought him down. Elano's sumptuous free kick soared over the wall and slapped Rost's left-hand post. As if affronted by Ireland's comments that he was lazy, the Brazilian was having the game of his life.

A minute after his free kick, Elano's flat corner surprised Rost and the overworked keeper could only flap the ball to Caicedo three yards out. In the tumult, the Ecuadorian flipped the chance over the bar. Chances would come and go thereafter but the tide was turning. With Dunne's red card (his ninth of a thunderously committed City career) went City's chances. The big Irishman clattered into Mladen Petrić like a combine harvester and City's long European adventure was over.

'City bought two of our best players in Kompany and de Jong but I still think we were the better side,' said manager Martin Jol, responsible for six straight wins over the Blues as Tottenham boss.

For Ireland, this was a demonstration of the spirit that had been missing. For the fans, a long and tortuous journey had been curtailed thrillingly at the quarter-final stage. For Hughes, the writing was on the wall. The league campaign would not deliver another European season in 2009–10. The next time City walked onto the fields of Europe, a new man would be in charge and a new era would begin.

For the UEFA Cup too, things would never be the same. It would be rebranded as the UEFA Europa League, losing mystique and gaining an unattractive Thursday-night match slot. For Hamburg, a semi-final derby with Hanseatic cousins Werder Bremen would end in defeat, as would the final for Werder against the omnipresent Shakhtar in Istanbul, for whom Fernandinho would star.

For City, the UEFA Cup would now remain for ever out of reach, Hamburg the best showing alongside the 1979 adventure in nearby Mönchengladbach. A weird Danish-flavoured odyssey that had begun in the Faroe Islands, progressed through three trips to Denmark itself and ended in a German port within 160 kilometres of the Danish border, with the prospect of a win taking them to yet another German port close to the Danish border, was over.

The days of geographical quirks making the headlines were drawing to a close, however. This would be City's last European campaign free of the dual burden of expectancy and scrutiny.

A new era awaited us all.

MANCHESTER CITY 2-1 SV HAMBURG | Att. 47,009 | Elano (pen.), Caicedo

Given, Richards, Bridge, Dunne, Onuoha, Ireland, Kompany, Zabaleta (Gelson), Robinho, Elano (Sturridge), Caicedo

TIME TO DELIVER

Atmosphere

> '*I have nothing against monkeys, because I am totally sure that monkeys are more intelligent than racists*'
>
> Mario Balotelli

The shaking of hands at pre-season training was unusually prolonged. Manchester City's rebuilding had taken on a life of its own with a sheikh's ransom (liberally estimated at £126 million by a greatly agitated press corps) dished out on David Silva, Yaya Touré, Aleksandar Kolarov and Jerome Boateng, with James Milner and the irrepressible Mario Balotelli waiting in the wings to join them.

The palace coup that had removed Mark Hughes and replaced him with the enigmatic Roberto Mancini had not just changed the lingua franca in the Eastlands corridors from English with a Welsh lilt to high-velocity Italian with added arm-waving, change everywhere was seismic. New faces; new strategies; new look. Some things, inevitably, stayed the same, however. Brian Marwood, City's director of football, had spent the summer pleading for patience from supporters besides themselves with excitement. A 35-year wait for a trophy, any trophy, was beginning to look like it might be actually coming to an end for the first time anyone could properly remember.

If the seeds of success had been sown by his predecessor with the purchases of Kompany, de Jong and Zabaleta, Mancini's summer spree would ignite the blue touchpaper with what would become the first strand of City folk heroes. In Touré and Silva the Italian had bequeathed to City perhaps the two greatest midfielders the club had seen since Colin Bell. In Balotelli, City would have a player deemed 'unmanageable' by José Mourinho and that Mancini himself would claim to be 'in need of psychiatric help' after one too many *unforeseen incidents* involving his player during his stint in Manchester.

A huge squad needed trimming before the big kick-off and departures included Ireland, Onuoha, Petrov and Vladimír Weiss, with the conundrum of how to get rid of Robinho and Jô troubling a second successive City manager. Cold-shouldered Craig Bellamy and injury-prone players like Michael Johnson and Roque Santa Cruz would also find themselves pushed towards the sidelines as City's journey towards the top took on more coal.

With rivals United limiting their summer intake to Javier Hernández and Bebé, it was clear that City were intent on gaining ground. A fifth-place finish in 2009–10 meant the Europa League would also be on the menu. With clear targets set, the appearance of the debonair Italian manager in the final training sessions before the off masked the cold steel of a killer. As a DHL van arrived at Carrington, Matt Lawton in the *Mail*, noticed a bin lorry exiting the same gates. Could one vehicle be depositing Milner and Balotelli, as the other removed Bellamy and Ireland, he mused. The glint in Mancini's eye suggested anything was possible.

The season started with the diminutive Silva taking a battering at White Hart Lane. Indeed, the whole team suffered, with Hart in superlative form between the sticks to ensure a 0–0 draw.

With the first big test of the season approaching in the shape of Liverpool's visit to Manchester, City set off for a midweek European qualifier in Romania. Timișoara had been the first city in Europe with electric street lighting, but it was a dim affair that the two teams produced for the 24,000 in the sweeping bowl of the Dan Păltinișanu Stadium.

The headlines, as they would be on frequent occasions during City's European campaign of 2010–11, were taken by debutant Balotelli. Entering the field for Gareth Barry on 57 minutes, he immediately produced two shots on goal. A third, just after Yaya Touré's effort had cannoned back off the post, put City into the lead, as he swept Emmanuel Adebayor's right-wing cross past the home goalkeeper, a certain Costel Pantilimon. What the BBC would later call a 'captivating cameo' concluded with a yellow card and an injury.

The Balotelli era was upon us.

If the Italian was continuing a solid line of daft behaviour through City's (European) history, other elements were being 'tidied up' to match the club's new elite status.

Daniel Taylor, reporting for the *Guardian*, remembers an eye-opening moment from Timișoara that would almost certainly have appealed to Balotelli's sense of fun. 'We had a bit of a problem with accommodation. Or at least the club did. City needed to swap hotels with the press. The original team hotel had a lap-dancing bar downstairs and lots of working ladies wandering around. The press ended up in there instead,' he added without blinking. 'In those days we were still travelling with the team. Then they started asking us to check in at a later time at the airport, so we didn't bump into any of the directors or management. Our instructions would be that we had to get on the plane an hour before take-off. It was all becoming very *MUFC*. I went for some food and ignored the instructions and there was a complete meltdown from one of the press officers.'

FC TIMIȘOARA 0–1 MANCHESTER CITY | Att. 24,000 | Balotelli

Hart, Zabaleta, K. Touré, Kompany, Lescott, Barry (Balotelli), Silva
(A. Johnson), de Jong, Y. Touré, Adebayor, Tevez (Jô)

In the staccato manner we would come to appreciate, Mancini
ran the rule over his new acquisition's debut. 'He had a great
debut. I am happy he scored. He's a good player.' The Italian's
economy of words had not been matched by his team, who had
needed many chances to come away with the one-goal advantage. 'Football is like this,' Mancini concluded wisely.

The City of Manchester Stadium contained broadly the same
number of supporters for the second leg that had been present in
Romania, though there was slightly less commotion. They were
soon on their feet as a mainly second-string eleven eased further
ahead after 43 minutes through Wright-Phillips. The geomet-
ric precision of the move was impressive, with Patrick Vieira's
through ball cutting straight into the box, where the diminutive
winger allowed it to run past him, as he altered its direction by
ten degrees to shoot cleanly past Pantilimon.

With Jô making his first start for nineteen months and Greg
Cunningham appearing for one of his five games in a Manchester
City shirt, Mancini was clearly keeping his powder dry. The scorer
of the second goal seemed to confirm this, although the provider
was a different story altogether. Dedryck Boyata's far-post header
was as simple as they come, but that was as a result of the flat,
deep, curving delivery from the right flank by David Silva, whose
arcing free kick completely flummoxed the future City goalkeeper.

Once again, Mancini was, much like Silva's passing, to the
point in his assessment: 'It is an important trophy. I think the
Europa League is difficult because you play more games. But if
we can change some players every game, I think we can arrive
at the end and play in the final. It is not like the Champions
League, but it is important.'

City had made it into the group stages, as had Liverpool with a win in Turkey, but Aston Villa, Motherwell, Celtic and Dundee United all ended their interest in the tournament at this point. The draw brought fresh new opponents, an odd new routine for the fans and one very old foe. City would be in Group A with Red Bull Salzburg, Lech Poznań and Juventus and the football world would be watching.

MANCHESTER CITY 2–0 FC TIMIŞOARA | Att. 23,542 | Wright-Phillips, Boyata

Hart, Richards, Boyata, Zabaleta, Kompany, Wright-Phillips, Vieira, Silva, de Jong (Cunningham), Adebayor, Jô

With little time to spare before the group got under way, City hurriedly arranged a dip in form to coincide with their big European entrance. Losing at Sunderland and being held at home by Blackburn was hardly the warm-up Mancini had in mind for the trip to Salzburg, but City made surprisingly light weather of the Austrians in their tidy new Red Bull Arena.

Ahead through Silva's first goal for the club – with his right foot – after Zabaleta's dangerous left-wing cross had been fumbled to him by Jô, City experienced few of the problems they had had in Romania.

A second-half goal from Jô, following up Carlos Tevez's raking right-foot shot, sealed the win for City. The lanky striker, having been on loan with Galatasaray and Everton, would complete an odd last season, with four of his six City goals coming in European competition. The uncharacteristically crisp finish here would be his penultimate, with one more to come in the strangest of situations.

With Jô beginning a long goodbye, Silva was about to become flavour of the month. In fact, flavour of every month for the next ten years. 'Silva is a fantastic player. For him it is a different situation now,' said Mancini, looking deep into his crystal ball. 'He is playing a different kind of football. But after one month, he is ready to go 100 per cent for the team. He will be an important player for the future. He is a strong player.'

Little did we know, a love affair was commencing.

RED BULL SALZBURG 0–2 MANCHESTER CITY | Att. 25,100 | Silva, Jô

Hart, Zabaleta, Bridge (Boyata), K. Touré, Kompany, Barry, Silva (Wright-Phillips), de Jong, Y. Touré, Jô, Tevez (Vieira)

With the likes of Juventus, Atlético Madrid, Liverpool, Borussia Dortmund, Zenit Saint Petersburg, PSG and Napoli involved, the 2010–11 edition of the Europa League resembled future Champions League campaigns. Here was a snapshot of the game's future power brokers making their way to the top rungs of the ladder. For City too, it would represent their last direct entry into the competition, before taking up residence in the elite tournament for successive seasons to the present day. It would be one of the last Europa League seasons to welcome so many big guns, before modern football's cash-flow regulations ossified the top strata.

'New money versus old lady'

The arrival of Juventus in Manchester, meanwhile, sent older supporters into a reverie of Brian Kidd (now happily ensconced on the bench in Mancini's extensive backroom staff), Peter Barnes and Jimmy Conway. Even the flowing blond locks of Mike Lester returned to the subconscious for a glorious moment or two. If the 1976 encounters had for all intents and purposes seen City taking on the Italian national team in black-and-white-striped disguise, the modern-day version of the Old Lady was also well endowed with future international big hitters such as Giorgio Chiellini, Leonardo Bonucci, 'the new Marco Tardelli'

Claudio Marchisio and a 35-year-old Alessandro Del Piero. In place of the steel-plated goalkeeper Dino Zoff, there was ex-Arsenal reserve Alex Manninger, however, and instead of Franco Causio and Gaetano Scirea, Eastlands feasted its eyes on Felipe Melo and Mohamed Sissoko. There was, as Mancini advised, 'nothing to worry about'.

With ex-Juventus players David Platt and Attilio Lombardo also on Mancini's staff and Patrick Vieira playing, City had information on what made Juventus tick. Their opening group game, a 3–3 home draw with Lech Poznań, suggested there would be little of the iron-clad rearguard that had thwarted City in 1976. Having warmed up by beating the intricate Italian defensive systems of Mancini's old adversary Carlo Ancelotti in the previous weekend's win over Chelsea, City looked ready for the challenge.

Mancini, ever the optimist, made future Juventus forward Carlos Tevez his captain. He would have need to rethink this wisdom in a year's time in Munich. Jerome Boateng also came in on the right side of defence for a debut delayed by an injury caused by an out-of-control drinks trolley on the flight over from Germany; a 'City injury' if ever there was one. Boateng's first touch in sky blue hardly confirmed his recovery, as he shanked a left-foot shot so wide it went out for a throw-in.

As early as the third minute, Juventus were laying down markers of their own, however, with Vincenzo Iaquinta's right-footer scorching past Hart's post. In the eleventh minute, the Italians were ahead with what was already their third attempt on goal. Again, Iaquinta was allowed space to advance, hitting a strong shot from distance, which nicked off the top of Kolo Touré's head and edged past Hart.

Tevez began to dictate play from the left, cutting in and crossing onto Gareth Barry's head. The backward flick from Barry hit the base of the post. On 37 minutes came the equaliser, with Touré's younger brother giving warning of what was to come with a slide-rule pass through a static defence. Adam Johnson, with a run that matched the penetration of the assist, only had to poke the ball past Manninger.

Del Piero's late free kick against the crossbar was as close as anyone would come to winning the game, as both sides appeared content with a point each, which kept them second and third in the group, respectively, behind Poznań, who had beaten Salzburg 2–0.

MANCHESTER CITY 1–1 JUVENTUS | Att. 35,212 | A. Johnson

Hart, Boateng (Milner), Zabaleta (Boyata), Kompany, K. Touré, Barry, Y. Touré, Vieira, A. Johnson, Tevez, Adebayor (Silva)

Tragically, between the Juventus and Lech Poznań matches, the death of Malcolm Allison was announced. The timing was also somewhat fitting, as it had been Juventus that had courted him in 1969 and it was against a Polish side that he and Joe Mercer had ushered in City's greatest-ever European moment. At the age of 83 the rigours of alcoholism and Alzheimer's had taken their toll on the greatest of City coaches. Although the fads and facets he had introduced to the game in the late '60s were now de rigueur throughout the football world, Allison had been at the vanguard of the Europeanisation of the English game. The modern-day City, managed by men of intelligence and capability, saw nobody matching the swagger and bravado of Big Mal.

The third group game brought the surprise Poles to Manchester and would bring Emmanuel Adebayor's plight at City into sharp contrast. A hat-trick from the lanky Togolese – the first in Europe by a City player – seemed to prove his worth, but he had been hitherto used sparingly by Mancini and the feeling was he was only playing while Balotelli recovered from injury.

Leading 2–0 at half-time, City showed how to bring the opposition right-back into the game with some shambolic defending early in the second half. First Joleon Lescott was lucky to escape giving away a penalty, then Zabaleta got himself in a tangle, allowing Joël Tshibamba to score, to the delight of the 7,000-strong travelling support. The fervour of the Polish contingent was in stark contrast to the paltry numbers Juventus had brought two weeks earlier, and their rendition of a mass turning away from the pitch, linking of shoulders and jumping up and down received the customary Manchester response of 'what the fucking hell was that?' However, the eye-catching spectacle had been noted and City fans would produce their own version of 'The Poznań' throughout the next season and a half.

As the stadium emptied, a giant banner reading '2011. The Wait Is Over' fluttered from the second tier. One wondered how long it would really be before the owner of the converted bedsheet was proclaimed a visionary.

MANCHESTER CITY 3–1 LECH POZNAŃ | Att. 33,388 | Adebayor (3)
Hart, Richards, Zabaleta (Bridge), Boyata, Lescott, de Jong, Vieira, Wright-Phillips (Jô), Silva (Y. Touré), Adebayor, A. Johnson

Wearing their stylish sash kit for the return game with Poznań, City's attire could have been a tribute to the departed Allison. First worn on his watch, Allison had wanted a continental look for City's kits to add style to the swaggering football he intended them to play. Sartorial elegance in Poznań was dimmed by a performance lacking the necessary colour, style and fabric, however, in a 3–1 reverse. A run of victories had carried City to second in the Premier League table but defeat in Poland was a third on the trot and provoked Mancini to state: 'Everything is against us.'

City had, in fact, been a little unlucky. Once Adebayor had equalised Dimitrije Injac's opener with City's 100th goal in Europe, the game evened out before being given an unbalanced look by two goals for the Poles in the final four minutes, the first of which the scorer Manuel Arboleda knew absolutely nothing about. 'We did not deserve this,' the manager lamented.

Poznań, fourteenth in the Ekstraklasa, were lifted to daring feats by a raucous, bubbling crowd and the enthusiasm of their debutant manager José Mari Bakero, freshly installed after the dismissal of Jacek Zieliński days before. With tales of unrest and squabbling coming out of the City camp, the 'lively squad' that the incoming de Jong had enthused about was threatening to bubble over. Mancini too was the focus of a hungry press pack, offering a glimpse into the future and the scrutiny successors Manuel Pellegrini and Pep Guardiola would receive. Heightened interest was now firmly fixed on the club. 'The club have asked me to qualify for next season's Champions League and we are going well. Why should I worry about being fired? This does not exist,' the Italian added with a shrug.

In truth, Mancini partly courted attention and partly attracted it. He was a driven character, but superstitious too and not a little vain. Daniel Taylor remembers: 'There was one incredible scene when he discovered the players could not have meatballs on the flight home. He wanted the same flight, same times, same in-flight food because City had won the subsequent league game after the previous trip away. There were no meatballs to be had and for Mancini it was the culinary equivalent of a plague of locusts coming City's way. Around the same time, he had ordered a disabled toilet at the training ground to be converted into his own personal bidet. He was quite something. When the club hired Pellegrini, it was on the express understanding that he was NOT like Mancini!'

LECH POZNAŃ 3–1 MANCHESTER CITY | Att. 43,000 | Adebayor
Given, Richards, Bridge (Kolarov), Boyata, Lescott, Zabaleta, Vieira, Milner (Kompany), Wright-Phillips (Silva), Adebayor, A. Johnson

December opened with the visit to Manchester of Alan. Here was a footballer who might not ever reach the heights of the world game, but on 1 December 2010 in a freezing cold northern English city, he played the game he will never forget. Fan Marc Starr explains: 'I turned on Thursday night Channel 5 and soon zonked out, waking sometime in the second half. I'd missed a heap of the action. Expletives. Then, an announcement in the stadium. I've been to Brazil five times. I remain fascinated by the impressive breadth of inspired, creative name choices there, from cultures all over the world. Few in the stands could have known the substitute's nationality. I still picture it now: "Alan. He's what? Brazilian? ALAN?" The crowd began to shout: "ALAN! ALAN! ALAN! ALAN!" Only City supporters could will you to score *purely on the basis of being called Alan*. The most MCFC-esque moment ever? More City supporters remember Alan than recall Jason van Blerk. And his middle name was Douglas. Into the pantheon he went.'

By this time, Adebayor's future was becoming clearer, with a loan deal to Real Madrid about to come to fruition after 'several bust-ups' with his manager. The Togolese's place in the side went to Mario Balotelli, who rewarded his manager's faith with a cornucopia of talking points. Alongside him, the presence of Jô in the starting line-up must have confirmed to Adebayor that his time was up.

Wearing gloves and a snood, the slope-shouldered Italian scored twice, celebrating Eastlands' first goal for 304 minutes with nothing more than a self-conscious smile, and saw the second half kick off while he was still exiting the changing rooms. If Adebayor's relationship with Mancini had produced metaphorical fireworks, here was the man with the genuine article.

'He never smiles when he scores,' Mancini said of his maverick striker. 'He's always been like this. Why? Because, for him, it's normal to score. He could score every day.'

'It's my job,' confirmed a non-plussed Balotelli.

Forty-three years on since the Ballet on Ice against Tottenham, Adam Johnson tiptoed through the Austrians like a figure skater to score a wonderful third as the snow fell ever thicker. 'I hope he can understand why I said these things,' Mancini said of his public criticism of the winger. 'I believe in Adam and if he works well, he can improve a lot. Maybe in three or four years when I have left, he will think "Roberto, he said some good things …"'

City's win confirmed not only qualification, as Juventus were knocked out with a single point in Poznań, but Mancini's growing list of running feuds. To the tetchy Tevez, we had now added Johnson, Adebayor and Balotelli. It would continue to be a feature of his tenure and would eventually be his undoing.

MANCHESTER CITY 3–0 RED BULL SALZBURG | Att. 37,552 | Balotelli (2), A. Johnson

Given, Boateng, Zabaleta, K. Touré (Richards), Lescott, Wright-Phillips, Vieira, Milner, A. Johnson, Jô, Balotelli (Adebayor)

With the trip to Turin to complete the group phase rendered meaningless, Mancini travelled south with an experimental squad. While there were plenty of absentees, the most contentious one was Tevez, the captain, who had put in a transfer request. Mancini had decided that on balance the player brought more to the squad than he took away, an opinion that would be sorely tested less than a year later, but unrest in the squad was growing as the team touched down in an icy Turin. As Daniel Taylor stated: 'The truth is City accepted a long time ago that what Tevez brings – the baggage, the bullshit, the occasional moments of brilliance – will always remind us of the gap between someone who is a great football player and a great football man.'

Mancini was no easy ride himself and this trip would prove the point well enough, but it was deemed essential to harness

Tevez's passion to a positive end. Convinced the striker was under the influence of his agent Kia Joorabchian, Mancini let his thoughts be aired to Ian Ladyman in the *Daily Mail*. 'It is an important season and he's an important player. I think we can change his mind.' With a rift between Joorabchian and chief executive Garry Cook, the situation remained sensitive, however. City's European games would be the playground for a long-running soap opera.

The match itself, played in freezing temperatures in front of a disinterested crowd of under 7,000, confirmed City as group winners, with Jô's final goal for the club sealing a 1–1 draw. To add to Mike Lester's unexpected appearance the last time City had graced Turin, Mancini now pitched an untried pair into this game. Thus, Alex Nimely played in his second and last game for the club, while Chris Chantler received a strange twentieth-birthday gift from his manager in the shape of appearing for the last four minutes at the Stadio Olimpico. He too would never again be seen in the sky blue of City.

Despite these oddities, the trip would have remained unremarkable but for Mancini's obsessive character rising once again to the surface. Daniel Taylor takes up the story: 'He didn't like the look of the plane for the return journey and made everyone get off and stay in a hotel. Noel Gallagher was on board too and it was still during the period when we could fly with the team. I had spoken to Noel on the flight out about the Tevez situation. It was access all areas. He had come out with the classic line that Tevez could be the first footballer to leave a club because he didn't like somebody in the office, meaning Cook. Meanwhile, Mancini thought the plane needed de-icing! You can imagine 200 of us having to get off a plane at 1am and hotels needing to be found for everyone, just because the manager didn't fancy it. It had classic Mancini written all over it. They stopped us all flying together after that. We don't get the same colour now, that's for sure.'

JUVENTUS 1–1 MANCHESTER CITY | Att. 6,992 | Jô

Given, Richards, Bridge, Boyata, Boateng, Vieira, Wright-Phillips (Chantler), Milner, A. Johnson, Nimely (Zabaleta), Jô

Hot on the heels of a double blow for the club, City prepared for the knockout rounds with a first-ever trip to Greece to play Aris Thessaloniki. Wayne Rooney's dubious-connection overhead kick had won the Manchester derby the previous weekend to halt City's progress at the top of the table and the terrible news that Neil Young's long battle with cancer had ended robbed the club of another hero from Vienna 1970, so soon after the passing of Malcolm Allison. Young's elegant, gliding forward play would have fitted seamlessly into any of City's modern-day sides, and his effortless style had been the perfect foil for the charging enthusiasm of Francis Lee and the gritty wing play of Mike Summerbee in City's first European success.

With the slightly more basic attributes of Wolfsburg's Edin Džeko now added to the squad, Mancini hit the Greeks with all the firepower he had but came up blank. Apart from the extravagant wall of pyrotechnics from the home fans before kick-off, the game fizzled and spluttered like a knock-off Roman candle. 'An ordinary match played in an extraordinary din,' as Daniel Taylor remembers it. Nevertheless, with Balotelli, Džeko and Tevez all on the pitch at the same time, there was clearly intent in City's strategy.

As press speculation grew over Mancini's treatment of certain players, his ill-conceived histrionics on the touchline when players did not follow his instructions and his abrasive relationships with all and sundry, the Italian began to wear a blue-and-white bar scarf, thickly knotted over his black Armani coat. Simple and chic, it told an adoring public to ignore the arguments and feel the commitment.

ARIS THESSALONIKI 0–0 MANCHESTER CITY | Att. 22,000

Hart, Richards, Kolarov, K. Touré, Boateng, Wright-Phillips
(Balotelli), Barry, Y. Touré, Silva, Džeko (Zabaleta), Tevez

Despite accusations of cautious tactics, a stereotypical nod perhaps to his Italian heritage rather than anything overtly visible in his team's style of play, Mancini again shoehorned plenty of attacking talent into his side for the return game. Thessaloniki, like Poznań before them, buoyed by a noisy yellow phalanx of more than 6,000 supporters, were steamrollered.

With Džeko twice pouncing with unerring finishes in the first twelve minutes, City's progress was swiftly assured. Mindful of his manager's early threats, the Bosnian was already responding with the most precious comeback of all: goals. If the open attacking was something of a prelude to City's future modus operandi in European competition, there were other pointers too to what we could expect. Kompany's groin injury necessitated his removal and the growing influence on the team of Silva and Yaya Touré, a little and large of silk and steel that would seal many a game against continental opposition in the ensuing years, was clear for even the most entrenched of football philosophers to notice.

For Džeko it was an early coming of age, the first time he had begun to bristle with the kind of confidence his manager sought. Having worked in tandem with another tricky, powerful South American at Wolfsburg, the Brazilian Grafite, the Bosnian looked a good fit alongside the wiry, effervescent Tevez. With Silva's slide-rule prodding opening avenues, the blueprint for future campaigns was taking shape under the canny Italian.

MANCHESTER CITY 3–0 ARIS THESSALONIKI | Att. 36,748 | Džeko (2), Y. Touré

Hart, Boateng, Kolarov, Kompany (Zabaleta), Lescott, Barry,
Y. Touré, Silva (Wright-Phillips), Džeko, Tevez (Vieira), Balotelli

Next up for City would be Dynamo Kyiv, 8–1 aggregate victors of the tie with Beşiktaş and another new destination on City's European odyssey: Ukraine. Long before the novelty wore off (City would play Kyiv again in the Champions League in 2015–16 and the fans would endure three consecutive trips to Shakhtar in the group stages (2017–18 to 2019–20), a trip this far east was breaking new ground.

With growing momentum in the FA Cup (a sixth-round tie at home to Reading promised City's first semi-final appearance since 1981) and a league campaign still threatening to deliver entry into the holy grail of the Champions League, resources, even of City's profundity, were beginning to feel stretched.

In the end, the match would hinge on two strikers coming in from the cold.

The first, Andriy Shevchenko, at the age of 34 and reaching the end of a stellar career, scored for the home side, his 67th in European competition, as he nipped in front of the horizontal Hart to nudge Andriy Yarmolenko's cross into the net. The second, Mario Balotelli, banned from wearing his snood in –8°C by UEFA's new edict on matchday attire, would be back in the warmth of the changing rooms quicker than anyone else.

Two minutes into the second half, Balotelli had not yet emerged from the tunnel to join his teammates, who were forced into the slightly unusual manoeuvre of playing on without him. This in itself was something of an innovation from the Italian, but what was to come next beat that into a cocked hat. Ambling down the touchline, clasping his face and shaking his head, Balotelli arrived pitch-side, followed by a gesticulating Mancini and an entourage of sponge-wielding gofers, all staring intently at the apparently distressed player.

You could not, as the saying goes, have made it up. Afterwards, Mancini, spitting feathers and whirling his eyes, spluttered the near-iambic pentameter: 'He had an allergy. I don't know what. His face was swollen. I don't know why.' Without adding his well-worn catchphrase *'ees normal'*, it was as close to poetry as anyone in the City camp had managed all night.

Continually pointing to his bloated face, the striker was looked over by the club doctor, while Mancini embarked on a long and picturesque rant nearby. It was just another incident in a career full of the unorthodox for the most high-maintenance player in the squad. For Mancini, it was another test for his blood pressure.

This tie would mark the first in the modern era of a succession of high-profile games that ran away unnecessarily from City. There were bigger disasters to come, that was for sure, but, looking back, Kyiv felt like the first of a series of missed opportunities. Assured at the start, City had fallen to Shevchenko's sucker punch in the 25th minute. Dominating possession in the second period, they were undone a second time when Richards dithered and Oleh Husiev hammered the ball high past Hart with thirteen minutes left.

Hart's opposite number, Oleksandr Shovkovskiy, enjoyed a charmed evening, saving everything that bounced his way on the rutted Lobanovsky Stadium pitch. With a bobble-hatted Mancini remonstrating acrobatically with Džeko on the touchline, things could have got worse, however, as Husiev again tore through at the end but was denied by a combination of Hart and Lescott.

Nigel de Jong's infamous 'lively dressing room' was in full flow afterwards, as doctors eased the swelling in Balotelli's face and staff tried to locate his raging manager.

DYNAMO KYIV 2–0 MANCHESTER CITY | Att. 16,000

Hart, Richards, Kolarov (Wright-Phillips), Kompany, Lescott, Zabaleta, Barry, Silva, Y. Touré, Džeko, Balotelli (Tevez)

Offering his expert opinion on BBC Radio 5 Live, ex-City stalwart Danny Mills claimed that 'City have been given a lesson in how to play two-legged European football,' this despite only one leg having been completed. 'At 2–0 down they can still turn it around in the second leg,' he went on, to give greater shape to his professional uncertainty.

The return leg had indeed been rendered challenging and it would be Balotelli once again who would complete his one-man trail of destruction to usher City's exit from the competition. Having helped put a hole in the ship in the first leg, Balotelli sunk the whole shebang without trace in the return. Fans arriving early might have had a slight inkling that all was not well when he failed to get into a succession of bibs during the warm-up. On top of his problems in the first leg, the penny was beginning to drop that Mancini had recruited an authentic *free thinker*. As the manager later reflected: 'I told him, if you played with me ten years ago, I would give you every day maybe one punch in your head. There are different ways to help a guy like Mario. I don't speak with him every day, otherwise I would need a psychologist.'

With a 6pm kick-off restricting the number of fans who could get to Eastlands on time, City hit the ground running and were beginning to make inroads when disaster and Mario Balotelli struck again. The Italian had already scooped a gilt-edged chance over the bar from three yards out when the mists of frustration descended and he planted a boot into Goran Popov's chest. Referee Cüneyt Çakir had little choice but to remove Balotelli from the fray, puncturing City's optimistic prancing with one dramatic flourish of his red card.

With ten men, City scored one of the two they needed through Kolarov's well-placed daisy-cutter but were unable to bring further discomfort to the Dynamo backline. A long trail through Europe that had started in Romania in August had come once more to an unsatisfactory conclusion. It would not be the last City saw of the Europa League, but it would be remembered for the high antics of one of City's most oddball players in recent generations.

That the season ended with Carlos Tevez hoisting the FA Cup, after victory over Stoke had given City their first trophy since 1976, meant Mancini, for all the shattered personal relationships, had some silverware to his name. City fans entered the summer in a euphoric state. The first great City side of the modern era was upon us. We could hardly wait to see what they could do in the cauldrons of Munich and Barcelona. As it turned out, there would be an unexpected upgrade to the already maverick behaviour displayed by Messrs Balotelli, Tevez and company. Only this time it would go out to a much wider audience.

MANCHESTER CITY 1–0 DYNAMO KYIV | Att. 27,816 | Kolarov
Hart, Richards, Kolarov (Milner), Lescott, Kompany, de Jong, Y. Touré, Barry (A. Johnson), Silva (Džeko), Balotelli, Tevez

RETURN TO THE TOP TABLE

Age of consent

Dressed head to toe in black, with the collar on his polo shirt turned up and an effortlessly expensive pair of Trussardi sunglasses sliding down his glistening nose, Roberto Mancini exuded anything but holiday cool. Gesticulating in his unmistakable way, the Italian paced nervously up and down, shouting at people and waving his arms indiscriminately. The Herbalife World Football Challenge was not supposed to be delivering these levels of stress.

City's high-profile status as trophy winners had suddenly catapulted them into a new world of club-monikered airliners and prestige American publicity tours. In Los Angeles, against local outfit LA Galaxy, star striker Mario Balotelli had just announced to the world that he was not taking the match too seriously by operating a dismal pirouette in order to back-heel the ball into the net. The ball trickled apologetically wide and his manager was now approaching levels of apoplexy that would have had a cardiologist advising him to sit down in the shade with a small bag of *biscotti di amoretto*.

If it was a snapshot in the sunshine for what was to come later in City's inaugural Champions League participation, we were not to know it at the time, but at least it told the watching world that City's endearing character had not been spoiled by winning their first trophy since 1976. Nor had Balotelli's by now high-profile contrary streak been ironed flat.

Ready or not, *the moment* had arrived.

The 2011–12 season would finally see City back in action in European elite competition. Their only previous outing was so deeply buried in the swirling mists of time that the tournament had since changed its name, changed its shape and form and shed its array of Nottingham Forests, Magdeburgs and Feyenoords to become a slick, sleek new reality of wall-to-wall Bayern Munich and Real Madrid.

Welcome to the Champions League.

After a sterling battle to finish 2010–11 in the top four, City had made it, with a first trophy in a generation thrown in for good measure. To many supporters the double achievement of finally winning something (beating United in the tense but deeply cathartic Wembley semi-final along the way), as well as finishing high enough in the league to enter the Champions League seemed like the lifting of a great weight from collective shoulders.

Malcolm Allison's brash promises from 1968 could finally be forgotten and a brand-new chapter could be written in bright, vivid colours.

Although City were Champions League novices, their expensively assembled squad was not. Fifteen of Mancini's squad had prior experience in the competition, led by Kolo Touré's 65 appearances and Owen Hargreaves' 52. Captain Vincent Kompany had also played fifteen games and City's ever-expanding ex-Arsenal contingent of Samir Nasri, Gaël Clichy and Kolo Touré could count on an accumulated total of 141 Champions League outings between them.

City fans may have been on the brink of a new experience, but the players were not. The theme of the crowd's fidgety uncertainty about big European nights – which would later become such a profound topic – was not entertained before the group stages in September. It was a club full of confidence and anticipation that received news of the draw that August.

The last time City had competed for the European game's biggest cup, there had been no seeding, no UEFA coefficients, no group stages to guarantee extra revenue and a near sure-fire method of gaining access to the even more lucrative knockout rounds. Things, over the period of 43 years that City had been idling around, had changed markedly.

Reward, if that was the correct word, came in the shape of the first of several groups of death that would litter the club's path in the early years of Champions League participation. City's first foray would take in the might of Bayern Munich, plus tricky Napoli and unpredictable Villarreal. Reaction was inevitably full of talk of what City's great potential might achieve. It would take supporters some time before drawing powerful elite clubs in tight, difficult groups became a bugbear and even longer before they could take the tournament properly to their hearts, but here was an exotic and enticing start to the relationship.

Manager Mancini stressed the profundity of the challenge facing his team: 'There are sides in the Champions League in this country, in Italy and in Spain, that have been doing this for many years and this will be our first attempt – but we have a great squad of players here, players who have played in and won the competition and who are used to the big stage with their countries.' He went on: 'We have been drawn in a very difficult group and that was always going to be the case because we were in pot three for the draw. I see it as a very even group though. There are four very good teams and only two can go forward. We must try to make sure one of them is us.'

As a rallying cry on the Malcolm Allison scale of grandiose rhetoric, Mancini's utterings were underwhelming and understated. At least one thing was for sure: City's first outing would surely not be shrouded in the controversy Allison had bestowed upon the club all those years ago. Mancini, a master of press conference non-committal and studio sound bites, gave everybody the quotes they needed in his charmingly *Italian* English. 'Football is this,' he would say time after time, or, when looking for variety: 'This is football.' These were his go-to answers for the vagaries and capricious turns of the sport that had made him rich, famous and undeniably fidgety.

The Italian had ex-City manager Sven-Göran Eriksson to thank for shaping his first steps in management. As assistant to the Swede at Lazio, he began to learn the ropes. 'He lives for football,' was Eriksson's summary. 'He drinks football. He probably dreams football.' As a player he had also soaked up the wily strategies of Sampdoria coach Vujadin Boškov, under whom he won a scudetto, two Italian cups and the Cup Winners' Cup. It was Boškov who would, in his own words, 'give the first five minutes' of the half-time break to Mancini to speak to the players.

'Everyone thought it was me and Luca [Vialli] that ran everything,' Mancini stated later, 'but Vujadin always had the last word. He was the cleverest coach I ever had.' In a 2020 documentary, Nigel de Jong would quip of Mancini: 'He was passionate about football, passionate about himself and passionate about winning.' It was almost certain, therefore, that any dressing room led by the Italian would contain characters and would see its fair share of honest opinions aired.

Mancini had already been credited with resurrecting the flailing career of Juan Sebastián Verón, an expensive flop at Manchester United and Chelsea. Brought back to life under his tutelage at Inter, the freedom offered to the graceful Argentinian was similar to that now being proffered to Yaya Touré in his City team. Mancini liked a midfield kingpin and he was betting his house on the muscular form of the Ivorian, with de Jong chugging around behind to mop up any potential mess.

It was undeniable that City's schedule looked tough. Opening at home to fellow debutants Napoli put Mancini's men under immediate pressure to kick off their inaugural campaign with a victory. To follow was a trip to Munich to play in the backyard of one of the tournament's long-time mainstays. The challenges were clear, the dangers obvious.

There was also the small matter of the even stronger domestic challenge that was being sought. The tear-drenched capture of the FA Cup was just the first step in City's bid to be considered elite challengers over the coming years. Mancini would be under pressure to deliver more signs of progress at home too.

City, with new signings Sergio Agüero and Samir Nasri showing strongly, had come out of the blocks flying. The opening day thrashing of Swansea had gone like a dream, with 30 shots on goal, four of which were converted, two of which were scored by the debutant Agüero, coming off the bench with a late flourish which gave the packed ground a little taste of the unmatchable avalanche of goals to come over the following decade. A 3–2 win at Bolton was followed by a scintillating demolition of Tottenham at White Hart Lane. Edin Džeko, looking sharp and menacing, notched four as City ran riot against the Londoners. A 3–0 home win over Wigan meant the team approached the Napoli game second in the Premier League and full of optimism.

UEFA edicts issued before the group stage announced that referees had been primed to be particularly strict on dissent and simulation. As City embarked on their first continental group stage, these elements seemed intangible dangers for a side – admittedly housing its fair share of off-the-wall characters – that was well drilled, focused and ready to give a good account of itself. There would be no dissent, no breaking of ranks, no more weird Balotelli pirouettes. City and their suave young manager meant business.

There would also be no Malcolm Allison. The likes of Balotelli, Tevez and David Silva would surely have had a place in any modern-day starting eleven put out by the ex-City coach. That they would have to play under the more practical auspices of Mancini did not seem to be something worth dwelling on at this point, but that standpoint would begin to change within weeks.

Forty-three years on from the debacle of Istanbul and City's only other participation in the European Cup, the two sides stood side by side in the Etihad tunnel, soaking up the cries of the 44,000 crowd assembled for the occasion.

Of the starting eleven, seven had already played in the tournament. Only four, Joe Hart, Joleon Lescott, Pablo Zabaleta and Gareth Barry, were making their Champions League bows. That all the newcomers were defensively minded players would have some resonance by the end of an evening of electrifying football.

Napoli arrived with a growing reputation. Like City, they had travelled successfully back from the ignominious domestic third tier to participate in UEFA's flagship event. Their three-centre-back system had brought them rich rewards in Serie A.

Walter Mazzarri, striding down the tunnel last (which was one of his Mancini-like superstitions that he insisted on following) in a luminescent blue bomber jacket and square spectacles was already cutting an agitated if curiously dressed figure. His other superstition, clearly visible on this occasion, was for him to be in what he called his 'good fortune pose' – arms crossed and holding his stopwatch – as the game kicked off. It was the only moment all night that he would stop moving.

Napoli were a powerful, counter-attacking team, based around the guile of Marek Hamšík and the lung-busting power of Walter Gargano and Juan Camilo Zúñiga. The duo in attack would also require some shepherding from Vincent Kompany and his teammates: the rangy Edinson Cavani had hit the goal trail after signing permanently at the San Paolo in the summer and in Ezequiel Lavezzi he had a tireless ratter just behind him.

An explosive start saw City racing at their guests with Samir Nasri going close. By the seventeenth minute, however, Napoli had found their feet and, as Lavezzi slipped inside Kompany's challenge, their first chance arrived. The stocky striker took two strides and opened his body to curl a side-footer over and around Joe Hart. The ball dipped violently but not quite enough and slapped noisily against the crossbar before flying to safety. With Napoli's hard-working midfield directing all of City's attacking inside from the wings, the home forays were becoming bogged down, but they almost found a way out after a swift break from a failed Napoli corner.

Yaya Touré, beginning one of what would become his trademark blasts down the field, carried the ball over the halfway line and fed the sprinting Agüero, who cut inside the wrong-footed Hugo Campagnaro to give it back to the supporting Touré. A curling right-footed shot by the African from the edge of the box arced past Morgan De Sanctis, addressing the bar with the same violence Lavezzi's effort had achieved before.

With honours even at half-time, Napoli's re-emergence into the game had come at a cost. Paolo Cannavaro and Salvatore Aronica had joined Christian Maggio in the referee's book, as the visitors employed a rotating system designed to avoid the same man making too many fouls.

If City were to rue a first half of growing dominance, they were to rue more seriously their lack of success in front of goal in the opening stages of the second period. Napoli flooded forward and Zabaleta's heroic block on Hamšík again saved the day. City were living dangerously and in Napoli's next surge up the pitch, apparently a little too dangerously. Touted all week by the press as a decent counter-attacking side, the Italians proved it adequately enough in the 69th minute with an attack as clinical as it was rapier fast.

Barry and Nasri were caught engaging in a moment of self-indulgent leg-waving near the Napoli box, which allowed Maggio to break through the middle and feed the rampaging Cavani to his right. Two strides later and the Uruguayan let go of a shot that flashed under Hart's body. City now needed a flash of inspiration.

However, this came almost immediately in the form of Aleksandar Kolarov's left foot after a foul on Zabaleta, who had been scurrying to collect the ball after Agüero's brilliant side-footed volley had again rebounded from the bar. The resultant free kick was slashed past a motionless De Sanctis for a thunderously received equaliser.

With Carlos Tevez completing a half-hearted warm-up routine on the touchline, City were about to bring on reinforcements. 'That's not the most enthusiastic warm-up I've ever seen,' said Ray Wilkins, summarising alongside Martin Tyler for Sky Sports. The question of how Tevez would react to Mancini relegating him to the subs' bench had been one of the pre-match topics in the media and his lethargic windmills and bored expression would become much more of a hot topic in the next match in Munich. For now, he looked non-plussed as he replaced the tiring Džeko.

Kolarov, his game framed between the elegant equaliser and the acquisition of a potato-shaped nose (flattened and broken just before the goal), had to come off too, with Clichy entering.

The most significant substitution was City's third, however, with Adam Johnson instructed to take the ball – and as many of Napoli's hard-pressed defenders as he could pick up along the way – out to the right flank. Suddenly, City had width and with it a new potency. For all Johnson's ten-minute menace, however, the game was run, with both sides able to reflect on a good evening's work. 'Any talk of a group of death was borne out tonight,' opined ex-City manager Mark Hughes on the Sky sofa afterwards. 'That was a very good Napoli side out there.'

Podcaster Howard Hockin also remembers being surprised by the quality of the opposition: 'I would be lying if I said I had vivid memories of the match itself, because I do not. But I do remember the feeling leading up to the match, and the emotions associated with finally feeling as if my team was a "player".

'What seemed so important at the time, ever since the day of the 2008 takeover, was the fact that until City were playing in the Champions League, they had not truly *arrived*. Perhaps I was blinded by the pomp and ceremony, and that damn theme tune, but that's how it felt. I mean, what was the point of billionaire owners if we weren't mixing it up with the European elite on a consistent basis? This meant the club had gatecrashed the traditional elite. It was a statement of intent more important than the result of the game.'

Meanwhile, the next day's *La Gazzetta dello Sport* knew exactly who the underdogs were: 'Napoli Stop the Millionaires' shouted the headline excitedly. '*Que bella figura*' from Napoli in their own '*primo Eurotest*', suggested Alberto Cerruti, the paper's English football correspondent.

For another Italian in Manchester, it had been an acceptable start: 'The first game is always difficult,' Mancini said. 'I told the players that Napoli would be difficult on the counter-attack. Maybe some of them wanted to win the game on their own tonight. They took too many touches and were a little bit nervous,' he concluded.

It was, however, impossible to complain after an entertaining match in which both sides had launched their campaigns by avoiding defeat. Those City fans casting their minds back to September thirteen years previously would have been even less inclined to grumble. On that occasion they had witnessed the club scramble to an unedifying 1–0 win against Macclesfield in front of 6,000 spectators at the Moss Rose. There had been no 'Zadok the Priest' featuring on that occasion, but the club's chaplain had been busy handing out the holy water before the game.

With Bayern winning 2–0 at Villarreal, it was already clear that City's next game, in Munich, would be of significance.

'Don't worry, we win our next game in Germany,' smiled Mancini as he turned away down the Etihad corridor.

MANCHESTER CITY 1–1 NAPOLI | Att. 44,026 | Kolarov
Hart, Zabaleta, Lescott, Kompany, Kolarov (Clichy), Y. Touré, Barry, Silva, Nasri (A. Johnson), Agüero, Džeko (Tevez)

The second match's scheduling brought it into direct conflict with Munich's Oktoberfest. Those of us planning eagerly to be present for City's re-emergence in the cathedrals of European soccer could hardly have been offered a stronger hand of cards. The prospect of the win that Mancini had *guaranteed* promised to make it a trip to remember. There would certainly be no lack of beer to accompany City's eye-opening return to A-grade football.

Carlos Tevez, washing away what little sweat he had accrued during his casual ten-minute jog out against Napoli, was about to give everyone a real reason to take to drink, however. If his postponed court case in Oldham for a driving offence had seemed to suggest a man happy to flout the rules, football etiquette on the grand stage was about to be the little Argentinian's next unwilling victim.

If Mancini's arms had been put to extravagant use in Los Angeles in the World Football Challenge, down on the Allianz touchline, they looked fit to spin clean off.

A match of cut and thrust had progressed to the 55th minute, with City's early surge resulting in two loud penalty shouts turned away, one against Silva and the other after Micah Richards was upended in full flight by ex-City defender Jerome Boateng ('The award of a penalty would not have been a mistake' suggested the next morning's edition of the *Süddeutsche Zeitung* drily). Two sucker punches from Mario Gómez just before the break had left them trailing 0–2. Having waited for the second half to settle, Mancini now needed to enforce his own alterations. Or at least, attempt to.

High in the upper tiers of Bayern's majestic home, it was impossible to follow the tragicomedy being enacted on live television for an audience of millions. Only a small portion of the 65,000 spectators were close enough to see exactly what was happening by the City bench.

The commotion on the touchline did not just involve Tevez, who, having warmed up in the nonchalant manner of a man fetching his bedtime hot chocolate from the kitchen, had decided to sit down again. Edin Džeko, the man apparently coming off, was also using his arms to good effect. Džeko is a tall man and has appropriately lengthy limbs. The Bosnian waved them at Mancini, remonstrated with the bench, jabbed his chest and then removed his boots and slammed them from a great height into the turf before him. As sideshows to match Bavaria's rich tradition of liberalist cabaret went, this was worthy of an Oscar.

Tevez, meanwhile, was refusing to budge. We were treated to the slightly less galvanising figure of Nigel de Jong entering the fray instead. In place of the whirring forward power of Tevez, City would be going sideways into yet more meaty tackles in midfield. As a calmer Mancini would later say: 'I need to speak to Edin. He was disappointed to come off, but a manager can do what he thinks.' Regarding Tevez's incalcitrant posturing, the Italian later suggested: 'Tevez refused to go on the pitch. It is a bad situation when a player refuses to come on and help the team. I cannot accept that.' The unblinking stare in Mancini's eyes told of a conversation behind closed doors that would make the wallpaper peel. Within days, Tevez would be on gardening leave and would not return until European football was a long way behind us all.

Suddenly, the centre of Munich with its packed *Bierkellers* and sizzling rows of multicoloured sausages seemed far away from a stadium perched on a patch of bald land beyond the airport on the edge of the autobahn to Ulm. As is often the case with modern football stadia, the televisual impact is sumptuous, but the actual on-the-ground logistics are less appetising. Munich would be closed by the time we fans stumbled back into its reluctant embrace.

While City's express-train start had petered out after the Richards penalty claim, Bayern had looked increasingly comfortable with their task, a club steeped in European history, knowing when to attack and when to drop back, when to press all the buttons, when to slow things down. With the final scheduled to take place in their own ground, they appeared to have all eventualities covered (this would finally blow up in their faces eight months down the line when Chelsea beat them on penalties at the very last hurdle, however).

For City, it was back to the drawing board and an autumn of uphill struggle to pass muster in Group A.

BAYERN MUNICH 2–0 MANCHESTER CITY | Att. 65,000
Hart, Richards, K. Touré, Kompany, Clichy, Nasri (Milner), Y. Touré, Barry (Kolarov), Silva, Agüero, Džeko (de Jong)

That City eventually lost out on qualification by a single point confirmed the damage was done not here in Munich, where deep down the club's strategists would have been prepared to accept defeat, but in drawing at home to Napoli in their inaugural game and losing the return at the San Paolo on matchday five. Two wins against Villarreal followed the Bayern setback, but by the time the group was closed with the home victory over an already qualified Bayern, qualification was resting on Villarreal gaining their first group points at home to a pumped Napoli. While this appeared a bit of a long shot, it would not even have merited a mention in the *City Book of Tall Stories*.

Hope was always the last flame to die out.

The chaos of those moments at the start of the second period in Munich would be repeated in the final game of the league season, when Džeko, Agüero and indeed the mavericks Tevez and Balotelli, would help haul City across the line against Queens Park Rangers in the most mind-numbingly dramatic way imaginable to end a 44-year wait to be crowned champions again. Ironically, it would be the plodding substitute in Munich, Nigel de Jong, who carried the ball the length of the field to set the final Agüero-flavoured histrionics in motion against QPR.

Between the defeat in Bavaria and City winning 3–0 at Villarreal in their fourth game, six consecutive wins fell the club's way. Twenty-four goals were scored in that period too. Mancini's side had found another gear. Beating Aston Villa 4–1 was followed by a tight home win over Villarreal in the first of two back-to-back encounters with the club hoisted to European prominence by future City boss Manuel Pellegrini. The real eye-opener and launch pad to a historic season end was the legendary 6–1 victory at Old Trafford, however, where Alex Ferguson's assurances of 'not in my lifetime' first began to look a little ropey.

The Villarreal home game had pitched City against their fourth Spanish opponents, after Bilbao, Valencia and Racing Club of Santander, and produced only their second win in six games against clubs from Spain. Even this one was in doubt until the very end. Juan Carlos Garrido's gutsy side held out with the scores tied at 1–1 until the 90th minute, when Agüero notched after intelligent prompting from Milner and Zabaleta. Both the scorer and the midfielder had been willing substitutes in an increasingly fraught second period, showing Tevez – now idly grilling *asado de costillar* back home in Buenos Aires – what positivity could achieve.

The win was City's first ever in the Champions League at the third time of asking.

MANCHESTER CITY 2–1 VILLARREAL | Att. 42,236 | Marchena (o.g.), Agüero

Hart, Zabaleta, Kompany, Lescott, Kolarov, de Jong (Agüero), Y. Touré, Nasri (Milner), Silva, A. Johnson (Barry), Džeko

In winning the return so comfortably in Spain, there had been only two real points of interest. Firstly, some of Villarreal's less well-educated supporters directed racist abuse towards Mario Balotelli after he had won and converted a penalty to make it 2–0 on the stroke of half-time. Touré had also been singled out for abuse. The ugly spectre of racism would rear its head later in the campaign in Porto and would be the catalyst for a testy relationship between the governing body and the club, when UEFA decided to fine City more for appearing late for the start of the second half than it did Porto for the grim behaviour of its supporters. A more serious ruckus would emerge from the behind-closed-doors CSKA Moscow game in 2015, but the first seeds of a labyrinthine story of bad will were sown on the parched grass of El Madrigal.

Secondly, Mancini, launching himself into yet another of his arm-waving episodes, banged his head so badly on the roof of the dugout, he could be seen crouching with an ice pack for a hat in the second half. Whether it helped cool the Italian's ardour was unclear, but he had certainly steered City into a good position in the group. No metaphorical headaches existed as the party rolled out of Alicante airport. Now lying second ahead of Napoli, who had been beaten in a five-goal thriller in Munich, City's trip to southern Italy would hold the key to qualification.

VILLARREAL 0–3 MANCHESTER CITY | Att. 24,235 | Touré (2), Balotelli

Hart, Zabaleta, Kompany, Savić, Clichy, Y. Touré (Agüero), de Jong, Nasri, Silva (A. Johnson), Milner, Balotelli (Kolarov)

As stories circulated that several Bayern fans had been stabbed in the buttocks by passing scooter riders in Naples city centre before their match, City's support was advised to keep a low profile.

Ian Cheeseman, preparing to report for BBC Radio Manchester, remembers the atmosphere well: 'It all looked stunning from the air, but Naples felt run-down and threatening once you were in it. I had to get the train to the ground to conduct interviews the night before the game and it brought me back into town just where we had been told not to go. To be fair the people were friendly, even though the environment seemed a bit edgy. It was total chaos around the ground on the match night, though. I got in late and found it near impossible to locate my press pass and after that where I was supposed to be sitting. I finally got seated and plugged in and the first voice I hear is saying: "Are you OK to go on in twenty seconds, Ian?" To think people reckoned it was a stress-free job reporting on City …'

The noise building up in the shattered old bowl of the San Paolo also told of an evening that would be memorable for all concerned. '90 Minutes of Fire' urged a huge banner hanging from the Curva Sud and that was precisely what Napoli delivered. Ahead early on through a near-post Cavani header, which crept in via the outstretched toes of Touré and Kolarov and evaded Hart, Napoli held on until Balotelli pushed in from close range. Cavani eventually made the difference, with a majestic right-footed volley from Lavezzi's low cross. With Hamšík's effort slapping the post, Napoli were good value for their win, despite a late City onslaught that saw Balotelli and Silva both go close.

The attacking verve that had carried Mancini's men to the top of the Premier League was conspicuous by its absence here, replaced by a nervous, cautious game plan that backfired. All the assured patience in dismantling Villarreal in their own backyard had disappeared in the noisy cavern of the San Paolo. City's apparent coming of age in the competition had been prematurely halted.

NAPOLI 2–1 MANCHESTER CITY | Att. 53,000 | Balotelli
Hart, Zabaleta (A. Johnson), Kompany, Lescott, Kolarov, Silva, de Jong (Nasri), Y. Touré, Milner, Balotelli, Džeko (Agüero)

Bayern's easy win over Villarreal meant Napoli would need just a point in Spain in their final game, whatever City could muster at home to Bayern.

The build-up to the decisive games was overshadowed by posturing by Karl-Heinz Rummenigge. This was the first of many times the ex-Germany international's strident opinions on City (and any other clubs with the nerve to spend more money than Bayern) would make the back pages. Now employed as chairman of the executive board of the Munich outfit, it was his remit to *protect the brand*. It was the likes of City, he insisted, that were undermining this crusade.

As stated in the German club's policy documents, Rummenigge's role was to 'represent the holding company on national and international bodies', a job which brought him into direct conflict with any club threatening Bayern's self-appointed seat at the top table of European football. To this day, Rummenigge appears unaware of the irony of Bayern's positioning. His club's own undermining of Leroy Sané through-out 2019 and 2020, by operating their bidding for the player publicly instead of through the usual channels, only served to bring Rummenigge and his modus operandi to the attention of those in Manchester. In 2011, Bayern represented just another exciting stopping-off point in City's brightly coloured journey back into European football's bosom. By 2020, they had become something akin to a sworn enemy.

Their visit on this occasion made them the fourth German side to play City in Manchester, after Schalke, Mönchengladbach and Hamburg, but only the second after Hamburg to visit the Etihad Stadium.

Mancini had stated that he would indeed be seeking out Rummenigge before kick-off, but their exchange of pleasantries pitch-side seemed innocuous enough from the safe distance of the stands.

On a night described by the *Daily Mail* as a 'Wipeout', both City and United left the Champions League. With only three survivors from the first game in Munich making the starting line-up, Jupp Heynckes, the Bayern coach, was giving City a reasonable chance. Choosing to rest Manuel Neuer, Franck Ribéry, Philipp Lahm, Thomas Müller and Mario Gómez, the German league leaders had a fragile look about them as the match kicked off in front of a buoyant 46,000 crowd. City, with the inexperienced Stefan Savić filling in at right-back for the injured Richards, started cautiously but got the break they wanted after 37 minutes when David Silva's crisp left-foot volley flew past Hans-Jörg Butt.

News from Spain at half-time revealed a goalless game that had City on course to qualify, but between Yaya Touré making it 2–0 (and pushing City's goal difference one better than Napoli's) and Gökhan İnler breaking the deadlock for the Italians in Spain lay only thirteen hope-filled minutes.

MANCHESTER CITY 2–0 BAYERN MUNICH | Att. 46,002 | Silva, Touré

Hart, Savić, Lescott, Kompany, Clichy, Y. Touré (Balotelli), Barry, Silva (A. Johnson), Nasri, Džeko (de Jong), Agüero

---

City's ten points in third place would have been enough to qualify from six of the eight groups and in two of them to finish top. In Group A, where it mattered, however, it was not enough. City would drop into the dark depths of the Europa League, a scene for also-rans they believed they had left behind.

Bayern would go on to face United's conquerors Basel, while Napoli would play Chelsea. The winners of those two ties would eventually meet each other in the Munich final. This in its way shows how well City had performed in the group. There had been mistakes to rue, but there was little beyond the shenanigans in the Allianz Arena to be ashamed of. The group winners, whom City had beaten at the Etihad, would lose the final in their own stadium to a Chelsea team that eliminated the runners-up in City's group. The symmetry of that and the ridiculously random nature of luck in cup draws was, as Mancini might have put it himself, football.

Between the 7 December defeat of Bayern and Thursday 16 February, when City's assault on the Europa League was due to start, the club played fourteen matches in three tournaments, winning only seven of them. Elimination from both cups at the hands of Liverpool and Manchester United suggested the so-called big guns still had Mancini's number. Yet City still led the way in the Premier League despite form that was beginning to stutter.

Having drawn FC Porto, matchday in northern Portugal dawned bright and sunny. From early on in the day, City fans had begun to make their way down to the Cais de Ribeira, a delightful setting in front of the River Douro under the great arches of Gustave Eiffel's iron bridge. It was an idyllic location to take in the warm weather and socialise. Traditional port barges puttered past, laden with barrels and the familiar-sounding English names depicted on the roofs of the port lodges on the south bank of the river seemed to confirm we were on friendly territory.

I met Porto *socio* Pedro Coelho in front of the Os Ribeirenses café, already doing a brisk trade in Super Bock beer and the omnipresent *Bifanas*, the hot pork sandwich that is the pre-match staple diet of the Portuguese. 'There is continuity in this great team,' he told me of Porto. 'What Mourinho started, André Villas-Boas continued. Villas-Boas was José's technical assistant and now it is Vítor Pereira who has the job. We won the league unbeaten last year, also the cup, we beat Benfica 5–0 and we won the Europa League final in Dublin against Braga. But the main man here is still the president, Pinto da Costa, and it is through him that this continuity comes.'

Indeed, making my way to the Estádio do Dragão to pick up press accreditation in the early afternoon, I descended upon a tiny café alongside the great white sides of Porto's redeveloped ground. Unlike the stadium, the café was blissfully untroubled by modernisation, with a narrow marble top serving as a counter, backed only by a toaster, a coffee machine and an enormous mural of the FC Porto president in power here for as many years as some of Africa's most entrenched leaders and far longer than any other club president in world football.

The president's ingenuity had led Porto to be the first big European club to properly develop ties with South America and it was now benefiting from this link in a big way. Of the talented squad about to face City, oddly no fewer than four would end up at the Etihad. Nicolás Otamendi, Danilo and Fernando were all part of the Portuguese club's remarkable South American scouting operation, while the less said about the fourth recruit, Eliaquim Mangala, the better.

With the likes of João Moutinho, Hulk, James Rodríguez and Lucho González, Porto would provide City with a proper test, despite the supposed drop down in level from the Champions League. 'I've been watching this team for years,' stated Coelho 'and this is just about as good as it has ever been. The players we get in from Brazil and Argentina come in under the radar. They get game experience of European football every season with Porto, which is good for us, because they get better, and good for them, because they are in the window and other teams can see how good they are. Each summer Pinto da Costa allows one or two huge transfers out to fill the till. Then the process starts again with the scouts in South America, all paid for by the transfers away from the club.'

Heading back to the tiny riverside bars of the Ribeira, it was clear that large hordes of away fans were now gathering to bask in the gentle sunshine. Thanks also to the welcoming nature of the locals, no one seemed troubled by the growing number of banners draped over the café fronts. 'Noisy Neighbours', 'Pride of Manchester', 'We've Seen Things', 'Pablo Zabaleta Corazon de Leon' all rippled softly in the gentle breeze as they hung above the Buraquinho Bar on the river front. Without a hint of trouble, City fans on the higher terrace appeared to have borrowed a number of tin trays and soup spoons from the bar and a small percussion unit had started banging out an a capella version of 'Oh, David Silva, he scored the fifth goal at Old Trafford'. Travelling to support British teams in Europe had come a long way from the violence and vandalism of City's earlier forays across the channel to Holland and Belgium in the '70s. 'Manchester's a shit hole, we want to stay here!' they sang on, as the sun baked the cobbles on the quayside.

By kick-off, a cold wind was whipping through the giant gaps at each end of the Dragao, redeveloped with warmer Euro 2004 summer evenings in mind. The stadium reverberated to the usual tribal sounds of the big match build-up, with a sell-out 47,000 crowd assembling. When I caught up with ex-City winger Paul Simpson, on duty for BBC Radio Manchester, he was circumspect: 'It's a shame it's come to the Europa League for City, but when you look around this ground and you look at the team sheets, you know that this is also worth being a part of,' he said. 'This can all be part of a learning process that stands the club in good stead for next season to try again in the Champions League. In the meantime, let's see if City can win the Europa League. That in itself would be a major step forward after winning the FA Cup last May.' Asked how it felt to see the club in such good shape after the trials and tribulations of the '80s and '90s, Simpson said: 'I was part of a team that came back out of the Second Division in 1985. It was done on a shoestring because there was no budget to strengthen. We were back down again two years later and we all know what happened in the '90s, so it's just fantastic to see City competing in Europe again and coming to places like this. It's magnificent, the stadium, the fans, the occasion. Just what the club and the fans deserve after all those struggles. And now there's money to prop up the challenge.'

If Porto's team sheet contained some of *the* names of European football, one big name of their own was conspicuous by its absence on the City list handed to UEFA before kick-off. Nowhere to be seen were the words *Carlos Alberto Tevez*. Recently returned from his unauthorised barbecue trip to Buenos Aires, Tevez was still to respond to the club's charge of gross misconduct. Excluded from Mancini's revised squad for the Europa League, Tevez would not be reintegrated in City's plans for Europe until the following season's opener with Real Madrid. Instead, Mario Balotelli – back from serving a suspension himself – would carry City's threat going forward, supported by a well-packed midfield, with Sergio Agüero on the bench if needed. The return of Yaya Touré after six weeks away at the Africa Cup of Nations with the Ivory Coast was also a major boost in what would be City's 75th European game.

By half-time, the Italian's pragmatism had backfired some-what. Despite several chances of their own, City were a goal down to Silvestre Varela's 27th-minute strike from close range after Hulk had powered past Kompany down City's right flank. Clichy, tracking Varela's run into the box, was just too late. In an all-action first 45 minutes, Fernando and Moutinho had bossed de Jong and Barry in City's engine room, but all of that was about to change. In fact, quite a lot was about to change.

As we waited high in the press area for the second half to start, the home side appeared on the turf first. There was nothing unusual in that, but City's tardy appearance, keeping the Porto players waiting for nearly a minute and a half would have its repercussions. As the match restarted, it had also become evi-dent that the local police were conducting some sort of sweep among the *Super Dragões*, Porto's main supporter group on the Bancada Sul.

At the other end, the 2,000 City supporters were soon warm-ing their hands, as Álvaro Pereira, in attempting to jostle himself ahead of Balotelli as the Italian chased Yaya Touré's long diag-onal cross into the area, only succeeded in knocking the ball past the startled Helton in Porto's goal. As the two players rose towards the arcing cross, the defender appeared to nudge Balotelli gently forward, but in doing so became unbalanced himself and diverted the ball into the net with his swinging arm. The Brazilian keeper made a point of approaching his defender afterwards with both gloved hands over his ears in a gesture suggesting Pereira had not heard his shout to leave it. Balotelli, sticking strictly to his own script, stood up, straightened his shorts and walked back to the centre circle without the slightest sign of glee. As goal celebrations went, it wasn't.

Suddenly, the tide had turned and it was City's chance to dominate. 'They obliged us to play at the top of our game,' the Porto coach Pereira would say afterwards. 'We played a beautiful first half but City started playing really quick transitions in the second half and that hurt us.'

What hurt even more was the winning goal, with just five minutes left on the clock. After Barry had won back possession on the halfway line, a quick one-two between Yaya Touré and Nasri put the Ivorian thundering through on the left side of the box. He drew three defenders and squared to the onrushing substitute Agüero, who had the simplest of tap-ins to complete a great night's work for the visitors.

Touré had assisted both City goals and Mancini's insistence on playing him direct from the Africa Cup of Nations under-lined the Ivorian's importance. I attempted to get the Italian to confirm the growing importance of Touré in the press conference after the game but he was as usual playing a straight bat. 'There was no doubt about this,' Mancini replied. 'Never any doubt about Yaya Touré. He is fit and is an important player for us, so I had no hesitation to play him, even though he arrived here yesterday direct from the tournament in Africa. He showed out there why we should play him.'

For the players, the line of questioning had turned to racist chanting from the Porto supporters towards Balotelli. UEFA announced shortly afterwards that they would be analysing video footage from the evening. For their part, Porto's directors offered the worthy explanation that they were 'proud to be a multiracial club' and that 'exhortations for "Hulk" and "Kun"' may have been misinterpreted by some to be racist chanting. At first sight, it appeared odd that they might have been shouting encouragement for one of City's players. UEFA's disciplinary board had already fined the Bulgarian FA after their fans had insulted Theo Walcott, Ashley Cole and Ashley Young in an international match. It remained to be seen what would follow this latest unsavoury incident.

Porto's rich history of failure in England (fifteen matches, thirteen defeats, no wins) suggested the tie might be over after the initial 90 minutes. With the next round threatening to take City straight back to Portugal (the draw had been made for the quarter-finals at the same time as the knockout round and had paired City with the winners of the match between Legia Warsaw and Sporting Clube de Portugal, which stood at 2–2 after the first leg in Poland), there was plenty to focus on.

FC PORTO 1–2 MANCHESTER CITY | Att. 47,417 | Pereira (o.g.), Agüero

Hart, Richards, Kompany, Lescott, Clichy, Barry, de Jong, Y. Touré, Silva (Kolarov), Nasri (Zabaleta), Balotelli (Agüero)

Porto's challenge in the return game was simple: to keep things tight and hope to edge through with a goal or two late on. After nineteen seconds that strategy had been tossed in the bin, with Agüero racing through the middle on to Touré's precision pass to score.

A crowd of nearly 40,000 settled down to watch a masterclass, including a neat preview of what was to come in future seasons, as Nicolás Otamendi left City with oceans of space through the middle, Agüero supplying Džeko with an easy chance to finish for the second.

Two more from David Silva, running things in his own inimitable way, and newcomer David Pizarro, a deadline day loan signing from Roma, meant the Europa League holders were out, beaten 6–1 on aggregate by a City side looking lean and hungry for the season's closing business. In truth, despite the early breakthrough, City's other goals had fallen in the 76th, 84th and 86th minutes, aided by Rolando's red card after the second, which made the game look easier than it was. Coach Pereira was adamant, stating: 'Anyone thinking City have dominated this game is wrong. The scoreline does not show what happened on the pitch. Up until the second goal, Porto were the better team. We played much better, but we know City have a good team and they used the counter-attack well.'

With Sporting finishing the job against Legia, it would be back to Portugal for those of us eager to see how far Mancini could take this exciting City side in a tournament well stocked with powerful teams. However, the City boss showed how his impression of the Europa League had changed radically from twelve months earlier, stating: 'We want to try to go to the final if possible but it will be difficult because the Europa League has top squads – Manchester United, Valencia, Schalke – *it is like the Champions League.'*

MANCHESTER CITY 4–0 FC PORTO | Att. 39,548 | Agüero, Džeko, Silva, Pizarro

Hart, Richards, Kompany, Lescott, Clichy, de Jong, Nasri (Džeko), Barry (Milner), Silva, Y. Touré, Agüero (Pizarro)

After waiting 40 years to return to Portugal to play a competitive game, there were less than three weeks between City's second-ever game in that part of the Iberian Peninsula and their third. City would be returning not only to Portugal but to the site of Malcolm Allison's last meaningful contribution to top-level football. As coach of Sporting Clube de Portugal in 1981–2, Allison had won the league and cup double. Still revered by the green-and-white half of the city of Lisbon, his swansong in the sunshine heralded an end to trophy winning for the man who had brought such pleasure to Manchester in the early '70s.

Housed in a belle époque hotel overlooking the Atlantic Ocean at Estoril, some twenty miles down the coast from Lisbon, the City squad prepared for a different kind of challenge against Ricardo Sá Pinto's hard-working side. As in Naples, Mancini had the entire squad stroll along the decoratively paved promenade on the morning of the match. While the players stopped for pictures and posed with the shimmering sea behind them, the supporters were gathering around Rossio Square in the heart of the old capital.

With Zabaleta injured and Yaya Touré serving a suspension, Mancini had been forced into making no fewer than seven changes from the 2–0 win over Bolton that had maintained City in top spot. This was Sporting's 250th match in European competition, revealing one aspect of the tie that was tipped heavily in favour of the Portuguese outfit. As winners of the 1964 edition of the Cup Winners' Cup, they shared an affinity with City for that discontinued tournament but had also finished as UEFA Cup runners-up in their own stadium when losing to CSKA Moscow in 2005, a self-destructive streak that seemed to mimic City's own unpredictable efforts down the years.

Coach Sá Pinto had even played against both James Milner (then of Newcastle United) and Adam Johnson (Middlesbrough) in that 2005 run to the final. The side was built in his own image, combative and technically adroit, with the national team goalkeeper Rui Patrício, Spanish right-back Diego Capel, Chilean playmaker Matias Fernández and Dutch striker Ricky van Wolfswinkel the stand-out performers.

In a sticky and featureless game, City's fortunes turned on a typically odd piece of ill-fortune in the 51st minute. The winning goal was scored by an on-loan Brazilian, his only goal for Sporting in just 23 appearances in total, before embarking on a career that has since taken in Kuban Krasnodar, Anzhi Makhachkala, Sporting Gijón, Cercle Brugge, Red Bull Brasil, Guarani and in 2020 saw him at Persija Jakarta. Xandão, a huge lighthouse of a central defender, flicked in the winner with an expertly back-heeled pirouette and his suddenly acquired balletic skills were, in high-profile terms, never seen again. He managed just 147 career games in the eight or so seasons that passed under the bridge thereafter.

Official pennant from
Bilbao vs City, 1969–70
Cup Winners' Cup.
Courtesy of Gary James

Official pennant from
Lierse vs City, 1969–70.
Courtesy of Gary James

A Bola newspaper,
Thursday 19 March 1970.

Programme from the home return
leg against Académica de Coimbra
on Wednesday 18 March 1970.

Poster advertising trip
to the 1970 Cup Winners' Cup final.

Match ticket for Valencia vs City in
the UEFA Cup, 27 September 1972.

Dave Watson fails to stop Gaetano Scirea putting Juventus in front in the UEFA Cup game against Juventus, 29 September 1976.

First day cover, City vs Juventus.
Courtesy of Simon Mullock

SUPER DINO TIPS SCALES!

Juventus 1, Manchester City 0
(Aggregate: 2–1)

THE OUTSTRETCHED fingers and swift reflexes of Italian goalkeeping idol Dino Zoff were all that stood between Manchester City and a sensational, if undeserved, U.E.F.A. Cup victory here tonight.

From BOB RUSSELL in Turin

Their moment of destiny came one minute from time of their second leg when big Joe Royle suddenly hurled himself to the near post and flicked a header towards the bottom corner.

But Zoff used all his expertise to get a hand to it and that was enough.

City were out, beaten by a well-worked 68th-minute winner from veteran striker Roberto Bonimsegna after Gaetano Scirea had levelled the aggregate scores in the 37th minute.

It was a night when City showed a lot of heart but none of the flair and finesse essential in such a demanding situation.

Brian Kidd, playing with a heavy cold, rarely got into it, neither did Royle, and Dennis Tueart, the

man with the speed and the style to shake Juventus, never really got into his stride, on a rain-soaked pitch.

So while it started optimistically with City comfortably absorbing early pressure and going forward in a manner which clearly worried the Italians, it ended sadly—with Royle the most disappointed of all.

From City's first raid, the Italians showed signs of nerves with Kidd just failing to connect from a link up between Hartford, Keegan and Royle.

But City lost some of their early authority and they were lucky to find such a brave referee as the Belgian Rion in the 37th minute when he

turned down an obvious-looking penalty with almost 70,000 Italian fanatics baying for his blood.

A rare slip by Doyle left Bettega clear, 16 yards out, and keeper Joe Corrigan had little option, but to take his ankles and send the Italians sliding, minus the ball, with the goalmouth unattended.

Ten minutes later, however, City were in deep trouble when Mike Doherty blocked a long shot by midfield man Scirea, only to put the ball back into the Italian's path.

The Juventus man picked his spot from 14 yards and stroked it beautifully into the far corner, past the out-stretched Corrigan.

City reshuffled in the second half with Tommy Booth in a more forward midfield role and Hartford dropping deeper.

But the fact remained that the Italians were gaining more and more possession.

Causio caused all kinds of problems slipping from flank to flank and twice in three minutes tested the courageous Corrigan to the limit, first with a thunderous swerving 18-yarder that the keeper punched out and then with a snaking cross-shot that was covered brilliantly.

The moment of truth came for City when defender Claudio Gentile floated a 30-yard free kick into the goal area and Bettega to head expertly across goal and leave Bonimsegna with a six yards volley that he couldn't miss.

Daily Mirror report on Juventus 2–0 City, September 1976.

Match ticket belonging to Graham Ward, City vs FC Twente, UEFA Cup, 27 September 1978.
Courtesy of Graham Ward

Match ticket, Widzew Łódź 0–0 City, 28 September 1977.

Lokeren 0–1 City,
UEFA Cup 2003–4,
Anelka about to score
the winning penalty with
the media double-decker
bus in the far corner.

Fan Erin Rose with City
defender Vedran Ćorluka
before City's game with
Midtjylland in August 2008.
Courtesy of Pat Rose

Half-time in City's first-round tie with
Omonia Nicosia, September 2008.
George Groutas, CC BY 2.0, via Wikimedia Commons

Poster advertising City's arrival in
Gelsenkirchen for Schalke vs City in
the UEFA Cup on 27 November 2008.

Roberto Mancini
addresses the post-match
press conference at the
Estádio do Dragão, Porto,
UEFA Cup, 2011–12.

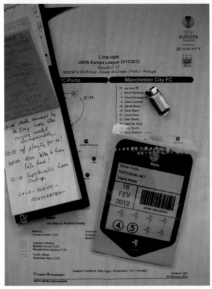

Press pack at
Estádio do Dragão,
Porto, 2011–12.

Headlines from
the Portuguese
press,
Porto 1–2 City,
UEFA Cup,
2011–12.

The steep stands in the Bernabéu for Real Madrid vs City, Champions League Group D, 2012–13.

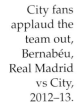

City fans applaud the team out, Bernabéu, Real Madrid vs City, 2012–13.

View from the away section, Real Madrid vs City, Champions League, 2012–13.

Fan Mike Hammond with CSKA supporter Sergei in Red Square, Moscow, October 2013.
Courtesy of Mike Hammond

Neil King in Moscow on the ill-fated trip to the behind-closed-doors fixture with CSKA in the 2014–15 group stages.
Courtesy of Neil King

TV still from the Moscow camera crew who joined City fans on a bus taking them to 'an alternative venue' to watch the match with CSKA.
Courtesy of Neil King

Mike Hammond at the start of the crucial Group E decider with Roma in the Stadio Olimpico, 2014–15.
Courtesy of Mike Hammond

View from the away end in the Ramón Sánchez Pizjuán Stadium, Sevilla, Champions League Group D, 2015–16.

Scene inside the Mercado
de San Miguel, Madrid,
before the Champions League
semi-final, 2015–16.
Courtesy of Glenn Ellaby

Fans and police
outside the Bernabéu
before the 2015–16
semi-final.

Real's fans welcome their side
for the semi-final, 2015–16.

City fans enjoying the sun
in the Plaza Mayor, Madrid,
before the 2015–16 semi-final.

View from the away end, Celtic Park, Champions League Group C, 2016–17.
Courtesy of Mike Hammond

2017–18 Group F match against Shakhtar Donetsk, played in Kharkiv's Metalist Stadium.
Courtesy of Mike Hammond

Pre-match press conference, Basel,
Champions League round of sixteen, 2017–18.

View from the away end, St Jakob-Park for Basel vs City.

OPPOSITE: View from the away section
Tottenham Hotspur Stadium, 2018–19
Courtesy of Mike Hammon

Fans gather before the round of sixteen match in Basel, 2017–18.

Pre-match press conference with Pep Guardiola and Vincent Kompany, St Jakob-Park, Basel.

Front cover of *MARCA* on the day of the match as news breaks that the outbreak of Covid-19 has reached Europe. Round of sixteen second leg with Real Madrid, 2019–20.

Mike Hammond, Murdoch Dalziel, Andy McNab and the author outside the Bernabéu, round of sixteen second leg, 2019–20.

Cais de Ribeira, Porto, on the day of the 2021
Champions League final with Chelsea.

Outside the Estádio
do Dragão before
the Champions
League final in 2021.

Smoke clears as
kick-off nears,
Champions League
final, Porto 2021.

Estádio Alvalade, Sporting Clube
de Portugal vs City, round of sixteen, 2021–2.

Front cover of *A Bola*, describing
City's 5–0 win over Sporting.

Outside the Estádio Alvalade,
Sporting vs City, 2021–2.

2021–2 semi-final first leg against Real Madrid. Fans welcome the teams.
Courtesy of Gareth Worthington

2021–2 semi-final first leg, City 4–3 Real Madrid.
Courtesy of Gareth Worthington

Pep Guardiola watches
from the touchline during
City's 4–3 win over Real.
Courtesy of Chris Dottie

Incomplete stadium
renovations at the
Bernabéu, semi-final
second leg 2021–2.

Night falling on
the Bernabéu for the
semi-final second leg.

Nigel de Jong's after-match assertion that the tempo had been too slow seemed accurate to those of us watching in the stands. 'We let the tempo drop too far to really open them up,' the Dutchman insisted. 'It doesn't matter which team is in front of us, if you do that, you're letting them back in the game. Fortunately, we've got the second leg and we can seal the deal at home.'

With night falling, the green-and-yellow panels of the Estádio Alvalade were lit up behind us as we left to go back into town. The bright light and gathering gloom would both be repeated in the second leg in Manchester seven days later.

SPORTING CLUBE DE PORTUGAL 1–0 MANCHESTER CITY | Att. 34,371

Hart, Clichy. K. Touré, Kompany (Lescott), Kolarov, Milner, de Jong, Barry (Nasri), Silva, Džeko (Balotelli), Agüero

Another one-goal defeat, this time at Swansea, separated the two games with the Portuguese. City were now off the top of the table and struggling for the form that had carried them ahead of Manchester United in what had developed into a two-horse race for the title. With Chelsea to face next, the Europa League suddenly began to look like a bit of a hindrance.

Mancini's programme notes for the Sporting game hinted at problems but concluded with comforting, familiar words for the jittery supporters: 'The last two games did not finish how we would have liked, but we can still win both competitions. *Football is like this.*'

As it turned out, the match would feature all the missing tempo that de Jong had mentioned after the game in Lisbon. Football *was* like this but not every week. So much tempo was pumped into the second leg, in fact, that every one of the 38,021 crowd would leave breathless and dizzy at the end of the evening's entertainment. Despite eventual failure in a match that Sporting had a half-time stranglehold on at 2–0 up on the night, Mancini would note what an influence the crowd could still have, even, or perhaps particularly, in moments of great adversity. Urged on by a wall of second-half noise, City came within a whisker of going through, when Joe Hart's lunging header in stoppage time was pushed around the post by the full-stretch Patrício. By this time, City had surged back to lead 3–2 with two goals from Agüero and a penalty coolly converted by Balotelli.

Having poached two dramatic first-half goals through Fernández (from a swerving 20-yard free kick) and van Wolfswinkel, Sporting ended the match hanging on for dear life. Afterwards, an electrified Sá Pinto paid tribute in the most appropriate way possible. 'I think Malcolm Allison would have been proud to watch a match between two great teams tonight,' he said. 'We at Sporting remember him too as a great manager of our club.'

MANCHESTER CITY 3–2 SPORTING CLUBE DE PORTUGAL |
Att. 38,021 | Agüero (2), Balotelli (pen.)

Hart, Richards, Savić, K. Touré, Kolarov, Pizarro (Džeko), Y. Touré, A. Johnson (de Jong), Silva (Nasri), Agüero, Balotelli

---

Thus, another European adventure had ended with sweat, tears and recriminations. For Mancini and City there would be fun and games of an even higher order than delivered against Sporting before the season finally chugged to a halt, with scenes of utter chaos against Queens Park Rangers.

City would be entering the 2012–13 edition of the Champions League as champions of the Premier League. For the Italian, though, glowing in the aftermath of a truly stunning achievement, he could expect to be judged next by his team's efforts overseas.

From a position of strength, it is always easier to keep building. In retrospect, what Roberto Mancini did in the summer of 2012 added precisely nothing to the range of qualities already in City's Premier League-winning stable. City's cash was splashed on Benfica's holding midfielder Javi García, Swansea winger Scott Sinclair, the ageing Inter right-back Maicon, Schalke's young centre-half Matija Nastasić and Everton's eternally promising Jack Rodwell.

None of them would go on to make an impression in a season that flattered to deceive, with the curtain coming down on the Italian's three-year reign at a sodden Wembley Stadium in dreadful, anti-climactic defeat to Wigan Athletic in the Cup final. Long before the sun went down at Wembley, however, an abject failure in the Champions League had already irrevocably sealed Mancini's fate.

If the previous season had seen City partake in a group of death, that all seemed like so much premature hyperbole compared to what the UEFA balls dealt them this time out. In Group D, there were two outstanding statistics before kick-off. City's three opponents – Real Madrid, Borussia Dortmund and Ajax – were all past winners of the trophy. It was also the only group to contain four league champions.

As groups of death went, this one had the air of absolute terminality.

On top of this, Mancini would be locking horns with Jürgen Klopp and José Mourinho, a battle royale of three of the game's most innovative thinkers. With Frank de Boer in charge of Ajax, the Dutch side would not be short of ideas either. City, it was widely agreed, had it all to do, but with the final scheduled for Wembley, a big effort might be worth it.

Where better to test your early season mettle than the towering ramparts of the Bernabéu. Those of us that had spent a lifetime waiting for a fixture like this to become reality, suspecting somewhere deep inside that we would probably have to carry those hopes to our graves with us, set out towards Spain with a spring in our step. Real, steeped in European football history, winner of this champions' trophy in each of the first five years of its existence, practically owned the rights to glory in Europe. City, the ragamuffins used to feeding off airborne scraps, would be dining first class at last. Naturally enough, the rich banquet would give us all indigestion, but that was for later.

First, there were the journeys to undertake, the arrivals, the meeting and greeting and the orienteering. I have watched City take on Real in their own palatial court three times now, but the first time is always an experience that widens the eyes and shortens the breath. Certainly, the prices of the *calamares a la plancha* at the Mercado San Miguel widened the eyes and attempting to keep a yard or two ahead of the local riot police would shorten the breath later too. Nevertheless, there was an exquisite irreverence about the yellow beach ball being lofted around the Plaza Mayor with its equestrian statues and marbled balconies. Sitting on the fringes of a site of coronations, public celebrations and executions, the ranks of travelling fans wondered which of the three we had come all this way for. As it turned out, we would be the lucky recipients of all three, one after the other, but in completely the wrong order.

Madrid is a place that likes to take itself seriously. The boulevards are impossibly wide and stuffed with honking traffic. Impossibly attractive women wear the dismissive manner of human beings who have spent many hours gazing in the mirror. They know they are beautiful. You look at them. They know that you are looking at them. They don't flinch. You wipe away a tear. They strut on. Men wearing suits as crisp as freshly rolled cigars stand laughing into mobile phones in a way only pricy lawyers can carry off. Everybody looks impossibly healthy. You daren't cough, in case you are carried away for being unfit for purpose.

And carrying us away seemed exactly the idea the local police were toying with.

Many of the pasty-limbed Mancunians stretching themselves in the late summer heat would not have been born the only time City's players graced the Bernabéu turf. For those that remembered a bizarre friendly here in 1979, illuminated by the presence of Bobby Shinton, Ray Ranson and Michael Robinson, *graced* was probably stretching things a little. Two red cards and seven goals later, five of them to the home side, whoever had had the brainwave of inviting City would be unlikely to do so again. Over 30 years had passed since then, a period decorated for Real by thirteen league titles, five Copa del Reys and six European trophies. In the same period, City had just the two pots won in a hurry in the preceding two years. The contrast sat loud and stark in anything and everything you contemplated about the two clubs. Yet, here we were operating on a level playing field of 90 minutes, eleven versus eleven.

Outside the cliff-like stands, a large and overdressed police presence was busying itself with the summary duties of grand European occasions against English clubs: baton-charging café terraces on the Castellano and moving people on roughly for drinking beer and laughing in an aggressive manner. It would become a feature of trips to both Madrid and Barcelona over the ensuing years that the police seemed to think they were welcoming visitors from an era not a place. Certainly, had the dubious section of City's support from the '70s and '80s descended on the Spanish capital, the armour-plated riot police would have had a lively afternoon. As it was, in the calmer days of 2012, it was they who seemed to be instigating the trouble.

Once inside, the walk to tier four of the Bernabéu is best partaken when in full control of your faculties, comprising as it does a couple of thousand greasy steps in a spiral of ill-defined light and sudden exhilarating shadow. Thankfully, the elixir of giddy optimism emanating from the visiting supporters made the climb bearable and stops were made on the ascent to genuflect, reorganise simmering tendons and bellow a few crude truths about just who was *the best team in the land and all the world*. At the summit, if the climb had not already taken your breath away, that crucial first glimpse of the green turf certainly did.

Like everything else witnessed in Madrid thus far, the Bernabéu spread itself loquaciously in front of the viewer, a gigantic cement-block monument to self-confidence, grandeur and prestige. It said: *Look at me, hold your gaze and tell me I'm not magnificent*.

What seemed less than magnificent was Mancini's team tinkering. The defence for this august moment would be Maicon–Kompany–Nastasić–Clichy. The Brazilian, still sporting the wide-eyed glare of a man asked to make his English Premier League debut at the Britannia Stadium, had been undressed two years previously by Tottenham's Gareth Bale. His career seemingly in tatters, he was now being asked to shore up the right side of City's defence against Real Madrid. Nastasić would be making his City debut. Elsewhere, the reassuring hulk of Yaya Touré had been given licence to roam, with García and Barry anchoring midfield. Up front the reintegrated Carlos Tevez would run the line alone.

This use of a double defensive-midfield pivot had become a growing feature of the season, allowing Touré – essentially a defensive bulwark in his Barcelona days, even playing outstandingly well in central defence against Manchester United in the 2009 Champions League final – to stride forward with real intent. Once unleashed, stopping him was akin to stepping in front of a tank. It would be a revolutionary tactical switch which would serve the club well over the coming years and turn Touré into perhaps the *one* figure above all others responsible for the club's surge to prominence.

As the game got under way, it became rapidly evident the defence would be given an examination of medical intricacy. Shots pinged in from all angles. Cristiano Ronaldo, taut and glistening, had four on his own in the first four minutes. There would be 30 Real attempts on goal by the final whistle, but, amazingly, painfully, it would not be until the minutes 87 and 90 that the last two meaningful shots of the match breached City's makeshift rearguard to steal away the points for the home side.

By then, a stunning final quarter of an hour had sucked the last drops of emotion from the occasion. Ignoring the obvious narrative, City chose the 68th minute to take the lead. Yet another thundering run from Touré took him through the middle like a minesweeper, with four home players in his wake. They looked like the tins carried behind a newlyweds' car, bobbing and tumbling as the Ivorian swept through the gears. The ball went left. Substitute Edin Džeko had matched his run and was available in space. The goal provoked delirium high under the rafters.

Marcelo, famed for his left-foot accuracy, wafted a delicious equaliser off García's thigh with his right foot, then Kolarov flipped a long free kick in low from the right flank. It evaded sixteen pairs of outstretched boots and drifted in at the far post. There were three minutes to go, but still City ended up losing the game, as Benzema slipped in an immediate equaliser, then Ronaldo's dipping shot skidded past a heroic Joe Hart. The shot did that *Ronaldo thing*, finding a trajectory that followed a weird dipping arc just like the beach ball on the Plaza Mayor hours before the match. Kompany somehow got under it, but it was down at hip height when it passed him. Mourinho's knee slide onto the pitch in a luxurious Pedro del Hierro suit would make the front page of *MARCA* the next morning. Night was falling like a lead weight.

Back in the Plaza Mayor, night had fallen completely. The yellow beach ball was now to be found impaled on a spike of the railings protecting the equestrian statue of Felipe III, the Miserable Monarch to his friends, as apt a member of Spanish royalty as one could have found. Back in the Museo del Jamon, made famous for its moody appearance in Pedro Almodovar's film *Carne Trémula*, the vast lines of skewered pork products produced one last metaphor for City's unlucky grilling.

REAL MADRID 3–2 MANCHESTER CITY | Att. 70,380 | Džeko, Kolarov

Hart, Maicon (Zabaleta), Kompany, Nastasić, Clichy, Barry, García, Y. Touré, Nasri (Kolarov), Silva (Džeko), Tevez

If the first two matches produced the same points tally as the previous year, the 2012 effort seemed doomed to failure. Gone was the optimism, replaced by the realisation that teams like Borussia Dortmund were still on another planet altogether. Jürgen Klopp's attack-minded team had come to Manchester with a line-up containing the future City midfield skills of İlkay Gündoğan and the forward thrust of Robert Lewandowski and Marco Reus, wrapped in an ambitious 4–2–3–1 formation that gave City problems from the very start.

Balotelli's last-minute penalty (his eleventh success from the spot in eleven attempts for City) may have delivered a point, but in truth a 90-minute blur of yellow and black had only been slowed *in extremis* by a virtuoso showing from Joe Hart, producing one of the best performances of his career between the posts.

Dortmund's goal, coming after a string of glorious saves by Hart, fell after the ponderous García had been replaced by the lightweight Rodwell. His dreadful attempt at a short, square pass across defence was easily intercepted by the rampaging Reus, who finished clinically to the far corner. Even then, the miraculously flexible form of Hart got a hand to the shot as it rocketed past him.

City were saved by the awarding of a light 89th-minute pen-alty by the referee for Neven Subotić's apparent handball. Waiting for Roman Weidenfeller to dive one way, Balotelli checked his run-up and dispatched the ball nonchalantly to the other side.

The Italian's talking-hand gesture to the keeper (who had followed him around before the spot kick imparting some no-doubt useful penalty-taking advice), as he collected the ball from the back of the net, suggested the German might like to consider talking less. In truth, it had been Dortmund loudly dictating everything from start to finish.

With Real easily beating Ajax 4–1 in Amsterdam, a gap of three points already existed between second-placed Dortmund and City. The next two matches, pitching City and Ajax together, home and away, would clearly decide the club's fate, but Group D already had the air of a fight for scraps for Mancini's men.

There was something prescient about the night's proceed-ings, however. Dortmund's withering possession stats and highly profligate finishing, which on another night would have finished off almost any other team, would mirror perfectly many of City's own performances in the fourth year of Pep Guardiola's tenure, when it would be City racking up the goal attempts and, occasionally, failing to bring home the bacon.

It would also mirror the infamous *gegenpressing* that trainer Klopp would bring to Anfield to defeat City in the Champions League in 2017–18 and in the race for the league title two years later. Journalist Raphael Honigstein called it the 'kill box', a sector high up the field where Dortmund, and later Liverpool, would savagely fight to regain lost possession before the ball travelled across the halfway line in their direction. 'The best playmaker on earth is *gegenpressing*,' Klopp insisted afterwards. With Sven Bender and Gündoğan pressing the life out of Yaya Touré, City's possession was funnelled to the crab-like García or wide to Silva and Nasri, where more energetic pressing forced the ball to be recycled to the full-backs. Perhaps more popular in the dugout than with the players tasked with delivering it, the tactic required incredible levels of fitness and concentration, selflessness and stamina, and Guardiola's City sides at the end of the decade would employ versions of it themselves.

This would not be the last time City's delicate fusion of passing and movement was stifled by Klopp's high-energy smothering blanket.

MANCHESTER CITY 1–1 BORUSSIA DORTMUND | Att. 43,657 | Balotelli (pen.)

Hart, Zabaleta, Nastasić, Kompany, Clichy (Balotelli), Y. Touré, García (Rodwell), Nasri (Kolarov), Silva, Džeko, Agüero

---

Joe Hart was by now the tournament's busiest goalkeeper, having seen a total of 50 goal attempts come flying his way in the first two group games combined. On Mancini fell the onus of restoring some sense of decorum to City's slipshod defence. Elsewhere in the competition, future figures of interest were having a better time of it. Fernandinho, the combative midfield leader at Shakhtar, had just masterminded his side's gutsy draw against Juventus and Chilean coach Manuel Pellegrini was sitting proud with Málaga at the top of a group that comprised AC Milan, Anderlecht and Zenit.

Another character set to become a Premier League mainstay was about to put paid to City's hopes of qualification on an eventful night in Amsterdam. A masterclass from Ajax playmaker Christian Eriksen secured their first points of the group and sank any slight hopes City still harboured of going through. In a match where possession was shared (51–49 per cent), chances were similar (thirteen to eleven) and City held the lead (Nasri, 22nd minute), the Dane's subtle midfield skills eventually made the difference.

'They played a different game to Madrid,' Eriksen affirmed later. 'Less zonal. That was better for our playing philosophy. We were able to find more space between their lines and I think we made good use of that.'

Micah Richards, meanwhile, was not at all sure what kind of game he had been ordered to play, stating that the manager had 'switched defensive formation three times'.

'He is a player I like with all my heart,' Dutch legend Johan Cruyff was moved to say afterwards of Eriksen, while Mancini, rueing a sloppy City performance, could only express his regrets, remarking: 'I take blame for this defeat. I did not prepare the players properly. It's my fault. I forgot to tell Lescott to jump ...'

This was Mancini beginning to let his slip show. The unnecessary poke at Joleon Lescott revealed a quirky character that was at once charming and sophisticated to the casual onlooker, but petty and vindictive to those who had to remain in close contact with him. The Italian still wrapped himself in a sky-blue-and-white scarf on matchdays, looking urbane and partisan, keeping the fans onside, but his relationship with the playing squad was beginning to unfurl. It would lead to a de facto downing of tools in the dreary conclusion to the season against Wigan at Wembley. Even now, at the graffiti-strewn Amsterdam Arena, the writing was clearly on the wall.

'It would be a miracle if we qualify now,' Mancini added, as he drifted away down the darkened tunnel towards the waiting coach.

De Boer was happy his side had finally stood up for itself. 'We played good football against a top team,' he said. 'We showed what we want to do. I get tired of people saying it was because our opponents played badly. Our players were dominating. City had no answers. We had most of the possession against Dortmund and Real but you can't afford to miss chances against teams like that. They present you with the bill only at the end.'

City's tab for missing out for the second consecutive year on the knockout rounds would be a sizeable one and there would be an Italian gentleman in a blue-and-white scarf asked to foot the bill.

AJAX 3–1 MANCHESTER CITY | Att. 47,743 | Nasri

Hart, Richards, Lescott (Kolarov), Kompany, Clichy, Barry (Tevez), Y. Touré, Milner (Balotelli), Nasri, Džeko, Agüero

---

If the game in Holland had been something of a disaster, seventeen minutes into the first half in the return, things looked even bleaker. Ajax, 2–0 up, were threatening to run riot.

That City eventually drew 2–2 and had two Agüero efforts ruled out for offside revealed a stoicism, which would serve them well on other occasions in this tournament, but the feelings of too little, too late would not go away. Dortmund's point at the Bernabéu meant that City's fourth place on two points was only six short of the Germans at the top of the group. Had they won this topsy-turvy encounter with Ajax, they would have been sitting pretty behind Real with the Spaniards due in Manchester next. As it stood, though, all looked done and dusted.

MANCHESTER CITY 2–2 AJAX | Att. 40,222 | Touré, Agüero

Hart, Zabaleta, Nastasić, Kompany, Clichy, García (Balotelli), Nasri, Barry (Kolarov), Y. Touré, Agüero, Tevez (Džeko)

Dortmund's next performance, whipping Ajax 4–1 on their own pitch, put City's troubles into deeper perspective. The same night, in a game City needed to win to keep their hopes alive, they drew with a Real Madrid side visibly stepping back off the gas in the second half and bade farewell to the Champions League for another year.

Once again, as with Dortmund, City had to rely on a late penalty to secure the point.

The situation posed several questions: City were unbeaten at the top of the Premier League, yet nowhere near the quality needed to proceed in the Champions League. The new signings had almost to a man had little impact. Mancini's man management was being called into question more and more. At a stage of the season where there was still plenty of domestic interest, the arrival of Txiki Begiristain to take up Brian Marwood's director of football role, seemed apposite. The former Barcelona winger had transformed a four-year barren spell at the Nou Camp into a glut of twelve trophies in the past seven years. The Spaniard immediately talked of short-term and long-term success. He was here to nail both. City's management's eyes were beginning to wander to an even bigger picture, and it was tempting to ask whether the new man's Barcelona links would hold any sway with the ultimate target, Guardiola.

For now, Roberto Mancini's reign was secure, but the Italian will have remembered that, as a part of the Sampdoria side beaten in the 1992 Champions League final by Barcelona, Begiristain could make a steely enough opponent if he was pressed. 'We have done well in the last two years,' Begiristain told a riveted press conference, 'Now we must do even better ...'

MANCHESTER CITY 1–1 REAL MADRID | Att. 45,740 | Agüero (pen.)

Hart, Maicon, Kompany, Zabaleta, Nastasić, Kolarov (García), Y. Touré, Silva, Nasri (Tevez), Džeko, Agüero (Milner)

Having gone out with ten points in 2011–12, City's three-point haul in 2012–13 replaced Blackburn's paltry 1995–6 four-point effort as the worst-ever English Champions League showing. From hot to cold within twelve months. No wins and a defeat at Dortmund which condemned Mancini's men to last place in the group. Ajax, finishing third, would move on into the Europa League.

A second-half goal from reserve Julian Schieber separated the sides at the end in the Signal Iduna Park. Hart, again the busier keeper, had prevented the scoreline going further in Dortmund's favour. Klopp, fielding five second-string players, felt City had fought hard throughout, but it was difficult to avoid the conclusion that this had been a meek effort after the relative heroics of the previous campaign.

BORUSSIA DORTMUND 1–0 MANCHESTER CITY | Att. 64,000

Hart, Maicon, Nastasić, Kompany, Lescott, Barry, García, Nasri (Zabaleta), Sinclair (Agüero), Tevez, Džeko (Balotelli)

Dortmund would go on to meet Real again in the semi-finals and lose to Bayern Munich in the first all-German final at Wembley. As had happened the year before, one of the clubs qualifying from City's group would reach the final. With Real dispatched in the semis, City could once again rue their misfortune.

League form would falter in the new year, leaving Mancini with only the FA Cup to cling on to in a season of growing unrest. Even that, after a demolition of Chelsea in the semi-final, would end in hurt and turmoil at the very same Wembley that Dortmund would grace two weeks later in the Champions League final.

News that Mancini's job might be on the line filled the papers on the eve of the Wigan final. For a club whose appearances in these kinds of festivities could still be counted by anyone with three fingers available, this was yet another criminal act of self-harm.

Mancini, no wet-behind-the-ears novice in matters of succession, having been caught behind the Etihad curtains himself before predecessor Mark Hughes had been moved out, looked to have been outmanoeuvred. From Machiavelli to the Medicis, the Italian powerhouses have always been able to handle themselves, but here was one having his exit strategy planned for him on the very eve of the Wembley showpiece.

For such a stubborn, forceful character to be suddenly painted as a lame duck seemed both a little harsh and a little odd, but that is how he finished, damp and bedraggled after a limp City lost to a last-minute Ben Watson winner. That one of Mancini's glut of summer signings, Jack Rodwell, failed to cover the scorer's near-post run seemed to sum the whole mess up perfectly. The Italian's nostrils seemed to gain an extra arch of disdain at the after-match questioning at the hands of the tabloid pack. Another relationship on the rocks. It was time to go.

Arguments about whether the manager should have been kept would last through the summer. Some maintained that he had underperformed given the limitless resources, while others reminded the doubters that he had been responsible for the most incredible moments of football drama any of us could remember witnessing, scenes that only people in the upper Amazon had yet to see images of.

But even in those moments of triumph, there had been doubt. How was it possible that the title could only be won with the miracle of two goals in injury time in the final game of the season? Surely it should have been simpler than that? How was it possible to look so underwhelming in continental combat? How could his final summer in blue render such a strange batch of hotchpotch footballers, when the only way to really improve on a title-winning side was to buy the very best on offer? There were almost as many questions as there were people wearing puzzled expressions.

What most surely could not be denied was the fact that this one man and his staff had brought City supporters the very best years most could remember. Only the so-called legacy fans could recall anything remotely similar to this glory. The club did for genial Joe Mercer then too, so this was not a new disease. Big Mal, Peter Reid, Brian Horton, Ron Saunders and others had all felt the cold steel on the back of the neck at the infamous *moment most inopportune.*

At a club like City, where the scaffolding of empire building continued to go up at some haste, the potent whiff of ambition was never far from the end of the nose. Some would say the scaffolding erected to hang Mancini had gone up with equally ill-judged haste.

With United and Chelsea starting the following season with new managers, City might have jumped the queue and opened up an advantage with a steady hand at the tiller. Was Mancini ever that, though?

Instead, they chose to go down the same perilous route of change as their rivals.

ENGINEERING IN PROCESS

Dream attack

Manuel Pellegrini arrived in Manchester as the Engineer and left as a shadow of his former self. In between he was thoroughly fêted as This Charming Man.

That alone suggests that the three-year reign of the then 59-year-old Chilean may have been something of a mixed bag. In many ways, it was a success. In a European sense, he would carry City to the very brink in the Champions League, breaking new frontiers for the club, but – much like Roberto Mancini before him – there would ultimately be an aftertaste of failure and missed opportunities at the parting of ways.

Having been responsible for two miraculous feats with Villarreal and Málaga, Pellegrini was deemed just the swashbuckling type to take City to the next level. Both Villarreal, in their semi-final with Arsenal in 2005–6 (a period when the height of City's continental involvement was a warm-weather Thomas Cook Trophy outing against Olympiakos), and Málaga, in their quarter-final with Borussia Dortmund in 2012–13, had reached unprecedented heights of European drama and achievement. Could he bestow the same effect upon the disjointed City side he had inherited?

Unlike his predecessor, Pellegrini had followed an understated one-club, thirteen-year playing career in the back four of Club Universidad de Chile. After completing an engineering degree, a mazy route through the Spanish-speaking football world led him to east Manchester. Speaking grandly of a 'responsibility to the aesthetic', his first moves did not necessarily rubber-stamp this line of thought, bringing in the eccentric wing skills of Sevilla's Jesús Navas (a player widely reported to suffer from homesickness as well as having more speed than direction) and the solid but apparently unspectacular midfield foraging of Shakhtar's Brazilian anchor Fernandinho.

With his assistants Ruben Cousillas and Xabier Mancisidor, Pellegrini had been responsible for eye-catching upturns in the careers of creative talents such as Juan Román Riquelme, Isco and Santi Cazorla, however, and hopes were high that certain elements of a bulging playing squad that had fallen dormant under Mancini could be reinvigorated.

The immediate targets for his tenure were clearly bookmarked: continuing growth domestically and a termination of the European dilly-dallying that had become a feature of City's modern efforts. At the very least, the new man was charged with hoisting City out of the group stages of the Champions League, as he had done so spectacularly with his previous two clubs.

Talk in Abu Dhabi was of a *five-trophies-in-five-years objective*.

The departure of Carlos Tevez to Juventus meant that discipline in the squad might also be tightened somewhat. To make up for the hole in the attack left by the Argentinian, Pellegrini summoned another Sevilla player, burly striker Álvaro Negredo alongside Fiorentina's enigmatic Stevan Jovetić.

By the time the squad flew on invitation to Abu Dhabi the following May to play a friendly with Al Ain, there could be few complaints about the Chilean's first season in charge. With a League Cup triumph over Sunderland and another Premier

League title to celebrate, it had been a roaring success. He was even up on his paymasters' supposedly ambitious *five-in-five* target. The smile on the watching Sheikh Mansour's face reflected work well done at home, but the story in Europe had been of altogether subtler gains.

Avoiding death

In the summer of 2013, there had been intriguing movement to the managerial merry-go-round, with Everton's David Moyes inheriting Alex Ferguson's hottest of hot seats at Old Trafford and José Mourinho returning to Stamford Bridge for a second swipe at things. Not since 1974, when Don Revie swapped Leeds for the England job, with Brian Clough replacing him, and Bill Shankly resigned at Liverpool, had there been so much managerial movement among the elite.

In deepest Bavaria, meanwhile, Bayern Munich had perhaps landed the biggest fish of all, as Pep Guardiola jetted in from his year-long sabbatical in New York to take charge of the self-proclaimed FC Hollywood.

Drawn in Group D, City for once could have little to complain about. If Bayern were old foes from 2011–12, the presence of CSKA Moscow and Viktoria Plzeň gave real hope of advance. Arsène Wenger, embarking on his eighteenth season in charge at Arsenal, could hardly say the same. In a group with beaten finalists Borussia Dortmund, Olympique Marseille and Napoli, Arsenal would be hard pressed to survive. For Celtic, bunched with AC Milan, Barcelona and Ajax, things also looked bleak. For City's third participation in the Champions League, at least they had not fallen into a group of death.

First up for City was a trip to the Czech Republic. Having won two of the previous three Czech titles, Pavel Vrba's Viktoria Plzeň were showing promising signs of staying power. Boasting a side full of internationals, they were expected to give City a tough start. A tough start was exactly what had been endured in the league, as the opening-day thrashing of Newcastle (4–0) had been followed by clumsy defeat at newly promoted Cardiff. Injuries to Nastasić and Kompany had also required Pellegrini to return to Málaga to buy stop-gap central defender Martín Demichelis to fill in. After a nervy first half in the radically down-sized Doosan Arena (reconstruction in 2011 had reduced capacity from 35,000 to 11,500), City had the game wrapped up within twelve exhilarating minutes of the start of the second period.

A tactical tweak by the Chilean would pay rich dividends on the evening and offer a pointer for the rest of the season. Anchoring Fernandinho as a shield in front of the back four, Pellegrini offered Yaya Touré licence to roam. Touré dominated proceedings from start to finish. It would be the beginning of a phase in his City career where the big man proved almost completely unstoppable, a battering ram through the middle that combined brute force with balletic foot movement and a shot that remained struck until it found a net, an advertising board or a spectator to halt its trajectory.

It was Edin Džeko who broke the deadlock, side-footing home after Agüero had wriggled free from boisterous marking on the left on 48 minutes. Thereafter, Touré took things into his own hands, curling in spectacularly from 25 yards after a quick interchange with Nasri. Agüero's clever swivel and left-foot shot from the edge of the box made it three and the curtain could come down on a comfortable start to the European campaign.

Playing in a smart new away kit of white shirts with a verti-cal side panel of dark blue and sky blue, City had once again looked like continental *fashionistas*. A growing belief that this time a squad had been assembled that would not just look the part but could cope with the vagaries of football at the high-est level would be tested to the limit in the next game, against Guardiola's Bayern at the Etihad, but, for now, it was job done.

Vrba's fondness for attack had left City with vast areas to exploit through the middle of the park, leaving them with eighteen goal attempts by the end of a comfortably handled first hurdle.

For those that had made the trip, there had been benefits beyond seeing such a clear-cut victory. Travelling fan Mike Hammond summed it up succinctly: 'Forty-five pence a pint and one of the best trips and greatest away ends of all the trips we've done.'

Pellegrini revealed a swift understanding of stock press-conference responses, stating: 'It will give confidence to all the players. We also have the derby next Sunday so winning away in the Champions League gives you confidence.' In times of greater tension, we would see how the manager's responses changed. Those used to Mancini's fireworks would for the time being have to put up with Pellegrini's platitudes. Daniel Taylor, tracing City's rise for the *Guardian*, could remember few histrionics from the new man, telling me: 'Pellegrini came in on the understanding that he would not supply the theatre that they had had to put up with under Mancini, although there would be one massive blowout that I can remember that required a public apology from him the day after ...'

In these early days of the Chilean's reign, such an occurrence appeared unlikely, but then he was not to know what kind of extravagant ill-fortune awaited his side deeper into the competition.

VIKTORIA PLZEŇ 0–3 MANCHESTER CITY | Att. 11,281 | Džeko, Touré, Agüero

Hart, Zabaleta, Kolarov, Kompany, Nastasić, Fernandinho, Nasri, Touré (García), Navas (Milner), Agüero, Džeko (Negredo)

Another principal actor in the City drama at this time was not to know what the repercussions of the home game with Bayern would have on his own career. Football is often an intricate jig-saw of chance happenings and little threads of coincidence, and Joe Hart was about to be caught out by one of them.

City were comprehensively beaten in their second group game by the five-time winners and defending champions. The 1–3 scoreline did not fully do justice to just how superior Bayern were on this occasion.

Right in the spotlight when the blame game began at full time was a crestfallen Hart. Having failed to stop an early potshot from Franck Ribéry, he was also slow to cover Arjen Robben's shot, which beat him by the near post for the third. The opposition manager, watching intently from the touchline, would sweep into the Etihad three years later and discard Hart as one of his first grand acts on becoming manager. Hart's career would go into nosedive from there and has never properly recovered.

Mancini had also been growing impatient with Hart towards the end of his third season, and Pellegrini's tenure at City had begun with his first-choice keeper being blamed for Andreas Weimann's winner for Aston Villa the weekend before the trip to Germany. Looking at a loss for one of the goals in the leaky defeat at Cardiff and letting a shot from James Morrison go straight through him in the early season England–Scotland international were also on Hart's lengthening charge sheet. Being the arch planner that he is, there was only a tiny chance that Guardiola was not already in possession of these details before his Bayern side strutted onto the Etihad turf to confront City.

Hart's diminishing profile in the eyes of those who were being paid good money to pick him or not mirrored the issues of City's earliest days in Europe, when Malcolm Allison had been forced to juggle the skill sets of Ken Mulhearn, Joe Corrigan and Ron Healey, with the former being notoriously ambivalent to his manager's tactical teach-ins, the affable Corrigan fighting weight problems and Healey never recovering from the enormous error that gifted Chelsea a place in the 1971 Cup Winners' Cup final.

Bayern's performance was an eye-opener from start to finish. Insisting that the transition from Jupp Heynckes to Guardiola would merely involve 'changes in detail', director of sport Matthias Sammer had underestimated the Catalan's meticulous approach to the game. With a new formation, an energetic pressing game and metronomic passing, Bayern were operating on another level. Pitching long-term right-back Philipp Lahm into midfield and winger Franck Ribéry as a false nine offered glimpses of the positional experiments that would take place when Guardiola took up the reigns at the Etihad. As the fastidious Catalan stated: 'You can win with the wrong strikers, but you can't play well without midfielders.'

Grilled on the tactical innovations that had seen City flatten Plzeň, then be completely undressed by Bayern, Pellegrini insisted: 'These things evolve, like a vaccination. After a disease, the antidotes follow.' This was three years before Guardiola's killer tactical planning would interfere with City again and seven before Covid-19 would shut down football all over the world.

Another element that the Chilean was unlikely to have been aware of at this early stage was a body of thought in the football press that was beginning to question the means City had used to make an assault on the higher echelons in the game. In a piece entitled 'Philosophy versus Money' in *World Soccer* magazine, Jonathan Wilson compared Guardiola's organic Bayern side, containing five home-grown players, with Pellegrini's £228m *construction*. 'Most teams, of course, fall between the two extremes,' argued Wilson, 'but it could be said that since systemised football took hold in the early 1970s, all the truly great sides – the Ajax of Rinus Michels, the Bayern of Udo Lattek, the Liverpool of Bob Paisley, the Milan of Arrigo Sacchi, the

Barcelona of Pep Guardiola – were based on a philosophy rather than enormous signings.'

Guardiola's philosophy would not always be coated with the same reverential tones when the Catalan applied it lock, stock and barrel to City, however.

MANCHESTER CITY 1–3 BAYERN MUNICH | Att. 45,021 | Negredo
Hart, Richards, Clichy, Kompany, Nastasić, Fernandinho, Touré, Nasri (Milner), Navas, Agüero (Silva), Džeko (Negredo)

The Bayern defeat also heaped pressure on the next two fixtures, home and away against CSKA Moscow. The Russians had beaten Plzeň 3–2 with Zoran Tošić and Keisuke Honda in scintillating form.

Despite being champions for the eleventh time in Russia, CSKA were a pale shadow of the Red Army side of earlier generations and came into this game in a state of crisis, having lost five of their previous seven matches, slipping to sixth in the league. Managed by the enigmatic Leonid Slutsky, whose playing career had come to an abrupt end after he fell from a tree trying to rescue a cat, they played a solid 4–2–3–1 with the emphasis on a well-drilled defence, featuring the combined age (92 years and counting) and experience of the Berezutski twins and Sergei Ignashevich, as well as Russia's best goalkeeper since Lev Yashin, Igor Akinfeev.

On top of that was the problem with their stadium. The Plzeň game had been played in Saint Petersburg owing to issues with their ground. The vast Luzhniki Stadium was in the throes of a major makeover in preparation for the 2018 World Cup and City would be hosted in the Arena Khimki, a compact new-build on the outskirts of the capital.

'I'm so gutted, it's difficult for me to find the words,' spluttered Slutsky at the end of a hard-fought match with City. With a rutted pitch that had been painted green to pass muster, the Russian's opposite number could have been forgiven for having to search for appropriate words too. In trying conditions, City had produced a gutsy performance to resurrect their hopes. If the pitch had received artificial colouration, there was no painting over the racist chanting that was directed towards Yaya Touré, however.

'I am very happy,' said Pellegrini, unaware of the commotion. 'The whole team concentrated with intensity on a difficult pitch.'

Ahead through Tošić's lob, CSKA were reined in immediately by Agüero's equaliser as he edged in front of the lumbering Sergei Ignashevich to convert Silva's pass. By half-time the comeback was complete, Agüero bravely getting his head to Negredo's delightfully flighted centre before the flying feet of Akinfeev.

Despite a host of other chances, City had Hart to thank for the win, with a flying block from Honda in time added on, which reduced Slutsky to a prone position on the CSKA bench. With six points and second place in the group, a first-ever qualification for the knockout stages was beginning to wink at City from behind the ex-iron curtains.

For the travelling fans, it had been a hazardous but worthwhile trip. Pat Rose, part of a group of comrades who would cover the best part of 4,500 miles following City that October alone, remembers leaving with anticipation and trepidation: 'Would our visas be accepted? Would we navigate our way round a city in which English seems to be an unused substitute? In the end, nothing disappointed us. Moscow was marvellous and the match was entertaining. The spectacle of Red Square, the Kremlin and St Basil's Cathedral by night surpassed the home fans' attempts at a light show, although I could find no City fans prepared to match their state of semi-undress in freezing conditions during the second half. Of course, the best bits were Agüero scoring two excellent goals.'

Mike Hammond also had good reason to remember the trip: 'I had promised myself if we ever got into Europe, I'd be there. Looking back, this was an easy promise to make, like saying I'd leave my wife if Michelle Pfeiffer ever turned up in my local. Anyway, we had made it to Moscow. Brilliant place. Our hotel was built on the outskirts in preparation for the 1980 Olympic Games. Sitting on a Metro line, it was only five stops from Red Square so easy to get about. That first night, however, was spent in and around the bars, restaurants and shops of the hotel, and I won't lie to you, it was a shambles. "Fancy another refreshing shot of ice-cold vodka, Mike?" "No thanks, Neil, I'm fucked." "Don't forget we're three hours ahead – it's only 2am at home!" ... This was the night we nearly stole a coach ...'

CSKA MOSCOW 1–2 MANCHESTER CITY | Att. 14,000 | Agüero (2)

Hart, Zabaleta, Nastasić, Kolarov, Fernandinho, García, Touré, Navas, Silva (Nasri), Negredo (Džeko), Agüero (Clichy)

If Moscow had been a struggle, the return was a breeze, with City 3–1 up at the break and 5–2 ahead by the end. After the trauma of Mancini's failures in the competition, Pellegrini had steered City out of the group with two games to spare.

One ahead after three minutes, when Silva was upended in the box by Tošić and Agüero netted the penalty, the win was sealed after twenty minutes when Agüero's flick, turn and acceleration made Alexei Berezutski look like he was playing in plaster casts. The finish was unerring. Agüero turned provider for the third, with a low cross that dissected the defence, leaving Negredo with a simple tap-in.

A growing theme of City's rise was highlighted by CSKA's response just before the break. If the attack was a wrecking ball, the defence sometimes looked like it was chained to the floor. Pontus Wernbloom made fortuitous progress past Fernandinho and fed Seydou Doumbia, who rounded European debutant Costel Pantilimon to score. The central axis of new man Demichelis and the raw Nastasić seemed brittle, a theme that would be returned to on many occasions in the future.

The three-goal cushion was restored in the 50th minute, when Touré's outrageous chip left the entire Moscow backline staring at each other and Nasri with the simple task of feeding the loitering Negredo. Doumbia's neat penalty made it 4–2 after Clichy had brought the Ivorian down in the box, but there was plenty of time for Negredo to complete a first hat-trick for the club with a simple header from Milner's deep cross.

Both Negredo and Agüero had scored in the previous weekend's 7–0 rout of Norwich, as Pellegrini's avowed commitment to the aesthetic began to produce the kind of attacking avalanche not seen since Kevin Keegan's best days. If CSKA had proved something of a disappointment, the win – however easy – was welcome, City's first at home in the competition since beating Bayern in 2011, as was the confirmation that Plzeň's home loss to the Germans had sealed qualification.

MANCHESTER CITY 5–2 CSKA MOSCOW | Att. 38,512 | Agüero (2, 1 pen.), Negredo (3)

Pantilimon, Zabaleta, Clichy, Demichelis, Nastasić, Fernandinho (Milner), Nasri (Navas), Touré, Silva (Kolarov), Agüero, Negredo

If a 7–0 win over Norwich had served as a useful warm-up for CSKA, so a 6–0 trouncing of Tottenham had the same effect before Plzeň's visit. This time the supporters had to make do with a 4–2 win, as the goals began to fly in from all angles.

Cort McMurray, a City fan from Texas, had made the game his first-ever trip to the Etihad: 'In July 2010, in the swelter of an Atlanta summer, my son Noah and I made our first sighting of fellow Manchester City fans. City were playing Mexico's Club

America in an exhibition match. A couple of hours before the match, we ran into a group of guys in City gear. They were from Manchester, sweating their way through City's tour of America. One of them, a gregarious railway engineer named Paul, asked for my email address. Over the years, we exchanged messages. It's been a cordial, but casual acquaintanceship. When our family was planning a trip to England, I contacted Paul and asked him for help in securing tickets to the Etihad. His response was immediate: "Leave it to me, mate. We'll get you sorted." He asked that Noah and I send him a photo of the two of us, wearing City shirts. This seemed reasonable: he hadn't seen us for more than five minutes, and that was three years earlier. The City shirt request seemed a little odd, but we complied.

'At every turn, people we barely knew treated us like long-lost relatives and reminded us that as City supporters, Manchester was our home. This wasn't a stretch for me: Manchester, great and grey and rainy, reminds me of Buffalo, New York, the ageing industrial city where I grew up. It felt familiar. It felt like home.

'Paul didn't give us much time to soak in the atmosphere. "Come on. There's something you need to see." He led us into the souvenir shop, where we met a man who looked official. "These here are all the way from Texas," Paul told the man, who shook our hands and handed us a couple of programmes. An envelope poked from the pages of one. "Welcome to Manchester," the man said, and disappeared back into his office. Paul was grinning. "Take a look on page 52." There was the photo Paul had requested, Noah and I posed in our City best, with a caption welcoming us to the Etihad. "Now look in the envelope." Our tickets had been upgraded to VIP "Platinum Box" status.'

Goals from Agüero, Nasri, Negredo and Džeko completed an unforgettable night for the McMurrays and continued City's rich vein of form. 'There are not many times when you're able to give one of your kids a truly unforgettable experience. Thanks to Paul, and the people at City, I had that privilege,' concluded Cort, as he left for the airport.

For many, the new stadium, lacking some of the intimacy and charm of Maine Road, would never quite be the same, but nobody could suggest that the warmth of the Manchester welcome had changed down the years.

MANCHESTER CITY 4–2 VIKTORIA PLZEŇ | Att. 37,742 | Agüero (pen.), Nasri, Negredo, Džeko

Hart, Richards, Kolarov, Demichelis, Lescott, García, Fernandinho (Touré), Nasri (Negredo), Milner, Džeko, Agüero (Navas)

In a season jam-packed with goals, City finished off the group games with a fabulous win at the Allianz Arena and followed that by beating Premier League leaders Arsenal 6–3 at the Etihad. If goals could guarantee prizes, City were on their way, but the feeling remained that somewhere along the line a really top opponent might take advantage of City's creaky backline.

That opponent might have been Bayern, had they not inexplicably taken their foot off the gas in the last game of Group D. Leading 2–0 and coasting, Bayern were caught out by a City side riding the crest of a goals avalanche and sank 3–2 with the ossified figure of Dante to blame. For a first six months of work, Pellegrini was pushing the envelope.

Two down after just twelve minutes in Munich, the Chilean could have been forgiven for taking players off to save legs, but instead he was forced into a change of right-backs when Richards pulled up injured and Zabaleta deputised. Boosted by the Argentinian's will to win, City suddenly attacked Bayern with an exuberance that stunned the European aristocrats. Silva reduced the deficit before half-time with a close-range finish to Milner's header into the box. He was also the instigator for the equaliser, putting Milner clear in the area only for dainty Dante to wipe him out. Kolarov stroked away the penalty. With Milner curling an exquisite third, City were now incredibly one goal from topping the group. However, this was the point at which the new coach produced the first decision that could have provoked doubts about his management of the very biggest games. It was a doubt that would resurface with a vengeance in his third and final season at the club, when it mattered most.

It would have been uncharitable in the extreme to criticise at this point of a goal-strewn season, but, with his side chasing a fourth and streaming all over Bayern's dithering defenders, Pellegrini brought on Jack Rodwell instead of the goal-hungry Agüero. Topping the group would have meant City drawing a second-placed side in the round of sixteen, which included Roberto Mancini's Galatasaray, Bayer Leverkusen, Schalke, Olympiakos, Milan or Zenit.

Instead, City finished second by the difference of one goal. Their goals tally of eighteen was only beaten by Real Madrid. All that muscle flexing suddenly seemed a little premature, though, as the Blues came out of the bag with Barcelona for the knockout round.

BAYERN MUNICH 2–3 MANCHESTER CITY | Att. 68,000 | Silva, Kolarov (pen.), Milner

Hart, Richards (Zabaleta), Kolarov, Demichelis, Lescott, Fernandinho, García, Navas, Milner, Silva (Negredo), Džeko (Rodwell)

For the purposes of contrast, two statistics suffice. This would be City's tenth game in Europe against Spanish opposition. Barcelona had played 60 games alone against English sides, scoring 98 goals.

If Pellegrini had seemingly failed his first test of courage with the Rodwell substitution in Munich, he had passed every other exam with flying colours. Blessed with the firepower of Agüero,

Jovetić, Džeko and Negredo up front, he had experimented with various permutations before revealing his hand. By pairing the Argentinian with the beefy Spaniard, he had hit the jackpot. Goals were flying in from both players at a rate of knots, but luck and misjudgement was about to rear its head again.

Having beaten West Ham 6–0 in the first leg of the League Cup semi-final, the Chilean made his second catastrophic error of the winter. Making sweeping changes for the second leg, the manager inexplicably picked Agüero and Negredo to start in attack for a game that palpably had no need for them. Agüero, recovering from a knock, survived, Negredo, in the form of his life, did not, scoring two then injuring his shoulder. Although he came back relatively quickly from the injury, something had shifted. His 23 goals for City in 2013–14 were scored in their entirety up to the West Ham second leg. City would end the season with two trophies and a lot of smiling faces, but Negredo's contribution would shrink remarkably.

For City, a match with Barcelona resonated in many ways. As well as testing themselves against the elite, the club was trying its utmost to catch up with them off the field too. It was to many an impossible task and one that would end with the club in court trying to shake off UEFA's punishments for apparently trying slightly *too hard*. City's commercial streams were beginning to ignite a swift closing of the gap. While the swashbuckling football was attracting plenty of plaudits, their new-found place among Deloitte's rich list was drawing a different kind of interest.

Pellegrini, gearing his side up for their game of the season, said: 'We are aiming to keep growing by winning many trophies. We are fighting for four titles this year. We have to be patient because we cannot change the team from one day to another. We have to keep the philosophy of the style and for that you need time.' Time had certainly allowed City's opponents to develop a *philosophy of style*. In Ferran Soriano and Txiki Begiristain, City now had the men to bring something similar to Manchester, at least off the pitch. On it, they would have to wait for Guardiola's authentic touch, but, in waiting, they had the intent to deliver that embodied Pellegrini's thought processes. Building a 'common football philosophy that links the youngest academy boy to the most senior first-team player' may have sounded like a cut and paste from the Barcelona manual, but City's own Manuel had a few ideas of his own. 'To be an attacking team is to know how to defend well,' he had said, but it wasn't clear if anyone was listening, let alone Martín Demichelis.

Barcelona also had another string to their bow, which was still out of City's reach and, despite a fly-past in the summer of 2020, would remain so: Lionel Messi.

As Daniel Taylor put it: 'How to stop Messi? Just hope he has a bad game …'

Barcelona manager, Gerardo Martino, was so fulsome with his praise, describing City as 'one of the greatest teams in the world', he might have been auditioning to replace Pellegrini, had he not already been in possession of the club game's number-one hot seat.

Although the two sides had totalled 34 goals between them in the group stages, recent history suggested the scoring on this occasion might be mainly by Barcelona. With two group-stage finishes to boast against Barcelona's five-year record of winner/semi/winner/semi/semi, City were massively up against it.

Demichelis, choosing to ignore his manager's mantra about how to attack through defending, slid through the back of Messi shortly after half-time to give Barcelona a penalty and get himself sent off all in one fell swoop. What Sam Wallace in the *Independent* had called a 'temptation to panic' had wrapped itself around the Argentinian, and the result was deadly. It would not be the last opportunity the Spanish press pack would have to call City's centre-back *'lento'* ('slow'). In this case it had been *lento* of mind and *lento* of body, although it had to be noted that his partnership with Kompany had looked solid enough up to this point. Initial contact may have even been outside the area, but referee Jonas Eriksson was keen to get things done and pointed to the spot instead. Pellegrini, doing a passable impression of predecessor Mancini's windmill arms and revolving eyes, already possessed his full-time conversation topic with Eriksson.

What the Chilean would produce to the press afterwards would necessitate a public apology. The Engineer had for the first time a serious spanner in his works.

From being on the rack as Barcelona closed in for the kill, City rallied valiantly late on, with Silva and Džeko going close, before Dani Alves broke in the 90th minute, exchanged passes with the elegant Neymar and finished between Hart's legs. It all seemed a little cruel, a little harsh, but to match Barcelona you have to be perfect, and City had not been that.

Pellegrini later spoke of Eriksson having to 'remedy a mistake he made against Barcelona in a quarter-final match with AC Milan two years earlier', at once revealing a mightily impressive grasp of football history and an outlandish attachment to conspiracy theory. Nobody had seen the Chilean this angry and animated before. The match had at least delivered us the knowledge that, underneath the placid exterior, deep, fast-flowing rivers ran.

MANCHESTER CITY 0–2 BARCELONA | Att. 46,030
Hart, Zabaleta, Clichy, Kompany, Demichelis, Fernandinho, Touré, Kolarov (Lescott), Silva, Negredo (Džeko), Navas (Nasri)

In preparation for what most saw as a tough challenge in the second leg, City landed the League Cup for the first time in 38 years, defeating Sunderland 3–1, with the two goals that turned the game around, from Touré and Nasri, that had to rank as the best quick-fire pair of cup-final goals ever witnessed.

Aqui se sufre mucho

With silverware on the shelf, Pellegrini and his staff could relax slightly. Ruffled and dishevelled from the first-leg 'injustices', the squad had had ample time to contemplate the next step. It was quite simple: win 3–0 in the Camp Nou.

Thronging the tree-lined precincts of Las Ramblas and Plaza Real with its Gothic arches and extravagant Gaudi lamp posts, fans clustered in expectant groups to drink in the sights. An Estrella Damm truck trundled gently up the middle of the square in case of emergencies.

Having draped little corners of this red-and-yellow-striped city with the sky-blue favours, preparation could begin for the inevitable disappointment. A pasting or a hard luck story? The voices expressing certainty of the three-goal win required were few and far between and those that whispered the magic score-line slurred it.

Outside the giant cliff face of the Camp Nou, quite a scene met the eye as 86,000 flocked in. The ticket that had been in and out of my pocket all day, just to make sure it hadn't melted, stated: '*General 3 Graderia, Acces 19, Boca 533, Fila 0027, sient 0016.*' Happily, the ticket also stated: 'Only for the visiting supporters.' Just how special Barcelona find their visitors would be revealed once we had climbed to the top of the mountain.

The Travessa de les Corts, once jam-packed with taxis, toot-ing cars and impatient pedestrians, by now lay miles below us, its traffic thinning, its population emptying into the big building with the tall sides. The last flight of stairs at the Nou Camp was an onerous task. Stewards shouting: 'Go! *Vale! Vale!*' encouraged one last effort to reach a section clearly already full. This cus-tom would be repeated in Seville and Madrid. All those little numbers printed carefully onto the tickets suddenly meant nothing at all. It was a little like boarding the late Ryanair flight from Magaluf, but with 5,500 other happy souls who have been at the trolley service all day. The treatment seemed to suggest employees of the club thought City's support had arrived on a direct flight from 1983.

Possessing only Catalan, Spanish and a rudimentary ability to wave his arms, a steward exhorted late arrivals to keep going. Facing the heavens, just under the clouds, there were no allocated seats. My *Boca 533* was correct enough, but the rest was as rooted in reality as referee Stéphane Lannoy's grasp of a good tackle. People were just being waved forward and upwards into already packed stands. Bewildered, frightened and in a hurry, the gangways were filling with fans too.

Heated words ensued between folk who knew no Spanish and bibbed representatives of Barcelona who knew no English.

At the top there was another issue. We would be the only fans in this vast place to be afforded the same view of the pitch as you would have watching migrating wildebeest from a helicopter through a thick camouflage tent. The *Daily Mail*'s Martin Samuel had noted other areas of discomfort visited upon the opposing fans: 'Barcelona officials invited the media to view plans for the redevelopment of the Nou Camp. The work will see a roof placed on the old stadium, something that will come too late for the 5,000 City fans shivering high up in the fourth tier.'

The teams entered to a mass of plastic red-and-yellow flags. The Barcelona anthem struck up. It would be days before the dry little military ditty exited my head. As the sides lined up, the first swell of 'Blue Moon' heaved out over the night sky. So high up, the noise doesn't usually register on TV, but the tightly packed City Curva was in tremendous voice. The home fans would manage two more flag-waving bursts after each goal and the occasional roll of tickled applause. The lack of passion was striking. To clubs like Barcelona, one Champions League game is much like another.

The next day, reasons for this soft-boiled atmosphere were revealed. The little red-and-yellow flags were everywhere. In the old town, at the cathedral, on Las Ramblas, at Plaça de Catalunya, each one neatly rolled up and poking from the back of a foreign tourist's rucksack.

Pellegrini, sitting up in the gods for talking too much, looked down on the embattled Gerardo Martino, prowling the touchline, as the home side swarmed forward with their short passes, grinding City into making mistakes in dangerous areas of the pitch.

In an increasingly dogged display, City had begun to win corners and keep possession against the owners of the ball. But Zabaleta's red card and Messi's famous little feint and dink routine from the penalty spot opened up the game. An 89th-minute equaliser dug out by Kompany provoked an immediate response: Dani Alves skipping in for 2–1. The following day, the Catalan press, who had murdered them all week, flushed up with hyperbole for Barcelona. Headlines exclaimed *'dios'* and *'pasión'*. We had seen great players play well, but little passion to go with it. A place swollen on history and self-importance, pumped by thousands of tourists, does not easily make for *pasión*. It is a process under way at the Etihad too. This is the cult of the super clubs.

BARCELONA 2–1 MANCHESTER CITY | Att. 85,957 | Kompany
Hart, Zabaleta, Kolarov, Kompany, Lescott, Fernandinho, Milner, Touré, Silva (Negredo), Nasri (Navas), Agüero (Džeko)

'One mistake is all it takes,' exclaimed Martin Samuel in the following morning's *Daily Mail*. 'Joleon Lescott got the ball tangled in his feet and the rest is history. As were Manchester City.'

History will also confirm that City recovered their nerve admirably to capture a second Premier League trophy in three years that season. Pellegrini's first season had delivered two of the five trophies the five-in-five plan demanded of him, but the club's European pedigree still needed looking at.

The summer brought City's first serious brush with UEFA's Financial Fair Play (FFP) regulations. Breaches by the club, regarding a £150 million accumulated transfer loss over the previous two years, invited a £49 million spending curb and a Champions League squad reduced from 25 to 21, bringing an immediate disadvantage for the 2014–15 campaign.

As if this was not bad enough, the coach embarked on a summer spending spree that smacked of Robert Mancini's own *badly spent summer*. The new alumni were to be Arsenal's Bacary Sagna, Chelsea icon Frank Lampard, Willy Caballero, plus Porto pair Fernando and Eliaquim Mangala.

Familiar faces

An uninspired transfer window was swiftly followed by an uninspiring Champions League draw, where City landed in a Group E that contained two of their opponents from the previous year, Bayern and CSKA Moscow. It would be the third time City had been paired with the Bavarians in their four-year history in the revamped tournament. If familiarity breeds contempt …

Italian runners-up Roma made up the foursome, giving City the look of second favourites in a close contest. If City-watchers thought the FFP issues were an ill omen, the match in Russia would, by reason of some creative rule-changing by UEFA, be a catalyst for the booing that still resonates around the Etihad to this day. After a season of glory, Pellegrini was about to see the other side of Manchester City.

Beginning away in Munich would get the worst out of the way quickly. City's season had started in erratic form, losing heavily to Arsenal at Wembley in the Community Shield and dreadfully at home to Mark Hughes' Stoke in the league. Convincing wins over Newcastle and Liverpool helped steady the hysteria, but City appeared ill-prepared for Bayern at this stage.

The reality, as is often the case, proved different. With a fragile-looking back four, City held their own for long periods, despite having Hart to thank for an imperious display which rivalled his efforts against Dortmund two years earlier. Hit by a late surge from the home side, the keeper saved a long-range stinger from ex-City right-back Boateng but was finally beaten by the same man in the final minute of the game. It was a tough pill to swallow.

It was the first time City had lost three consecutive games in Europe and, with Roma opening their campaign by beating CSKA 5–1, their place as second favourites was already under scrutiny. Keeping only three clean sheets in 21 Champions League games suggested the problems at the back were persisting, while the normally pivotal Yaya Touré's anonymity in the middle was a cause for concern. While Pellegrini had plenty to chew on, home boss Guardiola also looked to be struggling to galvanise the squad he had inherited from Jupp Heynckes. With rumours persisting that the Catalan was the ultimate target for City's ex-Barcelona head-hunters, it was interesting to note how much his side relied on grit, determination and a deflected shot in the last minute to get them over the line on this occasion.

With City's hierarchy eyeing him up, Guardiola had taken the opportunity to give City the once-over too. 'They are one of five or six sides that can win it this season,' he insisted to the press conference, maintaining an admirably straight face.

BAYERN MUNICH 1–0 MANCHESTER CITY | Att. 68,000
Hart, Sagna, Clichy, Demichelis, Kompany, Fernandinho, Touré, Silva, Nasri (Milner), Navas (Kolarov), Džeko (Agüero)

Meanwhile, the current incumbent was clearly doing a good job, despite a rocky start to the season. That September, I was asked by *Champions* magazine to track what had changed from the early days of the City empire. There seemed to be at least five clear categories where progress had been made through Pellegrini's change of tack:

1. *By keeping quiet.* Although he had been forced to watch the Bayern game from the stands, as part of his punishment for his referee outburst from the Barcelona defeat, Pellegrini's watchword on this subject would probably have been similar to that of journalist Sir Walter Bagehot, whose maxim was: 'An inability to stay quiet is one of the conspicuous failings of mankind.' Eschewing controversy meant his 'Charming Man' moniker continued to sit comfortably.

2. *By developing players.* The Chilean's approach had reinvigorated many members of the playing squad, notably the left-backs Clichy and Kolarov, wide midfielder Nasri and Džeko up front.

3. *By playing attacking football.* The title-winning season had been so laden with goals, opponents often did not know how to react. Mancini's more cautious, measured approach had been ditched for the cavalier style seen at Villarreal and Málaga.

4. *By man management.* Not only managing the egos but managing the numbers. The squad seemed more harmonious and more compact, shorn of Bellamy, Tevez, Balotelli and other awkward egos.

5. *By achieving his targets.* Having been set what many viewed as an over-ambitious target, the Chilean was already ahead of schedule after twelve short months.

Ahead after just four minutes in the home game with Roma, it seemed that City were trying to make up for lost time, but by the interval, Francesco Totti had equalised with a deft waft of his right foot and City were beginning one of their Champions League feuds with the Dutch referee Björn Kuipers. Totti's delicate finish made the inspirational playmaker the competition's oldest goalscorer at 38 years and 59 days. City's early penalty had also brought back reminiscences of ancient warriors of their own, as ex-right-back Maicon had pulled Agüero back in the incident. The Brazilian would later rattle Hart's bar with a degree of power not witnessed during his short stint in Manchester under Mancini.

A clutch of second-half substitutes, including Frank Lampard's first European appearance for the club, failed to change either the balance of the game or the score.

The ebb and flow smacked a little of City's entrance into the competition against Napoli, with a dangerous, well-balanced Italian side that seemed able to find all the necessary spaces on the counter. As in 2011–12, it looked like it would boil down to what City could do in Italy in the return game, providing of course they could deal with CSKA in the same manner they had done twelve months earlier.

By the time the trip to Moscow came round, even that had been thrown into doubt by a brouhaha that would cement the already frosty relationship between club and governing body.

MANCHESTER CITY 1–1 AS ROMA | Att. 37,509 | Agüero (pen.)
Hart, Zabaleta, Clichy, Demichelis, Kompany, Fernandinho, Touré, Silva, Navas (Milner), Džeko (Lampard), Agüero (Jovetić)

City warmed up for the trip east well enough, winning at Villa Park and knocking four past Tottenham. UEFA were about to unpack their highest-quality double standards for the occasion, however, and the after-effects would leave a sour taste in the mouth for years to come.

Neil King, a perennial City watcher since the early '70s, was booked up and ready to go to Russia. 'I booked my flights and hotel not long after the draw was made. The visa application form I found easier this time, as it was our second consecutive trip to Russia. On my return from the game in Munich said form was sent off and returned within the week. In the words of one of my friends, "What could possibly go wrong?"'

As it happened, plenty. UEFA had decided to punish CSKA by making them play a game behind closed doors, with the possibility of more sanctions if there were any further problems involving their fans. During City's loss to Munich in the opening group game, *further problems* were precisely what the CSKA fans in Rome decided to visit on the place. Days later (less than two weeks to the fixture with City), UEFA decided the CSKA–City match would also take place behind closed doors.

This produced an unsolvable problem for travelling City fans, Neil King among them: 'Well, nothing UEFA does surprises me, but to make this decision days before I was due to fly out beggared belief. So, OK … this means that UEFA will refund the £700 I have paid out I assume? Er … no, of course not. Although it is UEFA, who have refused me entry to the ground and the reason I have paid out my hard-earned money, arranged holidays from work and generally turned my life upside down, who say they have no responsibility for what now would be a pointless trip. *Merci, Monsieur Platini.* A few days prior to flying out, City sent an email invite to an event at the stadium on the afternoon of the match. Food, drink, entertainment etc. was all paid for and the match would be shown on a big screen. Now, considering this decision to play the game behind closed doors had nothing to do with the club, personally I thought this was a decent gesture. As much as I appreciated their efforts to dissuade me from going to Moscow, not going was not really an option.'

Bayern fans had managed to rent rooms in a tower block overlooking the Khimki Arena and this was the plan of the 40 or so City fans who had made it all the way to Moscow. This was dashed when the local police found out what they intended to do. Instead, bussed to a bar near the derelict Torpedo Stadium, the group watched on television as some 500 CSKA fans entered the closed stadium themselves.

That City had drawn a game they led 2–0 at half-time seemed almost irrelevant. A soft penalty awarded by István Vad on 86 minutes was responsible for producing the second face-like-thunder of Pellegrini's European slog with City. It matched those of the fans watching in Jimmy's Bar by the Moskva River. City had been short-changed on and off the field, and it would not be forgotten.

'I left this wonderful city with a sense of anger and disappointment to the UEFA hierarchy who had deprived me of watching City in Europe through no fault of my own. Their lack of thought and compassion for travelling supporters was quite frankly disgraceful,' said King.

CSKA MOSCOW 2–2 MANCHESTER CITY | Att. 350 | Agüero, Milner

Hart, Zabaleta, Kolarov, Kompany, Mangala, Fernando (Jovetić), Touré, Milner, Silva (Fernandinho), Džeko (Navas), Agüero

---

Despite the biting injustice, it was clear that the performance had been slipshod, that Eliaquim Mangala had looked like an accident waiting to happen at the back and that Yaya Touré's on-and-off form was a continuing source of mystery. The Chilean coach was beginning to realise that early success can act as much as a rod for your own back as a boost for future challenges. With Michel Platini unwilling to listen to the club's complaints regarding Moscow and the campaign to qualify stuttering perilously, CSKA visited Manchester to rub salt in the open wounds with a 2–1 win that virtually killed City's chances of progress. It left Pellegrini's men bottom of the table with two points from four games.

City conceded in the second and 34th minutes, CSKA weathered a storm of attacking and referee Tasos Sidiropoulos dismissed both Fernandinho and Yaya Touré, then ignored a more than viable penalty appeal when Agüero was felled in the box in the last minute. The hapless Greek then caused further uproar with a case of mistaken identity that spared Wernbloom a dismissal himself.

As exercises in bridge-building went, it had failed on every conceivable front.

Touré, absent-mindedly gazing at Doumbia (Demichelis had been equally rooted) as he rose to head the visitors into the lead, fired back six minutes later with a curling free kick. Clichy, scuffing a dreadful clearance straight into the middle of the pitch, set up CSKA's second, slotted in calmly by Doumbia again, notching his fifth goal against City in three games. With the scoring complete, the game had the unusual tag of having only Ivorian goalscorers. Two unnecessary red cards for a blatant block and raised hands on an opponent, respectively, and foul luck in front of goal all went together to make it quite the party package.

It was a year to the day that City had beaten the same opponents 5–2 in the same tournament with practically the same team, and three days since City had won the Manchester derby with verve and swagger. CSKA's first triumph on English soil at their sixth attempt came thanks to a striker who had not even rated his chances of playing. An elated Doumbia remarked: 'I was a bit surprised to be in the squad today, but I thank God everything went well.'

CSKA would be a difficult story to live down and, along with UEFA, CAS (Court of Arbitration for Sport) and TNS, another unforgettable acronym in City's ABC of European (mis)adventure.

MANCHESTER CITY 1–2 CSKA MOSCOW | Att. 45,143 | Touré

Hart, Zabaleta, Clichy, Kompany, Demichelis, Fernando (Džeko), Touré, Milner, Navas (Fernandinho), Jovetić (Nasri), Agüero

If the CSKA result had reduced City's chances to a twitching corpse, after 85 minutes of the penultimate group game at home to Bayern at the end of November, the body had gone cold and the vol-au-vents were being ordered for the service of remembrance. But the capricious beast that is Manchester City jerked into life and saved itself with two more prime examples of why Sergio Agüero was by now considered the most complete Premier League finisher since Alan Shearer. Twice he went through to slide the ball past Manuel Neuer, holding his nerve as all around him in the stadium melted. With CSKA being held in Moscow by Roma, all three teams would go into matchday six with a chance of going through with Bayern.

In truth, City had made an almighty meal of it. Ahead through Agüero's penalty, the awarding of which involved a red card for the perpetrator of the foul, Mehdi Benatia, City were facing 70 minutes against ten men. This being City, by half-time, they were 2–1 down to Xabi Alonso's surgical free kick and Robert Lewandowski's looping header.

And they were still trailing as the game entered the 85th minute. Then three early Christmas presents arrived, first from the normally immaculate Alonso, then ex-City man Boateng, who gave away possession cheaply. Both allowed Agüero to run at Neuer and twice the stocky Argentinian obliged with laser-precision finishing. CSKA's draw with Roma involved a Russian equaliser deep into stoppage time, constituting the third gift of the evening.

Were the Champions League gods beginning to change their minds about City?

City had now beaten Guardiola's Bayern twice in two seasons, on both occasions by 3–2.

'I have had some very good games this season,' admitted City's saviour Agüero. 'This is another one!' His captain Kompany was equally astute in his summary: 'Every team that wants to achieve special things in Europe needs a special player. He is our special player.'

The Stadio Olimpico would be a fitting venue for more special deeds at the eleventh hour.

MANCHESTER CITY 3–2 BAYERN MUNICH | Att. 44,502 | Agüero (3, 1 pen.)

Hart, Sagna (Zabaleta), Clichy, Kompany, Mangala, Fernando, Lampard, Milner (Jovetić), Nasri, Navas, Agüero (Demichelis)

The maths were clear enough. City needed to better CSKA's result in Munich to go through. This meant, dangerously for a club with City's tendencies, that even a score draw might suffice. After failing to qualify with ten points in their first season, it was now feasible for City to go through with six. In the end, it would be with eight points that City prevailed.

Doing things the hard way

'I wanted to play a pass to James Milner,' Samir Nasri explained with deadpan nonchalance after his goal rocketed City through the tightest of squeezes. Instead, the Frenchman had let go of a shot of ripping velocity that crashed past Morgan De Sanctis (another link back to Napoli 2011) off the goalkeeper's nearside post. Milner's decoy run had opened the gap; Nasri's shot had almost opened the net. The short distance to the away fans in the Stadio Olimpico allowed the team and supporters to celebrate together and, when Zabaleta crashed through to side-foot a second, the party could begin on one of City's most critical Champions League performances so far.

Ask any of those fans for a favourite memory and they will

almost certainly concur with supporter Andy McNab, who was busy dancing the fandango up in the stands, that Roma away reached parts that other football games don't always get to. 'We were still novices and the scribes were already in paradise as they had already written their match reports on our defeat. We had no Kompany, no Yaya, no Sergio and no fucking hope, and we hadn't even left Manchester airport ... The weather was a bit Manchester, the food was, to nobody's surprise, a bit Roman. The lads I go everywhere with following City were all in great spirits, mainly because we go in hope not expectation. We go because, well, you just do. It's four days with your mates talking football ... At the Stadio Olimpico things were very well organised. A cop each it seemed, armed with shields and large batons. Genuinely impressed with how much they were protecting us. Helping us into the stadium with a kind shove to show us they had our back. It was an amazing place; the stadium was loud and the Roma supporters bouncing without looking daft like we would if we tried. Nasri scored, I'd predicted it minutes before, not because I'm Nostradamus, but because people were giving him stick and well, that's how it works. Then Zaba, beautiful man. He kissed the badge, he could, he was allowed to then. You have to earn that right and he had done, many times. He meant it. One thousand five hundred City fans going wild. Then we got back on the buses ... Rome is fantastic, the Stadio Olimpico was vibrant, the win memorable and spending all that time with my mates and all those Italian police was special.'

If the fans had travelled in blind faith rather than any logical hope, the players saw it differently. 'It was the target at the start of the night,' offered Nasri afterwards, 'and we knew that if we were patient, we could do it.' Then a smile broke across the midfielder's face. 'You see, it's always the same with City. We always like to do it the hard way and here we are. We did it again!'

It was City's first clean sheet for thirteen European games, since the 3–0 win in Plzeň. In the shaky-looking defensive pairing of Demichelis and Mangala, Pellegrini had chosen bravely and come up trumps. Mangala, enjoying a baptism of fire in English football, had been just two years old when Totti began his senior career, while Demichelis was disproving the Samson theory, by playing better now his ponytail had been docked. Nevertheless, the Chilean's insistence on a perpetually high defensive line gave the Roma full-backs plenty of opportunity to try and get in behind City's supposedly frail central defence, which mostly held firm against the onslaught.

The result felt like a proper breakthrough. Not just in escaping a group in which City had been mired in last place as recently as matchday four, but also in the greater scheme of things. City's Champions League skirmishing had thus far not produced too many nights to add to the club's rich folklore, but here, in what Daniel Taylor called 'a shrieking, fire-cracking pit of noisy bias', they had finally laid down a marker. To do it without Touré, Agüero and Kompany only underlined how the club's mindset worked. With Agüero's replacement Edin Džeko playing in front of the fans who would adore him when he finally left Manchester for pastures new, and the indefatigable Fernandinho bossing a hectic midfield, City proved not only to the rest of Europe, but perhaps more crucially to themselves, that they could cut it in the most hostile venues when the chips were further down than the tricky moments at the start of a James Bond film.

With the water rising and the fuse running towards its end, they had freed the knots and taken flight. Now only a poor draw could bring them back in contact with the baddies.

AS ROMA 0–2 MANCHESTER CITY | Att. 54,119 | Nasri, Zabaleta

Hart, Zabaleta, Clichy, Demichelis, Mangala, Fernandinho, Fernando, Navas (Silva), Nasri (Kolarov), Milner, Džeko (Jovetić)

The draw for the knockout round took place in Nyon, Switzerland, on 15 December and brought immediate slumped shoulders all round. Pitched with Barcelona for the second year running, City's luck had turned again. The euphoria of Roman conquest disappeared faster than Antony and Cleopatra being pursued up the Nile basin by the *Legio VI Victrix*. The Great Manueline Empire, it seemed, might have to be put on hold for another year.

Pellegrini had two months to plan and get his best players in peak condition for the approaching challenge. In typical English fashion, there would only be the small matter of thirteen league and cup matches to negotiate in the ensuing period. To bolster the attack, the transfer window delivered Premier League top scorer Wilfried Bony from Swansea. It was an odd way to relieve yourself of £25 million, as the Ivorian quickly absented himself with Yaya Touré to play in the Africa Cup of Nations. He would be with City for a total of precisely fifteen months.

Although Chelsea had opened up a five-point gap at the top of the Premier League, a 4–1 win at Stoke and a 5–0 demolition of Newcastle steadied the nerves immediately before Barcelona's visit to Manchester. The Newcastle match saw David Silva in sublime form, Džeko score a wonderful goal and Bony finally make his debut. All seemed to be falling into place for the big challenge.

On 24 February, an expectant crowd gathered to see if City could control Messi and co. more successfully than the previous season.

Luis Suárez had made all the wrong kind of headlines the previous summer when he had bitten a chunk out of Giorgio Chiellini's shoulder in the Italy vs Uruguay World Cup finals match, but the Etihad was afforded a melon grin from the Uruguayan after he netted twice in the first half-hour. City had been caught cold by Barcelona's intricate, incisive forward play.

The Messi–Suárez–Neymar trident was quickly proving almost impossible for Kompany and Demichelis to shackle.

Pellegrini had spent much of the week promising that City would attack the Catalan aristocrats, but, by half-time, it had been a pretty lame showing. When Dani Alves' cross/shot skimmed the bar, it was beginning to look like the visitors would score a third if they wished. The trouble was not so much how good Barcelona were, everyone knew that, but the gap between them and City appeared to have widened instead of narrowed.

With a one-dimensional and understaffed City central midfield facing the beguiling movements of Messi, Ivan Rakitić and Andrés Iniesta, one could only imagine which words featured in the Chilean's half-time pep talk. With both Džeko and Agüero on the field, Barcelona found themselves with a man over in midfield. The spare man, Sergio Busquets, had time and space to pick out his passes, while Fernando and Milner ran around in ever-decreasing circles. The decision to take on the might of Barcelona with two out-and-out strikers in a 4–4–2 had seemed foolhardy at best.

The second half brought an improvement (tactically Fernandinho's introduction for Nasri had solidified City's presence in the middle), but chances went begging until Agüero's 69th-minute strike, reminiscent of the QPR title-winning goal for its oblique run and venomous finish. Within five minutes of bringing hope, City then removed it with Clichy's clumsy tackle on Alves bringing a second yellow card.

Messi's 90th-minute penalty should have sealed City's fate, but Hart parried it and the Argentinian produced a diving header to the rebound that was as inept as it was unexpected.

MANCHESTER CITY 1–2 BARCELONA | Att. 45,081 | Agüero

Hart, Zabaleta, Clichy, Kompany, Demichelis, Milner, Fernando, Nasri (Fernandinho), Silva (Sagna), Džeko (Bony), Agüero

Warming up for a difficult challenge at the Nou Camp by losing 1–0 at relegation-threatened Burnley was not a good look. In another way, it was perfect preparation, as that was exactly the score City achieved in Spain too. The difference was that the second defeat flattered City greatly.

Barcelona, with a swagger and a wiggle, appeared to be rewarding a local populace who had eagerly been awaiting what had been called 'a magical week' by *La Vanguardia*, in anticipation of games with City and Real Madrid within four days of each other. It was close to magic, perhaps even some form of wizardry, and City had nobody who could unravel the spell. Watching once again from the icy platform of tier four, individual players were hard to make out, errors were too many to catalogue, but the patterns of play were clear enough. Triangles, diagonals, corridors. City were pulled from pillar to post by their opponents' intelligent use of space, possession and movement. It would become a familiar sight to all of us with time, but for now it was a foreign body, an infestation of little legs, a symphony of pass and run that was not, at this stage, our own to enjoy.

With Sagna gazing dolefully at Neymar's hairdo, Rakitić – completely free at the back post – lobbed Barcelona ahead with nonchalant precision and for the rest of the match Hart stood tall to everything thrown at him. It was a performance to rank with his one-man shows against Dortmund and Bayern. At the end, Suárez offered the overworked keeper a long embrace, as if he wanted to get a closer look at the man who had stopped everything bar the kitchen sink.

Even when opportunity had briefly beckoned for City, Agüero going down in a sandwich between Gerard Piqué and Javier Mascherano, the Argentinian's penalty was saved by Marc-André ter Stegen. There were 77 minutes on the clock. Even slippery City, with their bent for the unusual, were not going to get out of this one.

'*Barbaro*', screamed the next morning's *Mundo Deportivo*. Messi: '*El mayor espectaculo del mundo*' had delivered his poetry and all around us were standing to applaud.

BARCELONA 1–0 MANCHESTER CITY | Att. 92,551
Hart, Sagna, Kolarov, Kompany, Demichelis, Milner (Lampard), Fernandinho, Touré (Bony), Nasri (Navas), Silva, Agüero

It would, by the season's end, be the story of 2014–15: a side going through the motions, with all of the swagger but none of the serious resolve, with a manager seemingly unable to push them to the next level. After his initial success, Pellegrini was learning what Mancini had learnt, that he was in charge of a quixotic beast that could blow hot and cold in two successive days. Whereas the Italian met fire with fire, the Chilean continued to avoid confrontation. Where they converged was in their stubbornness. City had failed to progress in four years of trying, owing to a number of factors: meeting high-ranked opponents to start with, but also because of how they set up against the big teams. Pellegrini's insistence on playing two up front against Barcelona smacked of naivety. With Villarreal and Málaga it had worked in an anarchic sort of way, proving the Chilean had the big game nous that City needed, but the club's overlords were demanding something more structured, more plausible and certainly more durable. Just like his predecessor, the Chilean would begin his third season under increasing pressure to find the balance that was still missing and deliver more. The press, hungry as ever for a story, were beginning to talk of 'greater scrutiny' and, as James Ducker put it in *The Times*: 'Growing uncertainty over the Chilean's position.'

From a position of some comfort twelve months earlier, Pellegrini would now experience the vice-like pressure that comes with a job heavy with expectation and littered with pitfalls.

King of the Kippax mark II

The summer brought in a mixed bag of signings, but the intent appeared to be returning. Liverpool's Raheem Sterling was a growing star, while Fabian Delph's on–off transfer left Villa fans furious and City's non-plussed. Who, even then, could have guessed that the August purchase of Wolfsburg's Kevin De Bruyne would see the first true imitation of Colin Bell step out at the Etihad? Certainly not the *Mirror*, who immediately dubbed the Belgian 'The £60m Reject'. In too came Valencia's Nicolás Otamendi to add cultured, patient defending to City's menu.

With the Barclays Manager of the Month Award for August tucked under his arm after a 'perfect start', few could have predicted how the season would pan out for Pellegrini. A fourth-place finish, squeezing back into the Champions League qualifiers ahead of United on goal difference, a 5–1 hammering in the FA Cup playing the youth team at Chelsea and growing dissatisfaction at the sloppy descent from the triumphs of his first season in charge. The season would be partially saved by the by-now customary success in the League Cup and, in some ways, by City's longest-ever run in the Champions League, but none of this would be enough to save the Chilean's job and even the European campaign would ultimately leave a sour taste in the mouth.

Drawn alongside the previous season's losing finalists Juventus, '70s powerhouse and group-stage debutants Borussia Mönchengladbach and back-to-back Europa League winners Sevilla, appetites had been whetted for what looked a finely balanced group. But with an away win at Selhurst Park, making it five wins out of five, came the first setback. Agüero's injury would keep him out of all but the last seven minutes of the opening game at home to Juventus.

The ribbing Wilfried Bony was getting from Giorgio Chiellini as the players left the pitch at half-time in the opening game told its own story. The Italian patted the Ivorian on the backside and appeared to share a joke, possibly about the eternal closeness of their engaging tussle, a 45-minute marathon of muscle and sinew, push and shove that had been – along with Fernandinho's ferocious long-range shooting – the feature of a pulsating half.

With 57 minutes gone, the deadlock was finally broken and from the most unexpected of sources. Direct from a corner, not one of City's party pieces on a normal day at the office, Kompany climbed untidily above Chiellini to head past Gianluigi Buffon. While the Italian complained, the Belgian cavorted. There had been a tangle of arms and a deflection off both bodies, but the ball was in the net.

There was just time for the first of what would become a long-running series of what-if moments involving the finishing of Raheem Sterling. A fantastic double save kept him out as City turned the screw. It would be the golden opportunity before the tide turned, new signing Mario Mandžukić drifting ahead of Mangala to net from Pogba's raking pass and Álvaro Morata scoring a stunning winner after freeing himself from Kolarov's freestyle marking.

City had endured another false start against Italian opposition. It would once again set tongues wagging in the press about naivety, ability, hunger and organisation. It was never dull on the undulating roads of Europe. Phil McNulty, writing for the BBC, asked the question on many people's lips: 'Do City believe?'

The fans' behaviour would become a moot point for many: booing the UEFA 'anthem' was now customary and enthusiastic, as for some was leaving before the end of the match to dodge the infamous traffic snarl-ups around the ground, but the support had been loud and boisterous for much of the game, the attendance a huge 50,000 after the summer's ground extension. On whether they had warmed to the Champions League or not, the jury was clearly still out.

MANCHESTER CITY 1–2 JUVENTUS | Att. 50,363 | Chiellini (o.g.)

Hart, Sagna, Kolarov, Mangala, Kompany (Otamendi), Fernandinho, Silva, Nasri (Agüero), Touré, Sterling (De Bruyne), Bony

---

Sevilla's 3–0 humbling of Mönchengladbach meant City's first meeting with the Germans since 1979 now became crucial.

With Mönchengladbach turning out in an all-black Champions League kit and City in a fluorescent colour that hovered somewhere between lime and traffic warden, the football was not the only thing that was dazzling on a night when City would escape by the skin of their teeth.

The foundation for the success, as had often been the case in the early years in the competition, was Joe Hart. Once again enjoying a fine game, he saved Raffael's first-half penalty to allow the teams to go in level at the break. Lars Stindl then put the home side ahead with an assured finish, before City finally came to attacking life. Demichelis would only score one European goal for the club and the equaliser against Gladbach that slipped in off his thigh and barely crossed the line will perhaps last long only in the memory of the perpetrator of the act. To allay any lingering doubts, Otamendi wellied it back into the roof of the net to make sure.

City were level and pushing for the win, which duly arrived off the 98th-minute boot of Agüero, his fifth penalty conversion in six attempts in the tournament. Sadly, the miss had been at the Nou Camp and there would be one or two more high-profile failures to add to the list by the end of the decade.

The match offered us views back into the past and views forward into the future.

Banishing memories of Malcolm Allison's introduction of the teenage Nicky Reid to deal with European Footballer of the Year Allan Simonsen at the old Bökelburgstadion, City had reignited their campaign at the first opportunity with a nerveless comeback against lively opponents in their new Borussia-Park stadium. They were, in doing so, the first British side to win at Mönchengladbach.

Another first was the sight of Sterling, Agüero, De Bruyne and Silva playing together. City's 61 per cent possession foretold much of what we would see from this talented group of players under the Chilean's successor.

Man of the Match Hart was unimpressed, however, stating: 'We didn't play well today. We were disjointed, as we have been for the last few games, but Sergio is a cool guy and he will score.'

BORUSSIA MÖNCHENGLADBACH 1–2 MANCHESTER CITY |
Att. 46,217 | Demichelis, Agüero (pen.)

Hart, Sagna, Kolarov, Demichelis, Otamendi, Fernandinho, Touré (Fernando), De Bruyne, Silva (Navas), Sterling (Zabaleta), Agüero

The 2–1 victory over Sevilla that stabilised City's bid to qualify from Group D followed a similar pattern to the German trip, with De Bruyne's fifth goal for the club only sealing the win in the 91st minute. Again, City had left it painfully late. 'Fight to the end' might have become the fans' defining chant, but it left nothing but shredded nerves in the stands. It did, however, leave City in second place in the group, a far better position than after the first round of games had been completed.

Sevilla's expertise allowed them to exploit the spaces left by the rampaging De Bruyne and wandering Sagna in a way Newcastle and Bournemouth had been unable to do in 6–1 and 5–1 defeats prior to this match. First, City had to make it uncomfortable for themselves, however, allowing Yevhen Konoplyanka to score from just inside the box.

The leveller six minutes later was rooted in Touré's persistence, as the giant Ivorian struggled past a challenge on the byline to set up Sterling for a shot. His effort was spilled by Sergio Rico, allowing an easy tap-in for the hitherto clunky Bony. Even easy tap-ins were not the Ivorian's speciality, and his mishit needed a deflection off Adil Rami to find the target from three yards.

As the game trickled into time added on, we were all treated to a little snapshot of what the *Mirror* had just weeks earlier labelled 'failure'. Touré began a break through the sparsely populated midfield. Ignoring the better option of Sterling to his left, he fed De Bruyne to his right. Faced with three covering defenders, the Belgian feinted to go outside, dropped a shoulder, moved instead to his left and, having worked the smallest of gaps, fired a low shot past the goalkeeper along the ground and inside the far post. Majestic, nerveless and classy, the Belgian had *arrived* and could now await more favourable headlines in the morning papers.

It was only City's third Champions League win against Spanish opposition (the ratio skewed somewhat by the four straight defeats applied by Barcelona over the previous two seasons) in nine attempts. Earlier efforts in different competitions against Bilbao, Valencia and Santander had not been much more encouraging. There would be work to do in Andalucía.

MANCHESTER CITY 2–1 SEVILLA | Att. 45,595 | Rami (o.g.), De Bruyne

Hart, Zabaleta (Kolarov), Sagna, Otamendi, Mangala, Fernandinho, Touré, Navas, De Bruyne (Kompany), Sterling, Bony (Fernando)

Casting minds back to the Chilean's inaugural season in the Premier League, a year that contained so much attacking football, so many goals, so many examples of cocksure exuberance, carefree exploitation of others' frailties, that it took the breath away, was doing the manager no good now. With a supposedly improved squad, the vivacity was missing, the goal flow irregular and the confidence intermittent. Success in the transfer market had also been patchy, with Pellegrini's decision-making being called into question too. Overuse of Vincent Kompany and over-reliance on certain other players was taking its toll. Otamendi and, to a greater extent, Mangala – the most expensive lumberjack partnership in Premier League history – continued to look ill-equipped for the job of shackling the world's top strikers.

At least City's luck seemed to be holding.

With the trip to Andalucía upon us, news that Sevilla had lost for the fourth time this season offered encouragement. Unai Emery's side had already been defeated in more home games than in the whole of 2014–15. Although City were by now top of the Premier League, Spanish scouts at the weekend's 2–1 win at home to Norwich would also have returned upbeat. City had limped home, saved by a late Touré penalty in a bizarre storm of uncontrolled football.

The heat and the general air of excitement led to some strange events in southern Spain. Fan Adrian Furness and his mates had misjudged kick-off time (9pm Spanish time) and a full day of enjoying the local red wine and tapas was beginning to have its effects. 'Well, it encouraged us to take an alternative mode of transport to the ground. We had hit the red wine a bit early, saw all those tourist carriages and it seemed obvious what to do next, so we ended up arriving at the ground by horse and trap singing the Zabaleta song all the way there.'

By the end of a wonderfully entertaining evening in the Ramón Sánchez Pizjuán, all talk of luck and horse-drawn carriages had been replaced by the usual bravado of the travelling hordes, buoyed by victory and cheap Rioja, singing of the things they were going to do to the next team to step in front of the juggernaut called Manchester City.

In a blistering first 45 minutes, City scored three, leading the home team a merry dance in the process. Six shots on target in the first twenty minutes had left Sevilla punch-drunk. How quickly Cityitis could deliver an about-turn in fortunes. Standing in the low sweep of the away section in the beautifully appointed stadium, it was easy to think the good times were rolling again. City's liquid football, with Sterling and Fernandinho leading the fight, tore the home side to shreds. It was so invigorating even the hitherto hapless Bony found his range, chipping in with a classy first-time strike for the third before the break. By the end, he had had seven shots, more than anyone, and only two of them had been fired into the crowd.

Better was to come. The 1–1 draw between Juventus and Mönchengladbach saw City go top of the group. Better still, remaining fixtures meant they could not be caught and had already qualified. Having started the group with a loss, City were through after four games. Having gained a reputation for pulling games out of the fire with late winners, City had demolished Sevilla with a burst of unstoppable power at the start. Being unpredictable had its obvious plus points. If the faithful following them across the continent were blissfully unaware of what to expect next, how could their opponents know any better? The fans, who had been reported to UEFA for their continued booing of 'Zadok the Priest', had arrived in Andalucía prepared, holding up a mass of messages for the watching governors of the game. They read simply 'Boo'.

The general urge of those standing on their red seats at the end was not to boo, however, but to applaud what had been one of City's most accomplished away performances in European competition.

SEVILLA 1–3 MANCHESTER CITY | Att. 39,261 | Sterling, Fernandinho, Bony

Hart, Sagna, Kolarov, Otamendi, Kompany, Fernando, Fernandinho (Demichelis), Touré, Navas, Sterling (De Bruyne), Bony (Delph)

Emery was magnanimous at the end. 'We have just played against a fantastic team,' he said. 'They were very fast and good at taking their opportunities.'

While Pellegrini spoke of the importance of trying to finish top, there was no denying that City's ills in the previous two seasons had come from second-placed finishes. Avoiding group winners would, all agreed, make a difference.

A sloppy 1–0 defeat in Turin would put this objective in jeopardy, but, when matchday six ended with a cascade of goals against the Germans, City could be happy with a job well done and their first group win in five attempts. While the Juventus game featured a goal that appeared to involve the scorer Mandžukić manoeuvring Otamendi out of the way, it was memorable for another of Sterling's special misses, when the striker bumbled his shot wide from De Bruyne's pinpoint cross from six yards out.

The blitz against Mönchengladbach involved a comeback from 2–1 down, a blistering opener from Silva, two cracking finishes from Sterling and another from the suddenly prolific Bony.

JUVENTUS 1–0 MANCHESTER CITY | Att. 38,193

Hart (Caballero), Sagna, Clichy, Otamendi, Demichelis, Fernando, Fernandinho (Delph), Touré, De Bruyne, Navas, Agüero (Sterling)

MANCHESTER CITY 4–2 BORUSSIA MÖNCHENGLADBACH | Att. 41,829 | Silva, Sterling (2), Bony

Hart, Clichy (Sagna), Kolarov, Otamendi, Mangala, Fernandinho, Delph (Bony), Touré, Silva, De Bruyne (Navas), Sterling

In qualifying relatively unscathed, Pellegrini had admitted defeat, ditching the twin-striker system that had unsurprisingly gone aground against Barcelona and introducing a single attacker plan, backed by an advanced three in midfield. The

4–2–3–1 offered greater security for European games. By dropping Touré in alongside Fernandinho, the 32-year-old Ivorian could conserve his energy a little, simultaneously bolstering the block in front of the central defence. Crucially too, City's attacking personnel had changed nature. Džeko, Jovetić and Negredo were all gone, replaced by the more enigmatic, flexible and pacey play of Sterling and De Bruyne, who could both play left or right at the drop of a hat. Added pace to the flanks meant opponents were being forced to sit deeper to combat City's shape, resulting in Pellegrini's team having a less vulnerable feel about it.

The draw for the knockout round brought Dynamo Kyiv back into City's orbit. The team that had knocked Mancini's side out in 2011 was back in the Champions League thanks to a double-winning season domestically. Taking advantage of Shakhtar's ejection from their home base in Donetsk, after the Russian invasion of the Donbass, Sergei Rebrov's side was on the up and had qualified ahead of FC Porto in Chelsea's group.

In the build-up to the first leg, UEFA managed to avoid further ire from City supporters by lifting the second of a two-match stadium ban for Kyiv, after racist chanting had marred their match against Chelsea. Having beaten Maccabi Tel Aviv in an empty ground, Dynamo's punishment had been downgraded and City fans would be allowed to travel.

For Pellegrini, things were turning sour. With confirmation that the much-courted Guardiola would replace him in the summer, he had the task of maintaining focus and command as his time ticked away. Feeling the pressure to concentrate on the Champions League, he fielded a quasi-youth team in the fifth round of the FA Cup at Stamford Bridge and saw his makeshift side ship five goals. With the end of his three-year reign at City now in sight, the knives were out for the quiet Chilean.

His indulgence of City's high-end stars had echoes of the last time City had come face to face with Kyiv, when the narrow twists of fate that sometimes decide a team's destiny had delivered a watery-eyed Mario Balotelli to the side of the pitch.

It was clearly a watershed moment for the coach, with dwindling opportunities to secure a positive legacy at the club where he had started so explosively.

Two crucial league defeats at home to Leicester and Tottenham, just before the FA Cup thrashing at Chelsea, had seen City lose three consecutive matches for the first time during his tenure. In a season that had singularly failed to take off, however, City had reserved some of their best performances and most spirited flourishes for the Champions League.

The accomplished win in Seville allied to late comebacks to defeat Mönchengladbach home and away and Seville at the Etihad, had proved that the team's spirit could still match its ability when there was proper focus. On this occasion, both sides had reason to be distracted: City by the following weekend's League Cup final against Liverpool and Kyiv by the fact that this would be their first match since beating Tel Aviv on 9 December.

Making ten changes to the side put out at Chelsea, the Chilean was clearly following orders to prioritise Europe. With Silva playing centrally behind Agüero and Fernandinho pushed wide to accommodate both Touré and Fernando in deep midfield, City were impressive, moving powerfully into a two-goal lead through Agüero's rapier-fast instincts and Silva's close-range finish. The Spaniard's shot, high into the roof of Oleksandr Shovkovskyi's net, came after Agüero had back-heeled Sterling into space on the left. When the cross flew across the edge of the six-yard box, Silva was left to pounce at the back post.

When Vitaliy Buyalskyi reduced the arrears with a long shot that swerved in off Otamendi's thigh, the home side began to push hard for an equaliser. Bolstered by an increasingly noisy crowd, they inflicted an uncomfortable twenty minutes on City, which saw Hart save at full stretch from the goalscorer, before their thrust was dampened by Touré's late curling left-footer. Suddenly, Pellegrini's team selection at Chelsea, for which he had been widely panned in the press, looked justified.

Despite his side's apparent rustiness, Rebrov was insistent they had lost for different reasons. 'The winter break didn't affect us. The fact is we have just played one of the best teams in Europe.'

'Is the tie settled? It is important in football to never think a tie is finished,' insisted the Chilean, aware of the irony of his own position, *finished but not finished* before the season's final whistle.

DYNAMO KYIV 1–3 MANCHESTER CITY | Att. 53,691 | Agüero, Silva, Touré

Hart, Sagna, Clichy, Kompany, Otamendi, Fernando, Touré, Fernandinho, Silva, Sterling, Agüero (Iheanacho)

The two matches that followed City's return from Ukraine cemented the season's course. Both were against Liverpool. The first landed the League Cup at Wembley after a tense penalty shoot-out, the second offered the customary Anfield league drubbing. It meant Pellegrini had a trophy to say farewell with and that the Premier League was out of City's reach, languishing ten points behind surprise leaders Leicester. Would this help train minds on the one trophy left within reach or would the early announcement of the manager's departure undermine his ability to motivate?

On 15 March, City made history in understated fashion by securing their first-ever Champions League quarter-final place with their first-ever goalless draw in the tournament. After 36 matches in the competition of varying hilarity and drama, they had finally achieved something via mundanity. Jesús Navas' shot against a post was the closest they got in a tight contest that betrayed the manager's tactical thinking for the rest of the campaign. Navas, a speedy but often wayward flank player had attracted the attention of Henry Winter, in the press box for *The Times*. 'He's like a racing pigeon that keeps flying into lamp posts.'

Told to sit tight, City allowed Miguel Veloso to dictate midfield for the visitors and had only Touré's second-half shot on target in the whole game. Kompany's cardboard hamstrings and Otamendi's gung-ho tackling meant City's defensive solidity was decimated, both men being taken off, and now depended on a Mangala–Demichelis partnership.

Pablo Zabaleta remained upbeat. 'This group of players are working hard to make this club even bigger,' he said. 'The Champions League, we are trying to reach at least a final. It's hard but today it was job done. Not a great performance but we are really pleased.' City were walking with giants now and the manager's tactics seemed to be acknowledging this.

Managing risk and reward was beginning to weigh heavily on Pellegrini.

MANCHESTER CITY 0–0 DYNAMO KYIV | Att. 43,630

Hart, Zabaleta, Clichy, Kompany (Mangala), Otamendi (Demichelis), Fernando, Fernandinho, Touré, Silva (Sterling), Navas, Agüero

---

If Kyiv had been stultifying, the next game City played in the tournament would be a firecracker.

The draw for the last eight brought City together with Paris Saint-Germain, busy completing a clean sweep of all four domestic trophies in France. By the time the first leg took place, they were already domestic champions, 25 points clear of Lyon with eight games still to play. In the eight short years that had passed since meeting in the lopsided Europa League groups of 2008, the potential interested audience in a PSG–Manchester City tie had gone through the roof. Thanks to huge investment from Qatar and Abu Dhabi, the two clubs had edged inside the walls as the drawbridge was being pulled up. For PSG this would be a fourth consecutive quarter-final appearance. If they seemed slightly ahead of City in development terms, being the one big fish in a relatively small Ligue 1 pond meant that they were not always best prepared for yearly tussles with European heavyweights.

The Paris match will go down as one of Pellegrini's last presents to the faithful; a rich tableau of colour and noise, of vivacious attacking and Keystone Kops defending. Above all, it was a match which started energetically, with David Luiz's booking after twelve seconds, and never let up. By the twelfth minute, the home side were already embarking on their second strong penalty shout of the evening. The first had been denied by referee Milorad Mažić, but Sagna's untidy swipe at Luiz could not be ignored. Zlatan Ibrahimović strutted forward and saw Hart save his third Champions League penalty with a magnificent stretch down to his right. The blond goalkeeper had been one of Pellegrini's most trusted European stalwarts.

In a rip-roaring contest it was City who took the lead, De Bruyne's sharp finish from Fernandinho's pass flashing past Kevin Trapp. Almost immediately, Fernando dallied on the ball, his panicky clearance ricocheting off Ibrahimović into Hart's goal. The French went 2–1 up when ex-City academy prospect Adrien Rabiot touched in at the far post after another desperate save from Hart. Showing fantastic spirit, City regrouped and got the equaliser they deserved when Serge Aurier miskicked, leaving Thiago Silva to deflect Fernandinho's shot with his backside. The ball entered the net apologetically on the opposite side to the one the Brazilian had been aiming at, but City had their precious away goals.

'If we want to win,' said a relieved manager afterwards, 'we cannot afford to make these kinds of mistakes, but we were trying to win the game from the first minute. It is the way we play.'

PARIS SAINT-GERMAIN 2-2 MANCHESTER CITY | Att. 47,228 |
De Bruyne, Fernandinho

Hart, Sagna, Clichy, Otamendi, Mangala, Fernandinho, Fernando, Navas, Silva (Bony), De Bruyne (Delph), Agüero (Kolarov)

With the Etihad a blur of blue tickertape for the return a week later, City were finally playing for the high stakes the owners craved. For the fans, the booing remained but, for matches like this, the crackle coming off the packed stands told a different story. The latter stages of the Champions League were special after all, a unique mix of elevated pomp and sophistication, with the electric snap of high-end combat.

This time it was City's turn to be awarded a penalty, as Agüero's surge was halted by a reckless lunge from Trapp. There was no Ibrahimović strut from the penalty-taker, but the result matched the Swede's from the first game, with Agüero side-footing wide of the target. With a match of epic ebb and flow heading towards its last quarter of an hour, De Bruyne under-lined why City had been happy to shell out £55 million for his services. With the merest of touches to slow down the ball on the edge of the box, the Belgian let fly with a low-raking effort that slid into the corner. A classic strike from an increasingly influential player, it was a goal fit to raise the Etihad roof and catapult City into the last four. With the ground engulfed in an intoxicating buzz from the 53,000 present, City held out to clinch a 3–2 aggregate win.

The embattled pairing of Otamendi and Mangala, as porous as a sieve in Paris, had played their part in keeping Ibrahimović and co. quiet. With only three clean sheets from the seventeen matches they had been paired in, they could add a well-earned fourth. As for De Bruyne, his potential as a leader and true great of European football was becoming more evident with every match.

MANCHESTER CITY 1–0 PARIS SAINT-GERMAIN | Att. 53,039 | De Bruyne

Hart, Sagna, Clichy, Mangala, Otamendi, Fernando, Fernandinho, Navas, Silva (Delph), De Bruyne (Touré), Agüero (Iheanacho)

By the end of the week, City – England's tenth Champions League/European Cup semi-finalists – knew the name of the side barring their way to the final in the San Siro, where Paul Power had weaved his magic four decades earlier. They would need to circumnavigate the most successful side in the history of the competition, bejewelled football royalty and the establishment's golden boys Real Madrid, while Bayern and Atlético Madrid would contest the other match.

With an expectant crowd roaring them on, City chose to play the percentages. A goalless first leg was clearly preferable to a scoring draw, leaving Pellegrini's side with the tantalising prospect of needing *only* a score draw in the second leg to proceed. Scoring, however, looked low down the home side's priorities, as the game ground on in a cat-and-mouse fashion. Real's midfield pass masters Luka Modrić and Toni Kroos were excellent in possession, while City's ball-winners Fernando and Fernandinho did their jobs to maximum effect. The result was a stalemate, as each side's outstanding players cancelled out the other's most dangerous individuals.

In the end, City had Hart to thank for the clean sheet, producing an excellent block from Casemiro's free header, then a miraculous save as Real came closer to breaking the deadlock.

MANCHESTER CITY 0–0 REAL MADRID | Att. 52,221

Hart, Sagna, Clichy, Kompany, Otamendi, Fernando, Fernandinho, Silva (Iheanacho), Navas (Sterling), De Bruyne, Agüero

There was noise aplenty, smoke and mirrors and lots besides, but at the end of the day, the return game in Madrid meant it was curtains for the side built by the delicate hands of Roberto Mancini and turned briefly into a fantasy goal-scoring machine by Manuel Pellegrini. The first great City side of the modern era was no more.

What a stage, what a place to bring it all to an end. And what an end it was too. Below the hulking, steep-sided cathedral of the Santiago Bernabéu, City's big-hitters finally ran aground. One sole shot on goal in the 88th minute was the total second-half effort for a side trying to save its skin in its first-ever Champions League semi-final. Fernandinho had earlier hit the outside of a post, but it was meagre gruel on a night of feasting.

Asked to produce one last earth tremor in a season of tumbling bricks, there was nothing left to give. Drifting out of a tournament that had played witness to exhilarating away performances in Mönchengladbach, Seville, Kyiv and Paris was deemed a stronger idea than throwing caution to the wind and going for broke.

The curtain that came down on City's season of European improvement was besmirched and of frankly dubious quality. Threadbare in the middle, see-through in parts, its fabric far from the Italian silks Mancini had bestowed upon us, far even from the early hand-knitted Andean rugs the kind Señor Pellegrini sneaked beneath our aching feet early on in his tenure. This was a quilt mottled with mould, hiding one of Manuel's half-eaten enchiladas.

For the fans, it had been a day in bright sunshine, cavorting from one plate of tapas to the next. With the sun dropping over the skyline, the trek up the Paseo de la Castellana began. In the heaving mess of excited traffic, Atlético-supporting taxi drivers tooted and wished us well against the sworn enemy. Still, there's nothing quite as historically relevant if you have followed City from Allison's 'cowards of Europe' speech through to the present day than to turn up boiling with intent and leave with your trousers around your ankles.

Swerving into one last café before the Bernabéu, the TV showed pictures of a flare-wielding crowd welcoming the Real team bus as it edged through the scrum. Throaty roars of 'City, the Best Team in the Land and all the World' drifted up through the smoke and firecrackers. So, this was what Champions League semi-finals were like. Passionate, intoxicating and bubbling over with intent.

A tingling vortex of noise and expectation carried us fans on through the ranks of nervous Madrid police and up the great spirals of Bernabéu *Fondo Norte*. The view from the top is exceptional, a great steep twist of tightly packed seats curving around in a wide bowl. This the scene of daring deeds from Gento to Zidane, Di Stéfano to Redondo, Camacho to Juanito.

The white-clad Madridistas in the Curva Sul added bounce and passion. High in the gods, a huge City following bellowed its throaty support.

Then silence followed by a whipcrack of noise. The ball, billowing in a strange arc off the stretching form of Fernando, drifted tantalisingly high and wide of Hart and into the top corner. The burst of noise rose into a stadium-round explosion from the home support, the like of which we hadn't heard in Barcelona; sharp, raucous and triumphant.

Gareth Bale, later to be chosen as *MARCA*'s '*el Dandy*' and the strutting, half-fit Cristiano Ronaldo kept City fully occupied. Pepe at the back could hardly believe his luck. The English scrappers had come in their carpet slippers.

And so, the story of Manuel Pellegrini ended.

Agüero fired a speculative effort over with two minutes to play. City's magnificent support began to try and suck the ball towards Keylor Navas' goal, but the players could not locate it, dared not risk it. Instead of the barn-storming finish, to go out with a defiant bang, all guns blazing, City spent the four minutes of injury time defending. Pellegrini's reign, seemingly intent on ending on the most imperceptible of light notes, would have no trumpet blast.

Despite the League Cup win, this was the end of a second consecutive season of considerable underachievement. It is surely a mark of where City had now arrived that a season involving this groundbreaking semi-final in Europe and a fourth League Cup win left some feeling underwhelmed.

In the harsh light of Madrid, the incoming Pep Guardiola would suddenly be aware that the initial tweaking job needed to be a touch more profound than at first thought. For Pellegrini, whose reputation grew from swashbuckling campaigns with Villarreal and Málaga, it was lights out on a feeble exit. The first great City side of the modern era was over.

As we filed out of that cavernous place, it was difficult not to feel a pang of regret. Pellegrini had brought us so much, brought us so far, but now, in the shadow of the great Bernabéu, it was time to take our leave of him.

REAL MADRID 1–0 MANCHESTER CITY | Att. 78,300

Hart, Sagna, Clichy, Kompany (Mangala), Otamendi, Fernando, Fernandinho, Touré (Sterling), Navas (Iheanacho), De Bruyne, Agüero

---

Football journalist and City watcher Stephen Tudor still sees the Madrid game as a pivotal moment in City's European development. 'This was the big missed opportunity,' he told me. 'We didn't turn up in that second leg and after going out – valiantly and with our heads held high – to Barcelona for two consecutive seasons, that felt like our time. Just wish we could have a second go at that night, only this time for Pellegrini to let us loose and go for it. Overall, there has been incremental progress made and experience accrued over the years of participation. We can look back to those early campaigns and highlight some shocking refereeing decisions, but there was also some poor game management from the players.

'Viewing the whole adventure from 2003, the UEFA Cup/ Europa League campaigns were a lot of fun for the fans. The early Champions League seasons were a learning curve. But then we get to Real Madrid and that was such a pivotal moment for City. It began to define them as *the nearly men* …'

GUARDIOLA:
A NEW KIND OF SERIOUS

Script of the bridge

The figure standing on the bridge over Ashton New Road patiently waited for the phalanx of jostling photographers to get their best shots. In an immaculately cut grey suit with a sky-blue scarf draped over his shoulders, Josep Guardiola Sala looked every inch the world's most talented football coach. Lean, expensive and ready.

With the sun blazing, the customary bank of grey cloud seemed to be exiting swiftly at the sight of the ex-Barcelona maestro. Could City's expectant fans take the unaccustomed dazzle as an early metaphor? Manchester's infamous weather held off longer than usual that day to allow the welcome to continue on the stadium concourse, where, backed by a giant awning claiming grandly 'It Begins', the Catalan greeted the crowd with the first warm words that would become a feature of his relationship with the people of a city he would take to his heart.

During an afternoon where the understandable hoopla took its toll on him, Guardiola was given ample opportunity to air as many positive thoughts on his new job as possible. In fluent, confident English he uttered a phrase which often flummoxes foreign users of the language but would become a sentence used perhaps more than any other during his time at the club: 'My priority is for us to play good. And after, try to win one game. And after that, another.' Little did the gathered throng know just how 'good' Guardiola's City would get.

With this long-awaited and much-heralded arrival, City's status as a club going places quickly rose several notches. The widely held belief among the watching press and City's gleeful support was that attracting what the world viewed as the sport's most coveted tactician and a serial winner would catapult the club to another level. And there was only really one other level to go to.

With this one single appointment, the aims of the club's Middle East owners to conquer titles on all fronts was suddenly brought into clear bright focus.

Here was a man, who – given a little time and the resources he had become accustomed to at Barcelona and Bayern Munich – could possibly carry City towards domestic domination and the promised land of continental glory too.

Since becoming the first English club to win a domestic and continental title in the same season under Mercer and Allison, City's European trophy cupboard had solely been employed for capturing dust and displaying the occasional obscure and oversized pre-season trophy from Ireland or Sweden. A generation of absence from continental competition had left the club with a mountain to climb in order to join a gilded elite that had in the meantime grown plump and comfortable at the top of a particularly well-protected and luxuriously decorated UEFA tree.

Since Silvio Berlusconi, the lugubrious AC Milan owner, had attempted a coup from within by shunting UEFA towards the formation of the quasi-closed shop of the Champions League in 1992, the polarisation of Europe's teams between a tiny elite and the rest had continued apace. City, in attempting to break into and solidify their presence within this elite, were one of the last clubs, along with the previous season's quarter-final victims Paris Saint-Germain, to scuttle in before the gates were padlocked. Despite this good timing, rising to the top rungs occupied by Real, Barcelona and Bayern would take something special.

The scamp in the welcome crowd who shouted: 'Are you going to buy Messi?!' had perhaps the most realistic idea of how City might prevail against the continental behemoths of Italy, Germany and Spain. Guardiola, as ever, would be doing it his way, however, and not with Lionel Messi but with Bacary Sagna.

As the Catalan got down to his first days in office, early thoughts were already turning to Europe and City's continuing quest, firstly, for acceptance at the UEFA high table and, secondly, for clear and unequivocal signs of progress towards the clearly desired goal of Champions League success.

As fans of rival clubs had intimated, particularly those of United, Liverpool and Chelsea, whose teams had already experienced the delights of being crowned kings of Europe: 'You aren't anybody in football until you've won the big one.' City were clearly now a top-six fixture in Europe – their exploits domestically had turned them into the club with the best average finishing position in the previous six years of Premier League football (that in itself was a totally unthinkable statistic just a few years earlier), but also (by Guardiola's second year in charge in 2017–18) the English club with the longest unbroken run in appearing in the Champions League.

Clearly on the up under Mancini and Pellegrini, the club now looked set to cement that progression with something altogether different. If those two men had helped hoist City towards the upper echelons, Guardiola was here to plant the flag on the snow-capped summit.

Did the clouds skipping away across the horizon that bright Manchester afternoon of Guardiola's unveiling hide one possible problem, though? His own record in the Champions League had not exactly been without blemishes. Since his Barcelona side had lifted the trophy in 2011, a succession of bad luck stories had stymied his progress. Of Guardiola's exits from the Champions League as a manager, three had been on away goals, and three had involved games with missed penalties by his sides. His Barcelona had been undone by an Icelandic volcano in 2010, meaning their trip to face Inter Milan had had to be undertaken by coach. On top of that, an underlying feeling that this most glamorous trophy was somehow meant to be the property of great rivals Real Madrid, winners of the first five editions from 1955–6 and the previous season's epic final with neighbours Atlético, had never completely left the scene either. Did some kind of a hex hang over the Catalan?

Describing Guardiola as unlucky in the light of his new club's history was certainly not an issue for fans brought up on a club capable of exiting the FA Cup to a ricochet off a balloon. While journalists prepared their theses for making sense of the chaos of football, the fans basked happily in the knowledge that tackling chaos had beaten tens of good men at the helm of City in the past.

Given the club's penchant for doing things the difficult way, perhaps the route to the top, although clearly marked with gaily painted flags and bunting, might not be quite as straightforward as everyone was hoping. For a club with such a strong reputation for shooting itself repeatedly in the foot, supporters would need clear proof that the old leopard had indeed managed to begin scrubbing off some of its most troubling spots. Unlucky or not, too intense or not, too committed to attacking or not, perhaps the most important aspect to the Catalan at this stage was that he bore little or no resemblance to Steve Coppell, Frank Clark, Ron

Saunders, Mel Machin, John Benson or any of the other *leaders of the lost cause*, whose efforts had become the cause of a million and one sleepless nights.

Thanks to the weak finish in Pellegrini's final year (City had only secured fourth place after a final-day draw at Swansea), a play-off match was needed before access to the group stage of the 2016–17 edition of the Champions League could be sealed.

Play-off games seldom cause seeded clubs problems, but for Guardiola the pressure was cranked up by the matches falling so early in his tenure. Fresh from a smattering of half-paced pre-season publicity games in the United States, City were thrown into a game against Romanians Steaua Bucharesti having played just one competitive match under their new coach.

The game in question had been typically riveting, owing to Guardiola's much-anticipated tactical tinkering.

On a sunny and relaxed afternoon, the opening Premier League game of the season had been won at home to Sunderland, but only thanks to a last-minute own goal by the deeply unfortunate Paddy McNair. Despite problems putting what seemed to be a straightforward match to bed (City had been in front from the fourth minute when Sergio Agüero netted from the penalty spot), Guardiola's debut game had nevertheless been quite an eye-opener.

With full-backs Sagna and Clichy cutting in constantly to play in midfield (at one point even crossing each other and heading to the other side of the pitch), the Catalan immediately invited the watching public to open their minds to a host of new and hitherto absurd possibilities.

One of the most startling was accepting Aleksandar Kolarov, a notoriously lethargic left-back, as a striding Franz Beckenbauer-esque figure on the left side of central defence.

There may have been other noteworthy occurrences, but the sight of the Serbian strutting through to midfield, ball obediently stuck to his instep, sent many in the full house into a parallel universe where just about anything might be possible.

Not everyone had been completely convinced by the opening day's activities, however, as the coach's desired playing style veered sharply away from what had gone before it. I wrote in my ESPN column the day after the Sunderland victory:

'The occasional grumbles rolling down off the stands at the Etihad last Saturday of "too much precision" and "not enough pace" will have been unusual noises to the ears of new coach Pep Guardiola. In what was only his fourth game in charge, after a sparse pre-season of three warm-up games, City's approach in the opening day fixture against Sunderland had surprised a few people.'

City had been undeniably slow in their attempts to circumnavigate an opposition packing its midfield with central defenders, despite being gifted the early boost of a fourth-minute penalty.

With Manchester agog at the new shape and ideas, Champions League football, and the away leg with Steaua, was already upon us.

Off the pitch, the squad revamp was well under way with Guardiola-sanctioned investments filing in one by one. İlkay Gündoğan arrived from Dortmund to provide box-to-box prowess, Celta Vigo's Nolito unorthodox wing play, Schalke's Leroy Sané an athletic streak down the left, John Stones a ball-playing presence out of central defence and Gabriel Jesus the prospect of some serious competition up front for Sergio Agüero after agreeing to move to Europe in January. At great expense and with considerable speed, the squad was being reorganised to suit the new man in charge.

In Bucharest, Guardiola persisted with Willy Caballero, who

had surprisingly been picked to play instead of England regular Joe Hart against Sunderland, and again fielded new man Nolito down the left and John Stones at the back, this time alongside Nicolás Otamendi, with Kolarov sliding five metres to the left to replace Clichy.

Having scored a penalty in the opening game, this tie would see Agüero hit two more from the spot, with neither of them counting. The first was saved by Florin Niță, but the second needed no intervention from the overworked goalkeeper as Agüero blasted high over the bar. Despite two misses from the spot, however, the stocky Argentinian secured a hat-trick, thus demonstrating a vast gulf between the two sides.

Long before the end, the 45,000 crowd had been cowed into polite applause by City's devastating counter-attacking which brought two more goals from Silva and Nolito and could easily have delivered considerably more than that. After the confused lethargy of the opening league game, this had been a free-flowing masterclass of dynamic pressing, counter-attacking and dizzyingly rapid interchanging of passes.

The Guardiola era at City was truly up and running.

What was already inescapable at this nascent stage of the season was the coach's inimitable influence. City's fast-flowing possession game ripped holes in the home side's shape and, through those newly drilled holes, Steaua were flooded by a series of killer passes by David Silva and Kevin De Bruyne. With so much of the season lying ahead, City fans were busy congratulating themselves on the new dawn rising before them. For the Romanians, squinting and squirming, there was no denying that this early-era Guardiola version of Manchester City had shown serious signs of being unstoppable. The domestic season ahead would prove it to be something of a false dawn, but the groundwork was being laid for something quite extraordinary a year down the line.

Statistics also revealed reassuringly revolutionary findings: City's 65 per cent ball possession was a taste of what was to come, while 24 shots to the home side's ten told its own eloquent story. Steaua were clearly not of the same calibre as the side that won the European Cup in Seville against Barcelona in 1986, but they were certainly no mugs either.

With this comprehensive dismantling of the Romanians on their own patch, City had – as the experts would have it – put down a marker. The giants of European football would be watching and taking note: Guardiola's side's first steps had been taken.

STEAUA BUCUREŞTI 0–5 MANCHESTER CITY | Att. 45,327 | Silva, Agüero (3), Nolito

Caballero, Zabaleta, Otamendi, Stones (Adarabioyo), Kolarov, Fernandinho (Iheanacho), Silva, Sterling, De Bruyne, Nolito (Angelino), Agüero

---

With a rampant 4–1 win at Stoke separating the first leg from the second, City entered the Etihad return with Steaua in good spirits and even better early season form.

The only real talking point to emerge from a low-key 1–0 win was the appearance of Hart between the posts. A conspicuous captain's armband appeared to suggest a going away tribute as the newspapers continued to speculate that Chilean captain and Guardiola favourite Claudio Bravo's arrival in Manchester was imminent. Several banners around the ground suggested not everyone in sky blue was ready to bid him farewell, however.

It had been widely mooted that Hart's lack of ability with his feet – as far as Guardiola was concerned, an essential part of any goalkeeper's repertoire – would count against him. His reputation for erratic distribution had on this occasion preceded him. The Catalan was to take no time in deciding that the young

England keeper was not what he was looking for as he strove to revolutionise a stagnant players' pool left behind by Pellegrini. It might even have been the case that he had made his mind up about Hart when his Bayern side had coaxed errors from the City man in 2013. Hart would not be the only focus of the new broom that was sweeping through the club, but the goalkeeper bought from Shrewsbury and groomed into the national team number one, would certainly be the highest-profile casualty of the new order settling over the Etihad. One remembered the games where he had stood between City and European drubbings and offered a moment of silent respect.

The match with Steaua also underlined something else: the new coach would not be afraid to throw unexpected figures into the fray, make wholesale changes and tinker with formation if and where he felt it beneficial. In came youngsters Pablo Maffeo and Kelechi Iheanacho, as well as the hulking mass of Yaya Touré, awarded a kind of slow-moving shuttle brief between midfield and a lightly manned attack.

Much would be made of what Pellegrini had left for his successor in terms of playing resources and, with a side containing Clichy, Navas, Touré and Fernando, with Kolarov once again switching to central defence, it was clear to see it would be an intriguing transition for all involved. Equally, Guardiola and his coaching staff knew full well that reinforcements were being made, but that in this first season they would have to make do and mend to a certain extent. A squad that had grown old and tired together under the Chilean coach still looked ill-equipped to attack on all fronts.

On this occasion, Steaua, tidy but light on ambition, restricted City to a single goal by Fabian Delph, headed in cleverly from an unusually accurate Navas cross from the right wing.

With so many first-teamers rested, Delph's performance gave the manager something to think about for the upcoming league games. The only casualty apart from the soon-to-be jettisoned Hart appeared to be Iheanacho, who pulled up after trying to outrun Bogdan Mitrea and left the pitch on a stretcher. For Delph, it was a first run-out under a manager who would find an increasingly important role for him.

MANCHESTER CITY 1–0 STEAUA BUCUREŞTI | Att. 40,064 | Delph

Hart, Maffeo, Stones, Kolarov, Clichy, Navas, Fernando, Delph, Nolito, Touré, Iheanacho

---

The draw for the group stages was made in Monaco a day after City had disposed of Steaua, on Thursday 25 August. Pellegrini's efforts in dragging the club to a semi-final against Real in his final season had helped push City – now with a higher coefficient – into the much more favourable pot two, meaning the groups of death that the team had had great difficulty avoiding up to now might well have become a thing of the past.

Not this time, however, as once again the little UEFA balls refused to roll for the club.

Out of the urns came Guardiola's old side Barcelona, familiar foes Borussia Mönchengladbach and Scottish champions Celtic. Initial reaction was favourable, with many suggesting second place behind the obvious favourites was within City's scope in a well-balanced group.

The opening game would be staged at the Etihad against the Germans and there would be little time to organise, have the Germans watched and get prepared, as the league season was now under way after an international break.

By 14 September, City had only had time to play two more league games, but it was becoming clear that the new coach was having an immediate effect both on and off the pitch. A home win over West Ham had been followed by a slick 2–1 win in the first Manchester derby of the season at Old Trafford, and City prepared to meet Borussia top of the Premier League table with a 100 per cent record, six wins from six games in all competitions.

Before the game could be played, however, the Manchester weather had something to say for itself. Graham Ward, watcher of City from the early '70s, explains: 'The weather had been so bad it led to the cancellation of the game for 24 hours, a blow for a few of the German fans, who had to return home. I met a Brazilian on the tram journey to the ground, and, as we chatted, he gave me a plastic poncho, which was to come in handy. As the tram pulled into Victoria, it halted as there was a huge flash of lightning over the CIS Tower and thunderous amounts of rain, the like of which I had never seen before – it reminded me of Honvéd nearly 50 years before.

'After a delay of 20 to 30 minutes, the tram set off, and the scenes on Market Street were remarkable, as office staff were vainly attempting to mop up flood water entering the Lewis' store. The tram arrived a few minutes before the scheduled kick-off, but, of course, it had been postponed. I had to make my way back home on the bus, as the tram service was suspended.'

Simon Hart, covering the match for the UEFA website, had noticed that not all the travelling fans had had to return home: 'I remember speaking to Borussia fans whose coaches were parked up outside the ground and some of them had slept on their coaches when the game was postponed 24 hours.'

Mönchengladbach, expected to provide a sterner test than in the 4–2 defeat the previous year, proved once again to be pliant opponents on the night, with another Agüero hat-trick helping City to a 4–0 win. The Argentinian had now scored six goals in three Champions League games.

With City fielding a strong side, Sterling shone down the left flank and busy debutant Gündoğan won a penalty after his ankles were swept from under him in the 28th minute. Indeed, Gündoğan fitted superbly into Guardiola's swift-moving possession game, leaving the Germans struggling to keep up.

The match also began to give pointers as to which players were likely to be favoured in Guardiola's first season. With Bravo newly installed in goal (he had already suffered a desperate Manchester derby), Otamendi and Stones formed the centre-back partnership, with Fernandinho shielding them in deep midfield. With David Silva's absence from injury, the attacking quartet in midfield comprised Gündoğan, Sterling, De Bruyne and Navas, with Agüero up front alone. Nolito's place on the bench suggested his initial impact had not been as great as hoped. The Spaniard's curious, hunched running style, making him look like an old lady escaping from a house fire, had not left favourable initial impressions.

At last, City's European entrance had been a positive one. After so many false starts in the Champions League, three points and a 4–0 goal difference provided them with a real platform to proceed with confidence.

MANCHESTER CITY 4–0 BORUSSIA MÖNCHENGLADBACH |
Att. 30,270 | Agüero (3, 1 pen.), Iheanacho

Bravo, Zabaleta, Stones, Otamendi, Kolarov, Fernandinho, Navas, De Bruyne, Sterling (Sané), Gündoğan (Clichy), Agüero (Iheanacho)

City's progress in the Premier League continued to be exemplary and, by the time the party flew north to Scotland for the latest of a long history of Anglo-Scottish skirmishes down the years, they were still sitting pretty at the top of the league, Guardiola was receiving a wildly positive press and the rest of the division were looking up at a team full of confidence.

The match turned out to be notable for two reasons. Firstly, it was a game of raw intensity that nobody present would forget in a hurry and, secondly, the final score of 3–3 meant City's ten-game winning streak from the opening day of the campaign came to an end. The game's intensity was matched throughout by the noise of the crowd and the amount of rain falling out of the sky. The tropical deluge in Manchester before the first game was more than matched by the Glaswegian elements in the second.

Before seeing what effect the weather would have on the game, the City support had other challenges to overcome, as Murdoch Dalziel recalls: 'This was infamously the first-ever away game where City fans had to collect their tickets from the venue beforehand. In this case, some old indoor market in Glasgow city centre. Thousands of inebriated Mancunians queueing in torrential rain, with many of them having forgotten to bring ID. What could possibly go wrong? What a mess it was.

'Pre-match there were Rangers fans everywhere, imploring us to win with language only suitable post-watershed. Getting to the ground was a weird experience as no taxis would take us and the only way we could get there was to take the bus in the general direction of the ground.

'I asked the driver which stop we should get off at and he said: "You'll know because everyone will get off," which I found weird because absolutely no one had any colours on. Anyway, the bus stops and everyone gets off. I asked the guy in front of me if he's going to the game and he says: "Aye, we all are, son." I asked him why no one was wearing colours and he said they all *were* wearing the shirts and scarves but that they were hidden under coats because this bus dropped off in a staunch Rangers area. "If they see any Celtic fans walking down the road to the game, Rangers fans will come out of the pubs and give them a slap!"

'Given that my brother and I are not only City fans but of Scottish descent, we thought we'd have a couple of quick ones.

Lo and behold, first bar we go in, head to toe, wall to wall in pictures of the Queen and a massive Union Jack behind the bar. It was moody to say the least. We got our beers and got the now familiar: "You better beat those Fenian bastards!"

'Anyhow, we had a couple more and got to the ground just as Fernandinho was equalising. I agreed to meet my brother at half-time, as he was sitting in a different area of the away end. Later on in the first half I saw my brother quite some way away; he was attempting to stand still but was swaying from side to side. Given he doesn't usually drink a lot, it appeared that drinking from 11am to 8pm, including cocktails, hadn't met with his body's approval.

'I went to meet him at half-time – nowhere to be seen. Rang him. Nothing. Later on, I got a message from him, saying he'd been escorted from the ground before half-time. You could say it was a memorable trip back to my homeland …'

That the weather had helped make the pitch greasy only heightened the spectacle. Three times Celtic went ahead, three times City – bedecked in a pina colada kit – pegged them back. If by the end everyone from players to supporters were utterly spent, it was hardly surprising.

With the hint of offside and a deflection off Sterling accounting for the home side's first two goals, Guardiola's side showed their character to keep coming back, firstly through Fernandinho's scuffed shot, then Sterling making amends for his own goal. When Dembele netted his second and Celtic's third just after the break, aided by Kolarov's balletic blunder in the box, things looked bleak, but the free-flowing football paid more dividends with Nolito tapping in after Agüero's shot had been parried by Craig Gordon. The winning run may have ended, but the Champions League start was on track with four points from two games.

On track was a phrase that ceased to be relevant after the next match, however, as Guardiola's Catalan homecoming turned into something of an embarrassment.

CELTIC 3–3 MANCHESTER CITY | Att. 57,592 | Fernandinho, Sterling, Nolito

Bravo, Zabaleta, Clichy (Stones), Otamendi, Kolarov, Fernandinho, Silva, Nolito (Fernando), Gündoğan, Sterling, Agüero

---

With the winning run ended at Celtic, City then lost at Tottenham and were held by Everton in the league. Suddenly, the reality of the struggle facing the new coach was laid bare. The performance of his defence, still majority-manned by players he had inherited rather than chosen himself, was a major focus, as was the dizzyingly erratic form of Bravo.

Although the final scoreline from the Nou Camp suggested obliteration, City had carried the fight to the home side during a first half where their own chances in front of goal outnumbered Barcelona's. A similarly bright opening to the second half belied the fact that City were about to finish such a distant second in this clash of the group favourites.

Undone by a catastrophic slip by Fernandinho, which allowed Messi to waltz into the box and score, the sudden deficit appeared to suggest an uphill struggle for the second half. However, chances continued to come City's way until the unstoppable Messi, in tandem with Luis Suárez and Neymar, finished the game off. By the time the second-half goals went in, City's goal was being guarded by Willy Caballero after Bravo received a red card in the latest instalment of his nightmare start in Manchester.

For Guardiola, it was a defeat to put alongside his Bayern side's 3–0 semi-final loss on the same pitch. For City, the heaviest defeat yet in their brief Champions League history. For Bravo, it was a public catastrophe beyond even the scatter-brained departure from his goal that had almost thrown away City's advantage in the Old Trafford derby. Here again, his poor delivery allowed Barcelona to come straight back at him before he had recovered his position, necessitating a save with his hands outside the box.

That his replacement ended up saving a penalty was academic as the three second-half goals gave the final score a flattering unrealistic tilt. City were lucky to remain second in the group after Celtic managed to lose at home to Mönchengladbach, but the gap to Barcelona was already five points.

The City coach, already proving a dab hand at chopping and changing to good effect, was widely criticised on this occasion for leaving out Agüero. Pushing De Bruyne forward as a false nine, chances had fallen City's way that Agüero would have put away without a fuss. City's new shape continued to puzzle, with Zabaleta encouraged to dig in alongside Fernandinho in midfield from his right-back position, a repeat of what we had witnessed on the opening day victory over Sunderland. Whether the shape had been a 3–2–3–2 or a 3–3–4, it had not worked, with chances missed and the opposition clinical with their own opportunities when they arose.

BARCELONA 4–0 MANCHESTER CITY | Att. 96,290

Bravo (Caballero), Zabaleta (Clichy), Kolarov, Otamendi, Stones, Fernandinho, Gündoğan (Agüero), Nolito (Caballero), Sterling, Silva, De Bruyne

If the manager's tinkering had been held partly responsible for the cave-in at the Nou Camp, it was only right that he should receive the plaudits for what happened in the return game. Having started the season with ten straight wins, by the time of Barcelona's visit to the Etihad, City were revealing their true colours to the new coach with a six-game winless streak before defeating West Brom prior to the game.

Lifting the roof

In what the Madrid-based *MARCA* gleefully called '*La Venganza de Guardiola*', City produced one of the Etihad's most enduring memories, wiping the floor with the aristocrats of Europe in an explosion of second-half fluidity. If Messi's hat-trick had illuminated the first game between the sides, then the return of his friend and compatriot Agüero to first-team duties tipped the balance City's way this time. Without getting his name on the scoresheet, the stocky Argentinian caused havoc in a destabilised visiting defence with a virtuoso display of selfless attacking play.

This was a heaving, bellowing tidal wave of an Etihad experience. A ground that so often struggled to come to life throbbed and fizzed as City wove their magic in a match which confirmed a kind of arrival, a blossoming into real big-stage participants. They had not just won but come from a goal behind and swept the masters away in a second-half blitz. If it was a triumph for Guardiola, it was a triumph too for the selflessness of Agüero, the imperious midfield prompting of De Bruyne and the fantastic opportunism of Gündoğan. It was vindication too for the owners and the dream that they had propagated. For the supporters, wringing their hands in disbelief, it was football of a kind that had only appeared in the most fevered dreams.

Tellingly, the City coach stated: 'In the first 38 minutes, we saw the best team in the world.' On the other hand, Barcelona coach Luis Enrique said after the first game that City had 'tried to press his side into the stands'. Here was much the same release of energy, this time with its rewards.

For the other 52 minutes of the match, City were the masters. Agüero pounced on the loose ball after Sergi Roberto attempted a suicidal lateral pass, fed Sterling on the right, whose cross was turned in by Gündoğan.

De Bruyne produced the *pièce de résistance*, curling in an inch-perfect free kick to put City ahead, then destabilised the visitors to prompt the move that produced a second tap-in for the lurking Gündoğan.

Andy Hunter's *Guardian* piece spoke of a 'team that looked like they had nothing to fear'. Perhaps he was right. Perhaps also he should have elongated the sentence slightly to add 'but themselves'. In any case, this was the kind of evening that everyone had been waiting for. At the sixth attempt, Barcelona had been vanquished.

MANCHESTER CITY 3–1 BARCELONA | Att. 53,340 | Gündoğan (2), De Bruyne

Caballero, Zabaleta, Stones, Otamendi, Kolarov, Fernandinho (Fernando), Gündoğan, Silva, De Bruyne (Nolito), Sterling (Navas), Agüero

---

The game represented a watershed for many. Colin Savage, veteran of many seasons watching City, had finally enjoyed a Champions League evening. 'I suppose I'm torn between three games that are my favourite memories of the tournament,' he reflected. 'Being in Madrid in 2012 when we were winning with a few minutes left on the clock and the PSG quarter-final win, but the 3–1 win over Barcelona just beats them. It really felt like we had come of age in the tournament that night. Really got the adrenaline going too. For once I actually enjoyed a Champions League occasion!'

By November, and with a game still to play, City had secured their fourth straight group-stage qualification. For those still bracketing the club in the naive newcomers section, the time had come for an upgrade.

Despite an erratic display in the 1–1 draw in Mönchengladbach, the point meant the Germans could no longer overhaul City for the second spot in the group. Barcelona's 2–0 win at Celtic Park meant the Scots would finish bottom.

With Kompany's string of injuries still not allowing him to be part of Guardiola's plans, the Catalan was again forced to deploy a patched-up defence. Only Otamendi, Stones and Kolarov could be called out-and-out defenders, while Sterling and Navas pushed on in the advanced wide positions.

It was another tactical gamble from Guardiola ('it will be sometimes three, sometimes four, we will see what works' he had joked beforehand) that occasionally reduced City's backline to a jittery mess. Confirmation that it had not gone to plan duly saw the coach revert to a traditional back four after half an hour, with Kolarov moving wider on the left to allow Navas in at right-back, but by that time, City had conceded to Lars Stindl's excellent approach play, setting up Raffael to shoot past Bravo.

A sliding near-post equaliser from David Silva and another red card, this time to Fernandinho, heralded a gradual closing down of the game as Borussia ran out of ideas. City, despite themselves, were through again, but the nature of this point left questions to be asked about whether Guardiola really possessed the personnel to achieve his high goals. League form had all but evaporated from the blitzkrieg start, with City conceding three goals at home to Chelsea and losing two players to red cards. Ill-discipline and a bedding-in period for Guardiola's unique ways meant patience was required.

BORUSSIA MÖNCHENGLADBACH 1–1 MANCHESTER CITY |
Att. 45,921 | Silva

Bravo, Otamendi, Stones, Kolarov, Navas, Gündoğan, Fernandinho, Sterling (Sagna), Silva, De Bruyne, Agüero

Closing the group affairs with a featureless (and meaningless) 1–1 draw with Celtic signified little more than City's bad run of four wins from twelve ticked on to thirteen. This was a far cry from Guardiola's sunlit honeymoon back in August and it would be a few more weeks before it dawned on everyone that the season 2016–17 might have to be confined to the bin marked 'experiments'.

With youngsters Pablo Maffeo and Tosin Adarabioyo featuring in another greatly reorganised side – nine changes from the weekend's game – and Zabaleta being asked to mimic David Silva in midfield, it was obvious from the outset that this was a further exercise in shuffling the pack. That the best City youngster turned out to be playing for Celtic (the on-loan Patrick Roberts) came as no surprise to seasoned City watchers well honed in embracing the ridiculous.

Naturally, it was Roberts who scored early for the visitors in the fourth minute and four minutes later the game's scoring had been completed with an equaliser from Iheanacho.

Six points adrift of Barcelona and four ahead of Mönchengladbach meant City secured the *safe second place* that had always been earmarked for them, but with experiments like Kolarov in central defence and Zabaleta as a midfield orchestrator, there seemed only limited mileage in such dabbling, even as short-term solutions.

MANCHESTER CITY 1–1 CELTIC | Att. 51,297 | Iheanacho
Caballero, Clichy, Adarabioyo, Sagna, Maffeo (Navas), Fernando, Sané, Zabaleta, Gündoğan, Nolito, Iheanacho

As ever, runner-up slots guaranteed a last-sixteen match with a group winner, however. City could look forward to a match-up with a team in strong form. That Bayern Munich and Real Madrid had also both finished second in their groups meant avoiding them, but old foes Napoli, dark horses Atlético Madrid plus the might of Juventus and Borussia Dortmund all awaited.

In the end, the draw for the knockout round on 12 December threw in a curve ball in the shape of Monaco. On the surface, it looked like a handy pairing for City, but Leonardo Jardim's technically adroit side had been uprooting plenty of trees in Ligue 1 and were expected to give a good account of themselves.

In my ESPN column, I spoke of City 'finally being blessed with the draw they would have yearned for. Monaco represent the easiest draw left open from the options restricted by UEFA's carefully arranged rules and regulations. Despite their good form in Ligue 1 – where they are currently running ahead of champions Paris Saint-Germain – and despite the fact that talented manager Leonardo Jardim is building a side to match the legendary 2004 team that reached the Champions League final in Gelsenkirchen, this Monaco side offer a great chance for City to reach the quarter-finals for the second year running …'

Having spent extravagantly in the recent past on the likes of João Moutinho, James Rodríguez and Radamel Falcao, the Monegasques were now concentrating enthusiastically on their youth policy. UEFA's notorious FFP rules had put a stop to a spending spree that Monaco vice-president Vadim Vasilyev had charmingly termed 'a bit too optimistic'. With 6,000 home gates, it was back to promoting youth by the time 2016–17 dawned. This had gone better than anyone could have expected and a side containing the talent of future City players Bernardo Silva and Benjamin Mendy, PSG-bound Kylian Mbappé, future Merseyside signings Fabinho and Djibril Sidibé and Chelsea capture Tiémoué Bakayoko would be hailed French champions by the end of the season.

Sitting in the press box at Huddersfield's John Smith's Stadium, watching a dreadful 0–0 draw in the fifth round of the FA Cup on Saturday 18 February, it was not immediately apparent what extravagant fare awaited us all at the Etihad three days later. The row of lukewarm pies and dented tea urns that represented Huddersfield's press buffet seemed to be shouting out for comparison with the extravagant seafood banquet Monaco residents might be familiar with. Nevertheless, if it were possible to get indigestion from fine dining, Monaco at home would be the game to supply it.

'The critics want to kill me,' Guardiola stated before kick-off. 'To be here in the last sixteen is not easy. People can think that City, with the most prestigious football, the most media, most advertising in the world, you have to be here. We are lucky guys. All the world will watch us. They will analyse us and kill us if we don't win.'

Intimating that *little City* were bobbing around among the big sharks was a narrative that some were beginning to tire of. With the Barcelona jinx seemingly overcome and successive group qualifications under their belt, City were transforming themselves into something of a safe bet, a far cry from the initial seasons battling – and losing to – the likes of Real, Bayern, Ajax and Dortmund.

While social media trolling would always involve ill-researched banter about 'scruffy Manc nouveaux riches', City were no wet-behind-the-ears novices, despite the cavernous gap between 1979 and the most recent European action. Even if the club's latest continental activity did not match up to the proud records of Arsenal and Manchester United, the squad of players were winners from the very highest levels of the sport.

If there was something to say for modern City supporters, it was that they had carried with them into the Years of Plenty a gallows humour that prepared them for a quick return to rhubarb and custard at any given moment.

A Barclays survey for the FA Premier League had uncovered the fact that the club had more season ticket holders of 25-years standing than any other club. Manchester City Football Club may have been almost unrecognisable from the team dumped out of the FA Cup by Halifax all those years ago, but many of the fans now entering the Nou Camp and the Parc des Princes had also been laid low at The Shay in an era when football smelled of moss and nettles.

Fragrant anarchy

In the impoverished relegation years of the '80s and '90s, preparing travel and accommodation arrangements for a City fixture in Monte Carlo would have had the perpetrator sectioned, but here we were.

That City should carry off the game 5–3 looked unlikely in the extreme for all but the last twenty minutes of this unforgettable encounter. Twice trailing at 1–2 and 2–3, it took a gargantuan effort by the players and an avalanche of attacking football to eventually prevail against a Monaco side that skipped and cavorted delightfully as they played their full part for two-thirds of the match. Leading the way in the game that would turn Manchester heads for ever in his direction was the diminutive Bernardo Silva. Twisting and turning, his darts into the middle areas from the right flank and metronome passing through City's defence with a wand of a left foot carried his side near to victory and entirely eclipsed his illustrious namesake in the City midfield.

A no-look nutmeg on the grand master Touré seemed to sum up the quicksilver performance of the Portuguese starlet. That it would be David and not Bernardo ruling the midfield roost by the end of a quite glorious turnaround spoke volumes for the little Spaniard's enduring influence on City's affairs.

Making seven changes from the turgid show at Huddersfield, Guardiola brought back all his favourites and then watched motionless from the sidelines as his plan dissolved before his eyes. Any thoughts of a cagey cat-and-mouse Champions League contest were quickly thrown out and replaced by the reality of yet another slapstick Manchester City evening. My ESPN column the day after the game suggested there might well be a spanner in the works: 'City's defence has been leaking all season and it appeared to have sprung the biggest hole yet when Monaco went 3–2 ahead. Both Stones and Otamendi were caught out by the thrusting counter-attacks. Unless Guardiola can shore up his backline, City may just be too open to actually get to within touching distance of trophies this season.'

In the *Guardian*, a breathless Daniel Taylor took up a similar theme: 'Where do you even start with a match of this nature? It was a thrilling night, full of mistakes, drama and controversy and, when everything was done, Manchester City could look back on a noteworthy feat of escapology.'

City had fought back with character. Even the erratic referee Antonio Lahoz, whom City would meet again at another vital juncture in the adventure a year later, seemed hell-bent on making life difficult, booking Agüero at 1–1 for a dive in the penalty area which television replays clearly showed was an infringement from Monaco's goalkeeper Danijel Subašić as he charged from his goal.

Guardiola's pre-match killing analogy had almost been re-enacted on the Etihad turf. This was not the Champions League that City's grand strategist was used to. His slide-rule precision victories with Barcelona and Bayern usually left little space for the kind of antics that City had been brought up on, but here he was presiding over a royal feast of fragrant anarchy.

It was *L'Equipe* who summed up a crazy match best. 'So beautiful but so hard,' it announced. 'Beaten in an exceptional match, *Les Monegasques* only cracked in the final twenty minutes,' journalist Régis Testelin stated. 'Qualification will not be simple in three weeks' time ...'

MANCHESTER CITY 5-3 MONACO | Att. 53,351 | Sterling, Agüero (2), Stones, Sané

Caballero, Sagna, Stones, Otamendi, Fernandinho (Zabaleta), Silva, Touré, De Bruyne, Sané, Agüero (Fernando), Sterling (Navas)

While *L'Equipe*'s assertion that Monaco's task would not be easy held firm, their eventual 3–1 victory in the second leg did not involve any of the convoluted narrative of the Etihad game. City were out at the last sixteen stage, Guardiola or not, outplayed and outrun by a mesmerising opponent, full of energy and verve. That Monaco would be the season's surprise team, reaching the last four, would be of little compensation to City, once again on their way home early with their tails between their legs.

City had been thirteen minutes from going through, after Leroy Sané had blasted the ball into the roof of the net from Sterling's parried shot to make it 2–1, but, undone once again by slack defending, they failed to hold out, allowing Bakayoko in for a headed decider.

It was the first time in Guardiola's managerial career that the Catalan had exited the Champions League so early. The City effect, loud and clear. On top of this, City became the first side to exit the Champions League after scoring five in a first-leg match, topping and tailing their notoriety nicely.

In a strange press conference admission, Guardiola expressed an inability 'to persuade' his players to attack 'until it was too late'. The thought of players doing anything other than carry out Guardiola's instructions to the letter raised a few eyebrows. Did some of them actually have their own ideas? 'All managers make mistakes, but I don't think it was a tactical mistake here,' he continued. 'The difference was between the first half and the second half. In the second half we tried to win the game. I did that way all my career. But the problem was the first half. We weren't there.'

Crucially, Guardiola would offer an identical excuse three years later in similarly grim circumstances against another French side, Lyon, suggesting some lessons are harder to learn than others.

Fan Simon Bell found himself watching the match from the section of the ground packed with the Monaco ultras. 'By the time of the Monaco game, ridiculous new away ticket control measures had been introduced, so I failed to source a second ticket for my wife. Knowing Monaco have a smaller crowd than you would probably see on any given Sunday at Hough End, I got straight on their website with my Letts French dictionary. Fifteen minutes later I was printing two tickets for the game – we were going to Monaco.

'The home stand behind the goal is quite small, and we found ourselves in the middle of their singing section. It is amazing how much racket can be generated by such a small group. Naturally, I refused to acknowledge their goals, drawing unwanted attention to ourselves. Internally celebrating a Sané goal in the last twenty minutes provided false hope, as they then got a third. Edging towards the exits, we managed to make a quick escape as soon as the final whistle blew. Catching the train back to Nice we found a small bar and some friends to help drown our sorrows of another unsuccessful European adventure.'

MONACO 3–1 MANCHESTER CITY | Att. 15,700 | Sané

Caballero, Sagna, Kolarov, Stones, Clichy (Iheanacho), Fernandinho, De Bruyne, Silva, Sané, Agüero, Sterling

---

Monaco would sail past Borussia Dortmund in the quarter-finals to confirm that their win over City had been no flash in the pan, before being dispatched by Juventus in the semi-finals. In the final, the Italians would be comprehensively taken to the cleaners in the Millennium Stadium in Cardiff by the one team that felt light years away from City, in European and any other terms. Real Madrid, serial winners of the tournament, added a twelfth European title to their sagging mantelpiece. There would be another for the Madrileños the following season as City combusted again at the crucial moment. To those pushing the club forward, it must have felt like lifting Europe's premier trophy was just a step too far for a ragamuffin club from West Gorton.

14

ANFIELD ANGST

Shot by both sides

Watching Liverpool's players warm up for a momentous occasion in Rome was painful viewing for all at City at the end of Guardiola's second season in charge.

Having rendered their Champions League semi-final second leg a near-formality, by winning the first 5–2, the old European masters were effectively stepping out in a game City had earmarked for themselves. A tie against Roma (at the venue where City had won so dramatically in 2014) rather than against one of the accepted giants at that late stage of the competition would have had City fans dreaming of a long trip to Kyiv for the 2018 final.

As it was, Liverpool were the ones genuflecting and waving to the crowd instead. It was yet another of football's delicious sliding-door stories. The tale of why it was Liverpool heading to the top table after a break of eleven years and not City for the first time in half a century of out-of-breath floundering is an intricate and emotional one that will unfold here.

City's sole experience of this stage of the competition was already a hazy memory. It had only been two years, but so much seemed to have happened since. From the early days when Paul Hayward in the *Daily Telegraph* had dubbed Pellegrini's tactics 'death by geometry', City's challenge had ended in oblique angles and an obtuse aversion to learning from their mistakes.

As if a domestic unravelling had not been bad enough, the lack of concrete progress in the Champions League seemed to hurt even more. True, there was the first-ever semi-final but even the legacy of that had been soured by a surprising outbreak of disciplined hiding, when gung-ho bravery befitting the club's colourful past had been required.

City's early Champions League disadvantage, borne of a UEFA quotient scheme that had often left them saddled with difficult groups, had ceased to be a problem. From the inaugural disasters against the big fish, City had grown teeth and scale of their own. Opening groups comprising Napoli, Bayern and Villarreal and Dortmund, Real Madrid and Ajax, had softened to Bayern, CSKA Moscow and Plzeň, CSKA Moscow, Bayern and Roma, Juventus, Mönchengladbach and Sevilla and Barcelona, Mönchengladbach and Celtic. Nobody was suggesting these were cakewalks, but – along with City's growth – they represented the dealing of a better, more manageable hand for a club trying to sustain a meteoric rise into the big-hitters' league.

While we had seen plenty of evidence of the early buzz City's supporters got at the prospect of visiting the cathedrals of Europe to watch their long-malfunctioning club in action, the directors' glances continued to fall on balance sheets and global projection. For City's *grand oeuvre* to come to proper fruition, serious progress needed to be achieved on a regular basis.

When Chilean cautiousness gave way to Catalan strategising, it was impossible to believe City's chances of success on the continent were being dealt anything other than a huge boost. Quite the contrary, this surely would herald the big push forward into the European elite. The tactical revolution that quickly unfurled seemed to stand City in good stead for significant progress. In Guardiola's trophyless first season, the run to the Champions League knockout round had included some of the season's most memorable moments but had been undone by a Monaco side busy playing out of their skins.

With City's league form untouchable in 2017–18, and Guardiola's bedding-in period complete, it was reasonable to expect big things from them. Until the quarter-finals the smooth procession had indeed begun to turn heads with four-goal victories in Rotterdam, Naples and Basel proof positive of a burgeoning power base.

Then came an evening of fire and brimstone at Anfield.

It had all started much more calmly in the south of Holland in September. De Kuip Stadium, Feyenoord's charismatic ground, was full to the rafters for the inaugural Group F game. Champions of Holland once again after an eighteen-year wait, the Rotterdammers were attempting to rekindle some of the old spirit that used to positively drip off the place. Facing City produced extra poignancy, as it pitted the 1970 European Cup winners against the 1970 Cup Winners' Cup winners, a blast from the past in shiny new clothes. If ghostly images of Ove Kindvall and Colin Bell, Willem van Hanegem and Neil Young drifted into the thoughts of older fans, it would be the likes of Nicolai Jørgensen and Kevin De Bruyne trying to stamp their names on European mythology this time around. Where once the charismatic figures of Malcolm Allison and Ernst Happel bestrode the corridors in improbably collared fur coats and kipper ties, now the sports-casual Pep Guardiola and Giovanni van Bronckhorst delivered the touchline instructions.

City's summer outlay had been spent mainly on a leaky defence, and three of those reinforcements – Benjamin Mendy, Kyle Walker and Ederson Moraes – made their debuts in a match which delivered the uncommon pleasure of a clean sheet. Stones took it upon himself to be decisive at the other end too, scoring twice. His header in the second minute was also City's fastest Champions League goal to date.

The two other debutants, Bernardo Silva and Gabriel Jesus, integrated well, with the latter also netting in a fluid opening half-hour. In between, Agüero's neatly clipped finish to Walker's cross increased the pressure, with City's new goalkeeper left inactive for long periods.

Guardiola's recipe for 'winning respect' was to put an end to a run of just one advance past the last sixteen in seven attempts. Allowing the Dutch champions just 34 per cent possession and one shot on target in their own ground was a start. 'We have made a huge effort to buy five players to make that step forward in Europe,' explained the coach afterwards.

Van Bronckhorst, meanwhile, sounded a little like Kevin Keegan, Tony Book and Roberto Mancini had done in simpler times, telling reporters: 'We couldn't get into the game. Maybe we were a bit anxious – the first time for a lot of players at this level. You could see the difference and the difference was too big.' City, the European juggernaut unsettling 'little' Feyenoord. How times had changed.

FEYENOORD 0–4 MANCHESTER CITY | Att. 43,500 | Stones (2), Agüero, Jesus

Ederson, Walker, Mendy, Stones, Otamendi, Fernandinho (Sané), D. Silva (Delph), De Bruyne, B. Silva, Jesus, Agüero (Sterling)

City warmed up for the home fixture with Shakhtar by walloping six past Watford and five past Crystal Palace. The immediate effect was to propel confidence through the roof, as Guardiola's new signings added a panache to proceedings that had been missing the year before. Paulo Fonseca's Shakhtar, neat and incisive, held City for 48 minutes of a match of intense ebb and flow, before De Bruyne decided enough was enough and, with one imperious swing of his right foot, planted the ball high past Andriy Pyatov.

With Stones again outstanding and Delph excelling at left-back for the injured Mendy, City's fluidity and understanding of one another had increased visibly. Despite meeting a Ukrainian side forming the strongest challenge of all the early season visitors to the Etihad so far, City had not only emerged unscathed, but sealed a two-win start to a Champions League campaign for the first time.

'A lot of credit to what we have done,' enthused Guardiola afterwards. 'The way Shakhtar play, very narrow, they demand a lot of us, but our high pressing was brilliant. We had problems in the first half, we did not make enough passes in a row, but the second half was much, much, much better. We are so happy for the win.'

MANCHESTER CITY 2–0 SHAKHTAR DONETSK | Att. 45,310 |
De Bruyne, Sterling
Ederson, Walker, Delph, Stones, Otamendi, Fernandinho, D. Silva (Gündoğan), De Bruyne, Agüero (B. Silva), Jesus (Sterling), Sané

City's performance in beating Napoli 2–1 in the third game of the group set hearts soaring in a way not thought possible. Manchester, this down-to-earth northern city of grit and hard work, was swooning.

In a place where chips come with gravy and where the simple form of a meat-filled pie is a paragon of virtue, Guardiola's masterpiece of geometry and physics was being welcomed as part and parcel of the new scenery. For 30 minutes against Napoli, City played the most eye-watering version of high-energy, high-precision swarming that fans had ever seen. The Italian league leaders, lauded beforehand for their measly defence and jet-heeled attack, their stylish midfield and their trusty goal-keeper, were reduced to a confused rabble by an onslaught that hit them between the eyes right from the off.

Many supporters struggled to remember the last time City had produced a passage of play so profoundly capable of obliterating opposition of this calibre. The nature of Manchester City, 100 years-plus of contrary occurrences, had been hewn from games where they managed to produce extremes of good and bad within the limits of a 90-minute match.

This, however, was very different.

Two up after thirteen minutes, the first half an hour involved a bewildering amount of possession, clever subtlety of movement and domination of all workable spaces on the pitch. The ball moved as if attached to an invisible thread, spinning delightfully from the boots of Silva and De Bruyne to the flanks, where Sané, Sterling and Walker continued the light-footed magic. Reward came in the shape of two early goals, but De Bruyne's immaculate no-look left-footed blast that came back from the underside of the bar and Jesus' shot stopped *in extremis* on the line between the jittery ankles of Kalidou Koulibaly could well have made it 4–0 before Napoli regrouped and produced a reaction of their own.

By this time, the delighted crowd was feasting on one of the best 30 minutes of football ever served up in the name of Manchester City.

Luck ran with City too, as Ederson parried Dries Mertens' penalty, the quick-thinking Fernandinho clearing the rebound off the line, and Stones miraculously deflected a second-half Marek Hamšík shot just wide of the post. Eventually, Napoli reduced the deficit with Amadou Diawara netting the second penalty awarded to the Italians.

Guardiola was bursting with superlatives by the end, saying: 'Today we won against an incredible team and to do that you have to make an incredible performance. They are one of the best teams I have faced, which is why I am so proud. It was perfect.'

Napoli's manager Maurizio Sarri was also impressed, stating: 'They are an extraordinary squad. They have tremendous physical, technical and tactical qualities and if they can maintain their physical shape they could go all the way.'

MANCHESTER CITY 2–1 NAPOLI | Att. 48,520 | Sterling, Jesus

Ederson, Walker, Delph, Otamendi, Stones, Fernandinho, D. Silva (Gündoğan), De Bruyne, Jesus (Danilo), Sterling (B. Silva), Sané

If the home game with the Italians had been a work of art, the return in the Stadio San Paolo resembled epic theatre. In a match which heaved into early action and never let up, City broke the resolve of a punchy home side with a performance as resolute as it was stylish.

The Italians, in danger of being knocked out of the tournament, had started with real purpose, taking a deserved lead through Lorenzo Insigne. Thirteen minutes later, the noisy patrons on the Curva Nord were treated to the sight of Otamendi 'the General' flicking them a rigid salute, after the defender's header from Gündoğan's cross had found the net. When Stones headed in off the underside of the bar (he had hit the bar with a thunderous header in the first half too), matching Lionel Messi's Champions League haul of three for the season so far, it stoked a hornets' nest response.

Insigne's drive slapped against the bar before Sané's mistake inside the box led to a penalty, which Jorginho dispatched calmly sending Ederson the wrong way. A talented Napoli side were pushing City to the limit. Midfield pivot Hamšík would say afterwards that it had been the best 30 minutes he had been part of in a Napoli shirt.

Having relied on a more agricultural style than usual, City got the ball back on the ground and began to dominate possession. By the end, the readily recognisable short-passing game was back in full flow, reducing the home side to chasing shadows. Make no bones about it, this had been an efficient dismantling of a significant European force twice over by Guardiola's men.

The 69th minute capped it all, with Agüero on the end of a sweeping counter-attack to break City's scoring record. The Argentinian disappeared under a pile of teammates and reserves on the touchline. It had been a fitting venue to achieve such impeccable heights of performance. Agüero's match shirt would, in an act of almost perfect symmetry, be given to his son Benjamin, the grandson of Napoli legend Diego Maradona.

Another counter-attack saw De Bruyne slot Sterling through, leaving the striker to dispatch his shot beneath Pepe Reina.

'City are the best team in Europe, managed by the best manager in Europe,' Sarri summed up succinctly afterwards. Few felt like disagreeing.

NAPOLI 2–4 MANCHESTER CITY | Att. 44,483 | Otamendi, Stones, Agüero, Sterling

Ederson, Danilo, Delph, Otamendi, Stones, Fernandinho, Gündoğan (D. Silva), De Bruyne, Sterling, Agüero (B. Silva), Sané (Jesus)

With qualification assured unusually early, City made heavy weather of Feyenoord in the fifth game. For a team that likes to pass and pass and pass again, it was the 88th minute before they finally found a meaningful one. Sterling, put through by Gündoğan's wonderfully measured pass, netted a neatly constructed winner.

From high in the press box, the lines were unmistakably City, even if the match had not been. Five seconds of one-touch genius had banished the lethargy and struggle of the previous

89 minutes. Winning ugly could also be of occasional use, Guardiola would have noted, but even then the goal had to be a thing of lustrous beauty.

A below-par performance had at least given the coach a chance to afford the crowd a glimpse of the future, with Phil Foden and Brahim Díaz getting late cameo roles on the European stage for the first time. It would be a snapshot of two very different Manchester City futures.

MANCHESTER CITY 1–0 FEYENOORD | Att. 43,548 | Sterling

Ederson, Walker, Danilo, Otamendi, Mangala, Touré (Foden), Gündoğan, De Bruyne (Jesus), B. Silva, Agüero, Sterling (Díaz)

Whether met by blessed relief or reluctant acceptance, City's long winning run at last came to an end with a 2–1 defeat in freezing Kharkiv, to a well-balanced Shakhtar Donetsk side.

This was always going to be a match pitched into the wrong place in City's calendar. With Champions League qualification already assured and a Manchester derby awaiting the following weekend, it was clear Guardiola – reaching the heady total of 100 Champions League games as a manager – had a tough decision to make, but ultimately also the easiest one. In saving his big-game players for the domestic spat, he may have handed qualification to the Ukrainians and ended City's record (28 games unbeaten), but – as it resulted in a win at Old Trafford – it was a worthwhile sacrifice.

In recent weeks, a glint of hope had appeared out of the grim struggles that had littered City's schedule. With the success of Feyenoord, Huddersfield, Southampton and West Ham – all relatively modest outfits that season – in closing down the space City could operate in and attempting to shut up shop for a point, City had been forced to call on an extra quality *in extremis*. That all four stubborn opponents had ultimately been beaten suggested two things: City's much vaunted spirit, encapsulated by the supporters' refrain: 'We'll fight to the end', was alive and kicking and the sheer weight of City's attacking possibilities meant that ultimately opponents would more often than not cave in whatever their stalling tactics might be.

For Foden (becoming the youngest Englishman to start a Champions League match at seventeen years and 192 days old), Tosin Adarabioyo and Brahim Díaz, the match represented welcome game time. For Shakhtar, it meant precious qualification in second place. Group winners City could look forward to the reward of a kind draw in the round of sixteen.

SHAKHTAR DONETSK 2–1 MANCHESTER CITY | Att. 33,154 | Agüero (pen.)

Ederson, Danilo, Adarabioyo, Mangala, Fernandinho (Agüero), Touré, Gündoğan, Foden, Jesus, B. Silva, Sané (Díaz)

Five days later, City knew their fate. It would be to Basel, and a first-ever game against Swiss opposition, that supporters would travel.

Swiss efficiency – from the herd of punctual trams to the hordes of office workers packing into Migros food market at 11.45 for their lunch – was everywhere to be seen when we arrived in a city freezing serenely by the banks of the Rhine.

Fountains pumped jets of water at vigorously timed intervals, while foggy-looking blokes with Manchester accents produced the full range of expletives to describe the privilege of paying '50 quid for a couple of Baileys and Amaretto'. The waiter in the Zum Braunen Mutz did what his profession suggested. He waited. He waited non-plussed as you rummaged for enough money to cover the modest round of drinks just ordered from him. The avoidance of eye contact allowed you to wipe away a tear unseen.

In among the plugs and sockets of a well-attended press conference the day before, Guardiola had appeared upbeat, a man
and a club on a mission, alongside an equally steadfast-looking
Vincent Kompany. There was levity too, when Guardiola was
asked if one training session after injury was enough to risk Sané
in the game, Kompany piped up: 'It's a bit longer than I usually
take to come back.' Snapshots of humour revealed how relaxed
it had become under Guardiola's guidance.

By the next day, the local lust for productivity must have won
City some new fans in this frozen corner of the country, after a
ruthless display of the by-now familiar passing routines ripped
the will to live out of Raphaël Wicky's team.

Basel, returning from a long winter break, seemed much less
enthusiastic at resuming work than the city's workforce had
appeared to be earlier in the day. Off the pace and outmanoeuvred by a City side as slick as they were hungry, the home team's
hopes had been demolished completely inside twenty minutes
of the first half.

Even City's back four seemed able to make mistakes and get
away with them. Basel's drowsiness undoubtedly played into
this, as Kompany prodded short passes to nobody in particular
and Ederson played his game of Russian roulette, slicing his
passes hither and thither through the narrowest of margins.

So underused was the Brazilian that you began to get the idea
that he was taking greater risks with his passing just to liven
affairs up for himself and his defensive colleagues. To labour
such elements, however, was to risk missing the point. City
appeared in such perfect harmony going forward that a special
kind of telepathy seemed to be at work. The ball zipped from
player to player as if along unseen strands being pulled by a
puppet master above the main stand.

This was City at their fluid best. Three up at half-time, the
rout was complete by 53 minutes. Gündoğan, smooth as silk,

with two well-taken goals, one each from Agüero and Bernardo Silva, the latter's finish as deft and delicate as a ballet dancer running through an adagio, but it had been so much more than four goals to the home side's nil.

For the fans, there had been sights to be seen: from the fast-flowing Rhine to the fast-running Raheem Sterling, everything was a blur of shining, liquid forward movement. As the Münsterplatz bells rang out, it was difficult to deny that this was another metaphor in a dimly lit town full of the things. As the moon rose high in the frozen night sky, you could imagine it falling from its majestic height and being trapped instantly on the instep of Bernardo Silva. We had been serenaded again and the art and poise of Guardiola's maestros had lit up this land of scientific exactitude.

In a season decorated so beautifully with the art and craft of talented men, there was perhaps only one fear: maybe it was only really City that could stop City now.

For some not steeped in the mysterious ways of this strange club, it was not a preoccupation. Maurizio Sarri, starry-eyed boss of previously beaten Napoli, was clear. 'I'm not watching Juventus, Tottenham and the others,' he laughed, '*I want to see Manchester City.*'

BASEL 0–4 MANCHESTER CITY | Att. 36,000 | Gündoğan (2), B. Silva, Agüero

Ederson, Walker, Delph, Kompany, Otamendi, Fernandinho, Gündoğan, De Bruyne (D. Silva), Agüero (Danilo), B. Silva, Sterling (Sané)

'We forgot to attack.'

As a manager's summing up, Guardiola's review of the meaningless home defeat in the return match was peculiarly distinct. Ahead as early as the eighth minute through Jesus, City sat back and seemed to ponder life. By the time they awoke from their reverie, the away side were ahead and hell-bent on holding on to their prize.

European debuts for Oleksandr Zinchenko and new signing Aymeric Laporte, and a rare outing for the cult figure of Claudio Bravo brought side interest to the occasion, but City stuttered to a stop in the second half and could not restart the motor. As Gary Owen told me of ancient times in Liège, once the foot had been taken off the pedal, it was a near-impossible task to re-find that fifth gear. His words rang as true in 2018 as they had in 1978.

Small consolation, then, in breaking the Champions League passing record of 978, a particularly Guardiola-esque statistic on a below-par night like this. For the near 50,000 who had spent good money to be present, it was meagre recompense, but City were through to the last eight and apparently in vivid good health. For the manager, the most high-profile advocate of neat passing in the world game, it was not enough either. 'Just to pass the ball for itself is nothing,' he said with a shrug, channelling his inner Mancini. 'When this happens it is not football.'

MANCHESTER CITY 1–2 BASEL | Att. 49,411 | Jesus

Bravo, Danilo, Zinchenko, Stones, Laporte, Touré, Gündoğan (Díaz), Foden (Adarabioyo), B. Silva, Jesus, Sané

Wicky was closer to the truth than he thought when he assessed City's chances of ultimate success in the competition after the match. 'We all know', he opined in the Etihad press conference, 'that the Champions League is a competition that depends on the form on the day and the draw has to go right so it is difficult to say how it will go for City, but in terms of quality and momentum then this team is clearly one of the top two or three teams.'

With restrictions lifted in the draw for the last eight, City eyed potential partners. Sevilla and Roma represented malleable opponents who had already been dealt with in recent campaigns. Bayern, Juventus, Real and Barcelona were grandees better kept at arm's length for another occasion. And Liverpool, the only other English side left in, represented the biggest, darkest nightmare of all.

Liverpool. Of course.

City would play their second-ever all-English European game, after the semi-final tussle with Chelsea in 1971. It was a bucket of the coldest possible water, thrown from the greatest possible height. Not only did Liverpool carry an other-worldly mystique on the continental front that appeared to stop opponents in their tracks, they possessed a record against City across all competitions that scarcely bore belief. Asking any City supporter to this day whom they would sooner avoid in any cup competition in any season, the answer will come quickly enough: Liverpool.

In the end, after a coach journey for the team made treacherous by the *Liverpool Echo*'s decision to publish City's proposed route to the ground in the days beforehand, unleashing a hail of missiles that hardly constituted a calm, measured build-up to their game of the season, City produced one of their most slapdash performances under the Catalan.

The club's historic failures at Liverpool were maintained and significantly augmented by a slipshod showing in losing 3–0, lacking practically any of the characteristics that had marked the season down as something unique. City were undone, step by painful step. It was ruthless against toothless. It had taken the home side only 31 minutes to build up the critical three-goal lead, with a whirlwind start whipped up by an electrified crowd that brought quick-fire goals from Mohamed Salah, Alex Oxlade-Chamberlain and, unbelievably as City staggered punch-drunk, a third from Sadio Mané.

As with the 4–3 league defeat at Anfield in January, City's defence had been quickly harried out of its stride, the midfield

– supposedly but not visibly bolstered by the presence of Gündoğan, replacing the apparently Anfield-phobic Sterling – proved to be anything but tight. The defence, with Laporte shunted out on the left, looked shell-shocked. In fact, with Gündoğan heading a presentable chance wide and City persisting with the rather obvious plan of unleashing Sané as a major threat against a wobbly Trent Alexander-Arnold, the one-dimensional response to the home side's hurricane was clearly not working. That most of the hurricane was blowing down the side occupied by a centre-half being asked to try out left-back for size was perhaps incidental, but further forward on the same flank Sané's touch seemed slightly off.

Guardiola had proved a master at getting his players to believe in the power of possession, but Klopp's own version of the doctrine included ceaseless pressing. Nonetheless, City had swarmed Napoli in a similar fashion to the scarlet waves that were engulfing them at Anfield, a comparison that bore some weight. All the pre-match kerfuffle of flares and smoke bombs had clouded the real threat, which was out on the Anfield turf.

A supposedly less talented midfield of ex-City man Milner, Jordan Henderson and Oxlade-Chamberlain laid waste to City's Rolls-Royce passers De Bruyne and David Silva. To top off a dim night's work, City's failure to register a shot on target – and that against the dubious goalkeeping of Loris Karius – was the first time they had attained that statistic since October 2016.

With Sané wasteful, the midfield corked and Jesus contributing fitfully in place of Agüero up front, the writing was on the wall. Oddly, the Champions League had produced four extremely one-sided games in the quarter-final first legs. All City could pray for was that their tie could provide the kind of dramatic turnaround that sometimes occurred at this prestige level. This was, after all, a club that had long proved capable of

Jekyll and Hyde performances, weird against-the-odds results and eye-opening surprises. Now would be a good moment to produce another one.

'Probably in this room there is no one who thinks we are going through,' admitted a deflated Guardiola later, while his counterpart Klopp, considerably more inflated after the remarkable events of the evening, was not counting his chickens: 'You have to celebrate a party when a party starts, not four weeks before.'

The Liverpool manager's assertion that 'it was not the result we were expecting' echoed the thoughts of many of us. Meanwhile, the final question went to the Catalan. 'Was replacing a forward [Sterling] with an extra midfielder [Gündoğan] the right thing to do?' he was asked. The reply would not be easily forgotten. 'We lost three–zero.'

For the fans present at Anfield, it had been a chastening experience too. 'I have very little recollection of that game,' says Murdoch Dalziel, 'because I watched most of it from behind my hands.'

Phil Hammond had also made the short trip west: 'There was clearly a lot of noise around this one. We had lunch and got stuck into the beers. We didn't know what to expect at Lime Street but it was quiet and we had a gentle walk to our usual spot for Anfield/Goodison, the Ship and Mitre. The atmosphere in there was good and there was a good mix of fans and everything was good-natured.

'And then we got the team news. That year we were absolutely sensational so to change the team round and play such a strange line-up/formation was incredible. It didn't really make any sense then and still doesn't now. We were a bit late so we headed outside and grabbed a taxi. That's when my friend Chris rang me asking if I was OK. I hadn't got a clue what he was talking about. He told us what they'd got up to, attacking our bus with bottles and flares. I confirmed I was still alive. We went a completely different way to usual and ended up high above Anfield walking down towards the Kop. We were a bit late so the majority of them were inside, which might have been for the best. There were no issues outside and we went in with hopes high.

'We started really well. Then we let one in and the rest is history. It was a really horrible feeling to blow it in the first leg and even worse to find out their first goal was offside and our disallowed goal was onside. That could have made a huge difference, but as they say: we never get anything at Anfield.'

LIVERPOOL 3–0 MANCHESTER CITY | Att. 50,685

Ederson, Walker, Laporte, Otamendi, Kompany, Fernandinho, Gündoğan (Sterling), De Bruyne, D. Silva, Sané, Jesus

---

There was at least some precedent for what City had to achieve for redemption in the Etihad return. Only the season before, Barcelona had come back from a 4–0 first-leg defeat against Paris Saint-Germain to knock the French side out 6–5 on aggregate. You had to travel back much further to find another example of a three-goal first-leg win being overturned, however, that of Deportivo la Coruña, who shocked Milan back in 2003–4.

City's players, nursing temporarily scorched self-confidence, were aware that it was still possible, if highly unlikely. The 5–0 league win in September bore proof of that and became the benchmark for what was required. That such a score against Liverpool had not, prior to the avalanche in the autumn, been reached since 1937 would not have been worth mentioning in the run-up to the all-important match. Some things are best left unsaid after all.

Although the eventual 5–1 aggregate in favour of Liverpool would suggest easy passage to the semi-finals for the Reds, there were distinct periods in the second leg when the Merseysiders were visibly wobbling. City, one up after two minutes, should have been two, perhaps three, ahead at the interval, but for more histrionics from Antonio Lahoz and bad luck in front of goal.

Eventually, they were undone by their own need to attack.

For much of a thunderous first half, City matched the energy and precision of Liverpool in the first leg. They were so incessant that one was left wondering why Guardiola had chosen a lethargic block a week earlier at Anfield. Similar questions would be asked of the Catalan in City's elimination to Lyon in Lisbon two years later and against Chelsea in the 2021 final.

City demonstrated capably enough on this occasion that they could flatten Liverpool down just as they had been crushed themselves in the first leg, making the manager's prescribed first-leg inertia all the more curious.

What *The Times* christened the next morning as 'teetering between brilliance and desperation' was all that City could offer the baying Etihad masses. With only two minutes gone, the seething ground exploded as Fernandinho found the calmest of passes in the confusion of tackles. Sterling, charging down the inside-right channel, tucked a quick ball inside to the onrushing Jesus, who hammered it home. Mayhem erupted.

When Bernardo Silva's raking left-footer bounced back from the inside of the post, everything seemed possible. Rather than weathering the storm, Liverpool were in danger of succumbing to it. With a minute to the break, Sané touched in to make it 2–0. What Klopp would later call a 'thunderstorm' looked to be drowning the visitors completely, but referee Lahoz was about to take centre stage, something that his wink to the camera during the pre-match anthem-sweep through the teams seemed to suggest he desired.

Holding up his arm, he ruled the German offside, which he was, marginally, but the officials had not noticed the ball had nicked off Milner, which rendered the goal legal. With apoplexy breaking out, Guardiola bestrode the white lines to remonstrate and was sent off by the straight-backed Spaniard.

Memories of the Monaco round-of-sixteen clash where Lahoz had also made contentious decisions against City were perhaps occupying the manager's mind. At this moment, the eye of the storm was passing. Dispatched to the sanctuary of the changing rooms, City could only rage about ill luck and Klopp could take advantage of the heaven-sent opportunity to reorganise his befuddled team.

A breakaway brought Salah his 39th goal of the season and Roberto Firmino made it 2–1 as City opened up to chase the game. While modern-day City have brought to a close decade-long losing runs in their rivalries with Arsenal, Tottenham and, most gleefully of all, Manchester United, the mental block against Liverpool is the only one that persists to this day.

MANCHESTER CITY 1–2 LIVERPOOL | Att. 53,461 | Jesus

Ederson, Walker, Laporte, Otamendi, Fernandinho, D. Silva (Agüero), De Bruyne, B. Silva (Gündoğan), Jesus, Sterling, Sané

There would be consolation for the crestfallen City fans, although *consolation* hardly covered it adequately. Of the six league games remaining, City would win five and draw one. The very last goal of the season, netted in the very last minute of the very last game in front of the packed away end at Southampton by Gabriel Jesus, would bring City to the hitherto unscaled heights of 100 points. With a goal difference of +79, the thought remained that it had been the –4 goal difference in the Champions League quarter-final that resonated more loudly.

Liverpool would reach the Kyiv final, where they would be beaten by the ultimate masters of the big European occasion, Real Madrid. For many of City's supporters, a record-breaking league campaign was compensation in kind for the never-ending continental woes, but the seemingly impossible dream was holding its distance from a club that so needed its embrace to rubber-stamp that place among the elite.

2019: THE BIG OPPORTUNITY

Movin' on up

The wait for another chance is never long. The Champions League bandwagon now chugs into life for City every September with the precise timing of leaves dropping off trees. Gone are the days when a European campaign was less likely than a relegation battle. Having moved in with the big boys, City now have their slippers under the bed too.

However, the 2018–19 season presented us with the usual candidates jostling for glory in Atlético Madrid's Wanda Metropolitano Stadium.

At the start of the season, with Guardiola's growing influence having landed the most spectacular of league titles, City were once again, to the bemusement of those who had watched them flounder for decades, being touted as one of the favourites.

Sooner or later, the club would have to deliver on the final promise left unfulfilled in a remarkable ten-year advance. With a well-balanced squad enhanced by the delicate wing skills of Leicester's Riyad Mahrez, but heavy-legged from a summer of arduous World Cup involvement, time would tell whether the new campaign would deliver beyond the high-water mark of Manuel Pellegrini's final season in charge.

On the wider front, more was expected from Barcelona and Bayern, who had both coped poorly with the challenges of domestic and international football the previous season. With Juventus bolstered by the acquisition of Cristiano Ronaldo and Real Madrid once again expecting to go far in 'their' tournament, the field would be strong, if a little familiar. Throw in a Paris Saint-Germain side coming under increasing pressure to match their dominance of French football with something concrete in Europe, and City could be forgiven for thinking the previous season might have represented something of a missed opportunity.

Missed opportunities, it seemed, were still something of an undeniable temptation.

For a club steeped in the tradition of doing things the hard way, however, there was no immediate reason to fear the worst. This feeling was given legs when the draw for the group stages pitted City against Hoffenheim, Shakhtar Donetsk once again and Lyon. With Liverpool and Tottenham drawing tough opponents and Manchester United thrown together with Ronaldo's Juventus, it was felt City had come out of the draw pretty well.

Having put together an eight-year unbroken run of Champions League participation, City were now England's longest-serving representatives in the tournament. This would have been an unthinkable statistic even five years earlier when, having finally made it into the elite, City were finding it difficult to extricate themselves from a string of treacherous first-round groups.

Here was another solid chance to progress. Guardiola, mindful of his own patchy record in the tournament, would be extra keen to fulfil the owners' dreams of landing the biggest trophy of all and at the same time bolster the one area the press could labour concerning his abilities.

The European campaign kicked off with City third in the nascent Premier League table, behind Sarri's surprisingly sprightly

Chelsea and a fully bolstered Liverpool. The opening day win at Arsenal and the 6–1 demolition of Huddersfield had both borne definite likeness to the scintillating football of the 2017–18 championship season. Despite this, a less than agitated crowd gathered for the opening fixture with Lyon on Wednesday 19 September and were rewarded for their own calmness with an obscurely inept performance. Lyon were quickly into their stride and had obviously decided to follow Jürgen Klopp's blueprint to unsettle City by pressing fast and direct in midfield.

Fielding Fabian Delph on the left side of a defence which twinned Stones with Laporte, Guardiola also included İlkay Gündoğan in a central role, which meant wide duties for Bernardo Silva and a place on the bench for Sané.

With a surprising 2–0 lead at half-time, the French side left the banned Guardiola (a touchline suspension was still in place after his sending off against Liverpool the previous season) with plenty to talk about.

Despite stirring from their slumbers in the second half, when Sané brought the left flank to life, little immediate change was evident until Bernardo Silva, moving inside for greater effect, got himself on the end of a jinking run from the German and found a space inside the far post with a raking left-foot shot past Anthony Lopes.

That was the extent of a muted comeback, however, leaving City playing catch-up from the very beginning of the group stage. Afterwards, the full force of a media duck-shoot broke over Guardiola and his players. It would be a taste of what was to come later in the season, an *amuse-bouche* before the spring banquet. In the *Guardian*, Jonathan Wilson pondered if City may not need a little *'mala leche'*, a phrase coined by Johan Cruyff when he had stirred the pot at Barcelona with the purchase of maverick Hristo Stoichkov in the '90s. Wilson wrote: 'There are – rare – occasions when it [City's tactical approach] can feel a little mannered, where the very purity of the style seems to make it vulnerable, just as pedigree dogs are more susceptible to disease. That is why Cruyff brought in Stoichkov at Barcelona, to add the *"mala leche"* – literally "bad milk" but more idiomatically, toughness, ruthlessness, capacity for improvisation – he felt the side were lacking.'

City's capacity for improvisation had seldom been questioned, but a single early-season defeat appeared to be working wonders on the country's journalists.

An ability to eke out favourable results from games closed down by timid opposition had been one of the features of a thrilling pre-Christmas run the previous season, when each game seemed to hang on a knife edge until desperately late winners, that always seemed to come, whatever the circumstances. Guardiola's micro-management from the touchline and his attention to the tiniest detail during strategy sessions had already become a thing of mystical authority. No stone was left unturned, ever.

There seemed plenty of room for *coached inventiveness*, but perhaps less for the off-the-cuff improvisation that was also occasionally needed.

Perhaps here, with the much-touted assistant Mikel Arteta in nominal charge of directing the course of the match, we were also being offered a glimpse into a grey and humourless future without the Catalan. Arteta it was who was left to try and put a realistic gloss on things after the game, stating: 'It could have been better. We started slowly, and we were inconsistent in the way we wanted to play. We lost too many duels. We gave the ball away in difficult circumstances and they scored twice, but after that, the reaction was superb. We tweaked a few things to control situations better and we created chances, but at this level, it wasn't enough. We were very aware of Lyon's strengths and weaknesses. They were well prepared.'

Having dispensed with Mario Balotelli, the last rascal to offer *mala leche* in the modern era, City's new *seriousness* was at the heart of the question being posed by Wilson in the *Guardian*. The Italian's grass allergy in Kyiv as well as his infamous bathroom firework display had turned him into something of a City legend.

It was ironic then that City's first-ever European triumph, all those decades ago in 1970, had come with a squad bristling with cheeky chappies. Francis Lee and Mike Summerbee had been notorious for their antics, as had Stan Bowles and Tony Coleman just before that triumph in Vienna, and Rodney Marsh just after. The early-'70s sides were brimming with strong characters and winning personalities. Perhaps Wilson's thoughts were – unknowingly – ruminating on something deeper in the club's character.

The lack of fervour from a below-capacity Etihad crowd also attracted customary press attention, with Miguel Delaney noting a clear difference with the previous evening's uproarious entertainment at Anfield for Liverpool's last-gasp 3–2 win over Paris Saint-Germain.

Writing in the *Independent*, Delaney opined: 'For all the cynicism about how much was made of the Anfield atmosphere before last season's quarter-final against Manchester City, the talk was all justified. The cynicism was all blown away by the boisterous noise of the crowd. Tuesday was a reminder of this, with the identity – and identity struggles – of opposition like the new Paris Saint-Germain only further emphasising it.

'This is not to say the sensation is exclusive to Anfield. You get the same thunderous reception on such nights at Old Trafford, the Bernabéu, Camp Nou, the San Siro and even now at the relatively new Allianz Arena and at Chelsea. You still don't get it at the Etihad with Manchester City, though. It's a great stadium, a great matchday experience, but you're not surrounded by a grandiose sense of history.'

With City's 1970 Cup Winners' Cup win coming before the first of Liverpool's continental trophies, the European *pedigree* outdated that of their rivals. However, the aching blank space that was the club's European record between defeat to Borussia Mönchengladbach in 1979 and a new beginning against Total Network Solutions in 2003 coincided with a period where Liverpool had reeled in no fewer than eight trophies (five European Cups/Champions League and three UEFA Cups).

MANCHESTER CITY 1–2 LYON | Att. 40,111 | B. Silva

Ederson, Walker, Laporte, Stones, Delph, Fernandinho, D. Silva, B. Silva, Gündoğan (Sané), Sterling (Mahrez), Jesus (Agüero)

City were perhaps falling between two stools in their attempts to be accepted by and in the gilded elite. Only time would heal the fissures caused by UEFA's FFP experiments on the club, the over-zealous fines after Porto and the ridiculous mismanagement of the match in Moscow with a supposedly banned CSKA crowd suddenly appearing out of the frozen Russian night.

The continued booing of the UEFA anthem at the beginning of matches had started – after four seasons of solid subscription – to act as an irritant to some, who thought it time to move on, time to assume their new role of big hitters and to stop looking like irritable agitators.

City would have to bite the bullet and ignore the brickbats. In order to ascend the steep slopes at the top of UEFA's football pyramid, it would take a steely resolve, sure-footedness and the kind of focus displayed on a week-by-week basis on the touch-line by the manager.

For a new generation of fans brought up on Wembley visits and trophies, self-confidence would soon challenge the old guard's inbred pessimism on the stands too.

Thus, the second game, an early-evening kick-off in Sinsheim, the sleepy hamlet home of the Bundesliga's only village team, Hoffenheim, brought early pressure.

Further dropped points would look like City's 2018–19 European campaign was doomed before it had even got out of the traps. With no margin for error, Guardiola wheeled out a familiar pre-match clarion call. 'We have five finals to qualify and this is the first one …'

Optimism remained widespread, however, as City's domestic form had really begun to fire in the interim, with the club now top of the Premier League table. Having put five past Cardiff, won heavily at Oxford in the Carabao Cup and disposed of Brighton with a powerful display, City were coming into a rich vein of form. With De Bruyne also back in training after a summer injury, the feel-good factor was back with a bang.

Captain Vincent Kompany, interviewed in the *Daily Mail* on the eve of the match, was circumspect: 'It's a tough competition to win. It's OK to say we want to win it, but there are seven or eight other teams thinking the same. They have just as big a claim as us.'

What City could expect from Hoffenheim was a fearless attacking policy under future Bayern coach Julian Nagelsmann. How do you stand up to a side like City was the widely asked question. City's attacking force had already been met by massed ranks of defenders in their games against Newcastle and Brighton, but Hoffenheim clearly had something else in mind. Midfielder Vincenzo Grifo stated: 'We want to give it all we've got. Attack, the whole 90 minutes!' Hungarian striker Ádám Szalai struck a similar note, saying: 'If you know Julian Nagelsmann, you know this match is going to be a tactical highlight for every fan.'

Within just 44 seconds of the kick-off at the Rhein-Neckar-Arena, City had their answer: Nagelsmann meant business.

Kerem Demirbay managed to slide Ishak Belfodil into a yawning gap between Laporte, being played as an emergency left-back, and Otamendi. The Algerian kept a cool head and slotted a low shot under Ederson.

City, stung into action by the early setback, were level seven minutes later. From just beyond the edge of the area, David Silva stroked an inch-perfect pass between two defenders to Sané. The German expertly dragged keeper Oliver Baumann from his goal, hesitating an instant to wrong-foot the backtracking defenders, before squaring it to Agüero. The Argentinian surged clear of a tackle and wide of the keeper's stretch to fire in low and true. After under ten minutes, the game was on fire.

With City dominating large chunks of what followed, the home side were happy to go in 1–1 at half-time. A cagier second half surprised those that had been enthralled by the open attacking of what had gone before.

With time running out, the player of the match decided to take things into his own hands. Stefan Posch, completing an admirable 90 minutes' work for the home side, dithered too long on the edge of the area. David Silva, anticipating the defender's brainstorm, nipped in to steal the ball and unleashed a left-foot strike under Baumann and into the far corner of the goal.

A distraught Posch later stated: 'It hurts to lose so late in the game. Nevertheless, we can be proud of our performance. We were missing a lot of players. For the winning goal, I couldn't see Silva behind me. Of course, I have to clear the ball. It's tough to take.'

Guardiola's pre-match comment that his side would 'have to suffer' if they wanted to go far in this edition of the Champions League was already running true.

In the German press, the *Sueddeutsche Zeitung* came up with the most eloquent analogy. Comparing City's 'Stradivarius' to Hoffenheim's 'standard concert violins', it noted that the hosts were 'like conductors, using their instruments and compositions to put together a nice score …' In the end, though, it had been a familiar Mancunian symphony that hit all the important notes.

TSG HOFFENHEIM 1–2 MANCHESTER CITY | Att. 24,851 | Agüero, D. Silva

Ederson, Walker, Kompany, Otamendi (Stones), Laporte, Fernandinho, Gündoğan (B. Silva), D. Silva, Sané, Sterling (Mahrez), Agüero

---

Following this up with a positive result in the Ukraine, where Shakhtar had never lost to an English club, was going to take something special, but a City side finding its stride in domestic competition travelled east in good mood.

Well organised by Paulo Fonseca, Shakhtar presented a familiar, if tricky, hurdle. With Lyon's victory at the Etihad and Hoffenheim's fearless approach, the group seemed more open than the others, where the stronger sides were already taking a grip on affairs.

In the end, there was no need to worry. City were simply stunning in everything they did on a fresh evening in Kharkiv's Metalist Stadium, the venue for Shakhtar's home games owing to the continued activity of Russian troops in the Donbass. The 3–0 final scoreline belied the fact that the goal frame had been hit three times and countless other efforts had been scraped off the line or narrowly missed their target.

With David Silva as captain, City began with the bit between their teeth. The home side, unable to gain any kind of foothold in the face of an onslaught of precision passing, looked disheartened as Guardiola's team cut them to shreds.

Although home captain Taras Stepanenko would later admit his side 'had made too many mistakes', it was not immediately clear what Shakhtar could have done better. They were simply overrun by a side firing on all cylinders. City's only weakness appeared to be Mahrez's shooting, which was narrowly wide on five separate occasions.

None of this mattered, as City employed the hitherto unknown sharp-shooting of Silva instead. The little Spaniard, once again at the heart of all that was progressive about City's movement, shot City into the lead with a raking shot that beat Andriy Pyatov at his far post.

Laporte, growing impressively into his first full season, headed home a second direct from a left-wing corner to put City two up by half-time. A third, passed in from the edge of the box by Bernardo Silva, who had appeared as a substitute just two minutes earlier, completed the rout.

A bewildered Stepanenko stated: 'We made lots of mistakes; we lost the ball too often. And, with the quality of their players, they created many opportunities. They deserved it.'

Fonseca was perhaps even more effusive, saying: 'We knew it would be very hard, especially without Marlos Moreno and Taison. We couldn't do much against City's quality in this game. They played superbly in the first half. We had more possession after the break, but it wasn't enough to threaten such a good team.'

With the next game scheduled between the same sides in Manchester, Fonseca hit a familiar note: 'It will be even harder to play in Manchester, but we will fight until the end and try to earn some points.'

**SHAKHTAR DONETSK 0–3 MANCHESTER CITY | Att. 37,106 |
D. Silva, Laporte, B. Silva**

Ederson, Stones (Walker), Mendy, Otamendi, Laporte, Fernandinho, D. Silva, De Bruyne (B. Silva), Jesus (Foden), Mahrez, Sterling

---

A thrilling 3–3 draw between Lyon and Hoffenheim meant results elsewhere had gone City's way, putting them top. After a stuttering start, the games at Hoffenheim and Shakhtar had confirmed the promise of a side that many were tipping to go all the way.

By the time Shakhtar landed in Manchester, two important developments were making headlines. Firstly, strong form had taken City clear at the top of the Premier League, with the 6–1 thrashing of a timid Southampton opening the tantalising possibility that it might even be possible to improve on the previous season's record-breaking haul. Secondly, and more significantly, German investigative journal *Der Spiegel* had printed three parts of a four-piece exposé on City. Under the title 'Bending the Rules to the Tune of Millions', they started: 'For years now, the Manchester City football club has vehemently denied that its owner, the sheikh of Abu Dhabi, broke financial rules. But internal emails tell a different story, providing evidence of backdated contracts, illusory sponsoring payments and cavalier, "We can do what we want", business practices.'

The magazine's low sliding tackle on the fabric of the club had appeared at first glance to be the precursor to a possible UEFA investigation (which would indeed take proper shape at the season's end), further wide-ranging sanctions or perhaps worse. The British press – with sections already harbouring what some fans thought to be a gigantic bee in their bonnet about City's growing domination – were sent into an immediate ferment.

The allegations would become progressively weaker as the magazine's serialisation ran towards its conclusion and, by the time City prepared to confront Shakhtar for the fourth time in two seasons, things were returning to relative calm.

On a damp evening in early November, City found the perfect response to the ire of their growing detractors. Despite this, the 6–0 crushing of Shakhtar was not without controversy. When Sterling stubbed his toe in the turf in the 24th minute, referee Viktor Kassai awarded a penalty, judging that the nearest defender, Mykola Matviyenko, had caused Sterling's tumble. By the end, the mistake seemed almost irrelevant, but, if nothing else, it allowed the *Sun* to remind us how the press had begun to turn in its reporting of the club's progress. The *Spiegel* exposé had evidently accelerated the process. The *Sun*'s back page had scrubbed through the 6–0 score and re-inked it as 5–0 below a headline that shouted: 'NO CLASS', a far cry from Ukraine's *Sport-Express*, which chose 'Masterclass' instead. 'City sporting shame' continued Carl Long's piece, completely ignoring the sublime performance that had been enacted either side of Sterling's comedy miskick. Long must have been sitting not more than a few metres from my own position, but he had chosen to concentrate on the one moment of poor ball control in the entire game for his story.

To every other pair of eyes in the 52,286 crowd, City were untouchable, playing their customary brand of one-touch football through spaces so small they could hardly be seen with the naked eye. Up in the freezing rows of the press box, it seemed – despite the fluidity and efficacy – this was a side yet to hit its proper stride. With De Bruyne again injured, it was also a side lacking its major pacemaker. Yet, those sky-blue shirts still seemed almost untouchable in their superiority. How far the club had come, since the opening European salvo fired into a somewhat warmer Istanbul night all those years ago. *Grande Pep* was fast overtaking *Big Mal* in City's pantheon of great managers.

The near-full house that had greeted City was also notable. It was a match that some could have been forgiven for foregoing. It had been raining all day in Manchester. The mucky day, the fact that Shakhtar were familiar and hardly blue-riband opponents and pre-Christmas budget strings would have been pulled tight for some, all served to act as deterrents. But, with a moody sky over the wet playing surface, there was only one place to be.

The effort of the fans was vindicated. Guardiola's men served up a show that left no one in any doubt that City were to be considered contenders this year.

City had lost their previous three home games in the tournament. Despite those defeats encompassing a dead rubber against Basel from the year before, the luckless defeat to Liverpool and the slump against Lyon, the coach was evidently smarting at such an ignominious run.

City shot out from the blocks, leaving their opponents pinned, stunned and a goal down after thirteen minutes. The author of the damage was Mahrez, jinking this way and that on the edge of the box, his final turn sending three defenders the wrong way, squaring to David Silva, whose first-time connection rocketed into the net.

The second, eleven minutes later, extracted what fight was left from the visitors and presented the *Sun* with their morning headline. It was unlucky in the extreme for Shakhtar. A through ball from Stones reached Fernandinho, who dispatched Sterling through the same central axis. As he shaped to scoop the ball over Pyatov, he appeared to rake his studs through the turf and comically fell in a heap. Sterling did not claim it. Indeed, down on the sidelines Guardiola could be seen telling the fourth official it was not a penalty.

City accelerated through the gears to tie the match up after 48 minutes. If Sterling's part in the second had been comical, his weaving, top-speed chase in the third bore all the hallmarks of a player on top of his game. Receiving the ball from David Silva, he made a beeline for the box, before swerving past two defenders to curl a rising shot past the flailing Pyatov.

Jesus then converted another penalty, this time after Taras Stepanenko had clipped Silva. Mahrez deservedly joined the scorers with a neat finish late on, and Jesus completed an unlikely hat-trick with a devious scooped finish over the demoralised

Pyatov after being slotted through by Mahrez. Shakhtar, flattened and outplayed, left the pitch knowing their chances of qualification now hung by a thread. City though, hoping results would have seen them qualify, would have to wait until the away game in Lyon to seal a place in the knockout rounds, after Hoffenheim completed a late comeback in France to draw 2–2.

Lyon sat in the driving seat to qualify in second place, with both Hoffenheim and Shakhtar still in with a chance of catching them if the French slipped up against City.

At least the manager's enthusiasm for City's performance was clear afterwards: 'We were brilliant in attack, brilliant in defence. It makes it all look easy, but it's not.' Although Jesus and Sterling had stolen the headlines for widely different reasons, the Catalan also praised one of the side's unsung heroes Zinchenko, completing an impressive game at left-back. 'He is a clear player, an intelligent player, so clever, so good, defensively, tactically, gives us an extra man in the middle too.'

MANCHESTER CITY 6–0 SHAKHTAR DONETSK | Att. 52,286 |
D. Silva, Jesus (3, 2 pens.), Sterling, Mahrez

Ederson, Walker (Danilo), Stones, Laporte, Zinchenko, Fernandinho (Delph), B. Silva, D. Silva (Gündoğan), Sterling, Mahrez, Jesus

Through again

A sixth successive qualification for the knockout rounds was secured in the penultimate match in Lyon, but not before the home side had run City ragged in a febrile atmosphere at the Groupama Stadium.

Twice taking the lead through Maxwel Cornet, Lyon were pegged back each time by a City side shaken out of their usual comfort zone. The home side's progress after the victory at City on matchday one had been odd to say the least. Unbeaten at this stage, all other games had been drawn, including two against

Hoffenheim in both of which the French had been ahead going into the 90th minute.

City's starting eleven showed three changes from the weekend stroll past West Ham. In a slightly lopsided line-up, Stones, Zinchenko and Mahrez came in for Otamendi, Delph and Gündoğan. Despite newspaper speculation, Foden had to be content with a place on the bench.

By half-time, with the game still goalless, City could count their blessings that they were not already two or three goals adrift of the feisty, fast-passing home side, with Cornet hitting the post.

By the 55th minute, City were behind to a scorching left-footer from the Ivorian, who was making sure his first appearance since scoring in Manchester would be a memorable one. Seven minutes later, City were level with the excellent Laporte heading in powerfully from Sterling's free kick. Within seconds, sloppy defensive play let in Sané down the left and his shot was fumbled onto the line by Anthony Lopes. Suddenly, City were giving Lyon a real game, but it was the home side who retook the lead when Cornet skipped through on the left, evaded Laporte's lunge with a clever touch and shot under Ederson.

Only a few seconds had elapsed before City came back with a second equaliser, this time Agüero getting up highest to Mahrez's cross to angle a header past Lopes. With Delph on to shore up midfield, the last minutes drew the sting from a terrific game. City were through, and Lyon would have some work to do against Shakhtar in the final game if they wanted to join them, after the Ukrainian side produced yet another late winner to edge past Hoffenheim 3–2.

LYON 2–2 MANCHESTER CITY | Att. 56,039 | Laporte, Agüero

Ederson, Walker, Zinchenko, Stones, Laporte, Fernandinho, D. Silva, Mahrez, Agüero (Foden), Sterling, Sané (Delph)

With City preparing to close out the group games against Hoffenheim, news broke that an investigation by UEFA into illegal payments – as reported by *Der Spiegel* – was imminent. David Conn, writing in the *Guardian* on 4 December, stated: 'UEFA officials are examining the allegations made against City based on the Football Leaks of the club's internal emails, to see whether the club may have conducted itself dishonestly or sought to illegitimately evade financial fair play rules. Cooperation is understood to have been sought from the Football Association and Premier League, who in effect take joint responsibility for working with English clubs to meet the requirements of UEFA's licence.'

City, hit by allegations that they 'cheated UEFA's rules' and presented 'a tissue of lies', had not at that time been contacted by the governing body, but rumours were rife that trouble was brewing. Alleged undeclared payments to Roberto Mancini, as well as doubts over the validity of the giant sponsorship fees paid by Etihad Airways had also been thrown into doubt.

With some writers jumping the gun, gleefully predicting a ban for the club if UEFA's finding's uncovered foul play, the build-up to the final group game was carried out in a tense atmosphere, as officials and staff alike went into something akin to lockdown.

With City qualified and Hoffenheim fighting for a third-place finish that would unlock spring participation in the Europa League, the game took on a muted feel. City had succumbed to their first league defeat of the season at Chelsea the previous weekend, allowing doubt to be aired about their title aspirations. With the injured Agüero, Mendy and De Bruyne joined on the casualty list by David Silva and Fernandinho, it was a significantly weakened side that took to the Etihad pitch to face the German side.

After only sixteen minutes, the gloom deepened as Andrej Kramarić stroked a penalty down the centre of Ederson's goal after Laporte had pulled Benjamin Hübner down. City huffed and puffed, hitting post and bar through Jesus and a deflection off Joelinton from Gündoğan's free kick, before Sané levelled with a blistering 30-yard free kick on the cusp of half-time.

Hoffenheim's increasingly devil-may-care attacking provided openings for City. Identical breakaways led to the enthralling sight of Sterling, Bernardo and Sané messing up a chance when all three were through on Baumann, but a second break finished more happily with Sané taking two deft touches before dispatching the ball crisply under the goalkeeper.

Foden, participating in his first Champions League game after signing a six-year contract, volleyed a spectacular left-foot shot which was tipped over, as City sealed top spot and eliminated Hoffenheim. 'He is a diamond,' enthused Guardiola. City had topped the group with thirteen points after a slow start, with yet another late goal in the other game sealing Lyon's second place ahead of Shakhtar.

Despite reluctance in some quarters to shower City with praise, Guardiola was not holding back. 'The managers are so good and the best teams in Europe are here,' he said. 'Some big, big teams have gone out. Inter Milan are an exceptional team, but they are in the Europa League. You sleep a little bit and you will be in the Europa League, so that is why I am so glad to be through.'

MANCHESTER CITY 2–1 TSG HOFFENHEIM | Att. 50,411 | Sané (2)

Ederson, Stones (Walker), Zinchenko (Delph), Otamendi, Laporte, Gündoğan, Foden, B. Silva (Kompany), Jesus, Sterling, Sané

Installed as one of the favourites, City awaited the Nyon draw knowing the proliferation of English clubs (Spurs, Liverpool and Manchester United had all made it through) and other factors introduced by UEFA left only four possible opponents: Atlético Madrid, Roma, Ajax or Schalke.

Only Atlético represented fresh opposition in Europe, while Ajax and Roma had been opponents in previous group phases. The draw duly paired City with Schalke. Although it would be a first in the Champions League, there had already been significant European action between the sides in 1970 and 2008.

Liverpool, facing Bayern Munich, Spurs, paired with resurgent Borussia Dortmund, and Manchester United, against Paris Saint-Germain, had all been saddled with tougher assignments. The infamous UEFA coefficients were now working more strongly in City's favour than in previous years.

To emphasise the feeling that greater powers were at work for City, domestic cup draws had also been kind, pairing the club with Rotherham in the FA Cup and third-tier debutants Burton Albion in the semi-finals of the League Cup. Those sides had been dispatched 7–0 and 9–0, respectively. To prove it was not just minnows getting pasted, however, title rivals Chelsea were hit for six in the run-up to the Schalke game too.

Düsseldorf: table dancing and *Schweinshaxe*

Seasoned travellers to see City in Schalke (this meant twice for most of us) knew that Gelsenkirchen held little interest bar being the royal-blues' home. The Veltins-Arena nestles in the visually decrepit coal belt of the upper Ruhrgebiet surrounded by industrial slag heaps. On our previous visit in 2008, Cologne had proved a match for our cultural appetites, but this time the bulk of City's support was housed in Düsseldorf. The day before the match saw large groups of City fans gathering in the city's sunny embrace to sample the delights of the famous Altstadt.

Finding accommodation at the Acon Hotel in Mintropstrasse, two minutes from the railway station, it appeared to be ideally located for the 45-minute rail trip north the next day. However, on closer inspection, it seemed also to be well positioned for would-be patrons of the Solid Gold table dancing bar, with the delightfully appointed Backstage Bar nestled next door. The Turkish grocer two doors up sold his own version of lady's fingers. Another twenty metres dropped you in front of the 'Authentic Flamingo American Table Dancing Bar'. What the Americans do differently on a table to the locals would never become completely clear during our brief stay.

The atmosphere in this part of town was downbeat, but at least the okra looked perky.

Düsseldorf's Altstadt presented a clearly different perspective. Twenty minutes' walk from the gently throbbing decay of Mintropstrasse, standing face to face with a bronze bust of Johannes Rau, Bundespräsident between 1999 and 2004, a period roughly spanning City's initial recovery from the horror days of the Third Division, one was reminded of the city's grand heritage.

Beyond Herr Rau, a short, brisk walk down the Rheinüfer, a broad boardwalk alongside the fast-flowing river, lay the Altstadt, an impressive accumulation of cafés, breweries and restaurants housed in narrow streets decorated with carillon bells and ornate Teutonic gables. The throbbing noise of 3,000 Mancunian voices called you in or drove you away, depending on your constitution.

Inside the Uerige brewery, proudly boasting more than 150 years of attempting to get the local population drunk, a homely welcome was assured. A man with a waxed moustache and a big white apron approached every five minutes or so with a huge tray of beer. The idea: to repeat his rounds until you cannot repeat yours.

The plate was the size of a tractor tyre. It contained what the locals call 'Schweinshaxe', supposedly pig knuckle, which did not sound OK but looked divine. It was, as it turned out, more than OK. A sumptuous slow-cooked shin of pork, with the meat falling away from the bone into a luxurious lake of onion gravy. This precious booty was guarded by three hills of, in order, sauerkraut, creamed potato and shredded red cabbage. A blob of volcanic mustard decorated the side. *Meatwear* to Germans is a little like lingerie to Parisians. It is an art form. It is culture. It fills stomachs. It tastes like heaven. After eating all of this, however, you cannot breathe and it was fully twenty minutes before we could walk properly down the street.

To mention Uerige without also mentioning Kürzer, Gattsweilers, Schlüsserl and Füchsehen would be remiss. For most of the raucously inebriated City fans making for their beds, it had been a grand night deserving of a grand match the next day.

The next morning, talk centred on the mysteries of good form, good luck, omens and superstitions. Stars were aligning. Cup runs decorated with Hoffenheims and Burtons, Rotherhams and Burnleys suggested something was in the air, but who could be sure. An incredible match suggested this may just be the case, although the way things had begun to unravel, one could have been forgiven for believing the opposite.

The game started at a fair crack, passes zipping, crowd humming and buzzing. City's lead, from a mistake by goalkeeper Ralf Fährmann on eighteen minutes had the effect of calming nerves and steadying the flow.

The referee then took over, awarding two penalties to the home side before half-time, the first a bizarre mix-up thanks to the newly installed but not fully functional VAR technology, which nobody seemed to be able to control. Little did we know what fun VAR would visit upon us in the coming months. Otamendi's arm was judged to be the culprit, but it took three minutes for the referee to point to the spot, with the away section spitting fire at the information-lite hold-up.

Both penalties were expertly converted by Nabil Bentaleb and City were left dishevelled, distracted and dumbfounded. The second half proved to be an exercise in regaining control, but Otamendi's 68th-minute red card (a second yellow after the penalty debacle) further skewed the balance. With time running out and City reorganised seemingly to maintain the status quo and take a one-goal deficit back to Manchester for the second leg, a strange energy began to grip the away side.

Kompany had been installed in Otamendi's vacant position, with Zinchenko asked to curb his attacking forays and dig in at the back, but suddenly City found an extra gear with one man less. It was not the first time that, from a position of unlucky disadvantage, a galvanised response had sprung. First substitute Sané, on his old Schalke stamping ground, curled in an unstoppable free kick to equalise on 85 minutes and then, with time running its course, a huge spearing pass downfield from Ederson fell next to Sterling, who – with a gentle nudge of the shoulder – eased his marker out of the way and advanced to slip the ball over Fährmann and into the net for a spine-tingling winner.

Most of the Veltins that had been regularly supplied during the match by a small army of men wearing rucksacks containing beer barrels and feeder pipes, was at this precise moment hurled skywards in a frenzy of lashing arms and legs. City had come back from the dead with a show of courage and character, which would surely bode well for the rest of the tournament. The famous 'Fight 'Til The End' song so beloved of the fans had never rung truer than in the deepening darkness of Gelsenkirchen, as the fans funnelled out to rejoin a public transport system that would carry us all around the highways and byways long enough to allow the Düsseldorf Altstadt to close its doors before we returned.

FC SCHALKE 04 2–3 MANCHESTER CITY | Att. 54,417 | Agüero, Sané, Sterling

Ederson, Walker, Laporte, Fernandinho, Otamendi, Gündoğan, De Bruyne (Zinchenko), B. Silva, D. Silva (Kompany), Agüero (Sané), Sterling

Within the space of four days, City had hauled in the first trophy of the season, beating Chelsea on penalties to secure the League Cup for the second consecutive year, the first time the club had ever retained a trophy, and managed to render the second leg of their Champions League tie less complicated.

Retaining the Premier League remained a priority, with Liverpool still making a holy fight of it, but the Champions League, for so long a distant and exotic dream, was coming into sharper focus with every step of the journey. City were clearly not taking things lightly. The courageous and resolute will to win looked set to see them through to the competition's last eight for only the third time in the club's history after 2015–16 and 2017–18.

By the second leg, the club was in the spotlight for all the wrong reasons. Having clawed back what at one time had been a seven-point Liverpool lead at the top of the Premier League and edged past them, City found themselves in the eye of a Europe-wide storm. With UEFA, FIFA and the English FA opening investigations into everything from Financial Fair Play breaches to illegal payments to youth team players, the press were splashing negative stories about the club on a daily basis.

City's football, however, in stark contrast to the maelstrom blowing around the Etihad, had remained measured and immaculate, a nine-game winning run lifting them to the top of the league and the brink of the quarter-finals of the Champions League.

In contrast, Schalke's Bundesliga form was wretched and they came to Manchester threatening to play a youth team to keep legs fresh for vital domestic clashes in the coming weeks.

In the end, they played as near to full strength as injuries would allow and were rewarded with a 7–0 caning at the hands of a magnificently fluid City side. Three goals up at half-time through a brace from Agüero (bringing him to 25 for the season) and a pinpoint finish from Sané after being slotted through magnificently by Zinchenko, City hit four more after the break through Sterling, Bernardo Silva and substitutes Foden and Jesus. It was City's largest-ever winning margin in the competition, beating the 6–0 demolition of Shakhtar earlier in the campaign, the 10–2 aggregate also a record-breaker.

The game was perhaps most remarkable for the five minutes lost to VAR, which held up three goal situations while officials deliberated off-pitch. The strange sight of an entire stadium and all the players and staff waiting patiently for the officials to make a decision was not made any more acceptable in its repetition.

MANCHESTER CITY 7–0 FC SCHALKE 04 | Att. 51,518 | Agüero (2), Sané, Sterling, B. Silva, Foden, Jesus

Ederson, Walker, Danilo, Laporte (Delph), Zinchenko, D. Silva (Foden), B. Silva, Gündoğan, Sterling, Sané, Agüero (Jesus)

Another remarkable feature of the game had been the performances of some of City's lesser lights. With injuries to Stones, De Bruyne, Mendy and Kompany and with the returning Laporte unlikely to make the full 90 minutes, Guardiola had decided to slot full-back Danilo in at centre-half, where he proceeded to excel. His manager was effusive in the post-match press conference, saying: 'I want to praise him as he was incredible. We play him at left-back and he doesn't complain; right-back, doesn't complain; holding midfielder in the final minutes against

Chelsea in the League Cup final, doesn't complain; plays central defender, doesn't complain.'

The continuing presence of stand-in left-back Zinchenko, ostensibly a creative midfield player, also caught the eye, with the young Ukrainian once again putting in a top-class performance, whilst Delph was finally back in from the cold after receiving a lesson in his manager's high standards (Guardiola was reputed to have been furious at two mistakes he had made in defeats at Newcastle and Leicester over the Christmas period).

Along with Zinchenko and Sterling, a decorative midfield display by Gündoğan also caught the eye, as did the masterful wing play of Sané against his former employers. The German flier had produced three assists and scored a wonderfully smooth goal of his own. He summed the situation up succinctly afterwards: 'Everyone knows we're a strong team and really aggressive at the front, but we also know it'll get tougher if you go further. It's a tough competition and you can play against really hard teams but it's exciting for us to see how the games will be.'

With surprises falling in the other games – Manchester United had come back from home defeat to somehow dismiss Paris Saint-Germain, while Ajax had walloped four past Real Madrid at the Bernabéu – the final eight had an unusual look about it.

Old England beckons again

Atlético's collapse in Turin meant both Madrid sides were out, while Tottenham had seen off Dortmund.

The prospect of a second consecutive all-English quarter-final thus loomed for City as they entered the draw with Spurs, Liverpool and United. This was the first time since 2009 that four English sides had made it to this stage and they were accompanied in the latter stages by Barcelona, Juventus, Ajax and

FC Porto. With Liverpool drawing the Portuguese for the second successive season, City avoided the most difficult of the home sides. The Merseyside club's dogged resistance in the Premier League was producing the closest title race for years. With six games to go domestically, Liverpool were two points clear having played a game more.

If there was no room for error in the league, being pitted against Tottenham in Europe offered little reprieve. Newly ensconced in their state-of-the-art stadium, the north London side would provide a stern test for City. Not as stern, perhaps, as Barcelona, who would visit neighbours United, or Juventus, who were paired with Ajax, and somewhere deep in the bowels of the Etihad, City's planners and plotters cannot have been displeased with the pairing.

With the strange spectacle of the semi-final draw being made at the same time, City now knew their possible path to European glory: beat Tottenham and a last-four game with either Juventus or Ajax loomed, before the final in Madrid. As he had done before the quarter-final with Liverpool twelve months earlier, Guardiola again chose the occasion of a knife-edge contest to put out a strangely unbalanced-looking side. His tinkering against Liverpool had partly been responsible for a dramatic Anfield defeat from which City found it impossible to recover in the second leg. In north London, the Catalan decided to pitch Delph back into the side at left-back for only his second full game of the season. With the blossoming form of Zinchenko cut short by injury and Mendy's weekend outing against Brighton in the FA Cup semi-final rendering him unable to play again, it was to the ex-Villa man that Guardiola now looked.

Agüero, missing against Brighton, was back in up front, as was Mahrez, chosen ahead of Sané, whose stuttering season and questionable attitude had removed him from automatic selection. In midfield, Bernardo's unexpected absence (having picked up an injury in training) gave Guardiola the chance to use a more defensive pair of Fernandinho and Gündoğan.

All in all, pre-match reaction among the fans travelling south for the third of four City games in London within two weeks ranged from surprise to consternation. 'If it works, Pep's a genius,' wrote one on Twitter. 'If not, he can expect to come in for some rightful stick …'

Inevitably, talk centred on an unusually cautious looking set-up from a manager who was beginning to gain a reputation for sclerosis in the latter stages of the Champions League. For those counting, and there were plenty in the morning's press, it had been eight years since the Catalan had led any side to victory away from home in the last eight or last four of the competition.

As things turned out, this night was not to be the one when he would turn that record around, although the start that City were given might on another occasion have led to a win.

Instead, a slow-burner of a game was ignited by a controversial decision awarded to City by VAR – again playing a prominent role in its inaugural season. A helter-skelter period of play had ended in Danny Rose deflecting a shot by Sterling away for a corner. Before it could be taken, but with not one City player appealing, referee Björn Kuipers suddenly held his finger to his ear to listen to instructions from elsewhere. Sure enough, slow-motion replays showed Rose's arm being raised as he skidded into the challenge, perhaps a normal physical response to the start of a fall, leading to him deflecting the ball away with his lower arm. A simple flourish from Kuipers told the stunned stadium that a penalty had been awarded from this innocuous-looking situation.

City's glee was both short-lived and a precursor to what would come in the second leg in even more generous portions.

In the furore, up stepped Agüero. City's all-time record scorer had a patchy record from the spot in European competition; a surprisingly erratic conversion rate of nine scored from fourteen taken became nine from fifteen as Hugo Lloris dived to his left to save comfortably.

City had started well enough, with Mahrez pressing down the right and Fernandinho managing his usual delicate balance of simple blocking-off manoeuvres and carefully disguised man-handling of Tottenham runners. One challenge on Harry Kane ended with Fernandinho casually cuffing the Tottenham man, which was unseen by Kuipers.

Having lost Kane to a robust 55th-minute challenge with Delph (the Spurs striker coming in hard on the City defender but ending up with ankle ligament damage himself), Spurs steadied themselves, withstood a period of increasing domination by City and grabbed the all-important goal. It fell in the 78th minute and was down entirely to Son Heung-min, who, having kept the ball in deftly by the dead-ball line, twisted back inside a lunging Delph to fire left-footed under Ederson. The City keeper, hurt in a fall earlier in the second half, was slow to get down to the shot, while Guardiola's on–off love affair with Delph would once again take a turn for the worst.

TOTTENHAM 1–0 MANCHESTER CITY | Att. 60,044
Ederson, Walker, Otamendi, Laporte, Delph, Fernandinho, Gündoğan, D. Silva (De Bruyne), Mahrez (Sané), Agüero (Jesus), Sterling

Afterwards, Guardiola testily defended his side's position in the face of some hostile questioning regarding his preference for Gündoğan over the recovered De Bruyne. Journalists and fans alike were also keen to know why – with his side struggling to get an equaliser – he had left it until the 89th minute to introduce fresh impetus in the shape of De Bruyne and Sané.

The Catalan explained: 'We played an incredible game and we controlled it. The result is not the best one but in the Champions League you have to make comebacks to go through ... Sometimes 1–0 is better than 0–0 because it's clear what we have to do. We know we have to score goals.'

For City fans, perhaps hoping a combination of Tottenham's perceived flakiness and a state of awe at their new surroundings might undo them, there was disappointment. At the end of the day, however, with some supporters already spitting fire at the defeat, City had returned from an away leg of the Champions League quarter-final a single goal down. It was all still to play for.

As Barney Ronay, writing in the *Guardian*, said: 'The South Stand held up its wall of plastic bags to spell out "To Dare Is To Do", an iconic image so iconic the Spurs media department had already called it iconic before it had even happened.

'Tempting fate, perhaps, with Manchester City's light-blue machine in town. It worked all the same. On a boisterous night on the Seven Sisters Road, Spurs produced the best result of the Pochettino era to date.

'City came here having won 22 of their last 23 games and playing with a thrilling fluency, but they never got started. Spurs were controlled and thrillingly assertive throughout, playing at the edge of their nerves but with a sense of poise too for a deserved 1–0 victory.'

A light-blue machine temporarily derailed – and in any case playing in yet another unloved Champions League change strip of maroon with orange sash – it seemed.

With work to do in the league, a looming FA Cup final against Watford and niggling injuries beginning to take their toll on an exhausted squad, the effort on this occasion had come to nothing. While some supporters claimed that of the three games with Tottenham coming in quick succession, this was the one that hurt least to lose, it meant that the return leg and the home league game would now *have* to be won.

In the press, a communal hand-wringing procedure was under way almost as soon as the players had cleared the pitch. In the *Guardian*, Jonathan Wilson asked whether City's manager was 'overthinking' his Champions League strategies: 'By definition, sample sizes for the latter stages of major competitions in football tend to be small, but this feels now like more than a blip. City's defeat here was the 10th straight away game in the Champions League quarter- or semi-final that Guardiola has failed to win.

'A skim down the list shows a range of games. Draws at Milan with Barcelona in 2012, or at Manchester United with Bayern in 2014, were good results. Nobody was initially concerned by what were widely seen as unfortunate 1–0 defeats to Chelsea and Real Madrid in the following round in those two seasons. But more recently results have become increasingly hard to explain. With Bayern there was a 3–1 defeat at Porto in the 2015 quarter-final, overcome in the second leg, as well as a very nervy 2–2 draw with Benfica in the 2016 quarter-final after a 1–0 win at home. And there have been the 3–0 shellackings with Bayern in 2015 and with City at Anfield last year.'

Suddenly, stories within stories, the characteristic that had served to mark out the Catalan as something special – his obsessive attention to detail – was being posted as a deterrent to City's progress.

What was certainly true was Tottenham's strengths had pushed Guardiola towards caution. The usual attacking down the flanks had been curtailed by selecting the slower, less-incisive Mahrez on the right and the *steady-Eddie* presence of Gündoğan in the middle. Fernandinho, meanwhile, had had his domineering presence clipped by a hustling Spurs midfield, typified by the burgeoning energy of Dele Alli. When City had cried out for more speed and width, nothing had changed until it was too late. A more vivid response was expected in the second leg in Manchester. Would Guardiola go hell for leather at a venue where City knew only success? Or would there be more strange tinkering in deference to the danger the opponent carried?

There would be only eight days to wait before we witnessed the nature of City's response.

UN-BE-LIEVABLE, JEFF!

City prepared to welcome Tottenham for the first of two consecutive home games that would shape their destiny. On the line: the fragile but real possibility of making history, not only for the club but for English football. A possible treble, or even the unthinkable quadruple, was still on, going into mid-April. Such riches had never fallen City's way in 125 years of existence. The following two matches would go a long way in deciding how the club and its ferociously focused manager would be viewed by history.

On the eve of the match, Guardiola was once again quizzed about his patchy Champions League record at this stage of the competition. The retort was firm but tetchy: 'Sorry, guys, I'm a failure in this competition, but many times I played in the semi-finals as a player.'

Touching on another theme that had taken root in the popular press, City's lack of full houses for home games and what talkSPORT Radio had laughingly regarded as a lack of character in the team and a lack of desire among the fans, the Catalan again mentioned the need for noise. 'The Liverpool game would be enough for me. We need it. Really we need it. I want to see that they want to get to the semi-finals. Not the players. The players no doubt after twenty months. I want to see my fans, our fans, that they really want the semi-final. I want to see that tomorrow.'

Perhaps some fire had been taken from the bellies of supporters, who had queued long hours in the rain for the right to watch defeats at Stockport and FA Cup first-round games at Darlington. Perhaps all that shouting defiance as City were relegated time and again in the '80s and '90s had left some fans running on empty. Perhaps the cosy years of the Premier League successes had taken that famous edge from the gritty City fans of yore. Maybe Guardiola, commenting from his position in the eye of the storm but on the periphery of the culture, had some sort of a point, however painful it might have been for the faithful to hear.

Valid point or not, nothing could hide the fact that tickets for Tottenham were £50 and above. Multiple Wembley trips and overseas jaunts had to be paid for one way or another. Those equating the club's new-found wealth with that of the supporters were busy missing perhaps the most important point of all. Those fans, in their thousands and thousands, had followed City through thin and thinner and their pockets were not bottomless pits. City's staunch but solidly working-class following had come in for criticism, but anyone who had been in Bilbao in 1969, in Liège in 1978 or in Hamburg in 2009 would vouch for the staying power of some of the most loyal fans in football.

What occurred in the return leg with Tottenham would prove to be almost unique, even to those droves of supporters who thought the club had already surprised them in every way possible. It would be a match – and a result – that would shape the rest of the club's season, their immediate future in European competition and leave an indelible mark on everyone who witnessed it.

On a crisp night, a packed house raised the roof for City, bringing memories of the UEFA Cup quarter-final with SV Hamburg during Mark Hughes' reign. What started as a memorable night of colour and passion developed into one of the most hair-raising and dramatic games of knockout football the stadium or indeed the tournament had ever seen.

With the crowd giving full voice to their hopes, the game kicked off before a sea of flags. City's need for a goal to even things up produced an early onslaught similar to the previous year's spat with Liverpool, but without such an early break-through. The packed house did not have to wait far beyond the second minute, when the deadline had been broken a year earlier, for the first goal to fall, however. Prised open by a precision pass by De Bruyne, the Tottenham defence could do little but admire Sterling's close control down the left. He cut inside and curled a perfect shot past Lloris into the far corner to level the scores after just four minutes.

If the fans were breathless at another dramatic and courageous start from the home side, seven short minutes later they were holding on to anything they could find just to remain upright.

By the eleventh minute of this astonishing game, the score was 2–1, following two opportunist goals from Son, assisted royally by some broad-dimension dithering in defence by Laporte. With City seemingly out for the count, Bernardo immediately made it 2–2 when jinking in from the right and sliding a shot through a slim space at Lloris' near post. It took a deflection before entering the South Stand net.

The unbelievable start already represented the fastest four-goal salvo at the beginning of any Champions League match. City were still behind on aggregate, as they had been when the game started, but four goals had been scored in the meantime.

It was clearly going to be quite a night and, with so long to go even to half-time, there was at this stage every reason to believe more goals might be scored. Certainly, a frantic-looking Guardiola on the touchline seemed sure he could squeeze some more out of his men, gesticulating wildly first at Walker, then at Kompany, to shore things up in a ragged rearguard. Often left to fend for itself, because of excessive numbers intent on going forward, the back four was always likely to come under pressure from any side prepared to attack it. In this case, Mauricio Pochettino's strategy appeared to be paying off with Son and Christian Eriksen finding space and discovering shooting alleys to test Ederson.

Incredibly, considering the electrifying start, only one more goal would come before referee Cüneyt Çakir blew for the break and it went to City to level the tie 3–3 on aggregate. With Tottenham's two away goals now bringing crucial pressure to bear on City, the home side still needed to raise the score to four to go through, however. The crucial third, Sterling's second of the night, once again put fire into the bellies of the 53,000 crowd.

Lloris had successfully slowed things down with a succession of dreamily executed goal kicks, but the goal brought this fascinating game back to volcanic life. De Bruyne was set free down the right by a clever flick and the Belgian sent in one of his trademark low arcing crosses. The ball eluded outstretched boots in the penalty box and ran to Sterling at the back post. His assured finish from close-in evaded the falling Lloris and slid into the net to raucous appreciation.

With half-time feeling like a kind of punishment, the break did at least offer the two coaches the chance to get the game back under control and the players to get their heads together. In such a frenetic atmosphere, it was clear neither Guardiola nor Pochettino were pleased at how things had gone. Both managers had reason to be proud of how their players had reacted to the crushing pressure of the game, but neither could say it was exactly going to their carefully planned pre-match strategies.

With the second period starting in a similarly gung-ho fashion, it was not long before City were pressing hard for the goal they needed. Five minutes into the half, Bernardo thought he had it, but – colliding with Rose running on to a spill from Lloris – the ball squirted wide.

Nine minutes later and City got the goal they wanted, as De Bruyne's peerless precision slid Agüero into the right side of the box and the little poacher's shot went past Lloris before the keeper could even react. Agüero's strike was his 28th of the season. For the first time in the two games, City had their noses in front. Would Guardiola now settle things down prudently to hold on to the lead, or would City continue to hammer forward in such unrestrained style? Note had been taken of the Catalan's growing penchant for closing games out with the introduction of an extra central defender (often Stones or Otamendi) or a deep-lying midfielder (Gündoğan or Fernandinho) to shore things up.

In the minutes immediately after the fourth goal, City did not seem to be sitting back in the slightest, but the 63rd-minute substitution of David Silva for Fernandinho appeared to be the first suggestion that Guardiola may be trying to shut down the middle corridor through which Spurs had been flooding happily all game. The match had provided royal entertainment thus far, but at no point could either manager have said to have been in control of proceedings.

Fernandinho would act as an anchor to the Tottenham pressure that would surely now come. Still, the twinkling close control of Sterling and Bernardo was being given free rein to attack an increasingly wobbly looking away defence.

With Tottenham withstanding City's growing midfield dominance, there appeared little sign of the late surge that Pochettino's men needed. However, a sudden attack produced a corner and, when that came to nothing, a second corner, which *did* provide something: a goal scored from Kieran Trippier's inswinger, off substitute Fernando Llorente's arm and hip and into the net. The Spanish striker, so often a square peg in a round hole since moving to London from Swansea, had known nothing of the skimming contact that had diverted the ball goalwards, but here he was milking the applause from the travelling Spurs fans, as his goal made it past the all-seeing eye of VAR.

It was now imperative for City to score again. The sinews straining in Llorente's neck during his celebrations would serve as a metaphor for the strained, bulging vortex of emotion that had by now gripped the Etihad. All or nothing, City threw themselves once more into all-out attack.

This raging, thundering match was still not done with us, with City now forced to surge forward without thought of defence. Spurs, operating right on the edge of their capabilities, seemed galvanised by the fact that the semi-final place drifting suddenly into focus had only been achieved once before in their history.

With City's efforts foundering on the visitors' massed ranks, one last agonising pulse of drama engulfed the stadium, sending both sets of supporters through an emotional wringer that would never be forgotten. Bernardo's deflected pass put Agüero through on the right side of the area and his ball back across the edge of the six-yard box was met gloriously by Sterling, stepping inside a challenge and planting the ball past Lloris.

As the Spurs players fell to their knees in tattered despair, City's jubilant players and fans raised the roof. Noise, elation and confusion gripped the 53,000 emotionally drained souls. If this was the height of emotion, seconds later, it got worse, as the roles were reversed. Referee Çakir, suddenly summoned by words in his ear to the side of the pitch, consulted VAR and signalled Agüero's position during the build-up to be offside. As the elation flooded out of the stadium like a reverse transfusion, the banks of Tottenham fans at the far end hauled themselves up from the floor to celebrate a truly spine-tingling survival story.

For the second consecutive year, City had been turfed out of the Champions League by a Premier League club, the first English club to be eliminated twice by fellow countrymen.

Tottenham, like Liverpool the year before, would go on to lose the final, after producing another minor miracle in winning the second leg at Ajax in the semi-final. For City, all that was left was to lick their wounds and gather strength for the rest of a domestic season which was ultimately to garner a magnificent, unprecedented and slightly under-praised treble of League Cup, Premier League and FA Cup (a staggering 6–0 defeat of Watford that would equal the final's biggest winning margin, standing since 1903).

MANCHESTER CITY 4–3 TOTTENHAM | Att. 53,348 | Sterling (2), B. Silva, Agüero

Ederson, Walker, Kompany, Laporte, Mendy (Sané), De Bruyne, Gündoğan, D. Silva (Fernandinho), B. Silva, Sterling, Agüero

City had produced yet another indescribable hotpot of emotional torture.

For fan Graham Ward, however, it would be extra poignant: 'The Spurs game was my mum's last, before she died in the May ... Mum had insisted on paying for hospitality packages and we were on the back row of level one of the East Stand, next to fans who weren't short of a bit (a huge amount) of industrial language, but, when you're a veteran of the '70s, it was water off a duck's back. "Seven goals and I never saw one!" was her verdict on the night.'

The season would long be remembered as a thing of beauty for a club that, twenty years before, had been sweating on a penalty shoot-out with Gillingham to climb out of the domestic third tier. The magnificent attacking football had seen records tumble, but the big target remained elusive. While the fans welcomed domestic successes over triumph in a Champions League that many still failed to muster any affection for, the goal of the owners and the target of their hugely decorated manager fell elsewhere. It would be to the European continent that their gaze would again fall in 2019–20, as City set out once again to capture the one trophy still on their wish list.

It was left to a pale-looking Guardiola to offer explanations for something that was impossible to categorise. Praising Spurs, who had become the seventh English side to reach a Champions League semi-final – after City, Manchester United, Liverpool, Chelsea, Arsenal and Leeds – the Catalan said: 'It is cruel but it is what it is and we have to accept it. I am so proud of the players and the fans. I have never heard noise like that since I have been in Manchester. Unfortunately, it was a bad end for us, so congratulations to Tottenham and good luck for the semi-finals.'

On the touchy subject of VAR, the City coach clenched his teeth: 'I support VAR but maybe from one angle Llorente's goal is handball, maybe from the referee's angle it is not. Today is tough and tomorrow will be tough too but the day after we will be ready.'

City, at times unplayable in their attacking effervescence with the often-injured De Bruyne the virtuoso performer, had been undone by two uncharacteristic slips at the back. Laporte, on his way to completing a near-immaculate season, had chosen an inappropriate evening to increase his errors quotient by 100 per cent. In many ways, City's exhilarating attacking display had confirmed why they had been considered one of the favourites to lift the trophy.

In exploiting a defence that had not been tested by many sides all season, Pochettino's tactical prowess and his players' bravery had come to the fore and prevailed in the most dramatic manner possible. Indeed, City's season had been one of high drama from start to finish, but – as far as European glory was concerned – the new era of rubbing shoulders with the game's historical giants was yet to yield the ultimate prize. A summer of relaxation and reassessing what and who would take the club to the game's pinnacle would follow, but with Manchester bidding farewell to Vincent Kompany and the roles of Sergio Agüero, David Silva and Fernandinho likely to be reduced in the coming months, it would be to City's new generation of talent that the club would have to look.

The first major era of success might well – when the whole story was told – have closed here in May 2019. What the next one would usher in was, as usual in these parts, anyone's guess.

CITYITIS HITS THE CONTINENT

That joke isn't funny anymore

> *'In recent years it's changed; I think now the club is desperately hungry to win the Champions League, and if I've learnt anything about City it's that whenever they set themselves a target, they are capable of achieving it.'*
>
> Vincent Kompany

The summer of 2019 involved a certain amount of soul searching if you were in the employment of Manchester City Football Club. If you were a fan, a similarly bleak period of introspection was also quickly under way as soon as the first jet of sun cream hit your pasty shoulders.

The club had just completed its most successful season ever, winning every domestic trophy available and, in doing so, becoming the first-ever English treble winners. On the back of the previous season's 100-point title win and the manner of the scintillating one-touch football that often looked like a different sport to that played by the rest of the Premier League, there was clearly reason for satisfaction.

The reality was quite different, however, as significant sections of the media had taken it upon themselves to become soldiers of a new moral code sweeping through the sport. City's Abu Dhabi-backing had already raised the suspicions of UEFA, urged on by vociferous members of football's elite, particularly Bayern Munich, Juventus and Real Madrid. Now, some sections of the British press became a moralising legion offering opinions on subjects as far ranging as child camel racers in the Abu Dhabi desert to bloody wars of succession in the imploding state of Yemen.

Whatever your thoughts on global socio-political affairs, the record-breaking of Guardiola's 2018–19 vintage was being partially buried beneath a hill of weirdly varied bad press.

In an era increasingly dominated by fake news and click-bait, where one person's agendas and biases are difficult to distinguish from the next person's objective platitudes, City occupied the centre ground. After the Cup final, beating Watford 6–0, Miguel Delaney, the *Independent*'s chief football writer, despaired: 'What's the point reporting on the football? The only relevant factor is that City are an infinitely better-resourced club, as they have proven every time these two teams have met since Watford's 2015 promotion … If by half-time it felt like any dull pre-season friendly in the United States, it by the end just resembled an evisceration. That's if any neutrals were actually still watching.'

Delaney had also taken to Twitter to remark: 'City will rightly celebrate their treble … but the rest of the game should not. That farce at Wembley reflected a huge problem rising in football, right across Europe.'

In contrast, Manchester United's 4–0 tonking of Chelsea in the 1994 final had the Sunday papers exploding in praise of a 'thrillingly powerful United performance'. There was evidently nothing thrilling about City's modern-day rise to power.

The problem, as it stood, was that City had just retained the league title for the first time in its history, separated by a single point from Liverpool, yet apparently the club's domination was so complete as to be *problematic*. Making parallels with the likes of Paris Saint-Germain, finishing their own domestic season top for the seventh year out of eight, or Bayern Munich, champions for the eighth time in ten years in Germany, seemed obscure. By 2022, at least one newspaper reporter would be calling City's dominance of a tournament they had never won as 'worrying'. Alice had heard fewer strange things over a cup of Vimto at the tea party.

Clearly, within the club, there was a resolute front, but it seemed that a major chunk of the reporting on City had turned swiftly and conclusively to bitter vindictiveness. Whereas past reporting had carried an undercurrent of the lovable old buffoon, unable to avoid constantly shooting itself in the foot, with the legions of supporters celebrated for their daft but unerring loyalty, things now looked different. Now even the football – sleek, elegant and otherworldly as it was – seemed fair game, or at least 'not worth reporting on'.

Perhaps City's rise had unearthed a cosy underbelly in English football, where the elite fed royally at the top table and had not really expected the feast to be gatecrashed. City's uninterrupted nine-year Champions League participation had meant one of the original gang of four of Arsenal, Manchester United, Liverpool and Chelsea had to miss out on the hill of money each year.

Tottenham's steady rise had dislodged another place and undiluted panic had set in. As it stood, Arsenal and Manchester United had largely been the fall guys. The two giants that had dominated the start of the new century were now struggling badly to keep up with progressively run clubs like Chelsea, Spurs and City. Liverpool's resurgence under Jürgen Klopp had further muddied the waters. With the Ferguson and Wenger dynasties long gone, the rot had truly set in. FFP had attempted to stall more clubs taking advantage of new investment, but the news in the summer of 2021 that Newcastle United, long since a loyal copy of the stuttering old Manchester City of the '80s and '90s, had been bought by an arm of the Saudi Arabian state, sent further shock waves through the establishment.

UEFA now suggested that they were studying the prospect of having 'permanent legacy invitees' in the future, a sure-fire vote winner with the likes of Manchester United, Juventus and AC Milan.

As the summer arrived, it was unclear where we were all headed. Certainly, for City, with their captain departed for a new challenge as player-manager of Anderlecht and the end in sight for David Silva, Fernandinho and Sergio Agüero, the first great trophy-winning squad of the club's modern times was coming to a close. Joining the likes of Nigel de Jong, Gareth Barry, Pablo Zabaleta, Yaya Touré, Mario Balotelli and Joe Hart, meant Kompany had ceded City's longest-serving mantle to David Silva. A gradual phasing-out of the old guard that had helped land City's first domestic trophies in nearly 50 years was nearly complete.

Phase two seemed to be upon us.

With the *Independent* categorising City in an elite group of transfer market 'sharks' who could buy any player they wanted, City's restocking would be watched with interest. Just how did you bolster a squad that had just won the Premier League, League Cup, FA Cup and Community Shield?

The answer was not slow in arriving with the much-coveted holding midfielder Rodrigo from Atlético Madrid. This meant competition, and a successor, for Fernandinho. In midfield, the return of De Bruyne would give the squad a similar shot in the arm to a new acquisition.

The much-awaited Champions League draw was something of a let-down, pitting City with Shakhtar Donetsk for the third consecutive season. To balance this, the other two sides in Group D were Dinamo Zagreb and debutants Atalanta. In a group that looked spectacularly bereft of booby traps, City were expected to prevail at a canter.

Even at this early stage, significant disruption had visited the City camp with injuries to Laporte and Stones reducing the central defence to a skeleton. In Ukraine for matchday one, Fernandinho took to the pitch as a central defender alongside Otamendi, with Rodrigo in the holding role in midfield.

The night proved memorable for several reasons, not least the power and composure with which City tackled what was supposedly the most hazardous fixture. İlkay Gündoğan's explosive midfield performance lit up a blistering first half, with the German hitting the post and seeing Mahrez bury the rebound, then scoring the second himself.

With De Bruyne performing strongly alongside Gündoğan and Fernandinho taking to his defensive role like a duck to water, City's movement and passing was too slick for Shakhtar. A late goal from Jesus wrapped up a comprehensive victory.

In the five encounters between the two sides, City had now run up a total of fifteen goals, the Ukrainians' most prolific opponent, while this was City's fourth clean sheet against them, also a record.

SHAKHTAR DONETSK 0–3 MANCHESTER CITY | Att. 36,675 |
Mahrez, Gündoğan, Jesus

Ederson, Walker (Cancelo), Otamendi, Fernandinho, Zinchenko, Rodrigo (Mendy), Gündoğan, De Bruyne (B. Silva), Sterling, Jesus, Mahrez

Next up were Dinamo Zagreb, who had inflicted a heavy defeat on Atalanta in their first game.

Questioned about City fans' apparent lack of love for the tournament by the *Guardian*'s eager Jamie Jackson, Guardiola produced the response the journalist was poking for by speaking of the need to 'seduce' City fans to the charms of the Champions League.

In a hard-fought contest, Dinamo held on until well into the second half, sometimes with luck on their side as Gündoğan's rasping shot hit the bar and cannoned back into play. The German's persistence eventually paid off in the 66th minute, when a smooth combination ended with a low ball from Mahrez being fired into the roof of the net by Sterling. More chances came and went before Foden buried a clinical right-foot strike in the 95th minute.

Responding to press reports that he should leave the club for more game time by holding the badge on his shirt out at arm's length and pointing to it, Foden was doing his best to quell the doubts. His manager's praise was not far behind. 'I am so sorry for him – he deserves to play more minutes. I am sure he will help us more,' said the Catalan. 'I am buzzing for Phil,' fellow scorer Sterling told BT Sport. 'I want him in the national team. If he keeps going, he will be there.'

With Tottenham conceding seven at home to Bayern, City's inability to score more than two against the Croatians illustrated the levels to aim at to match the giants. Profligacy on this occasion had not been fatal. But against a more ambitious team there could have been problems.

MANCHESTER CITY 2–0 DINAMO ZAGREB | Att. 49,046 | Sterling, Foden

Ederson, Cancelo, Fernandinho, Otamendi, Mendy, Gündoğan, Rodrigo, D. Silva (Foden), Agüero (Jesus), Mahrez, B. Silva (Sterling)

Patchy league form preceded the match with Atalanta, with a loss to Wolves and a win at Palace the only games since Zagreb. There was no such hesitation against the Italians, however.

Despite an eleven-minute hat-trick from Sterling and Atalanta's shock first-half lead, the main story of a drama-packed game was a hamstring injury sustained by Rodrigo, which threatened to further disrupt the season. The Spaniard had settled in well, providing such dominance that Fernandinho's switch to central defence was beginning to look semi-permanent.

With the other game in the group ending 2–2, City were left five points clear at the top of Group C after just three games, with a 100 per cent record.

Sergio Agüero, making his 100th appearance in Europe, had been responsible for dragging City back into a game in which Ruslan Malinovskyi's penalty had seen the visitors lead. A typical quick-fire double had City in front before the break.

With Sterling netting in the 58th, 64th and 69th minutes during a wild surge of attacking football, City were soon out of sight. Foden then received a second yellow card for pulling back Marten de Roon, after a tame incident with Malinovskyi had led to a booking six minutes earlier. It was a small blot on an otherwise good night's work and a strong response to Guardiola's harsh (but perhaps motivationally adept) pre-match doubts that 'this club is not yet ready to win the Champions League'.

Guardiola mused: 'Atalanta were a tough opponent. We knew they would be, after finishing third last season in Serie A. The result was good but it required an incredible effort.' Indeed, City's effort had produced the biggest winning margin of any English side against Italian opponents for nearly a decade. As if to further add proof that they were bedding into the Champions League, City had now managed to win three of the last five games in which they had fallen behind in, a sure sign if Guardiola needed one that his team was beginning to attain the mental toughness required.

MANCHESTER CITY 5–1 ATALANTA | Att. 49,308 | Agüero (2, 1 pen.), Sterling (3)

Ederson, Walker, Fernandinho, Rodrigo (Stones), Mendy (Cancelo), Gündoğan, De Bruyne (Otamendi), Mahrez, Foden, Sterling, Agüero

---

The return with Atalanta, played in Milan's Giuseppe Meazza Stadium, provided a second consecutive red card and further drama that had travelling fans turning up the volume to support their beleaguered side. Despite a bright start which saw Sterling score after just seven minutes, things quickly turned pear-shaped.

The problems started when Guardiola decided to replace the limping Ederson with Claudio Bravo to protect the Brazilian's fitness ahead of the forthcoming league game at Anfield. With ten minutes to go, Bravo clashed with the onrushing Josip Iličić and was shown a red card. Replays showed the Chilean to be slightly unlucky as no contact had been made as the striker cartwheeled over the goalkeeper. With nobody else available, Kyle Walker donned the baggy top and keeper's gloves for the final part of the game.

By this time, Atalanta had drawn level, but not before Jesus had failed to convert a City penalty, scraping a tame effort wide. Mike Hammond, watching enthusiastically among the noisy City contingent at the other end of the stadium, commented: 'That's the worst penalty we've ever seen.'

City had to a great extent brought about their own downfall, although a point seemed like a triumph by the end, with the supporters giving Walker a standing ovation. It turned out that Guardiola had replaced Ederson owing to a muscular injury that had been giving the Brazilian some discomfort. For City – to use an appropriate metaphor – it never rained but it poured.

ATALANTA 1–1 MANCHESTER CITY | Att. 34,326 | Sterling

Ederson (Bravo), Cancelo, Fernandinho, Otamendi, Mendy, Gündoğan, De Bruyne, B. Silva, Mahrez (Walker), Sterling, Jesus (Agüero)

Guardiola was a relieved man. 'We didn't exactly do what we were supposed to in the second half,' he explained. 'But it was a perfect result and now we need just one more point. In this competition, you know you have your chances and you have to take them.'

On the injury front, things were beginning to look bleak. To add to Leroy Sané, out since the first game of the season, and fellow long-term injury Laporte, Zinchenko and Rodrigo had fallen foul of the curse, with a serious doubt now hanging over Ederson too. If City were to prosper this season, it would be against the odds.

The 1–1 draw with Shakhtar in front of an expectant 52,000 crowd, confirmed City's smooth passage into the knockout rounds, but would hardly have put the fear of God into prospective opponents. Gündoğan, in a rich vein of form, again found himself on the scoresheet, but his close-range finish after good work by Jesus was cancelled out swiftly by Manor Solomon. The goal had come during a rare attack from the Ukrainians and was scored by a player who had been on the pitch barely five minutes.

City's inability to kill off games they were dominating was becoming a feature of the season. This would reach a peak in February when statistics from certain games would make scarcely believable reading. Qualification allowed Guardiola to rest players for the last game in Zagreb, as not only were City through, but, owing to Atalanta's surprise win over Dinamo on the same evening, they were also confirmed top.

'Seven years in a row means you have to qualify seven times,' said Guardiola. 'But now this competition in February will be completely different. We'll see in which conditions we arrive there. This competition is about the details.'

MANCHESTER CITY 1–1 SHAKHTAR DONETSK | Att. 52,020 | Gündoğan

Ederson, Cancelo, Fernandinho, Otamendi, Angelino, Gündoğan, De Bruyne (D. Silva), Rodrigo (Foden), Sterling, B. Silva, Jesus

---

Perhaps the biggest surprise of the final matchday occurred away from City's game in Zagreb, which was won comfortably enough with what amounted to a second-string side. Atalanta's spectacular 3–0 win in Ukraine meant the newcomers squeezed through in second place, a full seven points behind winners City.

City's match in a freezing cold Maksimir Stadium did not initially go to plan, as Dani Olmo smashed the home side ahead with an agile volley. A disputed equaliser from Jesus, heading in while two home players lay 'injured' on the turf, brought City back into things, and the Brazilian had completed his hat-trick by the 54th minute. Foden's stylish contribution was rewarded with a fourth, sliding in six minutes from time, in a display of some authority.

For the lad from Stockport, this was his 50th City appearance and his third Champions League goal, belying claims that he would be well advised to leave the club for more game time. Guardiola's nurturing of Foden, Eric García and Taylor Harwood-Bellis was beginning to become a feature of the season and seeing all three on the pitch in Zagreb helping close out the game was particularly satisfying.

DINAMO ZAGREB 1–4 MANCHESTER CITY | Att. 29,385 | Jesus (3), Foden

Bravo, Cancelo, Otamendi (Harwood-Bellis), García, Mendy, Gündoğan, Foden, B. Silva, Rodrigo (Sterling), Jesus (Zinchenko), Mahrez

---

With a winter of discontent setting in (Liverpool's lead had gradually stretched to an unbridgeable fourteen points), all eyes were now focused on Madrid, the venue for City's knockout-round tie.

Deemed a tough draw, Real represented a beatable version of earlier Madrid sides in recent history. Manager Zinédine Zidane certainly helped focus attention on their grand history in the competition, but the 2019–20 crop had finished a distant second to Paris Saint-Germain. In drawing 2–2 at home to Club Brugge and being thrashed 3–0 in Paris, Real revealed a soft underbelly that an in-form City could surely work on. The 6–0 thrashing of Galatasaray harked back to feasts of old, however. City would need to be at full strength, find some consistent form and hit Real with everything they could muster.

City's third modern-era visit to the Bernabéu could not come quickly enough for many, a February date with destiny for a club coming of age, timed to perfection regarding both growing confidence and returning casualties.

Speculation regarding Guardiola's ability to lift City to the necessary heights was never far away, however. In *World Soccer*, Jonathan Wilson suggested that the Catalan had failed to motivate players towards the end of his spells at Barcelona and Bayern, owing to the tactical onslaught inflicted upon them in the preceding seasons. Considering the coach's fierce and energetic approach to micro-planning everything from diet to match preparation, Wilson asked: 'How long is too long? At what point do players, on hearing a manager's motivational words, begin to shrug and think "we've heard all of this before"? … Guardiola is ferociously intense and that approach takes its toll on players.'

Guardiola in effect had a new squad of players to work his miracles on. Only David Silva, Fernandinho and Agüero had survived the revamp. Wilson's contention may have held some weight, but it was counterbalanced by the fresh blood attracted to the club specifically for the Catalan's rigorous focus. Whatever toll Guardiola's excessive attention to detail might have, most agreed it was small beans in comparison to the galvanising effect his presence had on all around him. Looking casually across the City squad, there was no single player who had not come on in leaps and bounds under his tutelage.

With this in mind, I posted a social media poll asking: 'What has had the most impact on City's season?' Of the 1,500 respondents, a huge 85.5 per cent voted for the long-time injury loss of Laporte and Sané, with a further 11 per cent citing Liverpool's massive improvement.

On 1 February, Real won the Madrid derby by a single goal to stretch their lead at the top of La Liga to six points. It took their unbeaten run to 21 games, in stark contrast to a City side whose profligacy was reaching new heights with defeat to José Mourinho's Tottenham, who scored with their only two shots on target while City missed from 22 of their own. Included was yet another penalty failure, making it five misses out of the last six.

With sections of the press mounting another attack on Guardiola, the wagons were being drawn into a tight circle as the Real showdown approached. The manager's quip after the win in Zagreb that 'this competition is weird, but hopefully we arrive in good spirits in February' was beginning to look a little ironic, given what had since befallen us. As the first leg moved into view, it was not just the Champions League that was looking 'weird' but life in general.

News of a serious viral outbreak in the Chinese province of Hubei meant that those arriving in Madrid for the game were met by the sight of some travellers wearing masks in the concourses of Barajas airport. An odd atmosphere gripped the Spanish capital as the City fans united in the usual watering holes around the Plaza Mayor and the Mercado San Miguel.

In those blissful pre-match hours, we were unaware of the two storms about to break, one on the pitch at the Bernabéu, the other through the streets of every town on the planet. On Tuesday 25 February, the day before the match, *MARCA* ran a front page the like of which few had seen before. It was completely dominated by the image of a football wearing a surgical mask, with the headline: 'With the Corona virus, there will be no play'. This did not refer to the Real–City match scheduled for the next day, but to the Europa League game in crisis-torn Lombardy between Inter and Ludogorets the previous evening, which was being played behind closed doors due to its proximity to Bergamo – where Atalanta hailed from – the epicentre of the European outbreak of the virus.

On matchday, *MARCA* repeated a front page last seen when City had been in town for the semi-final of 2016. Then, as now, the headline exhorted: 'For Another Night of Passion', asking Madridistas to pack the streets outside the Bernabéu. For that first match, the heady atmosphere had paralysed a City side asked predominantly to defend by Manuel Pellegrini. On this occasion, City's minds would be on the opposition goal, not their own.

What eventually played out on the night of Wednesday 26 February was a coming-of-age for Manchester City in Europe.

Into the lion's den swaggered City, treading unmentionable materials into the burgundy carpets of the house of the royal family of Spain, the aristocracy of UEFA, the charming white-clad heroes of world football.

City had taken on the team of Alfredo Di Stéfano and Santiago Bernabéu himself, of Butragueño the vulture and the carrion-pickers Camacho and Sanchís, of Puskás, of cavorting Hugo Sánchez and the goal machine Raúl, of Valdano and Steve McManaman.

Playing the role of the downtrodden outcast once again, City bestrode the palatial stage with such authority, the white scarves were soon hanging limp, the home eyes moist with frustration.

The morning's copy of *AS* had had a new role for the visitors, however, naming them grandly as 'the most expensive side in the world', as if Real's desperate rags were held together by glue and sticking plasters, Zidane's salary was counted out in Asturian carrots and Sergio Ramos' fines were paid by the local authorities.

Guardiola too, the Catalan artiste in the home of Castilian chest-puffing. The bestubbled arriviste pointing and genuflecting in the House of God. The so-called *Besta Negra* of all those Barcelona victories over the self-styled monarchs of the realm.

The day had been spent cruising the pristine concrete aisles of the city, shooting the breeze among the fragrant piles of tapas in the ornate Mercado de San Miguel. The Bernabéu rears up at you from the great car-infested sweep of the Paseo de la Castellana, built like the city itself on the concept of shock and awe. Everything is huge, noisy and ferociously busy. Real are the bumptious aristocrats, the landowners, the bull fighters, the silhouetted sherry drinker on the hillside.

This is what City were up against.

'Should be here earlier' snapped the nearest armour-clad policeman. This was City's (and my own) third visit, leaving few surprises at the over-officious policing. Being funnelled through small gaps from a large and boisterous crowd of away fans was nothing new, but nevertheless a perilous endeavour. That the local police did not fully grasp the idea of warm-weather drinking in preparation for the big night out should have ceased to be a surprise by now.

No heads were cracked this time in our vicinity, and we were past the thick line of black and facing the big climb to our places on the fourth and fifth tiers. The Bernabéu, like the Nou Camp, is a thing of solid beauty when framed by the lights and projected across the world on TV screens, but has its shabby corners behind the scenes. The crabby stairwells and the peeling paint, the rusty railings and the facility-lite concourses are all far from the glare of the TV arc lights and the banks of gleaming tapas in the VIP suites.

The usual view through a mesh of netting dropped from the roof edge met us at the top. It is another sign of how Real and others treat their visitors and expect them to behave. City's ranks were certainly in no mood for polite respect, a rasping chant ripping into the night sky as the teams came out.

Jesus, nominally alone up front, playing here, there and everywhere, started strongly, as did the probing De Bruyne. Ten, twenty, then thirty minutes of controlled possession, a Jesus right-foot chance parried away by Courtois and next to nothing from the Madrilenos.

De Bruyne skied another half chance and Ederson pulled off his one save of the match, an elastic stretch to Karim Benzema's downward header. Guardiola had asked Jesus to be mobile and for Rodri and Gündoğan to shuttle with care in midfield as City's flying Belgian roamed with more freedom to higher parts of the pitch.

The Catalan had decided controlled attacking was best, high on bravery but low on risky holes in a defence that had its slipshod moments during the campaign.

The *segundo ayuda* of meringues against chips and gravy steamed and bubbled. More control from City, two rasping shots from Mahrez within a minute suggested a breakthrough, but when it came, it arrived for the home side instead.

Back came City, raging on and off the pitch with indignant fury. Jesus, having a fabulous game, arced a header high over Courtois for a hysterically received equaliser. City were not finished with us yet. Everything was about to fall into place. In Daniele Orsato we finally had a referee who did not appear at all fussed by the white robes of the emperors. Boldly he pointed to the spot, as the fresh legs of Sterling took him beyond Carvajal's clumsy challenge. The right-back, run ragged by Jesus all night, had nothing but a late tackle to offer.

The wait seemed eternal as De Bruyne stepped forward. Could he improve City's execrable penalty conversion rate? In it went, low to the keeper's right. Better still and almost like a third goal, Ramos was red-carded as Jesus again turned the defence. The scruffy undesirables had sacked the fortress. UEFA's pet legal project had ejected the princes from their own glistening tower. Sixteen shots had rained down on Courtois' goal. This was no smash and grab while the guards were asleep. City had slept in the king's bed and left the soiled silk sheets on the bathroom floor.

Guardiola had out-thought Zidane and City had outplayed Real, making them look average in the process.

REAL MADRID 1–2 MANCHESTER CITY | Jesus, De Bruyne (pen.)
Ederson, Walker, Otamendi, Laporte (Fernandinho), Mendy, Rodrigo, Mahrez, Gündoğan, Jesus, De Bruyne, B. Silva (Sterling)

Within a week of this delicious spectacle, football, along with almost every other activity we treasure as our usual right, would be taken away from us. Europe was in lockdown against a deadly virus, and suddenly football was the last thing we were all thinking about.

Returning from Madrid, we reflected on how close we had been to the edge of the cliff. Considerably more people wearing masks at Barajas airport was the first sign that things were developing rapidly.

It took the best part of three months for some kind of balance to be found. Thousands of deaths worldwide, families fractured and broken, normal civil liberties curtailed. Covid-19 quickly saw to it that the world and all its familiarities was turned on its head. While one-way systems in supermarkets and socially distanced post-office queues became the bizarre new normal, the absence of football was an undesirable state thrust upon us all.

Despite the deaths, football had to come back, we were told by the FA and by UEFA. Contracts worth billions with global television agencies had been left hanging, unfulfilled until another ball was kicked towards the season's culmination. The sight of players returning to individual no-contact training sessions did not assuage fears that this was all happening too swiftly. With health systems at breaking point throughout the continent, unfinished football business seemed a moot point.

If Liverpool fans' 30-year wait for a league title was set to end with an empty coronation, City's seemingly never-ending quest for redemption on the continent also promised an audience-free denouement. A June date with destiny (set by the Court of Arbitration for Sport) in the courts to defend themselves against UEFA brought yet more layers of irony. Would a drastic two-year ban be upheld and, if so, could City raise a firm middle finger to UEFA by winning the Champions League just before they were removed from the next instalment?

Suddenly, the wheels are in motion

Rumours circulated concerning how UEFA intended to bring everything to a conclusion. With the club's legal staff busying themselves for one date and the training staff doing similar for another, the beginning of June saw focus drawn away from the carnage of the virus to how the end of the season might be managed. As premature as it seemed, the wheels were in motion.

By the time City returned to the pitch, beating Arsenal at an empty Etihad Stadium, the new reality had been mapped out. A packed calendar would be squeezed into the early summer to conclude domestic competition, while Champions League business would close in Portugal, with all remaining games played in Lisbon.

UEFA were immediately faced with a dilemma by the clubs whose knockout ties were half-completed. City's win at the Bernabéu had been won fair and square, but Real now mounted an appeal, suggesting it was not safe to travel to the UK for the second leg. Their title rivals had infamously finished off their own tie at Anfield in one of the last games to go ahead before the virus struck the fixture lists. A thrilling night at Anfield had, in retrospect, been a giant Petri dish for the virus.

With the league season squeezed into a behind-closed-doors schedule of two games a week, City struggled for consistency, beating Arsenal and Liverpool easily, but managing to dredge defeat from a game at Southampton, in which they had more attempts on goal than Leicester had had in beating the same team 9–0. City's challenge was clearly not just to win the Champions League for the first time, but to win it in the most *City* manner possible.

With the title safely delivered to Anfield, the long-awaited Court of Arbitration for Sport verdict was announced from Lausanne. The news could hardly have been better for City.

Complete exoneration it may not have been, offering the British press an opportunity to alight on sections of the 93-page document that suited their original narrative, but it could hardly have been clearer. The two-season ban was lifted, the original fine reduced to £9 million, the alleged breaching of UEFA's inconsistently applied FFP wiped out. That these had been flawed from the beginning, including the use of emails – supposedly incriminating – dated from before the birth of FFP, almost explained the club's reluctance to play ball. That the leaked *Der Spiegel* excerpts had come from five emails out of a total of many millions hacked by the Portuguese loner Rui Pinto also suggested desperately deep trawling to net the smallest possible sprats.

If City's behaviour looked calculating, UEFA's looked miserably mishandled.

The decision by the CAS to overthrow the UEFA ruling tossed the football world a story to chew on through the remainder of a sweaty, uncertain summer. It also opened a can of worms that the sport's governing body would have trouble keeping a lid on.

'Insufficient conclusive evidence'

That CAS dismissed many of the supposed wrongs on a time detail showed UEFA to have been inept in its most basic strategising. These, we were told, are the simplest of details, upon which the most hurriedly briefed legal teams would and should fix their expert attention. The CAS judgement that 'there was no evidence of wrongdoing' appeared in the verdict more times than Raheem Sterling pops up in the box in an average City match (eleven to be precise).

UEFA rapidly fell silent. Others not so coy alighted on the phrase 'insufficient conclusive evidence' to suggest City were still rotten, despite the findings. Well, there is no smoke without fire, that is certain. But smoke also prevents any of us from seeing anything as clearly as we would like, so it fell upon those experts who had taken the case apart line by line to be trusted in their judgement. They are, after all, the independent experts brought in *to arbitrate*, when all else failed.

In essence, the maintenance of an aggressive stance against UEFA seemed to have been vindicated. UEFA's clumsy hand had cuffed the club many times before, producing an uneasy relationship long before UEFA chief Aleksander Čeferin turned up the thermostat over FFP.

Wonky thinking

There had been fines for the late arrival on the pitch in 2012 in Porto that were heavier than those meted out to FC Porto for their fans barracking Mario Balotelli with monkey chants. There had been the grisly episode in Moscow too, another instance of ugly behaviour towards black players that eventually became a side issue to that of punishing City, cementing a relationship between the club, the club's fans and the governing body that has been at best frosty ever since. UEFA's wonky thinking had produced a fine for Beşiktaş having a cat on the pitch that was double that for Porto's racism. The bear-chested and racially dubious histrionics of Dinamo Zagreb's support in Manchester had not attracted UEFA's attention at all.

Michel Platini, that most graceful of midfield playmakers, but arguably not one of the modern game's most gifted administrators, devised FFP with good intention, but brought it to the table as a muddled mess that served the elite more cleanly than it served the clubs it was designed to assist.

That one of City's 'saviours' Rui Botica Santos should be Portuguese (he had presided over the three-man panel at CAS to judge UEFA's punishment), was ironic, as it was his countryman, Rui Pinto, who was responsible for the hacked documentation reaching the offices of *Der Spiegel* in the first place. That *Der Spiegel*'s giant glass and steel atrium overlooking the Ericusgraben in Hamburg harbour resembles a huge glass open goal is purely coincidental; that the journalists inside were suddenly reporting on a very different story today to the five-day bonanza they had had at City's expense two years earlier must have raised a smile in City's corridors of power.

I would catch up with Botica Santos later on in Lisbon, where he was kind enough to afford me two hours of his schedule to explain how CAS had come to their decision. It was a highly illuminating conversation, which served to emphasise that the CAS decision had been the right one, that the method of reaching it had been surgical and that – despite some time-barred elements that clearly raised some questions – the case City's legal team had brought had been meticulously planned and thoroughly argued. For a man used to presiding over high-level issues, from past Olympic Games to a spread of UEFA competitions, it would be quickly evident how impressed Botica Santos had been with every aspect of the club's approach to the case, and how UEFA and many sections of the British (and German) press had misread the way the ultimate decision would fall. That such a level-headed and cerebral man had presided over proceedings had clearly also been to the club's benefit.

City had already been punished for overspending in the early days after the takeover. Football's greased pyramid had successfully repelled all invaders. The barons in Paris had a foothold admittedly, but their *bling-bling* approach with Neymar and Mbappé reeked of wet hay. City may have splurged some of its cash poorly on Eliaquim Mangala and Wilfried Bony, but theirs was a strategy built to be inclusive, built to last the test of time.

A whole mini city was rising out of the besmirched dust of east Manchester. Regeneration was the name of the game. Community inclusion. Long-term thinking. Like it or not, the empire was being built brick by solid brick by people who had watched, learnt and listened.

And now the irony was almost complete. With FFP suspended for one summer, City would be able to build further with Champions League participation ensured. The fine that remained would trouble no one in their sleep and even that was for non-cooperation with a process that had been proved to be flawed. Whether FFP would survive in this form was also open to question. Its supposedly good intentions, ill-conceived and ill-deployed, had been shown up for what they were.

The irony would be complete, and UEFA's embarrassment too, if City could now hoist the trophy in Lisbon at the end of August. The gnashing of teeth that would follow if that transpired would be heard from UEFA's furthest outpost in the east to the westernmost cliff edges.

Pretty in pink

As might be expected, results off the pitch put a skip into the step on the field of play. Real Madrid, decked out from head to foot in pink, came bearing gifts too when the round of sixteen second leg finally went ahead, five months after City's historic win in Spain. The only regrets on a night of what felt once more as if destiny was calling was that there was no standing ovation for the last appearance in Manchester in sky blue from David Silva.

Silva's introduction to the action came as City were comfortably playing out another 2–1 win. Winning both legs against the original aristocrats gave Guardiola's side extra kudos for the final push. With UEFA deciding to play out the rest of the tournament in single-game fixtures in Lisbon over a two-week period, City had their goal in sight. Better news still, an inability on the part of Juventus to get past Lyon meant a quarter-final match-up with the French instead of a collision with a 'proper giant' of the European game.

Playing the usual 4–3–3 formation, City had harried a languid-looking Real, causing immediate problems. Raphaël Varane, caught in possession by Jesus, was the culprit as the ball was rolled into the box for Sterling to put City ahead 3–1 on aggregate after nine minutes. It was the 31st goal of an excellent season for Sterling.

With Sergio Ramos sitting the game out, his replacement Éder Militão was the only member of a beleaguered back four who did not go into meltdown as soon as he was pressed. City were rampant in those opening minutes, Madrid listless, looking like a team unused to being closed down with this degree of zeal. How could a team of such experience be so surprised by City's tactics?

By half-time, inexplicably, City had lost control and Madrid were level, Karim Benzema finding space behind Rodri to angle a header past Ederson. Would this be a classic Guardiola Champions League exit or could City pull themselves together?

Real's lively second-half opening was quickly snuffed out as City resumed their fast passing and hive-like pressing. By the 68th minute the aggregate had been widened once more with an exquisite finish from Jesus. Again, Varane was caught out, miscuing his header, then underpowering a second header back to Courtois. Jesus jabbed it over the oncoming keeper to put City back in front.

By the end, City's control had become total. Only the infamous profligacy had prevented more goals. Guardiola could take positives from his strikers and from the fact his midfield had passed their way through Madrid time and again, but questions remained about City's conversion ratio.

A joyous Guardiola nevertheless had words of caution to offer: 'For Real Madrid, to beat a big team in the last sixteen is normal. For us, if we are going to be champion, we have to beat these teams. This is important for our season and for our future. It is similar to when we beat Barcelona in the knockout stage. We don't have a lot of presence in Europe, so it is so important for the club. The big clubs lift the titles. We have to see how we recover. Last season we played Lyon twice and we could not beat them. We have to be calm.'

MANCHESTER CITY 2–1 REAL MADRID | Att. 0 | Sterling, Jesus

Ederson, Walker, Fernandinho, Laporte, Cancelo, Gündoğan, De Bruyne, Rodrigo (Otamendi), Foden (B. Silva), Sterling (D. Silva), Jesus

---

The Catalan was right. Lyon's effervescent counter-attacking had deposited psychological stains.

Guardiola would have eight days to prepare his squad for the Lisbon match. His side was in unquestionably good shape and, having eliminated one of the great sharks would not meet another until a possible semi-final with the winner of the Barcelona–Bayern quarter-final.

Watching Barcelona being dismantled 8–2 by Bayern Munich, a shiver must have run through Guardiola. Here was the club he grew up with being taken apart by the team he left to manage City. Although the draw would throw City into Bayern's path next, they were the only traditional giants left in the tournament. The other semi-final would feature Paris Saint-Germain, like City, terminally ill at ease in the tournament, and RB Leipzig, complete newcomers to the higher echelons of the sport.

Different year, same stuff

In the easy comfort of the Sheraton Hotel, Guardiola had been up to his old tricks again in the run-up to the match. The Catalan would once again deem it necessary to change the accepted wisdom of his 4–3–3 and face Lyon with a *new idea*. Afterwards, he would explain that the squad had been working on it solidly for three days in Lisbon, but the question would not go away: Why bother? Why now?

For the third season in succession, City did not pass muster when it came to the crunch. A quarter-final exit in itself was a poor showing after the build-up of expectation, but to lose to an outsider, accommodating a tactical switch the players looked ill at ease with, seemed in keeping with some of the false thinking that had crippled the club in earlier continental campaigns.

Switching to a five-man defence against Lyon? What had Guardiola seen that so mesmerised him? Or was the Catalan simply trying to live up to his reputation as football's innovator-in-chief? Afterwards, rumblings emerged from the dressing room that players were confused by the need to ditch the tried and tested, that others disagreed with the eleven chosen to start and yet others had begun to question Guardiola's powers to deal appropriately with the challenges of the very biggest games.

Certainly, since winning the trophy with Barcelona in 2011, things had begun to look bleak for Guardiola. Exits with City to

Monaco, Liverpool, Tottenham and now Lyon were compounded by high-profile disasters against Chelsea (with Barcelona) and three consecutive semi-final exits with Bayern (at the hands of Real, Barcelona and Atlético). His win rate of 60 per cent in the competition also compared unfavourably with his domestic win rate of 72 per cent at City and 75 per cent in Bavaria.

Biographer Martí Perarnau had quoted the City manager in 2015 as saying: 'I loathe all that passing for the sake of it, tiki-taka,' but here was a side set up to plod about with three holding midfielders seemingly tasked with flat-ball circulation until the opposition drifted off to sleep. But Lyon were wide awake and ready for the challenge. Taking advantage of an early lapse by the defence, Maxwel Cornet bent the French side into the lead with a shot around the retreating Ederson.

City spent the rest of the half trying to shake themselves awake, but the line-up was too heavily reinforced at the back, leaving a scarcity of creative talent to go forward. The one obvious outlet, De Bruyne, was sufficiently isolated to have little or no influence on the opening 35 minutes.

With the misfiring Fernandinho replaced early in the second half by Mahrez, City suddenly had traction, momentum and hope. De Bruyne charged through to convert Sterling's pull back with a force of shot that suggested City were about to make up for lost time.

It was at this point, with City coming to the boil, that the game took on familiar tones. That element of ill-fortune was threatening to raise its head once more. Seconds after Jesus squandered an excellent chance to put City 2–1 up, they were 2–1 down. Laporte, a beacon of tidy defending, fell to the ground under pressure and substitute Moussa Dembélé ran through to shoot straight at Ederson. The ball hit the underside of the goalkeeper's leg and drifted apologetically into the back of the net. By now the game had lost its self-imposed shape. Players were running with the wind. Another coruscating attack via Jesus on the right wing left Sterling with a glorious six-yard tap-in for 2–2. Thousands of nervous fans leapt to their feet in front of TV screens in Manchester and elsewhere to greet a second equaliser and a predictably drama-fuelled conclusion to the evening's activities. This was their City *doing it the dramatic way*.

Sterling shaped his body in preparation as the ball skimmed the turf and came straight to him at the back post. Then, aided by the gods of Jamie Pollock and Romark, of Alan Ball and every clown-painted Bramall Lane party balloon, England's number-one striker and scorer of 31 City goals inexplicably fired it over the bar. It was a truly horrendous miss, the sort of horror that tells you there and then it is not destined to be your night, nor your tournament, nor your trophy. Seconds later it was 1–3 through Dembélé again and the dream was done.

Those that had not witnessed 40 years of Manchester City's very best efforts to strangle themselves could scarcely believe their eyes. The rest of us shook our heads knowingly. The curse had returned. At a moment of high drama, with the world's attention fixed, City had done it again.

On the whistle, Lyon's players seemed dumbfounded at their achievement. City collapsed onto the turf. With 67 per cent possession, City were out. With nineteen shots to seven, City were out. With eleven corners to three, City were out. The story of the season had repeated itself one more time.

Summing up the game how thousands of others had no doubt also seen it, De Bruyne managed the simple eloquence 'Different year, same stuff' when the inevitable microphone appeared under his nose. Guardiola, meanwhile, talked of the club's inability to 'break the gap', an oft-raised point that City were still on the outside with their nose pressed against the window.

Once again, all that had been left as a memory was a greasy smudge on the outside of a window pane.

Certain themes recur when looking back at how this pattern could be possible. Guardiola has been quoted as saying 'tactics are not the most important thing' in the Champions League, but the evidence demands closer scrutiny. When it receives this scrutiny, a curious pattern emerges. It is of a coach prepared to roll out untried ideas in critical games.

Taking the three consecutive quarter-final defeats, Guardiola saw fit to offer Gündoğan an untested floating role at Anfield, where City had been beaten 4–3 previously; Laporte, a new recruit for central defence, was launched at left-back on that evening too. A year later, the first leg at Tottenham seemed to have been earmarked for experimentation too, with De Bruyne and Sané inexplicably dropped to the bench. Now, Guardiola threw in a three-man central defence, with Fernandinho a fish out of water on the right of the three, a role for De Bruyne which reduced his first-half influence to zero and five across the back to counter the evident danger of the seventh-placed side in Ligue 1. Starting the match without Mahrez, Foden, David or Bernardo Silva removed almost all the creativity with which City had swept all-comers aside over the previous three years.

In 'trying to cover the side's weak points against the opposition's strong points', the manager had yet again left himself open to the accusation of 'overthinking'. The concomitant danger of City's impasse – owners who covet the Champions League, fans who prefer domestic success and mistrust UEFA and their flagship tournament and a manager whose reputation hovers between genius and European failure – is that they will continue to fall between two stools.

Malcolm Allison's 'cowards of Europe' speech would not go away. Worse still, in a new and ironic twist, City's final effort had made *them* look like the cowards. The enigma that is Manchester City was still succeeding in confounding the very best brains the sport had to offer.

The big picture, however, was that City had once again found a way to fail when they had seemed all set to prosper.

LYON 3–1 MANCHESTER CITY | Att. 0 | De Bruyne

Ederson, Walker, Cancelo, García, Fernandinho (Mahrez), Laporte, Gündoğan, Rodrigo (D. Silva), De Bruyne, Jesus, Sterling

---

With the football world's constant need to construct and dismantle dynasties and explain their growth and diminishment, Guardiola's *death by passing* had been given its obituary in some circles, displaced by the high press of heavy-metal Klopp, new-wave Pochettino, Hansi Flick, Thomas Tuchel and Nagelsmann. After Liverpool's success the previous year, Bayern's high-energy swarming won the much-disrupted 2019–20 edition of the Champions League. Were we entering a new era? Had Guardiola's star already waned? The truth would take its time in revealing itself, but, in City's case at least, there seemed to be a strong argument to suggest they had been undone at the crucial moment by the kind of high theatre that the game has always thrived on. Mighty collisions of drama and weird luck that no single tactician could guard against.

Indeed, there was an argument that the Champions League had conjured as many of these kinds of winners as it had spawned winning systems. Moments of grand inspiration had littered past finals: Zidane in Glasgow, Ole Gunnar Solskjær in Barcelona, Messi's one-man dismantling of Manchester United. Spurs, in escaping the Etihad with a most electrifying *coup de théâtre* and repeating it in Amsterdam in the semi-final, proved the point to an extent. Without imposing any kind of system on their opponents, they had prevailed through magic acts of divine intervention.

Without doubt, huge strides had been taken. Whether a definable European identity had grown from the shreds of

City's earlier continental campaigns was unclear. Michael Cox, author of *The Mixer*, estimates that City's growth under three great managers coincides pretty cleanly to very different eras of how coaches have gone about trying to win in Europe. 'Mancini's period in charge was towards the end of an era when a predominantly defensive approach dominated,' he suggests. 'Pellegrini's appointment tied in with the possession approach that came after that and Guardiola bestrides the more tactically flexible and adventurous approach of the last few years, which, of course, he himself helped define.'

What was now intriguing the game's deep thinkers was, how – having completed the big strides – were City to complete the small, intricate steps to the top of the pyramid?

EMPTY PROMISES

Fool's gold

Emptiness, fear and reluctance greeted the start of the 2020–21 season. With a second wave of the pandemic gathering strength, football kicked off around Europe behind closed doors.

Players without time to recuperate from the late finish of the previous season were being asked not only to go again, but to do all the things the rest of the world were prohibited from doing.

If supporter ambivalence towards the Champions League had never really gone away, interest in football in general now waned in the face of the more practical issues of merely surviving and protecting those at risk in our communities.

Fear and loathing in Porto and Marseille

As irony would have it, the Champions League draw threw up, in the eyes of the travelling supporters at least, the most attractive group yet for City. Who would not have salivated wildly at the thought of supporting City among the sun, tapas and picturesque ruins of Athens, Marseille and Porto?

On the sporting front, it was clearly a kind draw for a club heralded on a yearly basis as 'one of the possible winners'. It remained a mystery from where this apparent predilection for a club with one semi-final to its name came. On a cultural front, it was sadly out of bounds.

While the fans digested the fact that they would be watching the show from their sofas, they could also appreciate how far City had come. Considered clear favourites in a group that six years earlier would have been declared too even to predict.

The opening match with Porto, just 67 days after the exit to Lyon, followed a worrying early season pattern. Indeed, it was a line that could be traced back considerably further than that. City, looking lethargic and disjointed, struggled to impose any form on the proceedings and duly trailed to a Porto side doing things in the spirit of their irascible manager Sérgio Conceição. As a metaphor for the unfolding season, the game bore signs of what was to come. City eventually came back strongly with İlkay Gündoğan to the fore, the German scoring the goal that put them in front after Agüero had equalised from the penalty spot.

The signs against Porto in the second half were there if you looked hard enough. Little clues were beginning to emerge, the green shoots of a floral tapestry that would ultimately bedazzle and beguile. Firstly, the presence of ex-Benfica lynchpin Rúben Dias in defence – despite an early error allowing Mateus Uribe to set up Luis Díaz to shoot past Ederson for 1–0 – meant City's backline was about to get a serious upgrade.

With Nicolás Otamendi the makeweight in a £65 million deal with Benfica, Guardiola had replaced gung-ho acrobatics with iron-plated reliability. Alongside Dias, John Stones, for so long cast into the shadows by a coach unconvinced of his ability to play in his system, was beginning his own march forward towards a place in Gareth Southgate's England squad.

This meaner defence would be the bedrock City intended to build upon. With a slower flow of goals at the other end, the Catalan was turning his team into a slightly different beast, with an unaccustomed central solidity that would turn them into a runaway success from the turn of the year. For Guardiola, the banishing of doom-mongers in the press would be an unexpected by-product of the resurgence.

With Porto beginning to flag, Gündoğan stepped up to flight a superb free kick past Wilson Manafá. Substitute Ferran Torres made it safe with a sharp finish to make it 3–1. City had their good start, Porto their baseless complaints. As Conceição charged away without offering a handshake, one could only imagine the welcome that would be waiting in Portugal in a month's time.

'We spoke before about being patient,' Guardiola explained. 'We had to be patient and at the right moment attack them, so we let them run.'

Conceição was more circumspect, stating: 'At the hour, the game changed. It changed in the sense that City were winning, which made our task more difficult. We had Díaz with limitations and then we had to change two players, the right-wing and the left-wing. Then we were looking to try to reduce City's advantage, but I feel very proud of what I saw from the team.'

If patience and control were the new watchwords ahead of verve and vivacity, the still unfamiliar landscape of empty stadia and silent nights would mean every team would be playing on an even playing field. There would be no local elements to tip the balance in favour of one club over another. It would be down to the players, the coach and the strength of their organisation, their tactics and their will to win.

MANCHESTER CITY 3–1 FC PORTO | Agüero (pen.), Gündoğan, Torres

Ederson, Walker, Cancelo, Dias, García, Rodrigo (Fernandinho) (Stones), Gündoğan (Foden), B. Silva, Sterling, Agüero (Torres), Mahrez

This point was admirably highlighted in City's second game in Marseille.

The Stade Vélodrome, normally a mosh pit of pyrotechnics and screaming, instead offered City a bowling-green surface and the calm simplicity of a training exercise, as Guardiola's men ran out 3–0 winners, with Gündoğan and De Bruyne again leading the charge.

With the giant slogan '*A Nous La Victoire*' emblazoned across the Vélodrome seats, City set about their task as if it had been placed there for them instead.

Ahead after eighteen minutes, when De Bruyne pounced on an error to angle a low ball to Torres to finish sharply, City hardly allowed André Villas-Boas' side to get a foothold. For the young Spanish forward it was a second Champions League goal in two appearances, for the Belgian it was a welcome return after two weeks out injured. With Gündoğan and Sterling adding second-half goals, City's position in the group was already looking secure.

City had already sauntered into a three-point lead at the top of the group after two matches, thanks to Porto's win over Olympiakos. Aware of the early season criticism, Guardiola kept his cards close to his chest, saying only: 'Part of the criticism was right, but you've got to accept it. It's part of our job. It's about where we've come from in the last month, with lack of preparation, injuries and Covid-19 but the Champions League is in a good place now. I'm sure we're going to find that consistency.'

OLYMPIQUE MARSEILLE 0–3 MANCHESTER CITY | Torres, Gündoğan, Sterling

Ederson, Walker, Dias, Laporte (Stones), Zinchenko (Cancelo), Rodrigo, Gündoğan (B. Silva), De Bruyne (Palmer), Foden, Sterling, Torres (Mahrez)

With games now coming thick and fast, a weekend win at Sheffield United was all that sandwiched the Marseille triumph with another three-goal European win, this time at the expense of Olympiakos. On this occasion, however, the only similarity was the early breakthrough from the fast feet of Ferran Torres. The other goals fell in the last ten minutes of an increasingly jittery display.

In a first-half onslaught praised by Guardiola, City ran at a befuddled-looking Greek side from all angles. A zippy move involving Mahrez, Gündoğan and a quick-fire one-two between Torres and De Bruyne saw the Spaniard net his third goal in three European outings with a crisp finish through the legs of José Sá.

With the City storm blowing itself out, the Greeks were tempted out of their shell. Guardiola, cutting an increasingly manic figure on the touchline, dropped to his knees as Mahrez again surrendered possession. With time running out, a classy finish into the roof of the net from wide on the right by Jesus and a long-range shot from Cancelo carried City over the line in better shape than their second-half showing deserved.

'Exceptional first half,' enthused Guardiola. 'The second half we struggled, but when we scored the second one the game was over. A good game, nine points, we need one more point to qualify.'

MANCHESTER CITY 3–0 OLYMPIAKOS | Torres, Jesus, Cancelo
Ederson, Walker (Cancelo), Stones, Aké, Zinchenko, Gündoğan, De Bruyne (Nmecha), Foden (Rodrigo), Mahrez (Jesus), Sterling (B. Silva), Torres

Requiring a single point from the return trip to Piraeus, City strolled through another game that might have been different had it been played in front of supporters. Olympiakos were as tepid as the atmosphere and, by the 36th minute, City had the match sealed, with Foden's cleverly worked goal the difference.

A sure sign of continental maturity was the side's ability to *manage* matches to a satisfactory conclusion. It was the 88th minute when the home side registered their single shot on goal, which also happened to include their first touch of the ball inside City's six-yard box, a truly damning statistic.

'It will come,' promised Guardiola afterwards, as if encouraging the press to believe in the Christmas post. 'We would love to do more but one day it will come and we will break everything.'

It was an interesting idea that conjured various images in the back of the mind. Foden's left-foot wizardry was perhaps as apt a deciding factor as any on the day that the world was delivered news of the death of Diego Maradona. As ever in football, the sad end of one era certainly felt like the ushering in of a new one.

OLYMPIAKOS 0–1 MANCHESTER CITY | Foden

Ederson, Cancelo, Stones, Dias, Mendy (Zinchenko), Rodrigo (Fernandinho), Gündoğan (Doyle), Sterling (Mahrez), B. Silva, Foden, Jesus (Agüero)

On 1 December, City secured top spot in the group, but it came from the only dropped points in the entire group phase. The 0–0 draw at the Estádio do Dragão would preface more discomfort in the same stadium in May, although quite how that might transpire at this stage nobody would have been able to guess.

A trip to northern Portugal had seemed almost a distraction from the push in the league. How times had changed from the nail-biting of the club's early attempts at Champions League joined-up writing. These days, poetry sprouted from every pen; rhyming couplets, metaphors and gushing prose decorated every step as the club underlined its new-found confidence on the continent.

Even here, with the home goalkeeper Agustín Marchesín playing perhaps the game of his career, City might have won had Rodri not been ruled marginally offside when substitute Jesus netted late on.

Marchesín appeared to have taken on the powers of an octopus as he continually blocked Torres and then Sterling. Even Jesus' disallowed goal had been a tap-in after another elastic save from the Argentinian. Porto had held on, aware that a point would see them through too. This was City's fifth advance in six seasons as group winners, a fact not lost on Conceição: 'We have raised standards high in the name of Portugal. It was difficult to get up front, because City react well when they lose the ball.'

It was Guardiola's first 0–0 draw in the Champions League in 59 games, stretching back into his tenure at Bayern, and Conceição's repeated rejection of a handshake at the end of the game confirmed how stressful extracting such a reward had been. City's eighteen shots on goal told another story, which had been, and would in the future be, a repeated theme.

FC PORTO 0–0 MANCHESTER CITY

Ederson, Cancelo, Dias, García, Zinchenko, Fernandinho, Rodrigo, Sterling, B. Silva, Foden, Torres (Jesus)

With the home tie with the group's worst side, Olympique Marseille, to wrap things up, City had cantered over the line in a manner which surely banished any remaining doubts in supporters' minds. This was now a truly thoroughbred European performer, reliable, consistent and trustworthy, a very distant cousin to the misfiring, mischievous child who had embarked on the adventure all those years ago in a cloud of inflated promises and mixed expletives.

As if this intangible upgrade was not enough, with a 3–0 mauling of the French, City also notched some milestones that were as notable as they were meaningful to a club that had struggled so hard to join the elite.

By gaining sixteen points in the group, they not only beat their own best in the competition but equalled the best by any English side. By conceding only one goal, they equalled Manchester United's record from 2010–11, a year before City had even set foot in the tournament. Records had been tumbling domestically year after year. Now, City were knocking European barriers down too.

Ederson had also equalled Pepe Reina's fifteen-year clean sheet record for first-round games. City were now clearly England's longest-serving Champions League contestants, with an unbroken ten-year sequence from the inaugural year under Roberto Mancini.

The Great Unpredictables had a shiny new look.

Against Marseille, a Champions League debut for Zack Steffen turned into a watching brief, as a fit-again Agüero added to Torres' 48th-minute opener and Álvaro González put the ball into his own net to close the scoring.

It was Agüero's 41st goal in the competition on a night when the statistics outdid the football.

MANCHESTER CITY 3-0 OLYMPIQUE MARSEILLE | Torres, Agüero, González (o.g.)
Steffen, Walker, García (Stones), Laporte, Aké, Fernandinho, Gündoğan (Sterling), Mahrez (Agüero), B. Silva, Foden, Torres

The draw pitched City with old foes Borussia Mönchengladbach. Rising pandemic figures forced the match to be switched to Budapest. The story of City in Europe appeared at this juncture to be taking on a symbolism of its own choice, following a pre-ordained route that mere mortals had no control over. City fans of a certain age will often vouch for the fact that the club has always had a wilful mind of its own, driven from deep within by some great malevolent force with an overdeveloped sense for the wicked.

Borussia had been Malcolm Allison's final European opponent as his second Maine Road tenure crumbled in 1979, and Budapest had been the city where he had been fêted in 1970 and taken by Honvéd club officials to visit the ancestral home of his spiritual mentor Ferenc Puskás.

The complete control exerted over the Germans resulted in a serene 2–0 victory. Employing a crushing possession and press game that took the wind out of their opponents almost immediately, City continued to showcase a new level of capability on the international stage.

Once again, defensive solidity made a palpable difference. This was the sixth clean sheet of the Champions League campaign, two better than the previous best effort. Despite Rodri's 93rd-minute aberration in putting Hannes Wolf through on goal, Ederson – completing a lonely night of spectating – was forced to dive smartly to his left to make a fantastic reaction save. It was his first stop of the game and the last action of a match controlled from start to finish by City.

Guardiola was insistent that his charges were accomplishing something beyond the normal. 'We played three days ago, travel, couldn't train much. In three days, we play at 12:30. It's an incredible challenge, everyone needs to be involved. Next game, we'll change five, six, seven players. The only way to sustain every player …'

When asked: 'What single element had brought City nineteen straight wins?' He responded wickedly: 'Having lots of money to buy a lot of incredible players.' For those struggling to keep up with the wave of negative opinions on a club that seemed damned if they failed to gain success by the riches of their owner but at the same time damned if they succeeded, it was the most apt answer available.

BORUSSIA MÖNCHENGLADBACH 0-2 MANCHESTER CITY | B. Silva, Jesus

Ederson, Walker, Dias, Laporte, Cancelo, Rodrigo, Gündoğan, Foden (Torres), B. Silva, Sterling (Mahrez), Jesus (Agüero)

With Covid protocols continuing to change on a daily basis, the second leg was also uprooted to Budapest, meaning City would play a home European tie away from their own ground for the second time in their history, after the 2008 game with EB/Streymur at Oakwell. That match had fallen victim to a plague of Bon Jovi fans. This time it was a real plague.

It was back to basics for Guardiola with the only outstanding quirk being the lack of a centre-forward. Both Jesus and the recovered Agüero featured on the bench, in case conventional tactics were needed at any point.

Guardiola's genius, downplayed by some because of the riches at his disposal, had City buzzing around their opponents with a ferocity of purpose that fairly made the eyes water. By the eighteenth minute, City were two up and the tie had been delivered. Both goals were works of art by a team whose creative purpose had always been underlaid by an innate sense of space, speed and timing.

The swiftness of passing, movement into holes and inventive thinking was all too much for Mönchengladbach, left chasing shadows in a series of impish opening thrusts from City. De Bruyne's strike for the first, rising off his left foot like a rocket that seared in off the underside of the bar, was aptly City's 100th of an increasingly persuasive season's work. We did not have long to wait for the 101st, featuring a surge from Foden, a no-look sliding pass to Gündoğan and a neatly lifted chip into the far corner.

A host of chances were created before City called it a day. Guardiola, perhaps still smarting at his Champions League record in Manchester, did not wish to hear of 'unfinished business' in the press conference, aware that three quarter-final exits, plus the manic last-sixteen departure against Monaco, could hardly be considered the success City's board desired. The mind-numbing defeat to Tottenham had been flushed from the system, but Lyon had already followed it in City's annals of doom in Europe. With the giants of European football again looking ill-prepared for the challenge, was this to be City's moment of glory?

If it was, then it would increasingly become remembered as the season all the major hurdles were German. The draw for the quarter-finals lumped City with Borussia Dortmund. In one of UEFA's let's-get-ahead-of-ourselves draws, the semi-finals were also mapped out, with a possible meeting with Bayern if they in turn got past fellow heavyweights Paris Saint-Germain.

MANCHESTER CITY 2–0 BORUSSIA MÖNCHENGLADBACH | De Bruyne, Gündoğan

Ederson, Walker, Dias (Laporte), Stones, Cancelo (Zinchenko), Rodrigo (Fernandinho), Gündoğan (Sterling), Foden, Mahrez, De Bruyne, B. Silva (Agüero)

City prepared for their biggest game of the season by winning two critical away games, at Goodison Park to reach the FA Cup semi-finals and then at third-placed Leicester in the league.

Now the focus fell on a club that had only visited the Etihad once, leaving on that occasion with plaudits ringing in their ears. A team constructed by Jürgen Klopp and containing İlkay Gündoğan and Robert Lewandowski had run riot on that occasion, City claiming an undeserved point by dint of one of Joe Hart's greatest nights and a last-minute penalty from Mario Balotelli.

Resisting the temptation to embark on one of his tactical adventures, Guardiola went with the same line-up that had polished off Mönchengladbach, with Foden and Mahrez lining up in a side again missing a striker. With Agüero, Jesus and Sterling available from the bench, more conventional shapes were available if necessary.

In the end, a fascinating game hinged as much on Dortmund's clever approach as City's slightly unorthodox shape. Pushing hard on those in possession and advancing with clever passing into space, the Germans proved a match for City for twenty minutes.

The first half revealed none of the weaknesses of a side being left behind in their domestic title race. When City took the lead, it was against the run of play and was the result of a flash of absolute brilliance that broke open the Germans.

Emre Can's terrible pass in midfield was intercepted by Mahrez. Feeding De Bruyne's run through the middle, the Algerian made for the far post. De Bruyne fed Foden through on the left and his arcing low ball reached Mahrez at the end of his long run. The winger still had work to do, his immaculate control stopping the ball from going out. Mahrez then aimed a shallow pass back to De Bruyne, who produced an unerring finish from the edge of the box.

City's domination was increasing markedly when the Germans suddenly drew level. There were only six minutes left when Erling Haaland, having had little opportunity to show his talent, finally worked himself clear of the limpet attentions of Rúben Dias, to put Marco Reus through. Although Ederson got a hand to the curling shot, Reus' accuracy was deadly, repeating his feat from 2012.

Not only had it been 84 minutes since the start of the match, but 788 since City had last conceded in the competition, Luis Díaz's strike in the first group game against Porto.

There were no slumped shoulders nor looks of resignation. Instead, City showed remarkable steel to ease back in front. The winner came not through throwing everything but the kitchen sink at the visitors, but by continuing to press carefully. With the clock ticking over the 90-minute mark, De Bruyne's laser-assisted pass covered 25 yards to the back post, where Gündoğan's immaculate touch dinked the ball back two yards onto Foden's left foot. The youngster spun the ball past the flailing Marwin Hitz for the winner.

No team in the competition had scored as many post-90th minute goals since their first appearance in 2011–12. This was the seventeenth time courage and character had pulled something from the fires of despair.

'Better to win than to draw,' was the coach's summary. 'We are going to Dortmund to attack. Every game we play to win.'

De Bruyne heaped praise on Dortmund: 'They played really well with the ball. It causes problems sometimes. I think in the first half we had a little bit of difficulty finding the chances. I think the reaction was really good, so to get the win is good. We know 2–1 is a tricky score but at least we are ahead.'

MANCHESTER CITY 2–1 BORUSSIA DORTMUND | De Bruyne, Foden
Ederson, Walker, Dias, Stones, Cancelo, Rodrigo, Gündoğan, De Bruyne, Mahrez, B. Silva (Jesus), Foden

If a week is a long time in politics, the week that Manchester City were about to put their supporters through would be better measured on the Richter scale than in simple minutes and hours.

Between the second leg in Dortmund on Wednesday 14 April and Wednesday 21 April, every emotion felt following this grand old club – from elation to despair, via revulsion and disbelief – would have a small red tick alongside it. The tired cliché of the emotional roller coaster would have to be updated with imagery befitting an era of Brexit, pandemics and global confusion.

First, to Germany, where both sides now knew that awaiting the victors in the semi-final would be Paris Saint-Germain, not holders Bayern.

Remarkably, City quickly put fans watching at home into a cold sweat by conceding the dreaded early goal. Jude Bellingham's expertly aimed shot avoided Ederson's grasp after a ricochet off Dias, and City found themselves having to mount a comeback from the fifteenth minute. Mahrez's goal-bound effort was cleared off the line by Bellingham, then perseverance from De Bruyne gave him the chance to hit a searing shot plum onto the bar. At half-time City were on their way out.

Within minutes of the second half, however, they were not.

Foden's cross from the left took a touch off Can's upper arm and referee Carlos del Cerro Grande pointed to the spot. Mahrez stepped forward for the most vital penalty of a season that had already seen four spot kicks missed by four separate colleagues (Agüero, Sterling, Gündoğan and De Bruyne). With no hint of his own sweeping miss at Anfield two years earlier, the Algerian's sureness of touch sent the ball arcing away from Hitz's left hand.

City plugged away assiduously but were made to wait until the 75th minute to seal their second appearance in the Champions League semi-finals. Foden's rocket, as the Dortmund defence parted in front of him, was the perfect denouement to a tie that had seldom looked beyond the Blues, even in those early minutes. As the youngster's jet-heeled celebration took him into the arms of his coach on the touchline, a pile of jubilant bodies confirmed that the calmness of City's execution of orders disguised a profound emotional attachment to the cause.

Chelsea would meet Liverpool's conquerors Real Madrid in the other semi-final. The previous year had seen two German semi-finalists. This time it was an English pair, as it had been in 2018–19, with Spurs and Liverpool.

BORUSSIA DORTMUND 1–2 MANCHESTER CITY | Mahrez, Foden

Ederson, Walker, Dias, Stones, Zinchenko, Rodrigo, Gündoğan, De Bruyne, B. Silva, Mahrez (Sterling), Foden

---

With all eyes on a Premier League run-in and a possible first-ever tilt at the Champions League final, City flopped in the FA Cup semi-final at Wembley, losing tamely to Chelsea. Then, suddenly, the headlines took on a life of their own.

The news lines first started to sputter as afternoon drifted towards evening on Sunday 18 April. Martyn Ziegler of *The Times* insisted that sources were suggesting that five of the Premier League's elite had signed documents to confirm participation in a breakaway Super League. Those clubs, Manchester United, Arsenal, Liverpool, Tottenham and Chelsea, would by nightfall be joined by a sixth: Manchester City.

It quickly became evident that Real and Atlético Madrid, Barcelona, Juventus, Inter and, somewhat surprisingly, AC Milan were also on board, but that European champions Bayern Munich and losing finalists Paris Saint-Germain were not. In the free-spinning vortex of a global news tsunami that was coursing its way across planet football, rumour and innuendo slowly gave way to confirmed facts. By 11pm that fateful night, each club had posted an identical statement on their websites, confirming adherence to a league that would be presided over by Real Madrid's Florentino Pérez, who was already managing to sound like a timeless Bond villain: 'We will help football at every level and take it to its rightful place in the world.' Just to set nerves jangling further, the structure's vice-presidents were Joel Glazer and Andrea Agnelli, two figures as well known for their altruism as the preening Real Madrid chief himself.

With a website that seemed to have been designed in a hurry by a distracted sixth-form student and a communications army that amounted to a Twitter feed that would remain blank throughout the fiasco, the operation smelled off from the first electrified moments. It appeared this elite break-out had instead been launched with only the assistance of J.P. Morgan, the giant American bank, and a team of half-briefed advocates as legal documents were swiftly dispatched to UEFA and FIFA dissuading them from issuing any knee-jerk sanctions.

The announcements brought an avalanche of vitriol from supporters' associations. UEFA were not shy to express themselves either, Aleksander Čeferin suggesting the clubs involved would be banned from the Champions League. 'We did not know we had snakes so close to us,' the UEFA president continued, visibly stirred. 'They have spat in our faces.'

With a power grab in full swing, fans everywhere took to social media to vent their fury. There was hardly a voice of consent to be found. As protesting Chelsea fans began to gather outside Stamford Bridge before their match with Brighton in a spontaneous show of disgust, City's formal withdrawal documents were already on their way to the Super League's organisers.

For 48 hours, football had apparently stood on the brink of a spectacular meltdown.

From Manchester to Miami and Lagos to Liverpool, the shock waves flowed out like an atomic bomb. The global obsession that football has become was stoking a charge of electricity through the wires that would have outed the Americas in one fell swoop. The threadbare piece of elastic that had held for decades between the game's organisers and the most powerful clubs in Europe (a system constructed painstakingly to protect the needs of the elite teams sufficiently to precisely hinder thoughts of breakaway leagues) had at long last snapped with a twanging noise reminiscent of Tarzan at the waning of his powers.

'Agnelli is the biggest disappointment of all,' Čeferin would say. 'I have never seen a person who would lie so many times and so persistently as he did.'

Telling lies at this point was chicken feed. Crucially, not all signees seemed as sure about it as the movement's leading figures. Pérez, unused to anyone questioning his motives, appeared on a late-night football show in Spain *El Chiringuito de Jugones* to talk up the project, telling his interviewer that the end point would be gifts of millions for everyone. Even more improbably, he insisted that the project was dreamed up to 'save football'. The profundity of the truth twisting was making people squirm. Even better, when it all collapsed just hours later, Pérez claimed that it was down to 'old people who had got scared'. At 74, the Real president was older than any of them.

How Ferran Soriano and City's power brokers viewed Pérez's performance is not recorded, but it is clear that lukewarm acceptance turned to cold feet within hours. With a growing backlash from players and media, it was becoming clear that this Super League had been launched down a slipway that had no water at the bottom.

But the impetus had gone, the tide had turned and water was beginning to enter Pérez's expensive suede shoes. It had taken little over 48 hours for normal service to be resumed. But a solemn shift *had* taken place, the size and effect of which would only become clear in the months to come. As more details appeared and Čeferin began to praise City for having the power of their convictions to conduct a U-turn, the UEFA president's immediate embracing of a club he had just eighteen months earlier tried to ban from his own competitions somehow provided a fitting epitaph for both the failed Super League and the soon-to-be-revamped Champions League. The rich clubs could apparently behave as badly as they liked and, as long as they were home before dark, the punishment would be mild.

Even as they sought to replace the Champions League with something bigger that would ultimately eclipse and end it, Pérez had insisted they would be taking those thirteen trophies, won with the skills of Santamaría, Puskás, Gento, Zidane and Juanito with them. Ironically, Bernabéu had already coveted a competition broadly like this, too. 'We would support without hesitation any move for a European League,' he had told English interviewers in a 1961 book that is effectively a manifesto of chest-puffed-out *Madridisimo*. 'Imagine it!' he had continued excitedly, 'Tottenham, Manchester United, Real, Barcelona, Reims, Juventus and more!'

The very fact that Reims, French champions and losing European Cup finalists to Real in two of the first four finals, had been included in this group of super clubs underlined why such a breakaway league was against the flowing fortunes of a sport rendered romantic and edgy by its embracing of underdogs. While City, with their backing of billions, were nobody's underdogs, their modern-day rise through the European ranks would have been impossible in such circumstances. This alone had been another reason for the incredulity of the fans back in Manchester at their acquiescence to Super League plans. Never mind climbing into bed with the very clan who had attempted to lock them out of the members-only club in the first place, why had Soriano and his acolytes wanted to join a league they would not have been invited to be a part of ten years ago?

In the meantime, City's season had reached a critical point. Could they still concentrate? Would the players still be giving it their all, despite the plotting going on behind their backs? Was City's old fragility about to resurface and scupper everything?

As usual, Guardiola was undeterred and faced up to the press with robust honesty. 'Football is nothing without competition,' he had said, even before the flames of the European Super League were snuffed out. Now, in preparation for the clash with Paris Saint-Germain, the Catalan relayed a story from the 1992 European Cup final, when he was asked how he would go about keeping his players relaxed ahead of the big game. As ever in times of need, the coach reached out for stories of Johan Cruyff. The Dutchman, manager of Barça at the time, was more than Guardiola's coaching mentor, a figure who had helped him form opinion and strategy on everything from dealing with stress to dealing with people.

Cruyff had told his players they should not be fearful of the game but to enjoy it because they had worked so hard to get there, Guardiola related. And the Dutch genius had not meant just the game itself. 'Enjoy the travel, the coffee in the terminal, the night and the dinner, watching the other semi-final, enjoy the press conference, the walk, the training,' said Guardiola, repeating his mentor's words. 'We are privileged to be one of the best four teams in Europe and we must enjoy it. Cruyff's idea was like this. Ours will be the same.'

And so, to Paris Saint-Germain, a side now marshalled by the man who had helped put City out of the Champions League in 2019 in the single most turbulent game in Guardiola's Manchester sojourn. Already during his brief tenure in the French capital, he had overseen pristine displays against blue-chip opponents Barcelona and Bayern Munich. Thus, even if City managed to do something noteworthy in Paris, it would not be game over.

Under the headline 'El Gasico or El Classico, why PSG v Man City is worth getting excited about', Jonathan Liew's *Guardian* preview began in classic form for the genre: 'Neither of football's great petrocarbon empires have won the Champions League and now they stand in each other's way ...'

Although City's involvement with the Super League project had helped paint PSG as the good guys, the old sportswashing clichés remained difficult for even the most talented scribes to avoid. What was equally evident, however, was the tingling anticipation the fixture engendered. Here was possibly Europe's best side pitched against its two best individual performers. Those still puffing and panting about oil derbies and the end of football would surely be putting their protest flags down before kick-off to concentrate on the sumptuous football show about to roll out, Liew claimed.

The club's chaotic recent history in the knockout stages suggested not everything could be planned for. Certainly, hatching a strategy to block Neymar, Mbappé and Ángel Di María would form a significant part of Guardiola's thinking, but City's chequered past meant there would always be that knife-edge element of *how the hell did that happen?*

Chelsea's success in holding Real in Spain the night before offered the tantalising possibility of a repeat of the all-English 1971 Cup Winners' Cup semi-final in the final, but first there was serious legwork to get through.

With the expected line-up announced an hour before kick-off, the players looked calm and collected as they stepped off the bus into a still evening outside the Parc des Princes. For once, Guardiola could not be accused of thinking up unexpected moves in the grand game of chess to come. He had used 49 different players in his 49 previous Champions League matches in charge of City. Despite being selected the most often (appearing 44 times), there was no place for Sterling in the line-up.

City were now a side completing a critical transition. No place either for Agüero, a reshaped defence founded on Stones and Dias, new men to the fore in Foden and Cancelo. The Catalan had overseen a quiet revolution in the playing staff and, almost inconceivably, the greats of the past had by now almost all been replaced.

As kick-off approached, the question on everyone's lips was:

How would City cope with the significant upgrade represented by PSG?

Within fifteen minutes, we had our answer. They were indeed a sizeable step up. Marquinhos wriggled free of Gündoğan's unorthodox marking to glance Di María's corner past Ederson. Faster, sharper, stronger, the French champions steamrolled City. Nothing seemed to be working. At half-time things looked bleak.

Guardiola had some talking to do.

Whatever happened in the dressing room at half-time, the game changed instantly. Gündoğan and De Bruyne began to dominate. Bit by bit not just a foothold appeared, but growing dominance. Suddenly, chances were falling City's way and the French side seemed cowed. De Bruyne's lofted cross curled in that inimitable way, deep into the area. But no heads made contact and the ball floated on. With Keylor Navas rooted to the spot, the cross gradually became a 'shot' and swept past the Costa Rican at the far post for a deliriously received equaliser.

Rather than provoke the home side, the goal further panicked them. City began to dominate possession in a way that should not happen in an away semi-final. The Blues, with their tails up, won a free kick deep in De Bruyne territory and, as the Belgian wiped himself down, he could be seen in conference with Riyad Mahrez. Afterwards, the Belgian would explain the nature of their brief chat, with the Algerian asking if he could take it and his captain agreeing 'as long as he scored'. Mahrez did just that, nipping in to whip a left-footer through the wall between Presnel Kimpembe and Leandro Paredes to beat Navas on his right side.

PSG had nothing more to give. A red card for Idrissa Gueye, raking his studs across Gündoğan's Achilles tendon, reduced them further. Foden surged through in search of a spectacular third, but his shot was straight, even if his mesmerising run had been anything but.

By the end, the statistics flowing from the game's number-crunchers were telling: this was the first time Mbappé had failed to register a single shot in a Champions League game. Dias and Stones had skilfully blotted out Erling Haaland and Harry Kane in recent weeks, making a hat-trick of the world's greatest strikers who had come up short against City's defence.

There were heroes in every position and, as always on such occasions, it seemed unjust to pick out some without mentioning others. A truly groundbreaking result had been achieved. For City and Guardiola, the moment of truth seemed nigh.

As ever with this chameleon club, there were more details that served to underline the magnitude of what was being achieved: in 105 Premier League games since 1992 where City had been behind at half-time, a grand total of one had been won. Now, in the space of two weeks, Guardiola's men had carried out the feat twice in successive knockout rounds of the Champions League. For this club of remarkable contrasts, it seemed only fair that this ridiculous stat should emerge from away legs at Dortmund and Paris Saint-Germain in the quarter-finals and semi-finals of the world's most prestigious club tournament.

'This landmark victory can lay the ghost of past Champions League failures,' gushed Phil McNulty of the BBC. 'There were two different halves,' spluttered a shocked Pochettino. As his coach delivered an excited summary of City's tactical evolution over 90 minutes, winning goalscorer Mahrez took to Twitter to voice everyone's thoughts in a more succinct fashion. '90mn left …' the Algerian tweeted. For once, nothing needed adding to that.

PARIS SAINT-GERMAIN 1–2 MANCHESTER CITY | De Bruyne, Mahrez

Ederson, Walker, Cancelo (Zinchenko), Stones, Dias, Rodrigo, Gündoğan, De Bruyne, B. Silva, Mahrez, Foden

The sight of an Etihad pitch covered in hailstones did not broker confidence. With heavy rain following, the surface began to look a little like it had in the hour before the Mönchengladbach game five years earlier.

Thankfully, the weather abated, but only in the sky. Down on the pitch it was swiftly apparent that the French had walked into a storm and it would not be long before PSG were losing control, both of the match and themselves. City, so long the team for whom the experts had to dream up clever new ways of describing an implosion, were magnificent, exerting total control on an opponent that could bear it no longer and simply blew up.

Before the petulance and the violence, however, a purring City side had a few things to say for themselves. Here was the power of the Premier League, here was the thrust of good planning and pinpointed spending, here was a group of winners gathering strength and pouncing at the optimal moment. A triumph of the collective unfolded before our eyes, if not a Ballet on Ice, then a certainly a Waltz in Hail.

With the surprise additions of Zinchenko at left-back and Fernandinho anchoring midfield, City offered their opponents no wriggle room whatsoever. Shorn of Mbappé, PSG looked to Neymar for inspiration, but he was swallowed whole by City's targeted pressing.

City had given us many memorable nights of European football, games that had brimmed over with goals and controversy, vivacity and carnage, but here at last was the pinnacle of controlled, calibrated high performance: a semi-final driven slowly and carefully through the gap marked 'final' with the precision and sangfroid of a team that looked like it had been there many times before.

The tighter the grip became, the more ragged French nerves got: a red card for the petulant Di María, who stamped on Fernandinho; a yellow for the over-excited Marco Verratti;

Danilo Pereira, newly installed as a substitute, carrying out a thigh-high lunge on Jesus as his first act on the pitch. They were not alone in what was a collective loss of control.

City were irascible, unstoppable in their tightening efficiency. Long before the final whistle – and this was perhaps the biggest eye-opener – the game was safe.

Mahrez's unerring finishes may have been the difference between the sides, but heroes were scattered liberally through the team: Dias again shoring up the defence to such an extent that Neymar had been completely snuffed out; Fernandinho, that evening to blow out the candles on his 36th birthday cake, a reassuring throwback to his greatest days; but perhaps outshining them all, the late-choice Zinchenko, a picture of calmness, composure and unhurried class on the left.

MANCHESTER CITY 2–0 PARIS SAINT-GERMAIN | Mahrez (2)

Ederson, Walker, Stones, Dias, Zinchenko, B. Silva (Sterling), Fernandinho, Gündoğan, Mahrez, De Bruyne (Jesus), Foden (Agüero)

From the frenzied oddity of goal-strewn exits to Monaco, Liverpool and Tottenham, here was progress to the fabled first-ever Champions League final at a controlled canter. Of all the things that were not on the menu for this most turbulent club, it was serenity.

As usual, there were more sub-plots, ironies and circular stories than a well-paced novel. City had confounded everyone again and would be going to Istanbul, the very city where their first-ever European away game had exploded in their faces back in 1968, to attempt to bring 'the cup with the big ears' back to Manchester as its sixth English winners.

Only it wasn't to be Istanbul, with all its imagery for City, after all.

With the pandemic still raging, a rethink was necessary. As the final came into focus, it was clear there were two venues where it could be played. Wembley, offering the logic of a London base to two English participants, would drop out owing to UEFA's needs for sponsor and VIP access. As with the previous season, Portugal – coping with Covid-19 as effectively as anyone – seemed the obvious choice, although this time it would be the Estádio do Dragão in Porto. This was a venue and a city that brought back happy memories for City, the sunny setting for a well-drilled 2–1 win in the 2012 Europa League. For City's travelling army of supporters, it was the scene of one of the most enjoyable away trips, with a large gathering enjoying the sunshine by the banks of the shimmering River Douro. How many would be allowed to return on this occasion was not clear, but a rush for tickets in a greatly restricted attendance began immediately.

With the venue set, the domestic season saw itself out, as City crossed the finishing line in a canter against Everton. The 5–0 win was in stark contrast to Chelsea's struggles, as the Londoners just about scraped into the fourth Champions League berth despite losing at Villa Park.

The final, it was announced, would also be the first European game of the season to have a crowd, with a modest 6,000 tickets for each club. With City's allocation snapped up, Chelsea returned some 800 tickets (the prohibitive cost of flights and obligatory Covid testing before and after meant many had had to call their plans off).

The coronation of Guardiola, ten years waiting to return to the club game's biggest occasion, was nearly upon us. The smooth demolition of Paris Saint-Germain in the last four had released many of us from the nagging fear that the Catalan would attempt to pull yet another tactical rabbit out of the hat. Apart from a slight doubt about the left-back position, where Zinchenko had seized his opportunity as Cancelo's form subsided, there were no arguments for the press to mull over.

The side, as they say, picked itself.

With the reality of participation in a final properly dawning, those intent on being there in person began the arduous task of claiming tickets, arranging transport and accommodation, updating passports and getting the obligatory tests completed, without which they could not even gain access to an airport departure lounge.

With the inevitable charge of adrenaline surging through the supporters, it was left to more objective bystanders to ask the pertinent pre-match questions. One, naturally enough, stood out: Having been responsible for defeating Guardiola twice in the previous month, could Thomas Tuchel do it again? A veneer of doubt had settled on matters. As with their previous Champions League victory against Bayern in the Allianz Arena in 2012, the Londoners' season had reached midway in dreadful chaos only to be turned around by the appointment of a new manager. For Roberto Di Matteo in 2012, read Thomas Tuchel in 2021. Man for man, the dark blues could not look their opponents in the eyes without fearing the worst, but finals demand nerves of steel, they demand brave men to step forward and they demand a good storyline.

Would it be Chelsea, turning carnage into gold dust, or would Pep's City finally cross the finishing line started in Istanbul 52 years ago, practically on the anniversary that they had been hauled kicking and screaming out of the Third Division in the unforgettable turmoil of the Gillingham play-off final in 1999? If Chelsea were fresh from chaos of their own, City had been rolling in the stuff for decades.

Dawn on 29 May saw thick mist shrouding the banks of the Douro. A foreboding gripped the quaysides as shafts of light slanted through the sea fog. As I walked down the Avenida dos Aliados, the great central thoroughfare of Porto, the first clanks and thuds were emanating from the humungous sound system in the Chelsea fanzone, a fenced-in 'funpark' opposite the Grand Hotel Monumental, where the BBC were conducting their matchday operations.

Interviewing Chelsea author Tim Rolls, presenter Chris Warburton asked if he feared for his side's chances. 'We are a different side with Kanté playing,' came the reply. 'It is essential he's passed fit to play.' From a City point of view, all that needed to be reiterated was that 'this side now picks itself'. It would within hours become a quote I wish had not been aired on national radio.

A walk down through the streets was clearing the heads of those preparing for another mammoth session of socialising down by the riverside. The tortuous route, through cobbled alleyways and impossibly steep streets made it feel like you had been dropped gently back into the '80s, with its ancient barber shops, wood-panelled *leitaria* (literally 'milk cafés') and its bizarre array of backstreet shops displaying dusty bric-a-brac. The final felt like a throwback too, with legions of paunch-bellied 50-somethings hauling themselves along the Cais de Ribeira in punishing 30-degree heat. There had even been a couple of chair-throwing episodes in the old town the night before to make us think lovingly of the unreconstructed 1980s, a grubby time when City and Chelsea had been aggressive foes in the old Second Division and bewildered counterparts in the final of the Full Members' Cup, ironically a competition foisted on English clubs thanks to the European ban after Heysel.

Those grey-haired gents in the slightly-too-tight Pringle polo shirts, now quaffing mid-morning glasses of red wine as the port barges glided serenely past in the background, had known worse times for sure. The grime of the mid-'80s seemed a long way back in the mists of time as these two clubs with stubbornly parallel histories faced up to each other on the grandest of football occasions.

From the swinging '60s, the early European triumphs of 1970 and 1971 (both in the now-defunct Cup Winners' Cup), to those death-defying days of Second Division struggle, Chelsea's fortunes had matched City's stride for stride. New investment, too, had come to both clubs in recent times, bearing fruit in a modern rush of majestic stars and glittering successes.

One element separated the two clubs, however. For City, this was virgin territory. A first Champions League final had been a long time coming. This tale has traced the myriad layers the struggle has taken on over the years. Was Guardiola's legacy to Manchester City watertight without this crowning glory? Could the second generation of super-talented City stars bring home the one trophy that had eluded the era of David Silva, Zabaleta, Kompany and Yaya Touré? Could this magnificent City side now seal its place in history as one of the Premier League's greatest ever sides?

A clue to where we were headed was to be found in the Portas de São Roque, another tiny café stuck in its own time warp down a cobbled street off the hill that the Estádio do Dragão clings gallantly to. In this tiny cave, with its scalding-hot soup and brisk chatter, scarves of every imaginable club hang from the ceiling.

Among photographs of the owner's family glad-handing officials from FC Porto were large pen pictures of the 2010–11 Porto squad. They peered down from the walls with unblinking eyes. At this point, those paying attention might have noticed bad omens were beginning to gather around us. Staring at me as I blew on my soup were the piercing gazes of Nicolás Otamendi, Maicon and 'the Octopus' Fernando, ghosts from a more recent Manchester City past, ghosts of collapses in Europe too. It was impossible not to drift momentarily into a reverie of horizontal Otamendi lunges and the fateful Bernabéu own goal off Fernando that prevented City reaching a Champions League final earlier than this. The air was tight, the noise was warping.

It was time to make our way up the great hill away from the fates and towards destiny.

The Estádio do Dragão is a modern reincarnation of the old Estádio das Antas, a colossal open bowl of concrete and barbed wire that occupied the same site before the construction frenzy that was Euro 2004 brought about its downfall. Its clean lines and open ends allow for light, air and, if you are lucky, a breath or two of Atlantic breeze to sweep gently across your features. With the sun dropping lazily past the giant roof tubes as kick-off approached, the relentless heat of the day was finally being extinguished.

Even at a third full, the atmosphere inside also leaned towards the 'old fashioned' with raucous and unrelenting support rolling off the City end. Chelsea too had brought their Old Brigade, white haired loudmouths happy to serenade us with some old classics. As UEFA's parping tannoys pumped out 'Blue Moon' and 'Blue is the Colour', you could squeeze your eyes a little and see Peter Osgood and Colin Bell striding the turf, Neil Young, Ron Harris and other faces of a bygone age. As Mark Lillis and John Bumstead danced across the subconscious, however, you knew that reveries of the past could only take you so far. A noisy present was now demanding our attention. A raw, old-time energy seemed to be gripping the place, despite the silken trappings of UEFA's blue-chip occasion.

Where the modernity was really supposed to kick in was in the form of City's penchant for a striker-less fluidity that would surely knock all ideas of glory out of Chelsea's heads. After all, the Londoners limp domestic finish had almost cost them a Champions League place, while City had finished the season wiping the floor nonchalantly with Everton.

But that would have been too simple. The plotline could not really advance on old times revisited alone. There was to be more, and news was now filtering through to confirm it.

Mouths were dropping around us as the team news was announced. A collective 'What the hell?' drifted around the great Curva like a proton bolt. City would be entering the most important game in their history *without* a holding midfielder. Hazy memories attempted to recall if this had been tried before (answer: just once, against Olympiakos), heads were scratched, then shaken slowly from side to side.

Señor Guardiola's heat rash was playing up again.

The coach, who has done so much to redesign the way we consume our football in England had chosen the very worst moment to scratch the top off the boil again. 'The side picks itself,' I heard myself saying as if in an echo chamber, but apparently for the Catalan physician, it doesn't and it didn't.

What had been working beautifully was changed for the event. Holding midfielder for the Champions League? No such thing. İlkay Gündoğan, City's top scorer this season, would apparently sit deepest. On top of this, the player benefiting from the reshuffle was Raheem Sterling, despite three months of almost relentlessly abject form. Neither Fernandinho nor Rodri would make it out onto the pitch in the starting line-up.

Was this the infamous overthinking taking root yet again or had the Catalan an urge to make it more challenging for his all-conquering troupe? The cult of greatness, of uniqueness, after all, keeps eating up the kilometres of praise and worship and spitting them out, ready for another heaped spoonful. Did Guardiola think the monster needed feeding again at this precise moment? Was it a stroke of genius to try and cut down football's granular chaos and chop it into ever smaller slices, another moment of horizon-affecting brainpower that mere mortals like us have to keep a safe distance from?

What, exactly, was going on?

Was Josep Guardiola Sala, shortly to be cast as the fidgeting, overactive arm-waver on the edge of the storm, racked with self-doubt or over-inflated with his own grandeur? A psychiatrist might well, one feared, have had something of a field day. Those of us creased up double in the stands were considering a trip to the shrink too.

And so it came to pass that yet another European custard pie (in the very country that fabricates them best of all) came straight for us and, yet again, every last one of us forgot to duck. But this one, had we had the chance to look under its base would have born the unmistakable hallmark: 'Made in Guardiola'.

Of all places, of all times, not here, not now. *Por favor*.

As the game got under way under a canopy of firework smoke, the fluidity was Chelsea's, the duels were theirs too, while City's well-oiled machine chose the worst moment to go rusty and seize up. Ben Chilwell pocketed Mahrez on the right, Mason Mount and the indefatigable Man of the Match-in-waiting N'Golo Kanté danced through City's understaffed midfield, Timo Werner and Kai Havertz played havoc with the exposed Dias and Stones. The list of tactical surprises seemed almost endless. Only Walker, Zinchenko and the surprisingly agile Sterling could claim to be playing anywhere near their best.

On half-time, Mount played in Havertz and the lanky German scored before Ederson could reach him. City's talisman Kevin De Bruyne fell to the calculated savagery of Antonio Rüdiger, a fractured nose and eye socket the Belgian's souvenir from a well-calibrated shoulder charge. Everything was going dark.

Slowly, the realisation dawned that we could add Porto 2021 to other outlandish tactical gigs foisted upon Liverpool, Tottenham and Lyon in recent years that City's opponents had gleefully played through, around and over.

Chelsea were swarming City in all areas of the pitch. Perhaps, after all, it was Thomas Tuchel, with his scientist's head, that was the Premier League's master tactician. He had seen off the champions three times in the space of little more than a month, after all.

But, for the legions in sky blue (local authorities in Porto estimated there had been many thousands more in the city than the 6,000 with tickets) this was beginning to hurt.

As the second half progressed, substitutions appeared, but in a manner that suggested a man fabled for seeking total control had lost it at the critical moment. Fernandinho's entry shored up some of the holes, but it was too late. Chelsea were running through ragged pockets and threatening a second, while City's forward movement had shrivelled to a lopsided effort, with Agüero and Jesus on the pitch as well.

That it took until the 96th minute for Mahrez to eke out meaningful space, sending a right-footer agonisingly over the bar, spoke volumes. The game was long gone. Mahrez's effort felt somehow typical of the whole thing. So close, yet miles away at the same time.

Agüero's last game before his move to Barcelona was ending with the wrong kind of tears. City's second great generation of winners was falling short of the European pinnacle. Bodies slumped to the turf, heads in hands in the stands. Trooping off down the hill, all that could be heard was the excited preparations for the handing over of the trophy. Triumphal music and exploding fireworks.

City in Europe remained a work in progress, albeit one with its foundations long laid. All that seemed to be missing was the author's bold signature to confirm an authentic masterpiece. Typically, for this chameleon club, the simplest thing was proving to be the most difficult.

CHELSEA 1–0 MANCHESTER CITY | Att. 14,110

Ederson, Walker, Stones, Dias, Zinchenko, Gündoğan, B. Silva (Fernandinho), Foden, De Bruyne (Jesus), Sterling (Agüero), Mahrez

BEAUTY AND CHAOS

Ruined in a day

There could be no denying the focus. The defeat in Porto, as painful as it was avoidable, had sharpened appetites for the new challenge. A summer spent chasing big signings that might make a difference ended in the strange acquisition of Jack Grealish, who might not. That a stellar £100-million acquisition (an English record) could lead to an anti-climax underlined just how high the stakes had become for City.

The disappointment did not surround the midfielder's signing. Grealish had blossomed into one of the star turns of the Premier League and had bolstered that impression on the international front with some decisive moments in England's appearance in the finals of Euro 2020. Rather, it was City's inability to force through the departure of the obviously interested Harry Kane from the grasp of Daniel Levy at Tottenham Hotspur. That City had spent much of the previous eighteen months playing without a recognised number nine seemed a moot point. 'They did it, yes, but they can't be expected to do it again,' came the ready replies.

In fact, the more understandable concern centred on the need for a powerful and reliable goal-getter for the high-intensity games likely to come City's way at the pointy end of the season. As had been ably demonstrated against Chelsea in Porto, when things were getting rough against high-calibre opposition, City would need the very best there was in order to maintain the control their manager demanded.

City found themselves in an even-keeled group, with a recognised giant in PSG, a strong dark horse in RB Leipzig and a thrusting underdog in Club Brugge. There was, as always, all to play for.

Any doubts about the Grealish signing were quickly diffused after his display against the Germans, however. In a match of unremitting action, City's new signing, given the misnomer 'shifty' by admiring opposition coach Jesse Marsch, scored a classy individual goal in a performance that belied the fact he was making his European bow. 'He played as if born to the Champions League,' gushed Mark Critchley in the *Independent*.

That Marsch could not remember whether Grealish had scored the fourth or fifth goal in the 6–3 rout of his team (*it was the fourth*) underlined the extravagant power that had been exerted on Leipzig in the midst of a crazy game that launched the 2021–2 Champions League campaign.

Against the 2020 semi-finalists, City could have been forgiven for harbouring some degree of trepidation. Instead, in a game that immediately revealed the two teams' kamikaze tendencies, Guardiola's charges managed to meld scattergun defending with rapturous attacking, bringing their total for the nascent 2021–2 season after just three home games to sixteen (after two 5–0 wins over Norwich and Arsenal).

If you threw in the last home game of the previous season (coincidentally a 5–0 win over Everton and the last home game City could count on the poaching instinct of a real striker, in this case Sergio Agüero, who bade farewell to Manchester with two goals), City had racked up 21 goals in four home games, with fifteen different scorers. Among the cascade of mouth-watering statistics, Guardiola's charges had also managed to become the fastest English team in Champions League history to record 50 victories in the competition. When one thought back to the tough-as-teak groups delivered in City's early days in the competition, this feat was even more astonishing. City had recorded a mere five victories in three of the first four seasons in the competition and now this. Undoubtedly jolted into proper action by Manuel Pellegrini, it was clear that Guardiola's tenure had catapulted City into the upper echelons.

A match that had simultaneously offered the impression that City were both European heavyweights while gleefully sticking to traditional historical club lines of gluey unpredictability would be a colourful microcosm for a campaign that would contain regal highs and scattergun moments of madness.

A fevered Guardiola, vividly explaining to goalscorers Mahrez and Grealish why they should be tracking back as well as showcasing attacking skills, revealed the fanatical attention to detail that had brought City this far under the Catalan. This may have ultimately played against the Blues in the Estádio do Dragão the previous May, but in loose-fitting early round games, his attention to detail remained a rivetingly important part of the coach's make-up.

In truth, sloppy starts were becoming difficult to avoid. A below-capacity crowd, including around 35 fans from eastern Germany, found it difficult going too, but, as the goals began to flow, so the evening's entertainment value suddenly sky-rocketed.

Nathan Aké's deft header put City ahead, while De Bruyne's renowned crossing forced Nordi Mukiele into a spectacularly headed own goal. It appeared that nobody could resist putting the Belgian's deliciously teasing crosses into the goal, even if it happened to be the one the Germans were meant to be defending.

Astonishingly, despite Mahrez's successful penalty, Leipzig were back to 3–2 by the 51st minute and more magic was needed; it duly came from the inspirational close control of the marauding

European debutant. Skipping in from his station wide on the left, he flat-footed two defenders and curled a beautiful right-foot shot past Péter Gulácsi. If stage fright on his Champions League debut was supposed to be the order of the day, nobody had told Grealish, who had taken to the big platform with consummate ease. Having delivered the ball in for Aké's opener, the former Villa captain became the first Englishman since Wayne Rooney in 2004 to both score and assist on a Champions League debut.

'The players are always talking about last season's final,' he said afterwards. 'They are determined to go one better this year.' Even at this early stage of the season, the focus was clear enough.

Two more goals, close-in from Jesus and from distance by Cancelo, kept Leipzig at bay, for whom the unlucky Christopher Nkunku managed the usually glorious feat of an away hat-trick, an achievement destined to be consigned to the narrow ground of German pub quizzes, along with the returning Angeliño's 79th-minute red card.

MANCHESTER CITY 6–3 RB LEIPZIG | Att. 38,062 | Aké, Mukiele (o.g.), Mahrez (pen.), Grealish, Jesus, Cancelo

Ederson, Cancelo, Zinchenko, Dias, Aké, Rodrigo (Fernandinho), De Bruyne (Foden), B. Silva (Gündoğan), Grealish (Jesus), Torres (Sterling), Mahrez

That the second game threw City into their most difficult challenge of the early phase was enough in itself to focus minds. That the trip to the Parc des Princes to tackle a PSG side with a probable striking trident of Neymar, Messi and Mbappé fell between away Premier League games at Stamford Bridge and Anfield felt almost cruel.

With the long-running Harry Kane summer saga over and the possibility of stealing Messi from a fast-disintegrating Barcelona unfulfilled, City's opening weeks domestically had been played out to the backdrop of media doubts about trying to win the league without a striker. This topic persisted despite the fact they had done exactly this the previous season and despite the fact that Grealish, Bernardo, Mahrez, Jesus, De Bruyne, Torres and Foden did constitute something approaching a reasonably potent attacking threat.

By the time City stepped out at Chelsea on a brisk Saturday lunchtime, the press had already managed to anoint Manchester United (with the returning Cristiano Ronaldo scoring twice on his debut), Liverpool (reacquainted with proper defending now that Virgil van Dijk had recovered from injury) and Chelsea themselves (*'Is Tuchel Pep's Kryptonite?'*) as would-be champions. Modern football coverage was nothing if not comprehensive in its profound observation of how a light hammer blow to the knee affects the movement of the leg.

City's dismantling of Chelsea on their own patch also turned out to be comprehensive, giving the media another name to throw into the hat of 2021–2 runners and riders. With a decisiveness going forward that had been missing in the early defeat at Tottenham and the dull 0–0 with Southampton, City's control of the team that had beaten them in the previous May's Champions League final was inarguable. Tuchel, vigorously rubbing what was left of his hair, stated that his side's game plan had been compromised almost completely by the lack of space and air City had given his players to operate in.

We had only three days to wait to see if a similar strategy was physically possible so soon after Chelsea and whether it was equally adept in suffocating the likes of Messi and Mbappé.

What transpired in Paris was a rerun of the wonderfully controlled Stamford Bridge performance, but with no tangible reward. An evening of growing control and regular chances to open the scoring was spoiled by the clinical sangfroid of the home side's obvious danger men. Messi's first goal for his club was as accurate as it was inevitable and followed an early break-through against the run of play by Idrissa Gueye.

City had demonstrated a degree of control over one of the favourites in their own backyard. That they had come away with nothing raised yet more questions about the legendary profligacy of Guardiola's sides, heaped pressure on the next game against Bruges and produced a theme that would haunt the club through to the end of the campaign.

PARIS SAINT-GERMAIN 2–0 MANCHESTER CITY | Att. 37,350
Ederson, Walker, Cancelo, Dias, Laporte, Rodrigo, De Bruyne, B. Silva, Sterling (Jesus), Grealish (Foden), Mahrez

Bruges proved a different story. The widespread talk of pressure seemed to galvanise City.

Naming another strong side, Guardiola went for the home team's jugular. The 5–1 win featured a flow, dynamism and balance that the Belgians failed to comprehend. The goal-scoring introduction of another gifted youngster in Cole Palmer was the cherry on the cake. Fellow youth product Foden's outstanding performance as a false nine even persuaded the *Manchester Evening News* to suggest somewhat prematurely that City's problems up front may have been solved in one fell swoop.

With De Bruyne yet to reach peak fitness after a summer of injuries and Sterling still misfiring badly up front, there was obviously more to come. Bernardo Silva, so close to a summer departure, and Rodri, much maligned for his moderately paced midfield movement, were leading the way in the new season thrust. With both Cancelo and Walker finding the net in the Jan Breydel Stadium, City looked full of ideas, full of options and, indeed, full of hope for the campaign to come.

There was a dark stain on the evening's proceedings, however, as news filtered through afterwards of an assault in nearby

Drongen, which left City supporter Guido De Pauw in a hospital bed in a coma. Here was a timely reminder that for the unlucky few, there were still dangers lurking, despite the sanitised world of modern Champions League football. For the vast majority, however, Bruges had been a calm, welcoming and beautiful host city and one which would leave those that had witnessed the match purring about it for years to come.

CLUB BRUGGE 1–5 MANCHESTER CITY | Att. 24,915 | Cancelo, Mahrez (2), Walker, Palmer

Ederson, Walker, Cancelo, Dias, Laporte (Aké), Rodrigo (Fernandinho), De Bruyne (Palmer), B. Silva (Gündoğan), Grealish, Foden (Sterling), Mahrez

The return with the Belgians came straight after a chastening home defeat in the league to a Crystal Palace side well marshalled by coach Patrick Vieira.

Phil Foden's early breakthrough against Bruges suggested another calm evening of European chess play, but a bizarre own goal off John Stones' face two minutes later brought new unease about City's *strikerless* limbo.

Growing superiority would eventually be rewarded with three more goals to give City a second big win against demoralised opponents. While Cancelo's triple assist made him the game's outstanding performer, it was Sterling's tap-in that perhaps carried the greatest hope that City could rely on his returning touch in front of goal to ward off the doubters.

At the top of the group, City's win practically sealed a ninth consecutive group stage qualification. Better still, a late equaliser for Leipzig against PSG meant City had leapfrogged the Parisians to lead the group. Beating Pochettino's men at the Etihad would now secure first place and a more favourable last-sixteen opponent in February.

MANCHESTER CITY 4–1 CLUB BRUGGE | Att. 50,228 | Foden, Mahrez, Sterling, Jesus

Ederson, Walker (Zinchenko), Cancelo, Stones, Laporte, Rodrigo, Gündoğan, B. Silva (De Bruyne), Mahrez (Sterling), Foden (Palmer), Grealish (Jesus)

And *beating PSG*, if the total swarming of the French champions could be called merely this, is exactly what came to pass as City turned on the style to mesmerise a Paris side unused to being given the tactical runaround. The visitors, fielding their dream attack, *'l'union sacree'*, according to the salivating French press pack, were defused, undressed and sent packing.

Such a thorough and intricate dismantling of one of the tournament favourites clearly boded well. In a scintillating night of one-touch football and bewildering pass and move, City were a step ahead of PSG right from Daniele Orsato's opening whistle.

In a first half where City completed 266 of 286 attempted passes, conjured eleven shots on goal and forced five corners, one felt the need to check that their dizzy opponents were in fact the serial champions of France and not a last-minute collection of part-timers. Without Foden, De Bruyne and Grealish, it would not have been unreasonable to expect trouble, but, galvanised by the emerging star of City's season Bernardo Silva, nothing could have been further from the case.

The little Portuguese, pirouetting, jinking and swerving, conjured masterful touch after masterful touch, culminating in a cushioned volley of a pass to set up Jesus for the winning goal. Here was the sacred union that the French journalists had spoken of, but it was dressed in sky blue and speaking Portuguese.

With Mahrez in equally unplayable mood, his velvet touch remarkably adhesive, City had all of the trump cards on this night of poker. That they had to come from behind, a rare link between Messi and Mbappé putting the French ahead, made the performance even more striking. City had hit perfect pitch and, even in these times of Guardiola-inspired majesty, this had been peerless fare.

'Yeah, we tried. It was good,' seemed overly simplistic from the City manager, when he was asked to describe his side's balletic efficiency afterwards. That they had done it against a top-six side in the competition, he admitted, was 'the most important thing'.

Perhaps the *Guardian*'s Barney Ronay's efforts to put appropriate words to City efforts were a little more illustrative, insisting: 'Frankly, this could have gone on all night. Did we have to stop? Did we really need to call an end to it? On a chilly, still night at the Etihad Stadium, Manchester City produced a performance that was oddly hypnotic: a brilliantly fluid, delicately stitched, oddly gentle display of how to win a game by simply picking your opponent apart.'

MANCHESTER CITY 2–1 PARIS SAINT-GERMAIN | Att. 52,030 | Sterling, Jesus

Ederson, Walker, Cancelo, Dias, Stones, Gündoğan, Rodrigo, Zinchenko (Jesus), Mahrez, B. Silva, Sterling

---

'We didn't get what we came for,' exclaimed Oleksandr Zinchenko afterwards, but a limp defeat in the final group game mattered little to the standings. Zack Steffen's four outstanding saves underlined City's defensive languor and the red card brandished to Walker would have repercussions later on as City's first trip to Leipzig drifted to an inglorious conclusion. With De Bruyne lethargic and alarming defensive lapses in concentration a major feature, City nevertheless wrapped up the group stage in pole position.

By the time Mahrez netted his fifth goal of the group stage,

Leipzig were two clear and coasting towards Europa League qualification. Guardiola, meanwhile, was gently fuming with his right-back. 'The red card hurts us, especially for the round of sixteen. Kyle Walker is an important player for us and it was unnecessary to lose him like this.'

Despite the unmistakable sound of gently grinding teeth, the defeat had little impact, bar producing a minor jolt to the free-wheeling machine that had gained such impressive momentum since the opening-match flattening of the same opponent. If we were to continue to believe in the mystic contrariness of this club, in fact, it would be asking a lot to find flaws, despite a frailty at the back and the lack of a striker, that might be serious enough to derail them.

RB LEIPZIG 2–1 MANCHESTER CITY | Att. 0 | Mahrez
Steffen, Walker, Zinchenko, Aké (Dias), Stones, Fernandinho, De Bruyne (Palmer), Gündoğan, Foden (Sterling), Grealish, Mahrez

A twice-attempted draw featuring the by now customary lack of UEFA sophistication eventually brought City together with Sporting Clube de Portugal in the first round of knockout ties. A true clash of history, between one of the original sixteen teams that took part in the very first edition of the tournament in 1955–6 and one of English football's earliest European trophy winners. It was also a tie between sides linked heavily by the sizeable shadow cast by Malcolm Allison, architect of City's 1970 triumph and a domestic double winner in Lisbon in 1982.

By the time the spring ties came about, City had put on something of a characteristic spurt domestically, powering to a twelve-point Premier League lead over Liverpool. A 4–0 stroll at Norwich revealed a side purring in cruise control with almost every player in rich, confident form. That they went one better in the Estádio Alvalade than they had at Carrow Road was testament to Guardiola's continuing brilliance in coaxing 98 season goals from a side still without a recognised central striker.

The enraptured City fans packed into a corner of the 48,000 crowd soaked it up as they had soaked up the *caipirinhas* in the spring sunshine by the expansive River Tagus that afternoon. A day of castles and precipitous cobbled streets, of salted cod and Super Bock was ending with the most potent cocktail of all, mixed and shaken by Portugal's own Bernardo Silva. The wiry little midfielder's miraculous seventeenth-minute connection on the half-volley produced warm applause from the home fans, as he dictated a sumptuous evening of pass and move. City were already ahead by then and would score two more before the break in a first half of breathless domination.

Silva would be denied a hat-trick by the offside flag, but Sterling rounded things off with a superb, curled effort that had home fans gawping at each other. The only reaction to this kind of dismantling was to applaud, regardless of whether it was your own team.

A growing media trend suggesting City's football might be boring had an answer yet again in the 43rd different match of the Catalan's reign to end with City five or more goals clear by the end. This represented 13 per cent of all matches under Guardiola, an astonishing figure. This 5–0 equalled City's best away score in Europe, achieved in the 2016–17 preliminary round tie in Bucharest.

For Sporting, in their first Champions League knockout game since 2009, it was over in a blur of passes and a blitz of goals. The home support had booed ferociously as City headed out with four ex-Benfica players in their ranks but were left with no option but to listen to the giddy travelling support yelling: '*You've had your day out, now fuck off home*'. It was as demoralising as it was blunt.

The manager was in blunt form afterwards too when asked what the rest of Europe would be thinking after the win: 'Last season we played thirteen games, we won eleven and drew one, we got to the final and lost and it was, "What a fucking failure is this team," but it's not true.'

With City reaching 200 Champions League goals, the fourteenth side to do it, but in 97 games, the quickest ever, it was a night full of intimidating statistics. The 21-year-old Phil Foden's 150th game for the club; City the first club to win five consecutive away games in Champions League knockout rounds. Even Sporting's own stats, among them a grand total of zero shots on target, bore testament to City's prowess.

On and on the plaudits rolled, but only one thing really mattered and that was that the rest of the field knew whom they had to avoid in the quarter-finals.

SPORTING CLUBE DE PORTUGAL 0–5 MANCHESTER CITY | Att. 48,129 | Mahrez, B. Silva (2), Foden, Sterling

Ederson, Stones (Zinchenko), Cancelo, Dias, Laporte (Aké), Rodrigo (Fernandinho), De Bruyne, B. Silva (Delap), Sterling, Foden (Gündoğan), Mahrez

With sights set on Saint Petersburg, the venue for the final, the football world was shaken to its core in unison with much of the rest of the planet for the second time in two years. Derailed previously by Covid-19, now came Russia's uninvited incursion into Ukraine. With Vladimir Putin visiting war on Europe's eastern front, the first football casualty of the conflict became Russia's second city, with the final switched rapidly to Paris by UEFA as a punishment.

With the world's attention once again diverted from the comparative unimportance of sport, it came as no surprise that the second leg with Sporting – a foregone conclusion anyhow – proved something of a damp squib, with City merely grateful for the exercise and the Portuguese embarrassingly pleased with themselves to gain a goalless draw against a side surprisingly well stocked with first-teamers.

City were neat without any great penetration, while Sporting were penetrative without any great neatness.

By the end, City had squandered the main chances and seen Gabriel Jesus' artistic effort ruled out by VAR. The Portuguese press' one-word headlines from the first leg ('Lesson' and 'Masterclass') had by now been revamped to 'Pride' for Rúben Amorim's willing young side.

For City fans, again turning out in large numbers for a dead rubber, the only levity in a dull evening was the substitute appearance of third-choice goalkeeper Scott Carson, a man last seen active in this tournament in 2005. The chant of 'England's number one' accompanied Carson's steady second-half progress, as City used the opportunity to blood a clutch of youngsters too.

MANCHESTER CITY 0–0 SPORTING CLUBE DE PORTUGAL | Att. 51,213

Ederson (Carson), Egan-Riley, Zinchenko, Stones, Laporte (Mbete), Fernandinho, Gündoğan, B. Silva (Mahrez), Foden (McAtee), Jesus, Sterling

There would be tougher days to come, beginning with the quarter-final pairing with Atlético Madrid, fluid victors over a seemingly terminally out-of-sorts Manchester United. After three visits to the city to play Real, Guardiola would be taking his team to the other side of the capital to face a war of attrition against Diego Simeone's renowned battlers.

Before that, Europe's governments had a war to deal with on its doorstep. With Russian assets being confiscated in an attempt to counter Putin's ill-judged belligerence, fellow Champions League qualifiers Chelsea entered a period of unique instability as owner Roman Abramovich headed quickly for the hills, his club seized by the British government. The theme of 'sportswashing' and the Premier League as a conduit for unacceptable investors with blood on their hands revisited the nation's sports pages. Some asked how sportswashing worked if all the new owners got was a severe public rinsing in the eager Western press. How could a sublime De Bruyne through-ball take anyone's minds off the shelling of civilians in Yemen? The *Mail*'s Nick Harris, a long-time and persistent critic of the club, went out of his way to produce a huge survey with predictable results along club-bias lines. Wolves, a club who had been found in breach of FFP, seemed to be held up as a club with virtuous owners, while City, a club with no debt, hoisted in March 2022 to the top of Deloitte's rich list for the very first time, was declared the epitome of what was least desired. The world was turning on a wobbly axis.

With dizzying developments at every turn, attempting to compartmentalise the meaning of football in the greater scheme of things was not getting any easier. Despite this, a meeting between the high priest of possession football and the cardinal of the main alternative to it began to focus attention. In a four-game spell that would involve having to face Liverpool and Atlético twice each, the mouth-watering prospect of City's keep-ball against Atlético's religious pursuit of success without it, kept everyone primed.

Simeone had once gone to visit a Barcelona training session, where the players were applying themselves to Guardiola's endless passing drills. Simeone's reaction, 'I don't like this', spoke volumes for the man's hot pursuit of practicalities.

The ambrosial prospect that an opponent as wired to anti-football as the Argentinian might provoke another spasm of tactical tinkering along the lines of the Porto final did not bode well, even if City's persistent excellence told us to expect a different story. Could the shadow of a manager whose vigorous chasing tactics had famously dumped Guardiola's Bayern out of this tournament in 2016 really set off a new episode of the Catalan's most debilitating affliction? In that game, shortly before he jumped ship for Manchester, a battle of wits ensued, on the one hand to carve out space, on the other to annex it.

Would the team that never seemed to lack an attacking option be defied by the one that possessed the maps and charts of every possible defensive encampment? Would the side that liked to be fed from the wings get sucked into the plots and schemes of the one that draws everything into a central quagmire?

Guardiola, fully aware of the furore, entered a kind of *banter overdrive* with 24 hours to the first leg, insisting: 'In the Champions League, always I overthink. I overthink a lot. Absolutely. That's why I've had good results. I love to overthink and create stupid tactics. Tonight, I take inspiration and there will be incredible tactics tomorrow. We'll play with twelve …'

City would start with eleven. The rest remained to be seen.

As it turned out, if you squinted a little, it was Atlético that looked to be playing with twelve, or even fifteen. 'They played with five at the back, five in midfield and gave us no space at all. Anyone commenting on this match should try this in training,' said match-winner De Bruyne – scoring his fifth quarter-final goal out of eleven in the competition. Atlético, with zero shots, zero goal attempts, zero corners and zero ambition, not only lived up to their reputation, but greatly enhanced it.

In a game that was being gradually throttled, it needed the inspiration of substitute Phil Foden, threading a magnificent pass through to his captain 79 seconds after coming on, to provide the one tiny spark that the Spaniards failed to extinguish. Exhibiting all the dark arts that have made them so notorious, Simeone's men chased, tackled and closed everything down, but the introduction of Foden and Grealish, who immediately succeeded in drawing a succession of fouls from a suddenly distracted Stefan Savić and Šime Vrsaljko, had made all the difference.

By the end of a punishing test, City had a slender lead to protect in Madrid. The manner that they would do it would surely be different to what had been witnessed here.

Guardiola, referring to Atlético's shape as '5–5', was content with the way his side had managed a truculent opponent. 'After 1–0 it was different. They pressed a little higher. I think the game in Madrid will be like the last fifteen minutes after the goal.'

MANCHESTER CITY 1–0 ATLÉTICO MADRID | Att. 52,018 | De Bruyne

Ederson, Cancelo, Stones, Laporte, Aké, Rodrigo, De Bruyne, Gündoğan (Grealish), Mahrez (Foden), Sterling (Jesus), B. Silva

---

It is not absolutely clear when and how the modern football term 'shithousery' was coined, but it was long associated with Diego Simeone's men before City arrived at the Wanda Metropolitano with a job to do in the return leg. On a night of extreme tension, Guardiola's flamboyant side suddenly found a darker side, however, and, to quote many, managed to out-shithouse the shithousers at their own game. By the end of this taut, goalless battle, Atlético had lost their nerve and were falling for the kind of extravagant acts of skullduggery that they had made their own during eleven years under Simeone's tutelage.

In a fraught, increasingly bad-tempered encounter, a lid of sorts had been kept on matters until the 89th minute, when it finally flew off and hit the roof. The spark was ignited by Felipe, already booked for cleaning out Foden in the first half, sliding into the youngster again and aiming a kick at him as an afterthought. Foden, using all his strength to roll back onto the playing surface 'in agony' after Savić had pulled him across the touchline, produced a cameo fit for the Royal Shakespeare Company. Felipe, the pantomime villain, was banished from play, while Savić, clearly on the point of combustion after aiming a head-butt at Sterling, was booked.

Referee Daniel Siebert, somewhat wide-eyed by this point, added twelve minutes of injury time to compensate for the shenanigans, booking seven more players to severely challenge the yellow-cards-to-minutes world record. Looking like a victim of Saint Vitus, the irascible Atlético manager also received official admonishment from Herr Siebert, as the temperatures inside the Wanda Metropolitano reached volcanic levels.

The *exchange of pleasantries* would continue in the tunnel afterwards, with Grealish introducing Savić to some of the more direct insults in the English language and the Montenegrin finding the silkiness of the City player's hair irresistible. With Siebert resting at this point, the local police finished off the evening's job.

City had struggled to get up the pitch in an increasingly choked second half. Foden, wrapped in head bandages after Felipe's close attention, and Fernandinho, introduced in the 79th minute, led the revolt of pretty football in a headlong charge towards game management. Time wasting, play-acting and distraction tactics showed Guardiola's men to be fast learners. City had prevailed in the most obtuse way imaginable, with a feat of Simeonian anti-football and sweat-drenched attention to closing down the game.

The reward would be a return to Madrid, this time to lock horns with Real, the self-styled 'owners' of the tournament, whose victory over Chelsea had been so free of structure as to resemble a different sport altogether. City would have to regroup, gather their frayed nerves and prepare for a very different opponent, with a very different mindset, in the last four.

ATLÉTICO MADRID 0–0 MANCHESTER CITY | Att. 65,675

Ederson, Walker (Aké), Stones, Laporte, Cancelo, Rodrigo, Gündoğan, De Bruyne (Sterling), B. Silva (Fernandinho), Foden, Mahrez

With rumours abounding that neither of the obvious fits at right-back, Walker and Stones, were going to make it (Cancelo was also suspended after his yellow card in Madrid), it came as a relief when the ex-Everton man was declared fit to play. That he lasted only 36 minutes in a game of churning drama was perhaps only a footnote in the end, but it did necessitate the inclusion of 37-year-old Fernandinho in his place, which directly contributed to two of the seven goals that were scored on a night of unremitting effervescence.

For those who had waited to see City pulverise the kings of Europe, here it was. For those that have always loved the club for its ridiculous penchant for tragicomedy, here it was too. Three times two goals ahead, but, by the end, pegged back to an amazing 4–3, a victory that once upon a time would have been beyond most fans' dreams but now allowed those filing out of the Etihad drained of emotion to shake their heads about *what might have been*.

How does a club manage such things? Two goals up after ten minutes on the back of De Bruyne's diving header (the fastest-ever Champions League semi-final effort) and Jesus' expert poaching, City were on fire, Real bereft. Chances came and went for a third, Mahrez striking the post, Foden's follow-up cleared from the line, before Real's danger man, Karim Benzema, reduced the deficit completely out of the blue. Still City pushed. Fernandinho, chugging up the right wing, served Foden who scored thunderously with his head. The Brazilian was then immediately caught out by Vinícius Júnior on the touchline and watched as his countryman streaked away to score an incredible breakaway goal for 3–2.

We weren't finished. Far from it. Bernardo whacked a sumptuous fourth and Mahrez swivelled through and shot inches wide before Laporte's handball gave Benzema the chance to finish with a Panenka for 4–3. The air was being sucked out of the place, the noise and sweat too. There was nowhere to go but home to restock, rethink and repair for the Bernabéu in a week's time.

'Are you disappointed to concede three goals here?' Guardiola was asked at the end by a foreign journalist. 'It's Real Madrid! This is Real Madrid!' he responded, wide-eyed, distilling in four short words the idea that, in this competition, against this opponent, you can swarm and choke, pulverise and perform to astonishing levels and still end up with the feeling that some grand failure has been visited upon you.

How could City have won so comprehensively yet also have left the tie on a knife-edge? Guardiola's men had been precocious, smart and devastatingly nimble and still managed to look naive at the same time. The old dog Real Madrid still had its teeth sunk deep into this tie. Would City, with this re-enactment of past *coups de théâtre* against Tottenham and Monaco in this very tournament, ever do it the easy way? Would Real, seemingly unable to admit their day was run, claw their way through to yet another final?

The questions kept coming and, as ever, the answers would not be long in arriving, although, when they did arrive, scarcely a single onlooker – or for that matter, scarcely a single participant either – would be able to make sense of a single thread of it.

MANCHESTER CITY 4–3 REAL MADRID | Att. 52,217 | De Bruyne, Jesus, Foden, B. Silva

Ederson, Stones (Fernandinho), Dias, Laporte, Zinchenko, Rodrigo, De Bruyne, B. Silva, Mahrez, Foden, Jesus (Sterling)

If the swirling, cavorting chaos of the first leg had taken the breath away, the closing of the second leg left many needing respirators, psychiatrists and a six-month retreat in a Himalayan tea plantation. Having been in nominal charge of this gigantic clash of football cultures from the 93rd second of the first leg to the last gasps of the 90th minute of the second leg, Manchester City reverted to age-old type at the very worst moment possible and succumbed, but not before teasing us all once again into thinking that a grand job had been carried out.

It is not easy to find new ways of describing the carnage visited upon City on this occasion, but it remains perhaps apt to say the club that produced the most dramatic single moment of Premier League history had themselves, on the greatest European stage of all, with all the spotlights shining down on them, been hit by an equivalent of the *Agüerooooo* sucker punch. Supporters of Gillingham, too, would have plenty of adjectives to aid those of us struggling for air and words, to describe the first-degree larceny of the 1999 Third Division play-off final that had seen them sailing into injury time with a two-goal lead, that would have taken them into the second tier, before City decided to wake up and save themselves from what many at the time thought could be football oblivion.

Here, an unnecessarily slim lead had been successfully, if fitfully, protected right through to the 73rd minute of a heaving, swaying tie, when Riyad Mahrez's stunning left-foot strike slid City into a seemingly conclusive two-goal aggregate advantage.

There had been clear chances along the way to broaden that gap, but sizzling efforts from De Bruyne, Bernardo and Foden were spectacularly dealt with by Thibaut Courtois, and Jesus' looping strike curled agonisingly past the post. Still, City thundered forward after taking the lead, with substitute Grealish rolling another effort along the goal line and out the other side without getting the minute touch it needed from Foden.

Grealish's next effort slipped Courtois but skimmed off the goalkeeper's studs, enough of a tiny deviation to take it millimetres past the post. Then, with the clock ticking inexorably towards Real's exit and City's second successive final, against, of all people, Liverpool in Paris, the match exploded in City's face like some vast, uncontrollable atomic soufflé.

With their very first attempt on target, Real pulled a 90th-minute goal back. With their second, an astonishing 88 seconds later, the same man – substitute Rodrygo – breached the quivering blue defensive line again. As unexpected collapses go, this one was untouchable in its power, its timing and its finality. Having slammed the door shut on neighbours Atlético in an epic 90-minute-long rearguard action in the quarter-final, City had now thrown their gains away in the time it takes to wipe away a tear. To make matters worse, within those 88 seconds, City had kicked off and thus been given possession of the ball, which was funnelled back to Ederson, normally a master of prissy sideways passes to his defenders. This time, the Brazilian, gripped by some form of tropical fever, launched the ball straight down the pitch to opposite number Courtois. Seconds later it was lying in the net behind Ederson for the most cataclysmic closure to a European semi-final anybody cared to remember.

That the ball had glanced very slightly off the head of Marco Asensio before Rodrygo headed it past the Brazilian just fried the mind that bit more. Could that tiny, inadvertent deflection have made the difference to where the eventual header went, just as the tiny glance off Courtois' studs moments earlier had taken Grealish's shot onto the outside of the post? If you thought about it too long, you would be interned. Add the fact that Real's first two shots on goal (in the 90th and 92nd minutes) had now produced the two goals they needed to survive this wobbling, bubbling event. It was mind-extending stuff.

With the place in transfixed uproar and many home fans already running around the precincts outside wondering what the deafening noise inside was all about, referee Daniele Orsato signalled extra time. City, operating like eleven ephemeral wisps of smoke, now required only one feather-light blow to disappear altogether. Dias, uncharacteristically wobbly all night, lifted a hesitant foot for Benzema to catapult over and the inevitable Frenchman dispatched his second penalty of the tie. City, moving like an invisible force, had siphoned concrete into their shoes, were already elsewhere, their power shrivelled, their thought processes utterly fried.

There could be no other denouement. Real, heading to their seventeenth final, had denied City their second. A team that seemingly not only needed to be killed off, but dismembered and buried a long way away, many fathoms down, under a six-lane motorway bridge, was still walking around applauding itself and kissing its regal badge. City's dagger thrusts had been delivered with cardboard swords. The great white-shirted beast was still breathing.

Match-winner Rodrygo was also struggling for air at the end: 'I don't have words for what happened today. God looked at me and said, "Today is your day."'

Was this more material for the Guardiola bashers? The cursed overthinker rides again for a record sixth semi-final defeat as manager, shared ironically with arch-nemesis José Mourinho. Or was it the fault of the intransigent club that he has gleefully hoisted to the heights of continental football, Francis Lee's mythical winners of the inaugural, the ever-lasting, eternally City's cup for cock-ups? Guardiola, for his part, could hardly be faulted. The best eleven players played. Even the substitutes had worked, Zinchenko and Gündoğan playing an integral part in Mahrez's opener and Grealish playing havoc in those last uncoordinated minutes before the newly raised roof flew off.

Here, instead, was what football at the highest level sometimes serves up: an inexplicably dramatic collection of events, set before us on a grand platform with the timing of the most adept stage director. For the global audience, unforgettable moments of theatrical chaos. For those of a Manchester City persuasion, yet another dangerously generous dose of the most deliciously stage-managed *dukkha*.

'Let God come down and explain it,' offered *MARCA*'s head-line the morning after, acknowledging the relatively small part a numinous and refulgent Real Madrid had played in their own phenomenal advancement.

If pressed, God might well have held that the tie had been lost in the welter of missed chances in Manchester, rather than a boiling moment of madness in Madrid.

For those lauding Real's 'big game management', there needed to be pauses for thought too. A team that tempts fate to this degree and only sporadically attempts to score a goal when goals need to be scored is one that must be supremely confident in its destiny, serene in the knowledge that a higher football power is busy looking after them. The polar opposite, perhaps, of how City supporters approach their club and its chances of suc-cess, even today. Or perhaps not, for City's European trajectory, with the unremitting chaos of Monaco, Tottenham, Liverpool and Madrid, also speaks of a destiny of kinds, a fight against the grain, a team ethos built on the smooth, unremitting control of the Guardiola era that regularly fails in the Champions League at the moments of greatest chaos.

The overthinking of team structure that led to collapses against Liverpool, Lyon and in the final of 2021 against Chelsea is one common criticism levelled at the Catalan, but there is a second pattern that has done for his City on frequent occasions: his team's reaction to sudden dramatic loss of control.

In all of the matches that mark Guardiola's most electrify-ing defeats, there have been uncatered-for moments where the unerring control exercised on the opponent has given way to eye-watering laxity, itself something of a false antithesis. In other words, when it goes, it really goes. And quickly. His Barcelona shipped two goals in thirteen minutes against Inter in 2010, his

Bayern side were catapulted from the tournament in 2014 by three Real Madrid goals in eighteen minutes and again a year later with three in seventeen minutes against Barcelona. With City the painful pattern has continued: two in eight minutes in falling to Monaco in 2017; three in nineteen minutes against Liverpool in 2018 and two in four minutes against Tottenham in 2019. Now, City had topped the lot conceding three in nine minutes in the white heat of Madrid.

Is it, in fact, rare outbreaks of chaos in a sea of calm control that undoes a philosophy constructed around the beauty of carefully calibrated returns?

REAL MADRID 3–1 MANCHESTER CITY | Att. 61,416 | Mahrez

Ederson, Walker (Zinchenko), Cancelo, Dias, Laporte, Rodrigo (Sterling), De Bruyne (Gündoğan), B. Silva, Foden, Jesus (Grealish), Mahrez (Fernandinho)

With faces reflecting the sourness felt, there was nowhere to go but home and nothing to do but try and focus scorched minds on a knife-edge title race with Liverpool.

Guardiola – allowing the immediate dust to settle – appeared remarkably lucid in the Friday press conference before a vital game with Newcastle. 'There is no time for mental,' he suggested, when asked about the eye-catchingly small span between Rodrygo's goals. 'It was 45 seconds later. There is no time to fall down. What happened, it's football. It's football.'

A tentative voice came out of the press pack: 'Pep, does this make you even hungrier?'

'No, always I am starving ...'

For the club he manages too, the hunger instilled in 1970 by Malcolm Allison has not been sated.

INDEX